Lecture Notes in Computer Science 16579

Founding Editors

Gerhard Goos
Juris Hartmanis

Editorial Board Members

Elisa Bertino, *Purdue University, West Lafayette, IN, USA*
Wen Gao, *Peking University, Beijing, China*
Bernhard Steffen, *TU Dortmund University, Dortmund, Germany*
Moti Yung, *Columbia University, New York, NY, USA*

The series Lecture Notes in Computer Science (LNCS), including its subseries Lecture Notes in Artificial Intelligence (LNAI) and Lecture Notes in Bioinformatics (LNBI), has established itself as a medium for the publication of new developments in computer science and information technology research, teaching, and education.

LNCS enjoys close cooperation with the computer science R & D community, the series counts many renowned academics among its volume editors and paper authors, and collaborates with prestigious societies. Its mission is to serve this international community by providing an invaluable service, mainly focused on the publication of conference and workshop proceedings and postproceedings. LNCS commenced publication in 1973.

Fuyuki Ishikawa · Alcino Cunha

Editors

Rigorous State-Based Methods

12th International Conference, ABZ 2026
Tokyo, Japan, May 18–20, 2026
Proceedings

 Springer

Editors
Fuyuki Ishikawa 🆔
National Institute of Informatics
Tokyo, Japan

Alcino Cunha 🆔
INESC TEC and University of Minho
Braga, Portugal

ISSN 0302-9743   ISSN 1611-3349 (electronic)
Lecture Notes in Computer Science
ISBN 978-3-032-26751-1   ISBN 978-3-032-26752-8 (eBook)
https://doi.org/10.1007/978-3-032-26752-8

© The Editor(s) (if applicable) and The Author(s), under exclusive license
to Springer Nature Switzerland AG 2026

This work is subject to copyright. All rights are solely and exclusively licensed by the Publisher, whether the whole or part of the material is concerned, specifically the rights of translation, reprinting, reuse of illustrations, recitation, broadcasting, reproduction on microfilms or in any other physical way, and transmission or information storage and retrieval, electronic adaptation, computer software, or by similar or dissimilar methodology now known or hereafter developed.
The use of general descriptive names, registered names, trademarks, service marks, etc. in this publication does not imply, even in the absence of a specific statement, that such names are exempt from the relevant protective laws and regulations and therefore free for general use.
The publisher, the authors and the editors are safe to assume that the advice and information in this book are believed to be true and accurate at the date of publication. Neither the publisher nor the authors or the editors give a warranty, expressed or implied, with respect to the material contained herein or for any errors or omissions that may have been made. The publisher remains neutral with regard to jurisdictional claims in published maps and institutional affiliations.

This Springer imprint is published by the registered company Springer Nature Switzerland AG
The registered company address is: Gewerbestrasse 11, 6330 Cham, Switzerland

If disposing of this product, please recycle the paper.

Preface

The 12th International Conference on Rigorous State Based Methods (ABZ 2026) was held in Tokyo, Japan, from May 18–20, 2026.

The ABZ conference series is dedicated to the cross-fertilization of state-based and machine-based formal methods. Abstract State Machines (ASM), Alloy, B, TLA, VDM, and Z are examples of these methods. They share a common conceptual foundation and are widely used in both academia and industry for the rigorous design and analysis of hardware and software systems. The ABZ conferences aim to be a forum for the vital exchange of knowledge and experience among the research communities around different formal methods.

ABZ 2026, to which this volume is dedicated, follows the success of the ABZ conferences from its first edition organized in London (UK) in 2008, where the acronym ABZ was invented to merge, into a single event, the ASM, B, and Z conference series. The Alloy community joined the event at the second ABZ 2010 conference, which was held in Orford (Canada). The VDM community joined the event at ABZ 2012, which was held in Pisa (Italy). ABZ 2014, held in Toulouse (France), brought the inclusion of the TLA+ community and the idea of proposing at each ABZ an industrial case study as a common problem for the application of different formal methods.

The ABZ 2016 conference was held in Linz, Austria, and ABZ 2018 in Southampton, UK. In 2018 the steering committee decided to retain the acronym ABZ and add the subtitle 'International Conference on Rigorous State Based Methods' to make more explicit the intention to include all state-based formal methods. The two successive ABZ events were organized in Ulm (Germany) as virtual events, while ABZ 2023, 2024, and 2025 were held in Nancy, France, in Bergamo, Italy, and in Düsseldorf, Germany.

ABZ 2026 was co-hosted with FM 2026, the 27th International Symposium on Formal Methods, the flagship conference of FME (Formal Methods Europe). This year, the doctoral symposium, tutorials, and workshops were managed by the FM symposium, including the Rodin workshop traditionally affiliated with ABZ.

ABZ 2026 received 25 submissions. At least three program committee members reviewed each submission, and 20 papers were accepted for publication in this volume and presentation at the conference: 13 long papers covering a broad spectrum of research, from fundamental to applied work, 4 short papers on work in progress, and 2 papers on the ABZ 2026 case study about an autonomous planetary rover. One journal-first talk was accepted in addition to the papers.

The ABZ program also included three invited talks by Toshiaki Aoki, Jin Song Dong, and Dominique Méry.

Organizing and running this event required a lot of effort from several people.

We are grateful to all the authors who submitted their work to ABZ 2026. We wish to thank all members of the Program Committee and all the additional reviewers for their precise, careful evaluation of the papers, and for their availability during the discussion period which considered each paper's acceptance.

Furthermore, we thank Marie Farell and Tsutomu Kobayashi for managing the case study for ABZ 2026, and Yamine Ait Ameur and Elvinia Riccobene for their useful advice.

For readers of these proceedings, we hope that you find them useful, interesting, and inspiring for future research

May 2026

Fuyuki Ishikawa
Alcino Cunha

Organization

Program Committee

Yamine Ait Ameur	ENSEEIHT, France
Toshiaki Aoki	JAIST, Japan
Paolo Arcaini	National Institute of Informatics, Japan
Richard Banach	University of Manchester, UK
Silvia Bonfanti	University of Bergamo, Italy
Chiara Braghin	University of Milan, Italy
Maximiliano Cristia	Universidad Nacional de Rosario, Argentina
Alcino Cunha	INESC TEC & University of Minho, Portugal
Catherine Dubois	ENSIIE, France
Guillaume Dupont	ENSEEIHT, France
Marie Farrell	University of Manchester, UK
Flavio Ferrarotti	Software Competence Centre Hagenberg, Austria
Marc Frappier	Université de Sherbrooke, Canada
Stefan Hallerstede	Aarhus University, Denmark
Thai Son Hoang	University of Southampton, UK
Akram Idani	Université Grenoble Alpes, VERIMAG lab, France
Fuyuki Ishikawa	National Institute of Informatics, Japan
Eunsuk Kang	Carnegie Mellon University, USA
Tsutomu Kobayashi	Japan Aerospace Exploration Agency, Japan
Regine Laleau	Paris-Est Creteil University, France
Thierry Lecomte	CLEARSY, France
Michael Leuschel	Heinrich Heine University Düsseldorf, Germany
Frederic Mallet	Université Côte d'Azur, France
Atif Mashkoor	Johannes Kepler University Linz, Austria
Dominique Méry	Université de Lorraine, LORIA, France
Stephan Merz	Inria, France
Alexander Raschke	Ulm University, Germany
Elvinia Riccobene	University of Milan, Italy
Asieh Salehi Fathabadi	University of Southampton, UK
Patrizia Scandurra	University of Bergamo, Italy
Gerhard Schellhorn	Universität Augsburg, Germany

Emil Sekerinski   McMaster University, Canada
Neeraj Kumar Singh   ENSEEIHT, France
Maurice ter Beek   CNR-ISTI, Italy
Laurent Voisin   Systerel, France
Fabian Vu   Heinrich Heine University Düsseldorf, Germany

Invited Talks

Practical Applications of Formal Methods to Automotive Systems: From In-Vehicle Systems to Autonomous Driving

Toshiaki Aoki

JAIST, 1-1 Asahidai, Nomi, Ishikawa, 9231292 Japan
toshiaki@jaist.ac.jp

We are working on the practical application of formal methods to automotive systems. So far, we have conducted joint research with more than ten companies in the automotive domain. Our research has consistently focused on applying formal methods to real industrial products.

Our first major project focused on automotive operating systems compliant with the OSEK/VDX standard, which later evolved into AUTOSAR OS. In this project, we conducted practical verification by combining model checking and formal specifications with software engineering techniques such as testing. This collaboration continued for more than ten years, during which we verified two commercial operating systems. Following this, we received many joint research offers from suppliers and achieved several practical outcomes. We applied formal methods to support ISO 26262 compliance for a commercial electric power steering system. We also developed verification techniques for microcontroller-based systems and applied them to MCAL (Microcontroller Abstraction Layer) modules. Furthermore, we proposed methods to support coverage requirements in model-based development using MATLAB/Simulink, leading to the development and release of the commercial tool PROMPT.

Today, autonomous driving has become a global focus. Our previous work mainly targeted individual modules of automotive systems, namely in-vehicle systems. In contrast, autonomous driving systems are fundamentally different from these systems, as they generate control commands that are executed by in-vehicle systems. They integrate AI technologies with image processing, sensing, and control. However, since AI systems often behave as black boxes, methods for ensuring their reliability and safety are not yet fully established. In response to this shift, we have expanded our research focus to include autonomous driving systems. Recently, we launched a JST/CREST project titled "Formal Methods and Verification Tools for Next-generation Automotive System Platforms." This project aims to develop formal methods and verification tools to ensure the safety and reliability of autonomous driving systems. As in our previous work, we continue to emphasize applying formal methods to real systems, currently using Autoware as our target platform.

In this talk, I will first present the research results we have achieved so far, as well as the practical lessons learned from our industrial collaborations, and then introduce an overview of the JST/CREST project.

Reasoning Beyond LLM: Formal Methods Agents

Jin Song Dong[1], Yufan Cai[1], Zhe Hou[2], and Xinyue Zuo[1]

[1] National University of Singapore, Singapore
[2] Griffith University, Australia

The rapid emergence of code-centric Large Language Models (LLMs) has fundamentally transformed modern software engineering practice. Tools such as Copilot, DeepSeek, and GPT-5 now enable developers to generate substantial amounts of code with minimal effort, significantly improving productivity and lowering barriers to programming. However, despite these advances, a critical challenge remains: LLM-generated code lacks formal guarantees of correctness. Due to the well-known hallucination problem and privacy issues [4], these models may produce syntactically plausible yet semantically incorrect or unsafe programs, raising concerns about their reliability in safety-critical and high-assurance systems.

This talk addresses this gap by integrating formal methods with LLM-based code generation. In the first part, we demonstrate that program refinement calculus can be utilized as a principled "formal chain of thought" to guide LLM reasoning and verify the correctness of LLM-generated code. Instead of relying on purely heuristic or probabilistic generation, LLMs are steered through a sequence of formally justified refinement steps, ensuring that each transformation preserves correctness. This approach not only improves the quality of generated programs but also enables machine-checkable verification of their correctness [1].

The second part of the talk shifts focus from code generation to system-level design and validation. We investigate LLM-aided system design and validation, where LLM-enhanced model-checking agents are developed to collaborate with formal verification engines [3]. These agents assist in tasks such as model construction, property specification, counterexample interpretation, and iterative refinement. By combining the expressive power of LLMs with the rigor of model checking, this paradigm enables more scalable and user-friendly verification workflows, bridging the gap between domain engineers and formal methods experts [6, 8, 7].

In the third part, we highlight the limitations of LLMs in solving planning and strategy analysis problems that require formal symbolic reasoning techniques. Empirical studies show that, despite their fluency, LLMs struggle with problems demanding precise logical inference, long-horizon reasoning, and combinatorial search. These findings underscore the necessity of integrating LLMs with formal symbolic methods rather than treating them as standalone solutions [2, 5].

Overall, this talk presents a unified perspective on trusted AI for software engineering, advocating a synergistic integration of LLMs and formal methods to achieve both scalability and correctness in next-generation software systems.

References

1. Cai, Y.,et al.: Automated program refinement: guide and verify code large language model with refinement calculus. In: ACM Principles of Programming Languages (2025)
2. Cao, Y., Song, W., Wang, D., Xue, J., Dong, J.S.: Failures to surface harmful contents in video large language models. AAAI Conf. Artif. Intell. **40**(42), 35331–35339 (2026)
3. Dong, J., Sun, J., Zhang, W., Dong, J.S., Hao, D.: Contested: consistency-aided tested code generation with LLM. Proc. ACM Softw. Eng. **2**(ISSTA), 596–617 (2025)
4. Jin, W., et al.: Whispering under the eaves: protecting user privacy against commercial and llm-powered automatic speech recognition systems. In: 34th USENIX Security Symposium, USENIX Security 2025, Seattle, WA, USA, 13-15 August 2025, pp. 4643–4662. USENIX Association (2025)
5. Ma, M., Liu, R., Lin, Y., Huang, Z., Dong, J.S.: Trainref: curating data with label distribution and minimal reference for accurate prediction and reliable confidence. In: The Fourteenth International Conference on Learning Representations (2026)
6. Zhang, Y., et al.: Position: trustworthy AI agents require the integration of large language models and formal methods. In: International Conference on Machine Learning (2025)
7. Zhang, Y., Emma, S.Y., En, A.L.J., Dong, J.S.: RvLLM: LLM runtime verification with domain knowledge. In: The Thirty-ninth Annual Conference on Neural Information Processing Systems (2025)
8. Zuo, X., et al.: PAT-Agent: autoformalization for model checking. In: 2025 40th IEEE/ACM International Conference on Automated Software Engineering (ASE), pp. 2122–2133. IEEE (2025)

Systematic Development of Distributed Algorithms using Event-B- Experiences, reviews and prospects -

Dominique Méry ⓘ

LORIA & Université de Lorraine, Vandoeuvre-l'es-Nancy, France, Vandoeuvre-lès-Nancy, France
dominique.mery@loria.fr
http://members.loria.fr/Mery

The Event-B language, with the refinement, provides a framework for developing distributed algorithms that are correct by construction. The first application concerned the IEEE1394 leader election protocol in a connected network and opened up a field of significant applications, some of which related to security. This presentation aims to provide an overview of distributed algorithms developed according to the correct-by-construction paradigm and to illustrate this approach using the problem of termination detection. We review the various elements related to distributed algorithms from the perspective of modelling and verification using refinement. In particular, we compare this approach with other approaches based on state-based formalisms, notably TLA. The illustration of the methodology serves to enrich the practical method of distributed algorithm design based on refinement and to illustrate this method in the context of verifying the termination detection distributed algorithms, in particular the Dijkstra-Scholten algorithm and associated algorithms. Beyond the development of the algorithm, we address the localisation of events and the transformation of the local Event-B machine into a distributed algorithm. In particular, we focus on the algorithmic form generally used in the literature (such as G. Tel or L. Lamport) and we enrich the description of the algorithm by specifying the required properties of the algorithm. This formal exercise has led us to relevant observations regarding the Event-B language and the capabilities of the tools, notably theorem instantiation techniques. Beyond the treatment of termination detection, we also show how our teaching of distributed algorithms has evolved and has enabled a better explanation of how they work. Finally, this work continues by considering other distributed algorithms that pose new challenges both to the refinement technique and to proof tools. In this way, we are enriching the algorithms we teach and developing an atlas of distributed algorithms constructed by refinement.

Contents

Case Study Track

Journal-First Talk

Research Track

Counterexample-Guided Interval Weakening

Ben M. Andrew[(✉)] [iD], Louise A. Dennis [iD], Michael Fisher [iD],
and Marie Farrell [iD]

Department of Computer Science, University of Manchester, Manchester, UK
`benjamin.andrew@manchester.ac.uk`

Abstract. Systems deployed for long periods of time in dynamic environments may experience performance degradation that affects timing guarantees, even when their functional behaviour remains unchanged. In the design and verification of critical systems, such timing guarantees are often expressed using Metric Temporal Logic (MTL). Under degradation, these specifications may no longer hold as stated, although weaker variants that relax timing bounds may still be satisfied and remain meaningful. For example, while an elevator may initially be required to arrive within 30 s of a request, degradation of its motor may only allow us to guarantee arrival within 60 s. Although weaker, this guarantee is still useful and allows the system to maintain a reasonable level of operation. In this paper we present CEGIW, an iterative, counterexample-guided algorithm for automatically weakening timing intervals in MTL specifications so that they hold for a given system model. The algorithm preserves the logical structure of the original specification and weakens only interval bounds. We prove the correctness and optimality of CEGIW, and conduct an empirical evaluation to demonstrate the practicality of interval weakening using formalised requirements from a number of real-world case-studies. Using a model checker to produce counterexamples, CEGIW either identifies the strongest interval weakening under which the specification holds, or determines that no such weakening exists.

Keywords: System degradation · Specification weakening · Formal methods · Metric temporal logic

1 Introduction

Temporal properties of systems are often specified using logics such as Metric Temporal Logic [26] (MTL), and these properties can be verified to hold using model-checking [12]. However, in the real world, system failures or degradation can invalidate these proofs by breaking their assumptions, in which case the

This work is partially supported by EPSRC grant EP/Y001532/1, the CRADLE project under EPSRC grant EP/X02489X/1 and the Royal Academy of Engineering through both a Research Fellowship and a Chair in Emerging Technology.

© The Author(s), under exclusive license to Springer Nature Switzerland AG 2026
F. Ishikawa and A. Cunha (Eds.): ABZ 2026, LNCS 16579, pp. 3–21, 2026.
https://doi.org/10.1007/978-3-032-26752-8_1

desired properties may no longer hold. Yet, under degradation the system may still have some useful capabilities for reduced operation, and so *logically weaker* versions of these properties may hold. Given a degraded system and an ideal MTL property that does not hold in it, we aim to derive the strongest possible logical *weakening* of that property. To constrain the search space, we focus on modifying the intervals of MTL formulae while preserving the structural form of the specification. For example, we may want an elevator to always arrive at least 30 s after calling it, represented by

$$\Box(\texttt{callElevator} \rightarrow \Diamond_{[0,30]}\texttt{elevatorArrives}) \tag{1}$$

(where $\Box$ is the *always* operator and $\Diamond_{[0,30]}$ is the *eventually* operator bounded between zero and thirty time units). However, if the main motor breaks, a weaker backup motor may start, slowing the system down. In this case the ideal property may not hold, and we may only be able to guarantee that the elevator will arrive within 60 s, represented by

$$\Box(\texttt{callElevator} \rightarrow \Diamond_{[0,60]}\texttt{elevatorArrives}). \tag{2}$$

This property is logically weaker than the original, but still guarantees a useful level of functionality. We would like to be able to derive this new property automatically from the system model and the original property.

Related Work. Many works consider *unrealisable* sets of requirements—where conflicts mean that no satisfying implementation exists—solving the problem by weakening specifications. Some use counterstrategies to strengthen assumptions [6,28] in the LTL fragment $GR(1)$, while others use heuristic-guided genetic algorithms to mutate assumptions and guarantees towards realisability [11]. However, this is different from the problem of weakening specifications relative to an existing implementation, which we are concerned with. We use a counterexample-guided approach, which has been applied to a large variety of problems including abstraction refinement [1,14,24], program synthesis [4], and learning assumptions for compositional verification [16], but not yet to the problem of specification repair in the presence of an existing implementation. This has been explored using techniques from the field of program repair [20], typically heuristically-guided *generate-and-validate* approaches like mutation-based repairs [13] and dynamic invariant detection [2]. We, however, are concerned with correct-by-construction, *semantics-driven* approaches, which have only been explored in the case of propositional logic specifications [7].

Contribution. We present our Counterexample-Guided Interval Weakening (CEGIW) algorithm that, given a degraded system and a desired MTL property that does not hold on the system, produces a new optimal MTL property that both is weakening of the original property and holds in the degraded system. The weakening is optimal with respect to a formally defined interval order, ensuring that no strictly stronger interval weakening satisfies the degraded system. We use a counterexample-guided approach, generating counterexamples with the

NUXMV model checker [12], weakening the property to hold on the counterexamples, and iteratively weakening in this way until the property holds in the system. This approach is aimed at engineers in the design phase of safety-critical systems, who are trying to understand how resilient the timing properties of their system are to various proposed degradations, and how the system's formal guarantees are thus impacted.

The paper is organised as follows: Sect. 2 sets up the weakening of MTL formulae within contexts, Sect. 3 describes CEGIW and proves its correctness and optimality, Sect. 4 demonstrates CEGIW on an example and considers its usefulness in real-world case-studies, and Sect. 5 concludes and outlines future work.

2   Weakening Within Contexts

We briefly state the syntax and semantics of Metric Temporal Logic [26] (MTL). Let $\mathcal{P}$ be a set of propositional variables. Well-formed MTL formulae are formed according to the rule:

$$\phi := p \mid \top \mid \neg\phi \mid \phi \wedge \phi \mid \phi\,\mathcal{U}_I\,\phi \mid \phi\,\mathcal{R}_I\,\phi \tag{3}$$

where $p \in \mathcal{P}$ and I is an interval, $[a,b]$, for $a \in \mathbb{N}$ and $b \in \mathbb{N} \cup \{\infty\}$ and $a \leq b$. Other constructs can be defined as usual, e.g. $\Diamond_I\phi \equiv \top\,\mathcal{U}_I\,\phi$. We consider MTL formulae with a pointwise semantics over the set of natural numbers [5], defined according to a trace π which is an infinite sequence of states in which atomic propositions can hold, and an index of the trace $t \in \mathbb{N}$. The set of atomic propositions that hold in the t-th state is denoted by $\pi(t)$. A trace π satisfies an MTL formula ϕ, denoted by $\pi \vDash \phi$, if and only if $\pi, 0 \vDash \phi$.

$$
\begin{aligned}
\pi, t \vDash p \quad&\text{iff}\quad p \in \pi(t) \\
\pi, t \vDash \neg\phi \quad&\text{iff}\quad \pi, t \nvDash \phi \\
\pi, t \vDash \phi_1 \wedge \phi_2 \quad&\text{iff}\quad \pi, t \vDash \phi_1 \text{ and } \pi, t \vDash \phi_2 \\
\pi, t \vDash \phi_1\,\mathcal{U}_I\,\phi_2 \quad&\text{iff}\quad \exists i \in I.\,((\pi, t+i \vDash \phi_2) \wedge \forall j \in [0,i) \cap I.\,(\pi, t+j \vDash \phi_1)) \\
\pi, t \vDash \phi_1\,\mathcal{R}_I\,\phi_2 \quad&\text{iff}\quad \forall i \in I.\,(\pi, t+i \vDash \phi_1) \\
&\qquad\quad \vee\, \exists j \in I.\,(\pi, t+j \vDash \phi_2 \wedge \forall i \in [0,i] \cap I.\,(\pi, t+i \vDash \phi_1))
\end{aligned}
$$

Note that $\phi_1\,\mathcal{R}_I\,\phi_2 \equiv \neg(\neg\phi_1\,\mathcal{U}_I\,\neg\phi_2)$. CEGIW weakens a constituent subformula of a larger formula. We show, using the notion of *contexts*, that a weakening of a subformula implies a weakening of the larger formula.

Definition 1 (Contexts). *MTL Contexts are like MTL formulae with a single hole $[-]$, and are formed according to the rule:*

$$C ::= [-] \mid C \wedge \phi \mid \phi \wedge C \mid C \vee \phi \mid \phi \vee C \mid C\,\mathcal{U}_I\,\phi \mid \phi\,\mathcal{U}_I\,C \mid C\,\mathcal{R}_I\,\phi \mid \phi\,\mathcal{R}_I\,C \tag{4}$$

where ϕ is an MTL formula and I is an interval. Our definition of contexts does not allow negations on the path to the hole $[-]$, similarly to the restriction imposed by negation normal form (NNF). However, adjacent MTL subformulae ϕ are not required to be in NNF and can contain negations.

We define the notion of *context substitution*, where an MTL formula ψ is substituted into the hole of a context C to produce an MTL formula $C[\psi]$. By pushing negations inwards, an arbitrary subformula ψ of an MTL formula ϕ can always be extracted to get a context C where ϕ is logically equivalent to $C[\psi]$.

$$
\begin{aligned}
[-][\psi] &= \psi \\
(C \wedge \phi)[\psi] &= C[\psi] \wedge \phi & (C \, \mathcal{U}_I \, \phi)[\psi] &= C[\psi] \, \mathcal{U}_I \, \phi \\
(\phi \wedge C)[\psi] &= \phi \wedge C[\psi] & (\phi \, \mathcal{U}_I \, C)[\psi] &= \phi \, \mathcal{U}_I \, C[\psi] \\
(C \vee \phi)[\psi] &= C[\psi] \vee \phi & (C \, \mathcal{R}_I \, \phi)[\psi] &= C[\psi] \, \mathcal{R}_I \, \phi \\
(\phi \vee C)[\psi] &= \phi \vee C[\psi] & (\phi \, \mathcal{R}_I \, C)[\psi] &= \phi \, \mathcal{R}_I \, C[\psi]
\end{aligned}
\tag{5}
$$

Definition 2 (Weakening and strengthening of MTL formulae). *Let ϕ and ϕ' be MTL formulae. ϕ' is a weakening of ϕ, denoted*

$$
\phi \sqsubseteq \phi'
\tag{6}
$$

if and only if, for all traces π and time-points t, if $\pi, t \vDash \phi$, then $\pi, t \vDash \phi'$. In this case, symmetrically, ϕ is a strengthening of ϕ'. Note that an MTL formula ϕ is always both a strengthening and a weakening of itself, i.e. $\phi \sqsubseteq \phi$.

Theorem 3 (Weakening of contexts). *Let C be a context and ψ and ψ' be MTL formulae. If $\psi \sqsubseteq \psi'$, then $C[\psi] \sqsubseteq C[\psi']$.*

Proof. We do a proof by induction over the grammar of contexts using the induction hypothesis $P(C)$, that $C[\psi] \sqsubseteq C[\psi']$. The non-temporal inductive cases are omitted for brevity.

BASE CASE $[-]$: We assume that $\psi \sqsubseteq \psi'$, and by the definition of context substitution we have that $[-][\psi] \sqsubseteq [-][\psi']$ and thus $P([-])$.

INDUCTIVE CASE $C \, \mathcal{U}_I \, \phi$: Assuming $P(C)$, we take an arbitrary trace π and time-point t, assume $\pi, t \vDash C[\psi] \, \mathcal{U}_I \, \phi$, and want to prove $\pi, t \vDash C[\psi'] \, \mathcal{U}_I \, \phi$. We know that there exists an $i \in I$ such that $\pi, t+i \vDash \phi$, and that for all $j \in [0, i) \cap I$ we have $\pi, t + j \vDash C[\psi]$. Taking arbitrary i and j, by the induction hypothesis we have that $\pi, t + j \vDash C[\psi']$, and so by the semantics $\pi, t \vDash C[\psi'] \, \mathcal{U}_I \, \phi$. Thus, we have $P(C \, \mathcal{U}_I \, \phi)$.

INDUCTIVE CASE $\phi \, \mathcal{U}_I \, C$: Similar to the above case.

INDUCTIVE CASE $C \, \mathcal{R}_I \, \phi$: Assuming $P(C)$, we take an arbitrary trace π and time-point t, assume $\pi, t \vDash C[\psi] \, \mathcal{R}_I \, \phi$, and want to prove $\pi, t \vDash C[\psi'] \, \mathcal{R}_I \, \phi$. By the semantics of $\mathcal{R}$ there are two cases:

1. For all $i \in I$ we have $\pi, t + i \vDash \phi$, thus we have $\pi, t + i \vDash C[\psi']$, and so we have $\pi, t \vDash C[\psi'] \, \mathcal{R}_I \, \phi$.
2. There exists an $i \in I$ such that $\pi, t + i \vDash C[\psi]$, and that for all $j \in [0, i] \cap I$ we have $\pi, t + j \vDash \phi$. Taking arbitrary i and j, by the assumptions we have that $\pi, t + i \vDash C[\psi']$ and $\pi, t + j \vDash \phi$, and then by the semantics we have $\pi, t \vDash C[\psi'] \, \mathcal{R}_I \, \phi$.

Thus, in both cases we have $P(C \, \mathcal{R}_I \, \phi)$.

INDUCTIVE CASE $\phi \, \mathcal{R}_I \, C$: Similar to the above case. $\square$

We show that, depending on which temporal operator is used, by expanding or contracting its interval we can weaken or strengthen the surrounding formula.

Definition 4 (Right-bound modifications of intervals). *Let $I = [a, b]$ be an interval. For any $i \in \mathbb{N}$, a right-bound modification of I is either a right-bound extension $[a, b + i]$, or, provided $i \leq b - a$, a right-bound contraction $[a, b - i]$. A right-bound modification is* strict *if $i > 0$. The set of all right-bound modifications of I is denoted $\mathcal{B}_R(I)$.*

Lemma 5 (Weakening of $\mathcal{U}$ interval). *Let ϕ and ψ be MTL formulae, and I and I' be intervals, where I' is a right-bound extension of I. Then, $\phi \, \mathcal{U}_I \, \psi \sqsubseteq \phi \, \mathcal{U}_{I'} \, \psi$.*

Proof. We assume that I' is a right-bound extension of I, and so, taking an arbitrary trace π and time-point t, we assume $\pi, t \vDash \phi \, \mathcal{U}_I \, \psi$ and want to prove $\pi, t \vDash \phi \, \mathcal{U}_{I'} \, \psi$. We know that there exists an $i \in I$ such that $\pi, t + i \vDash \psi$, and that for all $j \in [0, i) \cap I$ we have $\pi, t + j \vDash \phi$. Taking arbitrary i and j, we have that $i, j \in I'$, and so $\pi, t \vDash \phi \, \mathcal{U}_{I'} \, \psi$. Thus, $\phi \, \mathcal{U}_I \, \psi \sqsubseteq \phi \, \mathcal{U}_{I'} \, \psi$. $\square$

Lemma 6 (Weakening of $\mathcal{R}$ interval). *Let ϕ and ψ be MTL formulae, and I and I' be intervals, where I' is a right-bound contraction of I. Then, $\phi \, \mathcal{R}_I \, \psi \sqsubseteq \phi \, \mathcal{R}_{I'} \, \psi$.*

Proof. We assume that I' is a right-bound contraction of I, and so, taking an arbitrary trace π and time-point t, we assume $\pi, t \vDash \phi \, \mathcal{R}_I \, \psi$ and want to prove $\pi, t \vDash \phi \, \mathcal{R}_{I'} \, \psi$. By the semantics of $\mathcal{R}$ there are two cases:

1. For all $t' \in I$ we have $\pi, t + t' \vDash \psi$. Then, as $I' \subseteq I$, we know that for all $t'' \in I'$ we have $\pi, t + t'' \vDash \psi$, and so $\pi, t \vDash \phi \, \mathcal{R}_{I'} \, \psi$.
2. There exists a $t' \in I$ such that $\pi, t + t' \vDash \phi$ and for all $t'' \in I \cap [0, t']$, we have $\pi, t + t'' \vDash \psi$. As I' is a right-bound contraction of I, there are two further cases:
   (a) If $t' \in I'$, then we still have that $\pi, t + t' \vDash \phi$ and for all $t'' \in I' \cap [0, t']$, we have $\pi, t + t'' \vDash \psi$, and so $\pi, t \vDash \phi \, \mathcal{R}_{I'} \, \psi$.
   (b) If $t' \notin I'$, then $I' \cap [0, t'] = I'$ and so we know that for all $t'' \in I'$, we have $\pi, t + t'' \vDash \psi$, and so $\pi, t \vDash \phi \, \mathcal{R}_{I'} \, \psi$.

Thus, in all cases we have that $\phi \, \mathcal{R}_I \, \psi \sqsubseteq \phi \, \mathcal{R}_{I'} \, \psi$. $\square$

Often in CEGIW, recursive calls will generate a set of intervals from which either the strongest or weakest must be chosen. We show that there is a total order of implication over the set of right-bound modifications of an interval, which allows us to make that choice.

Lemma 7 (Extension-weakening order of right-bound modifications). *Let I be an interval. Then, $\mathcal{B}_R(I)$ has a total order $\supseteq$, where for all MTL contexts C, MTL formulae ϕ and ϕ', and all $I', I'' \in \mathcal{B}_R(I)$, if $I'' \supseteq I'$ then we have $C[\phi \, \mathcal{U}_{I'} \, \phi'] \sqsubseteq C[\phi \, \mathcal{U}_{I''} \, \phi']$.*

Proof. For any pair of intervals I' and I'' in $\mathcal{B}_R(I)$ we can order the resulting subformulae by applying Lemma 5 to get $\phi\,\mathcal{U}_{I'}\,\phi' \sqsubseteq \phi\,\mathcal{U}_{I''}\,\phi'$ (or the reverse), and then order the full formulae with their contexts by applying Theorem 3 to get $C[\phi\,\mathcal{U}_{I'}\,\phi'] \sqsubseteq C[\phi\,\mathcal{U}_{I''}\,\phi']$ (or the reverse). $\qquad\square$

Lemma 8 (Contraction-weakening order of right-bound modifications). *Let I be an interval. Then, $\mathcal{B}_R(I)$ has a total order $\sqsubseteq$, where for all MTL contexts C, MTL formulae ϕ and ϕ', and all $I', I'' \in \mathcal{B}_R(I)$, if $I'' \subseteq I'$ then we have $C[\phi\,\mathcal{R}_{I'}\,\phi'] \sqsubseteq C[\phi\,\mathcal{R}_{I''}\,\phi'].$*

Proof. Similar to the proof of Lemma 7, but uses Lemma 6 to order $\phi\,\mathcal{R}_{I'}\,\phi'$ and $\phi\,\mathcal{R}_{I''}\,\phi'$. $\qquad\square$

3   Algorithm for Interval Weakening

CEGIW is split into two levels. At the top-level, there is an iterative process that finds counterexample traces to the MTL formula ϕ by model checking (Sect. 3.1). At each iteration, once a counterexample trace π is found, we weaken a given interval in ϕ such that the new formula ϕ' holds on π (Sect. 3.2). However, this does not guarantee that ϕ' holds on the model itself, and so we need to repeat the process, finding a new counterexample trace for ϕ' and weakening the interval again, driven by the iterative process. We finish once we produce a ϕ' that holds on the model.

3.1   Iterative Weakening

Assume that we have an MTL formula ϕ that has a temporal subformula $\psi\,\triangle_I\psi'$ with an interval I that we want to weaken. ϕ can be split into $\psi\,\triangle_I\psi'$ and the surrounding MTL context C, such that ϕ is logically equivalent to $C[\psi\,\triangle_I\psi']$. Assume we also have a transition system $\mathcal{M}$. Using a model checker, we check whether ϕ holds on $\mathcal{M}$. If it holds then we are done, but if not, we will receive a counterexample trace π through $\mathcal{M}$ for which $\pi \nvDash C[\psi\,\triangle_I\psi']$. We can then weaken on this counterexample with

$$I' = Weaken(C, \psi\,\triangle_I\psi', \pi, 0) \tag{7}$$

which is described in Sect. 3.2. By Theorem 19, if $I' = None$, then there exists no weakening I'' of I such that $\pi \vDash C[\psi\,\triangle_{I''}\psi']$, and so the same holds for the model $\mathcal{M}$. Otherwise, I' is an interval such that $\pi \vDash C[\psi\,\triangle_{I'}\psi']$. However, $C[\psi\,\triangle_{I'}\psi']$ does not necessarily hold on $\mathcal{M}$, and so we model check again, creating an iterative loop that ends when we either produce an interval I'' that is a weakening of I such that $C[\psi\,\triangle_{I''}\psi']$ holds on $\mathcal{M}$, or show that no such weakening exists.

3.2   Weakening on a Counterexample

Model checkers generally produce a specific type of infinite counterexample trace, called a *lasso trace*.

Definition 9 (Lasso traces). *A trace π is* lasso *if it can be separated into a finite prefix π_{pre} and an infinitely repeating finite suffix π_{suf}, forming*

$$\pi = \pi_{\mathrm{pre}}(\pi_{\mathrm{suf}})^{\omega}. \tag{8}$$

This restricts us to a subset of infinite traces that can be finitely represented. The finite length of a lasso trace is then defined as $|\pi| = |\pi_{\mathrm{pre}}| + |\pi_{\mathrm{suf}}|$. Both π_{pre} and π_{suf} must be minimal.

We show that we can prove properties of an entire infinite lasso trace using only a finite *covering interval*. Without this, we may need to iterate over the entire infinite trace, impacting completeness.

Definition 10 (Covering intervals). *The suffix-covering interval of π, defined with respect to an interval $[a, b]$, is*

$$\mathrm{cov}_{\pi}([a, b]) = [a, \min(b, \mathrm{end}_{\pi}(a))] \tag{9}$$

where we specify a finite end *of the infinite trace with*

$$\mathrm{end}_{\pi}(a) = \begin{cases} |\pi| & \textit{if } a < |\pi_{\mathrm{pre}}| \\ a + |\pi_{\mathrm{suf}}| - 1 & \textit{otherwise.} \end{cases} \tag{10}$$

Lemma 11 (Lasso trace coverage). *Let ϕ be an MTL formula, π be a lasso trace, and $a \in \mathbb{N}$. If for all $t \in [a, \mathrm{end}_{\pi}(a)]$ we have $\pi, t \vDash \phi$, then for all $t' \in \mathbb{N}$ with $t' \geq a$ we have $\pi, t' \vDash \phi$.*

Proof. We assume that for all $t \in [a, \mathrm{end}_{\pi}(a)]$ we have $\pi, t \vDash \phi$, and, taking an arbitrary $t' \in \mathbb{N}$ with $t' \geq a$ want to prove that $\pi, t' \vDash \phi$. There are two cases. Firstly, if $t' < |\pi|$ then we know that this is within the $[a, \mathrm{end}_{\pi}(a)]$ range and so we have $\pi, t' \vDash \phi$. Otherwise, if $t' \geq |\pi|$, we split π into its prefix π_{pre} and infinitely repeating suffix π_{suf}, and want to prove that $\pi_{\mathrm{pre}}(\pi_{\mathrm{suf}})^{\omega}, t' \vDash \phi$. As $t' \geq |\pi|$, we can split it into $t' = |\pi_{\mathrm{pre}}| + n \cdot |\pi_{\mathrm{suf}}| + m$ for some $n, m \in \mathbb{N}$ with $n \geq 1$ and $m < |\pi_{\mathrm{suf}}|$.

$$\begin{aligned} &\pi_{\mathrm{pre}}(\pi_{\mathrm{suf}})^{\omega}, |\pi_{\mathrm{pre}}| + n \cdot |\pi_{\mathrm{suf}}| + m \vDash \phi \\ \implies &(\pi_{\mathrm{suf}})^{\omega}, n \cdot |\pi_{\mathrm{suf}}| + m \vDash \phi \\ \implies &(\pi_{\mathrm{suf}})^{\omega}, m \vDash \phi \\ \implies &\pi_{\mathrm{pre}}(\pi_{\mathrm{suf}})^{\omega}, |\pi_{\mathrm{pre}}| + m \vDash \phi \end{aligned} \tag{11}$$

We know that $|\pi_{\mathrm{pre}}| + m$ is in the $[a, \mathrm{end}_{\pi}(a)]$ interval, so we have $\pi, t' \vDash \phi$. $\square$

We also define the *optimality* of weakenings, used to prove that CEGIW will not produce an interval weakening that is any weaker than it needs to be.

Algorithm 1: Weakening within a context C; non-temporal cases elided

1 **function** $Weaken(C,\ \psi\,\triangle_{I_{\mathrm{orig}}}\psi',\ \pi,\ t)$
2   **if** $C = [-]$ **then**
3   **if** $\triangle = \mathcal{U}$ **then**
4   **return** $Weaken\mathcal{U}Direct(\psi,\psi',I_{\mathrm{orig}},\pi,t)$
5   **else** // $\triangle = \mathcal{R}$
6   **return** $Weaken\mathcal{R}Direct(\psi,\psi',I_{\mathrm{orig}},\pi,t)$
7 $\cdots$
8   **else if** $C = C\,\mathcal{U}_J\,\phi$ **then**
9   **return** $Weaken\mathcal{U}Left(C,\phi,J,\psi\,\triangle_{I_{\mathrm{orig}}}\psi',\pi,t)$
10   **else if** $C = \phi\,\mathcal{U}_J\,C$ **then**
11   **return** $Weaken\mathcal{U}Right(\phi,C,J,\psi\,\triangle_{I_{\mathrm{orig}}}\psi',\pi,t)$
12   **else if** $C = C\,\mathcal{R}_J\,\phi$ **then**
13   **return** $Weaken\mathcal{R}Left(C,\phi,J,\psi\,\triangle_{I_{\mathrm{orig}}}\psi',\pi,t)$
14   **else if** $C = \phi\,\mathcal{R}_J\,C$ **then**
15   **return** $Weaken\mathcal{R}Right(\phi,C,J,\psi\,\triangle_{I_{\mathrm{orig}}}\psi',\pi,t)$

Definition 12 (Optimality of right-bound extensions and contractions). *An interval I' is an optimal right-bound extension (resp. contraction) of an interval I with respect to a context C, MTL formulae ψ and ψ', a temporal operator $\triangle \in \{\mathcal{U},\mathcal{R}\}$, trace π, and time-step t, if*

$$\pi, t \vDash C[\psi\,\triangle_{I'}\psi'] \tag{12}$$

and either (a) $I = I'$, or (b) there exists no strict right-bound contraction (resp. extension) I'' of I' such that $\pi, t \vDash C[\psi\,\triangle_{I''}\psi']$.

The entrypoint of CEGIW is Algorithm 1, which recurses following the inductive structure of the MTL context grammar[1]. The proof of correctness and optimality follows the same inductive structure, with base cases for directly weakening the intervals of $\mathcal{U}_I$ and $\mathcal{R}_I$ (Lemmas 13 and 14), and inductive cases for weakening subformulae on either side of both operators (Lemmas 15 to 18).

Intuitively, to weaken a $\mathcal{U}$ formula $\psi_l\,\mathcal{U}_I\,\psi_r$ in Algorithm 2, the algorithm considers how the interval can be adjusted so that the formula becomes satisfied. Starting from time t, if the formula does not hold under the original interval, the only admissible weakening is to extend the right bound, thereby allowing additional time for the right subformula ψ_r to become true while the left subformula ψ_l continues to hold. The algorithm therefore extends the right bound incrementally until either the $\mathcal{U}$ formula holds on the given trace or no further extension is possible. In the former case, it returns the smallest such extension, yielding an optimal weakening; in the latter case, it reports that no interval weakening exists.

---

[1] Implementations of elided cases are in the public repository.

Algorithm 2: Directly weakening interval of $\mathcal{U}$

---

1 **function** $Weaken\mathcal{U}Direct(\psi_l, \psi_r, [a,b], \pi, t)$
2 $\quad$ **for** $i \leftarrow a$ **to** $\mathrm{end}_\pi(a)$ **do**
3 $\quad\quad$ **if** $\pi, t + i \vDash \psi_r$ **then**
4 $\quad\quad\quad$ **return** $[a, \max(b, i)]$
5 $\quad\quad$ **if** $\pi, t + i \nvDash \psi_l$ **then**
6 $\quad\quad\quad$ **break**
7 $\quad$ **return** $None$

Lemma 13 ($\mathcal{U}$ base case). *Let I be an interval, ψ_l and ψ_r MTL formulae, and π a lasso trace. Then, for all timepoints $t \in \mathbb{N}$ with*

$$I' = Weaken\mathcal{U}Direct(\psi_l, \psi_r, I, \pi, t), \tag{13}$$

either I' is an optimal right-bound extension of I such that $\pi, t \vDash \psi_l \, \mathcal{U}_{I'} \, \psi_r$, or $I' = None$, in which case there exists no such interval.

Proof. We take an arbitrary t. Our proof for Algorithm 2 uses the loop invariant that $\forall j \in [a, \mathrm{end}_\pi(a)]$ with $j < i$ (where $I = [a, b]$), we have that $\pi, t + j \nvDash \psi_r$ and $\pi, t + j \vDash \psi_l$. On first entry to the loop there is no such j, so this is trivially true. On reaching the end of the loop body, we know that $\pi, t + i \nvDash \psi_r$ and $\pi, t + i \vDash \psi_l$, and so in combination with the loop invariant we know that $\forall j \in I$ where $j \leq i$, we have $\pi, t + j \nvDash \psi_r$ and $\pi, t + j \vDash \psi_l$. Thus, the loop invariant is preserved. Suppose at the start of iteration i that the loop invariant holds. If $\pi, t + j \vDash \psi_r$ on Line 3 then we return $I' = [a, \max(b, i)]$. This is an optimal right-bound extension of I and we have that $\pi, t \vDash \psi_l \, \mathcal{U}_{I'} \, \psi_r$.

If $None$ is returned, then either we broke out of the loop early because for some $i \in [a, \mathrm{end}_\pi(a)]$ we have $\pi, t + i \nvDash \psi_l$ at Line 5, or we ran the loop to completion. In the first case, we know that $\pi, t + i \nvDash \psi_r$ as this is checked before at Line 3, and so combining with the loop invariant we know that ψ_r never held up until ψ_l stopped holding, and so there is no right-bound extension I' for which $\pi, t \vDash \psi_l \, \mathcal{U}_{I'} \, \psi_r$. In the second case, by the loop invariant we have that for all $i \in [a, \mathrm{end}_\pi(a)]$ we have $\pi, t + i \vDash \psi_l$ and $\pi, t + i \nvDash \psi_r$. By Lemma 11 we then have the same for all $i \in \mathbb{N}$ with $i \geq a$, and so there exists no right-bound extension I' of I that satisfies $\pi, t \vDash \psi_l \, \mathcal{U}_{I'} \, \psi_r$. $\square$

Lemma 14 ($\mathcal{R}$ base case). *Let I be an interval, ψ_l and ψ_r MTL formulae, and π a lasso trace. Then, for all timepoints $t \in \mathbb{N}$ with*

$$I' = Weaken\mathcal{R}Direct(\psi_l, \psi_r, I, \pi, t), \tag{14}$$

either I' is an optimal right-bound contraction of I such that $\pi, t \vDash \psi_l \, \mathcal{R}_{I'} \, \psi_r$, or $I' = None$, in which case there exists no such interval.

Proof. Full proof and pseudocode is available in our public repository. $\square$

Algorithm 3: Weakening within $\mathcal{U}$ on the left

---

1 function $Weaken\mathcal{U}Left(C,\ \phi,\ [a,b],\ \psi \triangle_{I_{\text{orig}}} \psi',\ \pi,\ t)$

  2 $b_{\text{fin}} \leftarrow \min(b, \text{end}_\pi(a))$

  3 $intervals \leftarrow [\,]$

  4   **for** $i \leftarrow a$ **to** b_{fin} **do**

  5   **if** $\pi, t + i \vDash \phi$ **then**

  6   **if** $i = a$ **then**

  7   **return** I_{orig}

  8   **return** interval in $intervals$ with maximal absolute difference to I_{orig}

  9 $I \leftarrow Weaken(C, \psi \triangle_{I_{\text{orig}}} \psi', \pi, t + i)$

10   **if** $I = None$ **then**

11   **return** $None$

12   append I to $intervals$

13   **return** $None$

We prove the inductive cases with an MTL context C, an interval I, MTL formulae ψ and ψ', a temporal operator $\triangle \in \{\mathcal{U}, \mathcal{R}\}$, and a lasso trace π. We use the induction hypothesis $P(C)$, that for all timepoints $t \in \mathbb{N}$ with $I' = Weaken(C, \psi \triangle_I \psi', \pi, t)$, if I' is an interval then $\pi, t \vDash C[\psi \triangle_I \psi']$, and

1. If $\triangle = \mathcal{U}$, then I' is an optimal right-bound extension of I;
2. If $\triangle = \mathcal{R}$, then I' is an optimal right-bound contraction of I.

If $I' = None$, then there exists no such interval in each case.

Intuitively, when weakening within the left subformula of a $\mathcal{U}$ operator in Algorithm 3, we must ensure that the left subformula holds at every relevant timestep until the right subformula becomes true. Starting from time t, the algorithm therefore examines each timestep $t + i$ within the original interval and determines the interval weakening required for the left subformula to hold on the given trace at that point. Because the left operand of $\mathcal{U}$ is interpreted universally over the interval, the overall weakening must be strong enough to satisfy all such requirements. The algorithm therefore selects the weakest interval that subsumes all interval weakenings computed for individual timesteps. If no such interval exists, or if weakening fails at any timestep, the algorithm reports that no valid weakening can be found.

Lemma 15 ($\mathcal{U}$-left inductive case). *Let C be an MTL context, I and J intervals, ϕ, ψ, and ψ' MTL formulae, $\triangle \in \{\mathcal{U}, \mathcal{R}\}$ a temporal operator, and π a lasso trace. If $P(C)$ holds, then so does $P(C\,\mathcal{U}_J\,\phi)$.*

Proof. For Algorithm 3 we assume the inductive hypothesis $P(C)$ and want to prove $P(C\,\mathcal{U}_J\,\phi)$. We take an arbitrary t and distinguish two cases, according to whether $\triangle$ is $\mathcal{U}$ or $\mathcal{R}$. In either case, by the induction hypothesis each recursive call evaluates to either *None* or an optimal interval I' related to I by the corresponding relation (right-bound extension or contraction respectively) such that $\pi, t + t' \models C[\psi \bigtriangleup_{I'} \psi']$.

We use the loop invariant that, for all $j \in \mathrm{cov}_\pi(J)$ with $j < i$, we have that $\pi, t + j \not\models \phi$ and that $I' = Weaken(C, \psi \bigtriangleup_I \psi', \pi, t + j)$ is an interval such that $\pi, t + j \models C[\psi \bigtriangleup_{I'} \psi']$. On first entry to the loop there is no such j, so this is trivially true. On reaching the end of the loop body, we know that $Weaken(C, \psi \bigtriangleup_I \psi', \pi, t + i) \neq None$ from Line 10, and so by the induction hypothesis the recursive call must have produced a suitable interval I'. As we also know that $\pi, t + i \not\models \phi$ from Line 5, the loop invariant is thus preserved for $j \leq i$. Suppose at the start of iteration i that the loop invariant holds. If $Weaken(C, \psi \bigtriangleup_I \psi', \pi, t + i) = None$ at Line 10 then by the induction hypothesis we know that there is no suitable interval I'' for which $\pi, t + i \models C[\psi \bigtriangleup_{I''} \psi']$, and by the loop invariant that there is no $j < i$ for which $\pi, t + j \models \phi$. Thus, there is no suitable interval I'' for which $\pi, t \models (C\,\mathcal{U}_J\,\phi)[\psi \bigtriangleup_{I''} \psi']$. If $\pi, t + j \models \phi$ at Line 5 then we split on whether it is our first iteration or not. If $i = a$ (where $J = [a, b]$) then we know that $\pi, t + a \models \phi$, and so any interval will work. We simply return the original interval I_{orig}.

Otherwise, by the loop invariant we know that for all $j \in \mathrm{cov}_\pi(J)$ with $j < i$—of which there must be at least one as $i > a$—we have an interval I' such that $\pi, t + j \models C[\psi \bigtriangleup_{I'} \psi']$. Applying Lemma 7 if $\bigtriangleup = \mathcal{U}$, or Lemma 8 if $\bigtriangleup = \mathcal{R}$, we obtain a maximum interval I'' such that for all $j \in \mathrm{cov}_\pi(J)$ with $j < i$ we have $\pi, t + j \models C[\psi \bigtriangleup_{I''} \psi']$. If $\mathrm{cov}_\pi(J) = J$ then we have

$$\pi, t \models (C\,\mathcal{U}_J\,\phi)[\psi \bigtriangleup_{I''} \psi']. \tag{15}$$

Otherwise, if $\mathrm{cov}_\pi(J) = [a, \mathrm{end}_\pi(a)]$, then by Lemma 11 for all $k \in \mathbb{N}$ with $k \geq a$ we have $\pi, t + k \models C[\psi \bigtriangleup_{I''} \psi']$, and so the above holds here too. $\square$

Lemma 16 ($\mathcal{U}$-right inductive case). *Let C be an MTL context, I and J intervals, ϕ, ψ, and ψ' MTL formulae, $\bigtriangleup \in \{\mathcal{U}, \mathcal{R}\}$ a temporal operator, and π a lasso trace. If $P(C)$ holds, then so does $P(\phi\,\mathcal{U}_J\,C)$.*

Lemma 17 ($\mathcal{R}$-left inductive case). *Let C be an MTL context, I and J intervals, ϕ, ψ, and ψ' MTL formulae, $\bigtriangleup \in \{\mathcal{U}, \mathcal{R}\}$ a temporal operator, and π a lasso trace. If $P(C)$ holds, then so does $P(C\,\mathcal{R}_J\,\phi)$.*

Lemma 18 ($\mathcal{R}$-right inductive case). *Let C be an MTL context, I and J intervals, ϕ, ψ, and ψ' MTL formulae, $\bigtriangleup \in \{\mathcal{U}, \mathcal{R}\}$ a temporal operator, and π a lasso trace. If $P(C)$ holds, then so does $P(\phi\,\mathcal{R}_J\,C)$.*

Full proofs for Lemmas 16 to 18 are available in our public repository. We use these supporting lemmas to prove the correctness and optimality of CEGIW.

Theorem 19 (Correctness for weakening). *Let C be an MTL context, I and J intervals, ϕ, ψ, and ψ' MTL formulae, $\bigtriangleup \in \{\mathcal{U}, \mathcal{R}\}$ a temporal operator, π a lasso trace, and $t \in \mathbb{N}$ be a timepoint. Let $I' = Weaken(C, \psi \bigtriangleup_I \psi', \pi, t)$. If I' is an interval then $\pi \models C[\psi \bigtriangleup_{I'} \psi']$, and*

1. *If $\triangle = \mathcal{U}$, then I' is an optimal right-bound extension of I;*
2. *If $\triangle = \mathcal{R}$, then I' is an optimal right-bound contraction of I.*

If $I' = None$, then there exists no such interval in each case.

Proof. We use the same induction hypothesis $P(C)$ defined for the preceding inductive lemmas. The non-temporal inductive cases are omitted for brevity.

BASE CASE $[-]$: By Lemma 13 if $\triangle = \mathcal{U}$, and Lemma 14 if $\triangle = \mathcal{R}$, we have $P([-])$.

INDUCTIVE CASE $C\,\mathcal{U}_J\,\phi$: Assuming $P(C)$, by Lemma 15 we have $P(C\,\mathcal{U}_J\,\phi)$.

INDUCTIVE CASE $\phi\,\mathcal{U}_J\,C$: Assuming $P(C)$, by Lemma 16 we have $P(\phi\,\mathcal{U}_J\,C)$.

INDUCTIVE CASE $C\,\mathcal{R}_J\,\phi$: Assuming $P(C)$, by Lemma 17 we have $P(C\,\mathcal{R}_J\,\phi)$.

INDUCTIVE CASE $\phi\,\mathcal{R}_J\,C$: Assuming $P(C)$, by Lemma 18 we have $P(\phi\,\mathcal{R}_J\,C)$.

$\square$

The time complexity of Algorithm 1 is $O(|\pi|^{\mathtt{td}(\phi)})$. where π is the counterexample trace and $\mathtt{td}(\phi)$ is the *temporal depth* of the MTL formula ϕ, i.e. the maximum number of nested temporal operators along any path in the syntax tree. In practice, $\mathtt{td}(\phi)$ is typically very small.

4   Evaluation

We evaluate how *effective* interval weakening is in understanding the temporal behaviour of specifications, and how applicable it is to real-world requirements. To this end, we investigate the following research questions:

RQ1: How can CEGIW be used to explore and diagnose timing margins in MTL specifications during early design? (Sect. 4.1)

RQ2: To what extent do existing real-world requirements provide practical targets for interval weakening, and are such weakenings meaningful in their application domains? (Sect. 4.2)

Choosing a model checker. There are no industrial-strength model checkers for MTL with pointwise semantics [3,10], yet many efficient tools exist for linear temporal logic [12,23] (LTL). Thus, we translate MTL formulae into LTL using the *next* (X) operator [8, Remark 5.15] and use an LTL model checker. During preliminary investigation, it was found that symbolic LTL model checkers such as NUXMV [12] and SPIN [23] typically generate minimal counterexample traces. Weakening intervals with these usually only increments or decrements the bound rather than modifying it by a larger amount, which increases the number of calls made to the model checker dramatically. Our implementation uses NUXMV in bounded model checking (BMC) mode, producing multiple counterexamples for a specific bound length, finding the optimal interval for each of them and returning the weakest, making it more likely that we make fewer calls to the model checker, thus improving the algorithm's efficiency. For our implementation we require the user to choose the BMC bound; while theoretical completeness can be preserved as completeness thresholds do exist for BMC [15], choosing a suitable bound still requires experience.

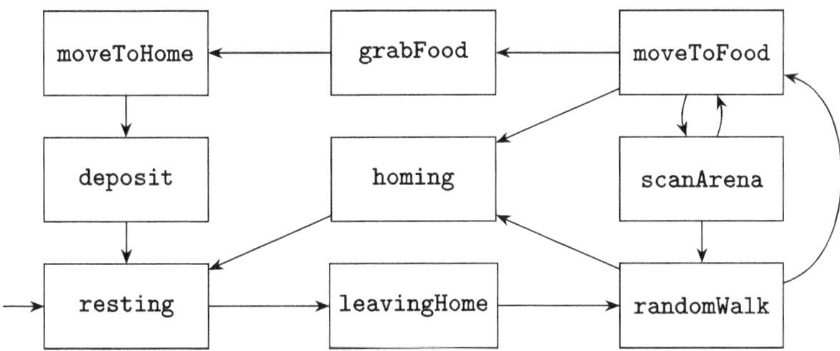

Fig. 1. Abstract state transition system for the robot's foraging behaviour. The robot begins in a resting state, then searches for, collects, and deposits food.

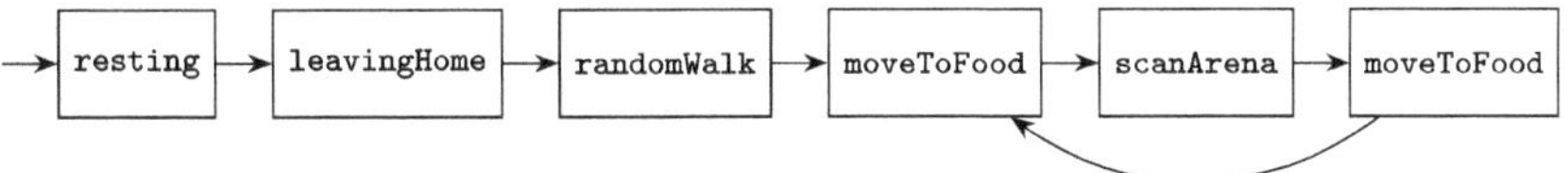

Fig. 2. Infinite lasso counterexample trace for the property in Eq. (16).

4.1 Demonstration of CEGIW (RQ1)

To address **RQ1**, we use an example based on a model of a foraging robot swarm [27]. Robots are located in an arena and do a random walk to find food, which they then carry back to their home. Here they recharge and then repeat their foraging task. We model a single robot with a state machine, depicted abstractly in Fig. 1. In the concrete transition system $\mathcal{M}$ the robot can remain in a given state for a configurable amount of time before it is forced to move to a next state. The transition system is specified concretely using SMV, the language of the NUXMV model checker [12]. We would like to prove that, after leaving the `resting` state, the robot will return to `resting` in at most 3 time units, represented by

$$\mathcal{M} \vDash \Box(\mathtt{resting} \to \Diamond_{[1,3]}\mathtt{resting}) \tag{16}$$

and translated from MTL to LTL as

$$\mathcal{M} \vDash \Box(\mathtt{resting} \to X(\mathtt{resting} \lor X(\mathtt{resting} \lor X(\mathtt{resting})))). \tag{17}$$

If this does not hold in the transition system, we would like to weaken the interval to produce a new, weaker property that does hold. Using CEGIW, we find in the first iteration that no suitable weakening of the interval exists based on the counterexample in Fig. 2, which shows an infinite loop between the `scanArena` and `moveToFood` states. This suggests a mistake in the modelling of the system, as in the real world the robot's battery would run out of charge. We amend the design by including in the requirements the notion of a battery that decreases as transitions are taken. While we are in `randomWalk, scanArena,` or `moveToFood`—in other words, searching for food—we monitor the battery level, and if it decreases below a certain threshold we abort and return home to recharge. The modified state transition system is depicted in Fig. 3. We check our desired property (Eq. (16)) against our amended model, and can see in Fig. 4a that in four iterations of CEGIW we extended the interval, and ended with the optimal interval which was then verified to hold in the system. So, the optimal property that holds in our amended system is

$$\mathcal{M} \vDash \Box(\texttt{resting} \rightarrow \Diamond_{[1,20]}\texttt{resting}). \tag{18}$$

Another property we are interested in is not the maximum time that the robot can spend away from home, but the *minimum*. We wish the robot to spend at least 20 time units away from home, formalised as

$$\mathcal{M} \vDash \Box((\texttt{resting} \wedge \Diamond_{[1,1]}\neg\texttt{resting}) \rightarrow \Box_{[1,20]}\neg\texttt{resting}). \tag{19}$$

Again, we check this against our modified model and can see in Fig. 4b that it took only one iteration to contract the interval, reaching the optimal interval which was then verified to hold in the system as

$$\mathcal{M} \vDash \Box((\texttt{resting} \wedge \Diamond_{[1,1]}\neg\texttt{resting}) \rightarrow \Box_{[1,3]}\neg\texttt{resting}). \tag{20}$$

By using CEGIW, we first identified that the original specification had a design flaw that allowed unwanted infinite loops. While a traditional model checker would conclude that the given specification does not hold, it cannot itself deduce that *no* weakening exists. After modifying the specification, we then deduced both the maximum time that the robot can stay away from home, as well as the minimum time. CEGIW can thus provide value in both analysing existing requirements and supporting system modelling.

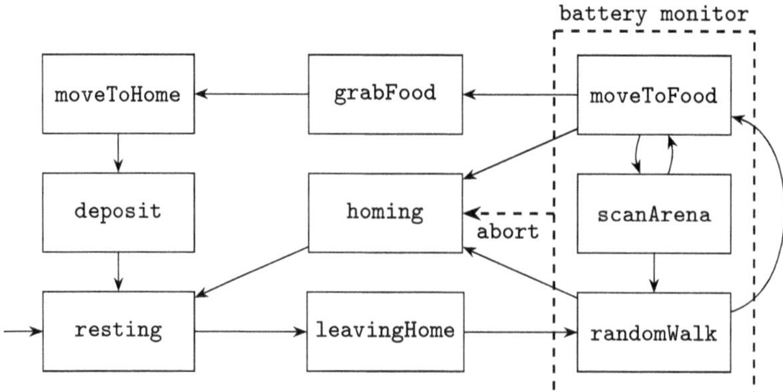

Fig. 3. Abstract state transition system for the robot's modified foraging behaviour. The battery monitor is represented by the dashed section on the right.

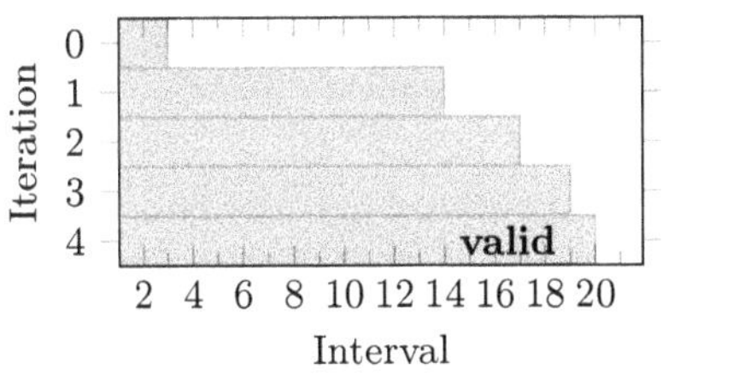

(a) Interval extension for Eq. (16).

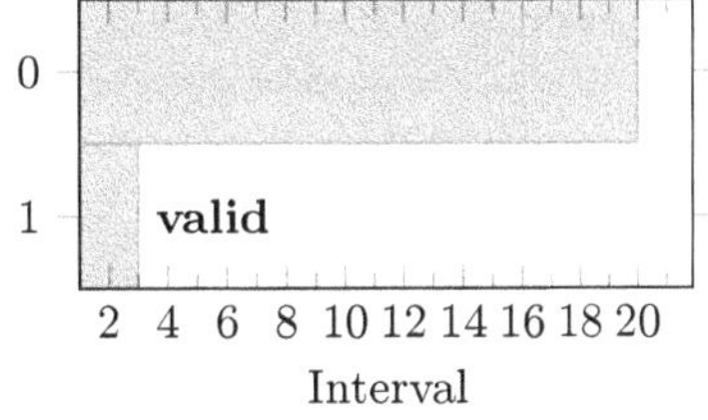

(b) Interval contraction for Eq. (19).

Fig. 4. Iterative interval weakening to generate optimal, valid intervals.

Table 1. Interval-weakenable requirements in FRET case studies.

Case study	Total requirements	Weakenable requirements
Mechanical lung ventilator [17]	121	57
Autonomous drone [31]	62	19
Lift-plus-cruise aircraft [30]	49	29
Aircraft engine controller [18]	42	0
Inspection rover [9]	15	1
Grasping for debris removal [19]	20	0
Robotic patterns [32]	36	11
LMCP challenges [29]	74	7
Total	**419**	**124**

4.2 Applicability of Interval Weakening to Real-World Requirements (RQ2)

In this section, we analyse existing requirements from a number of real-world case studies to assess how often interval weakening is applicable, and how weakened timing bounds can be interpreted in their respective domains. These requirements are formalised using the Formal Requirements Elicitation Tool (FRET) [21] and are written in FRETISH, a structured natural language that can be translated to MTL [22]. FRETISH requirements can have a **timing** field, on which we can use interval weakening to weaken the requirement itself. The number of requirements that can be weakened using interval weakening per case study is shown in Table 1. As an example, the requirement in Fig. 5a from the autonomous drone case study [31] uses the **within 12 milliseconds** timing which specifies that if the condition holds in one state, then the consequent must hold within the next twelve states (assuming that state transitions correspond to a millisecond of time passing). The MTL translation of this timing corresponds to the MTL temporal operator $\Diamond_{[0,12]}$, and so the requirement corresponds to

$$\Box(\texttt{ControlLoopStart} \rightarrow \Diamond_{[0,12]}(\texttt{ControlLoopFinish})). \tag{21}$$

<table>
<tr><td>

```
upon ControlLoopStart System shall
within 12 milliseconds satisfy
ControlLoopFinish
```

</td><td>

```
if powerFailure System shall for
120 minutes satisfy !off
```

</td></tr>
<tr><td>

(a) Autonomous drone requirement REQ018 describing the maximum time the control loop can take to complete.

</td><td>

(b) Mechanical lung ventilator requirement FUN37 describing how long the system must stay on after power failure.

</td></tr>
</table>

Fig. 5. Example FRETISH requirements from the case studies. Both are taken from systems that are fully implemented and operational in real-world settings.

Under system degradation, for example if the onboard communications network is degraded so that commands take longer to reach control surfaces, we may not be able to guarantee this and so would have to weaken the property by extending the interval, giving more time for the system to run its control loop, with an example weakening in

$$\Box(\texttt{ControlLoopStart} \rightarrow \Diamond_{[0,24]}(\texttt{ControlLoopFinish})). \tag{22}$$

An example requirement from the mechanical lung ventilator case study [17] is shown in Fig. 5b, and as the FRETISH timing `for 120 min` corresponds to the MTL temporal operator $\Box_{[1,120]}$, the corresponding MTL property is

$$\Box(\texttt{powerFailure} \rightarrow \Box_{[1,120]}(\neg\texttt{off})). \tag{23}$$

This is a regulatory requirement [25] and so, if it does not hold in the degraded system, it is critical to know by exactly how much it is violated. We may only be able to guarantee that the ventilator will stay on for at most 90 min after `powerFailure`, producing the weakening

$$\Box(\texttt{powerFailure} \rightarrow \Box_{[1,90]}(\neg\texttt{off})). \tag{24}$$

Of the 127 interval-weakenable requirements in Table 1, 116 can be weakened by interval extension as in Eq. (22), and 11 by interval contraction as in Eq. (24).

Several case studies in Table 1 have few or no requirements that can be weakened with interval weakening. These requirements are typically liveness properties specified with the **eventually** timing, which cannot be weakened further, or safety properties specified with the **always** timing, for which interval weakening would not be appropriate. For example, from the grasping for debris removal case study [19],

$$\texttt{SV shall always satisfy !collide(SV, TGT).} \tag{25}$$

To answer **RQ2**, we have shown that interval weakening is applicable to a substantial proportion of existing temporal requirements, and that such weakenings have meaningful interpretations in safety-critical domains. We have also answered **RQ1** by using CEGIW to identify problems in a specification, and then deduce useful timing properties in the fixed system.

5   Conclusion

We present CEGIW, a novel algorithm for weakening intervals in MTL properties of degraded systems, and prove its correctness and optimality. We demonstrate how CEGIW can be used during the design phase to understand system limitations under degradation, and explore how the formalised requirements of a number of real-world systems may be weakened against real implementations. This shows the applicability of CEGIW in the design of safety-critical systems for understanding the impacts of system degradation.

Future Work. A current limitation is that we only weaken on the right-hand-side of intervals, when both left- and right-bound modifications can produce valid weakenings. Restricting to only right-bound modifications creates a total order over the search space, so there is always a single optimum when multiple choices exist. Expanding to both left- and right-bound modifications creates a partial order over generated intervals, and so choosing between intervals is much less obvious. Future work will also explore other types of weakening, making syntactic changes to formulae beyond intervals.

Another limitation is that only a single interval can be weakened, and that the user must choose which one. Expanding to use multi-objective optimisation with Pareto optimality will improve the usability and applicability of this approach.

Availability. The implementation of CEGIW, full proofs, and all case study artefacts are available in our public repository[2]. Scripts are provided to reproduce all tables and examples reported in Sect. 4.

References

1. Aarts, F., Heidarian, F., Kuppens, H., Olsen, P., Vaandrager, F.: Automata learning through counterexample guided abstraction refinement. In: Formal Methods (2012)
2. Abreu, A., Macedo, N., Mendes, A.: Exploring automatic specification repair in dafny programs. In: International Conference on Automated Software Engineering Workshops (2023)
3. Akshay, S., Contractor, P., Gastin, P., Govind, R., Srivathsan, B.: Efficient verification of metric temporal properties with past in pointwise semantics. https://arxiv.org/abs/2510.14699v1. 2025
4. Alur, R., et al.: Syntax-guided synthesis. In: Formal Methods in Computer-Aided Design (2013)
5. Alur, R., Henzinger, T.A.: Real-time logics: complexity and expressiveness. Inf. Comput. **104**, 1 (1993)
6. Alur, R., Moarref, S., Topcu, U.: Counter-strategy guided refinement of GR(1) temporal logic specifications. In: Formal Methods in Computer-Aided Design (2013)
7. Andrew, B.M.: Weakening goals in logical specifications. In: Rigorous State-Based Methods (2026)
8. Baier, C., Katoen, J.-P.: Principles of model checking (2008)

---

[2] https://github.com/benmandrew/CEGIW.

9. Bourbouh, H., et al.: Integrating formal verification and assurance: an inspection rover case study. In: NASA Formal Methods (2021)
10. Brihaye, T., Geeraerts, G., Ho, H.-M., Milchior, A., Monmege, B.: Efficient algorithms and tools for MITL model-checking and synthesis. In: International Conference on Engineering of Complex Computer Systems (2018)
11. Brizzio, M., Cordy, M., Papadakis, M., Sánchez, C., Aguirre, N., Degiovanni, R.: Automated repair of unrealisable LTL specifications guided by model counting. In: Genetic and Evolutionary Computation Conference (2023)
12. Cavada, R., et al.: The NUXMV symbolic model checker. In: Computer Aided Verification (2014)
13. Cerqueira, J., Cunha, A., Macedo, N.: Timely specification repair for alloy 6. In: Software Engineering and Formal Methods (2022)
14. Clarke, E., Grumberg, O., Jha, S., Lu, Y., Veith, H.: Counterexample-guided abstraction refinement. In: Computer Aided Verification (2000)
15. Clarke, E., Kroening, D., Ouaknine, J., Strichman, O.: Completeness and complexity of bounded model checking. In: Verification, Model Checking, and Abstract Interpretation (2004)
16. Cobleigh, J.M., Giannakopoulou, D., Păsăreanu, C.S.: Learning assumptions for compositional verification. In: Tools and Algorithms for the Construction and Analysis of Systems (2003)
17. Farrell, M., Luckcuck, M., Monahan, R., Reynolds, C., Sheridan, O.: FRETting and formal modelling: a mechanical lung ventilator. In: Rigorous State-Based Methods (2024)
18. Farrell, M., Luckcuck, M., Sheridan, O., Monahan, R.: FRETting about requirements: formalised requirements for an aircraft engine controller. In: Requirements Engineering: Foundation for Software Quality (2022)
19. Farrell, M., Mavrakis, N., Ferrando, A., Dixon, C., Gao, Y.: Formal modelling and runtime verification of autonomous grasping for active debris removal. In: Frontiers in Robotics and AI, vol. 8 (2022)
20. Gazzola, L., Micucci, D., Mariani, L.: Automatic software repair: a survey. In: International Conference on Software Engineering (2018)
21. Giannakopoulou, D., Pressburger, T., Mavridou, A., Rhein, J., Schumann, J., Shi, N.: Formal requirements elicitation with FRET. In: International Working Conference on Requirements Engineering: Foundation for Software Quality (2020)
22. Giannakopoulou, D., Pressburger, T., Mavridou, A., Schumann, J.: Automated formalization of structured natural language requirements. In: Information and Software Technology, vol. 137 (2021)
23. Holzmann, G.J.: The model checker SPIN. IEEE Trans. Softw. Eng. **23**, 5 (1997)
24. Howar, F., Steffen, B., Merten, M.: Automata learning with automated alphabet abstraction refinement. In: Verification, Model Checking, and Abstract Interpretation (2011)
25. ISO. Particular requirements for basic safety and essential performance of critical care ventilators. 80601-2-12 (2023)
26. Koymans, R.: Specifying real-time properties with metric temporal logic. Real-Time Syst. **2**, 4 (1990)
27. Liu, W., Winfield, A.F.T.: Modeling and optimization of adaptive foraging in swarm robotic systems. Int. J. Robot. Res. **29**, 14 (2010)
28. Maoz, S., Ringert, J.O., Shalom, R.: Symbolic repairs for GR(1) specifications. In: International Conference on Software Engineering (2019)

29. Mavridou, A., et al.: The Ten lockheed martin cyber-physical challenges: formalized, analyzed, and explained. In: International Requirements Engineering Conference (2020)
30. Pressburger, T., Katis, A., Dutle, A., Mavridou, A.: Authoring, analyzing, and monitoring requirements for a lift-plus-cruise aircraft. In: Requirements Engineering: Foundation for Software Quality (2023)
31. Sheridan, O., Becker, L.B., Farrell, M., Luckcuck, M., Monahan, R.: Sharper specs for smarter drones: formalising requirements with FRET. In: Requirements Engineering: Foundation for Software Quality (2025)
32. Vázquez, G., Mavridou, A., Farrell, M., Pressburger, T., Calinescu, R.: Robotics: A New mission for FRET requirements. In: NASA Formal Methods (2024)

Fuzzing Executable ASMETA Models

Gabriele Bellini[iD] and Elvinia Riccobene[(✉)][iD]

Computer Science Department, Università degli Studi di Milano, Milan, Italy
`gabriele.bellini@studenti.unimi.it`, `elvinia.riccobene@unimi.it`

Abstract. Specifications of modern complex systems can become so large that model cutting or abstraction is required to enable automatic analysis by model checkers. Moreover, relying solely on model simulators or scenario-based validation does not provide sufficient guarantees regarding the model's compliance with requirements or its satisfaction of desired properties.

Building on the idea of code fuzzing and leveraging the executability of models, this paper introduces a model fuzzing approach for Abstract State Machine specifications developed in ASMETA. The supporting tool, specified in ASMETA, enables randomized executions of models with the aim of triggering unexpected behaviors such as crashes, assertion failures, or security vulnerabilities. To evaluate our approach, we consider two well-known case studies from the literature, one from security protocols and one from concurrent systems, to demonstrate its analysis capabilities.

Keywords: Formal Models · Fuzzing · Abstract State Machine · ASMETA · Security Testing · Hyperproperties · Model Evaluation

1 Introduction

Formal methods provide a rigorous foundation for specifying and verifying system behavior, ensuring correctness at an abstract level before implementation. Among these, Abstract State Machines (ASMs) [14–16] offer a powerful and expressive framework for modeling system behavior through precise, executable specifications. The ASMETA framework [2] has further extended the practical applicability of ASMs by offering a comprehensive toolset for editing, validating, simulating, and analyzing ASM specifications. Through tools such as model simulators, invariant checkers, and translators, ASMETA enables ASMs to be treated as executable models, allowing early validation and iterative refinement.

Despite these advantages, as system complexity increases, ASM specifications can become extremely large and intricate. Large models may include extensive parallelism and numerous interacting components, leading to state-space explosions that make exhaustive techniques such as model checking computationally impractical. Even with the support of ASMETA's validation and verification (V&V) tools, complete formal analysis often becomes infeasible once specifications exceed a certain level of complexity.

© The Author(s), under exclusive license to Springer Nature Switzerland AG 2026
F. Ishikawa and A. Cunha (Eds.): ABZ 2026, LNCS 16579, pp. 22–42, 2026.
https://doi.org/10.1007/978-3-032-26752-8_2

To address these scalability limitations, we investigate integrating fuzzing [35] as a complementary execution-based analysis technique for ASMs within the ASMETA environment. Borrowing the concept from the software domain, where code fuzzing is well established [33], a fuzzer automatically generates a wide range of environment configurations and nondeterministic choices to explore multiple execution paths of an executable model. Unlike exhaustive model checking, fuzzing trades completeness for scalability, enabling the exploration of a large behavioral space at relatively low computational cost. This perspective is also closely related to statistical model checking (SMC) [3], which similarly relies on execution sampling when full state-space exploration is infeasible. Moreover, generating and analyzing multiple execution traces naturally supports the validation of hyperproperties [21, 25], i.e., properties defined over sets of traces rather than individual executions.

In this paper, we introduce model fuzzing as a scalable validation approach for ASM models and integrate it as a first-class analysis technique for executable ASMs within the ASMETA framework. Our novel contributions are threefold:

- An ASMETA-based fuzzer model capable of driving executable ASMETA specifications through randomized environments and nondeterministic choices.
- A runtime checking mechanism for (i) invariants and user-defined termination conditions, and for (ii) trace-set properties (hyperproperties) across multiple executions.
- Support for quantitative evaluation of model behavior via aggregated metrics over states or conditions of interest across multiple executions.

By integrating fuzzing into the ASMETA tool chain, we provide a lightweight and scalable complement to exhaustive verification, enabling the validation of large or highly nondeterministic ASM models when full formal analysis is impractical. Our model fuzzing approach increases the likelihood of uncovering specification defects, unintended behaviors, invariant violations, and missing rule guards that may remain undetected by traditional V&V analyses. Thus, it enhances the reliability of complex specifications and offers a pragmatic approach for analyzing systems that exceed the limits of traditional verification techniques.

Although our contribution focuses on ASMETA models, the approach can apply to other formal methods that provide executable simulation platforms, which constitute the essential prerequisite for model fuzzing.

The remainder of the paper is organized as follows. Section 2 briefly recalls the ASM formal method and the ASMETA toolset. Section 3 introduces the idea of model fuzzing by leveraging the executability of specifications. In Sect. 4, we present the ASMETA-based model of our fuzzer and explain how it captures the essential requirements of a fuzzer for state-based executable models. Section 5 reports the results of applying the fuzzer to two well-known case studies: the Needham–Schroeder public-key protocol, known to be vulnerable to Lowe's attack [32], and the classical dining philosophers problem. These examples illustrate the applicability of our method across different domains and computational paradigms, highlighting its effectiveness in analyzing relevant behavioral properties. Section 6 discusses our approach in relation to complementary V&V techniques supported in ASMETA, outlining how fuzzing can be integrated into the ASMETA tool chain and analyzing its strengths and limitations. Section 7 compares our work with existing approaches, and Sect. 8 concludes the paper and outlines future research directions.

2   Abstract State Machines and ASMETA in a Nutshell

The *Abstract State Machines* (ASMs) [14–16] is a state-based formal method. *States* are mathematical algebras specifying a system configuration by means of arbitrarily complex data, i.e., domains of elements with functions defined on them. State *transitions* are expressed by transition rules describing how the data (function values saved into *locations*) change from one state to the next one.

Functions that are not modified by rule transitions are *static*. Those that are updated are *dynamic*, and are further classified into *monitored* functions—read by the machine but modified by the environment—and *controlled* functions, which are both read and written by the machine.

To specify different control structures, we use the rule constructors for guarded updates (`if-then`, `switch-case`), parallel updates (`par`), and nondeterministic updates (`choose`), etc.

An ASM *computation* (or *run*) is defined as a finite or infinite sequence $S_0, S_1, \ldots, S_n, \ldots$ of states, where S_0 is an initial state and each S_{n+1} is obtained from S_n by firing the unique *main rule*, which may in turn invoke other rules. At each computation step, a set of locations is updated simultaneously, thereby changing the interpretations of the corresponding dynamic functions and determining the next state. Any inconsistent updates cause the model run to fail and stop.

ASMETA. It is a toolset built around ASMs [11]. It enables integrated use of tools for model editing (using the `AsmetaL` notation) and V&V activities, and has a well-defined process [6] for system modeling and analysis.

Model validation exploits the characteristic of the ASMs to be *executed*. A model can be validated by simulation (using `AsmetaS`) – interactively or randomly –, animation (using `AsmetaA`), and scenarios execution (using `AsmetaV`).

Model verification is performed by proving properties expressed in temporal logic. The tool `AsmetaSMV` [8] maps `AsmetaL` models to the `NuSMV` [20] model checker, which verifies whether the specified properties hold over all possible executions of the model.

For further details on tool usage, the reader is referred to the tutorial in [11] and the public GitHub repository [2].

3   Fuzzing an Executable Model

Our approach follows the classical fuzzing paradigm [35]: an external agent repeatedly executes a target program until allocated computational resources are exhausted or unexpected behavior –such as a crash or an invariant violation– is detected. If formal models are executable and a simulation platform is available, the same idea can be used for fuzzing models. A visual comparison between the traditional single-run simulation and our fuzzing-based approach is shown in Fig. 1. In the case of a model single-run simulation, invariants are checked at each execution step. These are logical formulas expressing properties that must hold in every state, and reflect requirement properties or any kind of assertions that must always holds. A violation of an invariant indicates that the property is not satisfied, revealing incorrect behavior. In case of automatic fuzzing, an apriori fixed, but large, number of runs are sequentially executed, and possible invariants violation stops fuzzing, revealing the incorrect behavior. Note that, in the case of infinite runs, the fuzzer observes a fixed number of steps.

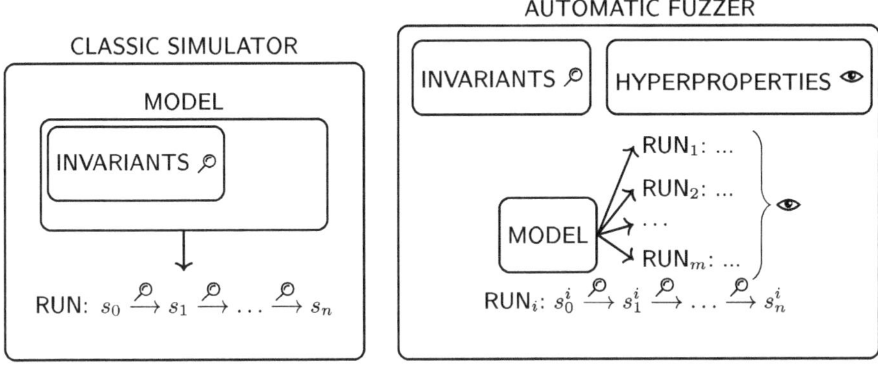

Fig. 1. Comparison between classic simulator and fuzzing approach

Automated multi-run execution strengthens the assessment of how well a model adheres to its specification and also enables the detection of potential security vulnerabilities. While specifying desired properties is often straightforward, verifying that the model actually satisfies them can be far more challenging. By exploring a wide range of execution paths, the fuzzer can expose behaviors or corner cases that a single run would likely never encounter. In particular, violations of specified invariants indicate that either the model or the underlying specification requires revision. Moreover, since model fuzzing has access to information aggregated across multiple runs, it enables checking *hyperproperties* [21], i.e., properties defined over sets of execution traces. For example, "stipulating a bound on mean response time over all executions is an availability policy that cannot be specified as a property of individual traces" [21]; similarly, enforcing a lower bound on "the percentage of requests that are serviced

```
1   asm fuzzer                                    30      if run = −1 then
2                                                 31        par
3   import ../../STDL/StandardLibrary             32          r_reinitializeSimulatedModel[]
4   import ./targetModel                          33          run := 1
5                                                 34        endpar
6   signature:                                    35        // check invariants
7     controlled hyperpropertyLocations:...//     36      else if not(invariants) then error := true
        to measure observed runs of the           37      else if not(hyperproperties) then error
        target model                                       := true
8     controlled error: Boolean                   38      else
9     controlled steps: Integer                   39        // do one run step of the target model
10    controlled run: Integer                     40        if not(terminatedRun) then
11    derived hyperproperties: Boolean            41          par
12    derived invariants: Boolean                 42            r_measureHPs[] // optional
13    derived terminatedRun: Boolean              43            choose $varList in DomainList
14    static maxRun: Integer                      44                with propList($varList) do
15    static maxStep: Integer                     45                    r_simulatedMain[
16                                                                        $varList]
17  definitions:                                  46          steps := steps +1
18    function maxRun =... // max number of       47          endpar
        runs                                      48        // reset the target model run and
19    function maxStep =... // max number of               simulate again
        steps                                     49        else
20    function terminatedRun = steps>=            50          if run < maxRun then
        maxStep or ... // complete from           51            par
        the target model                          52              r_measureHPs[] // optional
21    function hyperproperties =... // H1 & ...   53              r_reinitializeSimulatedModel[]
        & Hn, (optional) to define                54              run := run + 1
22    function invariants =... // I1 & ... & In,  55            endpar
        import from the target model              56          endif
23                                                57        endif
24    rule r_reinitializeSimulatedModel =... //   58      endif endif endif
        import from the target model              59
25    rule r_simulatedMain =... // import         60  default init s0:
        from the target model                     61    function hyperpropertyLocations =...
26    rule r_measureHPs = // (optional) to        62    function steps = 0
        manage hyperpropertyLocations             63    function run = −1
27                                                64    function error = false
28  main rule r_Main =
29    // initialize the target model for the
        first run
```

Listing 1. ASMETA fuzzer

within a specified time" [21] requires reasoning over sets of execution traces. By leveraging hyperproperty monitoring techniques [25], violations can be detected by correlating behaviors across different runs. This capability opens the door to detecting sophisticated classes of bugs, particularly those related to security, confidentiality, fairness, or nondeterminism.

Our automatic fuzzing approach makes it possible to determine whether a given hyperproperty fails within the observed set of runs. This feature distinguishes classical code fuzzing from this model-based perspective. Thanks to white-box access to the model during simulation–allowing the fuzzer to inspect internal state memory–it can measure additional system characteristics. In particular, by persisting observed data across runs, the fuzzer can compute metrics such as the average number of runs in which a condition of interest occurs. Such hyperproperty-based analyses are not possible in a single-run setting or when using a black-box external tool, and therefore substantially enhance our ability to evaluate the model's robustness.

4   ASMETA Fuzzer Development and Usage

We describe here how we have concretized the approach of fuzzing ASMETA models. According to the intended behavior described in Sect. 3, we have specified a fuzzer model in ASMETA, running on the ASMETA simulator. Listing 1 presents the skeleton of this model.

Fuzzer Operation. According to the r_Main rule (see line 28), the fuzzer first initializes (rule r_reinitializeSimulatedModel at line 32) the target model based on the initial state defined in the target specification.

It then executes the target model by invoking, at each run step, the model's main rule via r_simulatedMain (see line 45). Execution continues until the fuzzer detects a violation of an invariant (line 36), a hyperproperty (line 37), or a run-termination condition, terminatedRun. This condition reflects both the predefined limit maxStep on the execution length of the simulated model and any additional constraints derived from the specific target model. Indeed, depending on the model imported for analysis (line 4), further termination conditions may be introduced, either due to the model's internal logic or to delimit the scope of the fuzzing analysis.

At each step, the fuzzer provides randomly generated environment values by nondeterministically assigning values to the monitored variables varList[1] from their respective domains DomainList (line 43), while ensuring that the assigned values satisfy all required properties propList (line 44). The nondeterministic updates are implemented using the **choose-with** rule constructor, which enforces the conditions specified in propList() over the generated values.

If no violation is detected, the target model is executed repeatedly until the terminatedRun condition is satisfied. If the fuzzing process has not terminated (line 50), the simulated model is restarted; each execution begins from the same initial state (line 53), as defined by the rule r_reinitializeSimulatedMode (line 24).

An error condition is reported when an invariant or an hyperproperty (see line 36–37) is violated. In practical experiments, instead of using Boolean error flags, each invariant or hyperproperty can be associated with an integer code or a descriptive message, replacing lines 36–37 with a sequence of if statements.

To support the evaluation of model behavior, the fuzzer records the values or the occurrence of specific conditions in the simulated model. This is performed by the rule r_measureHPs, which updates the relevant measures both at each step within a run (line 42) and at the end of each run (line 52). These recorded data can then be used as quantitative metrics to derive further insights about the target model or to assess whether hyperproperties hold.

---

[1] There are some syntactic constrains in the AsmetaL syntax [11]: $var denotes a variable var, r_rule[] denotes a macro call rule.

Fuzzer and Target Model Configuration. To effectively fuzzing a target model, the skeleton of the fuzzer model and a target model must be instrumented and configured according to the following steps.

- The target model's monitored functions are converted into controlled functions managed by the fuzzer, since the environment is now provided by the fuzzer, which handles these functions either randomly or according to predefined rules.
- The invariants are extracted from the target model and converted into derived functions within the fuzzer's model. These will be used during fuzzing to check for possible violations.
- The main rule of the target model is moved into the fuzzer's model and renamed as r_simulatedMain. The fuzzer will invoke this rule at each step of the single run.
- The initialization logic originally defined in the init section of the target model is moved into a dedicated rule, r_reinitializeSimulatedModel, in the fuzzer's model.
- The target model, instrumented as above, is imported into the header of the fuzzer model.
- Before starting the fuzzing process, we specify, in the fuzzer model, the maximum number of simulations to run (maxRun), the maximum length of each run (maxStep), and refine the model-specific termination condition that applies to all executions (terminatedRun).

This process of configuring the fuzzer and the target models can, in principle, be automated, although it is not at the moment. Listing A in the Appendix shows the fuzzer model configured for fuzzing the ASMETA specification of the Needham–Schroeder public-key protocol, introduced in the next section.

The fuzzer, as ASMETA model, is executed by the AsmetaS simulator [11].

5   Fuzzer Applications

To evaluate our approach, we consider two well-known case studies from the literature: one from the domain of security protocols—the Needham–Schroeder public-key protocol, known to be vulnerable to Lowe's attack [32]—and another from classical concurrent systems—the dining philosophers problem. These examples demonstrate how our method supports the analysis of relevant properties, highlighting its applicability across different domains and its effectiveness in scenarios with varying scalability and computational paradigms.

5.1   The NSPK Protocol Case Study

The Needham–Schroeder public-key communication protocol [34] (NSPK, for short) consists of a sequence of messages exchanged between two principals, A

for *Alice* and B for *Bob*, with the goal of achieving mutual authentication.

$$\begin{aligned}
&\textit{Protocol}: &&\textit{Legend}: \\
&\text{M1. } A \to B : \{A, N_A\}_{K_B} &&N_A, \text{ nonce generated by A} \\
&\text{M2. } B \to A : \{N_A, N_B\}_{K_A} &&K_A, \text{ public key of A} \\
&\text{M3. } A \to B : \{N_B\}_{K_B} &&\{\dots\}_{K_A}, \text{ encryption with } K_A
\end{aligned}$$

It consists of three messages: in the first message, principal A sends to B a message containing her identity, A, and a nonce, N_A, to avoid replay attacks, that only B can decrypt with his private key. B's answer (message M2) is ciphered with A's public key and contains nonce N_A to authenticate B, and a nonce N_B to authenticate A with B. Since message M2 is encrypted with A's public key, she is the only one who can decrypt it, thus if B receives message M3 containing nonce N_B encrypted with his public key, A is authenticated, too.

The protocol exhibits a well-known vulnerability, known as the Lowe attack [32]: an intruder (the Spy) intercepts the private nonce N_B generated by B and reuses it to engage in a parallel session with A. This violates *entity authentication*, the property ensuring that each participant in a protocol session can be confident of the identity of its peer.

We would like to emphasize that our goal is not to analyze the protocol in order to discover new vulnerabilities, as it has already been extensively studied in the literature. Rather, we selected it as a case study because its known vulnerability allows us to demonstrate that our fuzzer can automatically rediscover such flaws. We started from an ASMETA specification available in the ASMETA repository, which we modified in two main respects.

First, we replaced the original multi-agent model with a single-agent orchestrating the execution of all principals. This restructuring ensures that, after each transition, control returns to the main rule, enabling the fuzzer to simulate the protocol step by step. At each step, the acting principal is selected nondeterministically, allowing us to encode all possible interactions among principals within the protocol.

Second, we revised the Spy's behavior to conform to the Dolev–Yao adversary model [23]. In this setting, the Spy can intercept, modify, forward, and replay messages, while remaining unable to break the underlying cryptographic primitives. This change produces a more realistic and general adversarial model, better suited to demonstrating the fuzzer's ability to automatically uncover failures and security flaws. In contrast, the original repository version manually encoded the Spy's behavior specifically to reproduce Lowe's attack.

We specify this model by introducing nondeterministic choices that span the admissible adversarial actions. The Spy is implemented as a protocol-aware stochastic agent that can dynamically interleave honest and adversarial behaviors during a single execution. Rather than encoding fixed attack strategies, adversarial behavior is constructed as a sequence of fine-grained decisions (e.g., whether to intercept, replay, or modify a message, and how to transform its fields). Message manipulation is restricted to well-typed substitutions: each field may only be replaced with another element of the same type (e.g., principals, nonces, keys), ensuring that all generated messages remain well-formed. This Spy's behavior enables systematic exploration of diverse and previously unknown attack traces without requiring manually specified attack scenarios.

Although this generalization introduced behaviors that are not directly useful for attack discovery—for example, intercepting a message and returning it to its original sender—, it also revealed previously unmodeled behaviors in the honest receiver. These behaviors had remained unnoticed in the original specification available in the ASMETA repository due to the more limited attacker model.

Starting from the revised model of the NSPK protocol, following the model and fuzzer configuration steps described in Sect. 4, we obtained the ASMETA model of the fuzzer customized to analyze the NSPK model. It is reported in Appendix A and available, together with the original and the revised NSPK models, online [1].

We defined four invariants and one hyperproperty.

Invariants. The first two invariants verify whether the model correctly implements the protocol specification:

1. *Honest users never reuse the same nonce with different receivers*:

$$\neg\big(\exists s, r_1, r_2 \in \mathit{User} \; \exists n \in \mathit{Nonce} : \neg\mathrm{isSpy}(s) \wedge \neg\mathrm{isSpy}(r_1)\wedge$$
$$\neg\mathrm{isSpy}(r_2) \wedge r_1 \neq r_2 \wedge \mathrm{sent}(s, r_1, n) \wedge \mathrm{sent}(s, r_2, n)\big)$$

   where, the predicate *isSpy(u)* evaluates to true if the user is a Spy, and *sent(s,r,n)* holds when the principal s has sent a message to r containing the nonce n.
2. *The number of completed sessions never exceeds the number of initiated sessions*:

$$\mathit{terminatedSessions} \leq \mathit{startedSessions}$$

   The other two invariants examine whether the specification actually satisfies the intended security goals of the protocol.
3. *Upon termination, the protocol successfully enabled two users to exchange nonces*:

$$\mathit{termination} \implies \exists u_1, u_2 \in \mathit{User}, \; \exists n_1, n_2 \in \mathit{Nonce} : u_1 \neq u_2 \wedge n_1 \neq n_2\wedge$$
$$\wedge \, \mathrm{know}(u_1, n_1) \wedge \mathrm{know}(u_2, n_1) \wedge \mathrm{know}(u_1, n_2) \wedge \mathrm{know}(u_2, n_2)$$

   where, the predicate *known(u,n)* holds when the principal u knows the nonce n.
4. *Confidentiality*: for any number of completed protocol runs, each exchanged nonce is shared between no more than two participating agents.

$$\mathit{terminatedSession} \geq 1 \implies \neg\big(\exists u_1, u_2, u_3 \in \mathit{User} \; \exists n_1, n_2 \in \mathit{Nonce} :$$
$$u_1 \neq u_2 \wedge u_1 \neq u_3 \wedge u_2 \neq u_3 \wedge n_1 \neq n_2 \wedge \mathrm{know}(u_1, n_1) \wedge \mathrm{know}(u_2, n_1)$$
$$\wedge \, \mathrm{know}(u_3, n_1) \wedge \mathrm{know}(u_1, n_2) \wedge \mathrm{know}(u_2, n_2) \wedge \mathrm{know}(u_3, n_2)\big)$$

Hyperproperty. It checks a robustness requirement: after a sufficiently large number of protocol executions, the presence of an attacker should not reduce the termination rate below 70%.

5. *The protocol terminates at least 70% of the time*:

$$run \geq 100 \implies \left(totTerminatedProtocols \cdot 100 \geq 70 \cdot totStartedProtocols\right)$$

The fuzzer proved valuable both during model development and in the final analysis. Throughout the construction phase, it served as an effective debugging tool by generating traces that revealed invariant violations, enabling us to identify the source of each issue and refine the model accordingly. In this respect, the fuzzer represents a practical alternative to the `AsmetaA` animator, especially for complex models in which identifying property violations through the graphical interface is challenging.

The fuzzing analysis of the final model showed that the second invariant detected a replay attack targeting the third message of the protocol, thereby highlighting a discrepancy between the model and its specification. In the original specification available in the ASMETA repository, the third message verified only that the received nonce had been generated by the intended receiver, but did not ensure that the nonce was fresh (not previously observed). Thus, beyond assisting with model refinement, the fuzzer also exposed a security flaw in the specification itself: when invariant 4 is violated, the fuzzer successfully uncovers the Lowe attack on the protocol (a corresponding trace is provided online [1]).

In addition, the fuzzer was successfully applied to the evaluation of hyper-properties. By introducing a limited number of controlled locations, suitable to specify the hyperproperty, into the fuzzer signature, we were able to express quantitative constraints over multiple executions and detect violations of hyper-properties at runtime. This demonstrates that the proposed approach is not limited to single-run invariants, but can also support the analysis of more expressive security properties.

Evaluating Fuzzer Scalability. In the baseline scenario with two users and one spy, the attack is detected after only a few executions. To assess the scalability of our approach, we systematically increased the cardinality of several domains, substantially enlarging the model state space. Although these scenarios expose the same vulnerability as in the two-user case, they do so within a significantly more complex setting. The median execution time for each configuration, measured over 11 runs, is reported in Table 1[2].

These results confirm both the simplicity and scalability of the proposed method. Obtaining comparable results through an automatic translation to model-checking techniques would be impractical, primarily due to state explosion and also due to expressivity limitations. In particular, our model defines the function *messageNNK*, which maps a message identifier to the corresponding NNK message content, i.e., from *MessageID* to *Prod(Nonce, Nonce, PubKeyID)*. However, this function cannot be automatically translated into NuSMV

---

[2] The experiments were performed on a machine equipped with 32 GB of RAM and a 13th Gen Intel(R) Core(TM) i5-1335U processor (up to 4.6 GHz).

Table 1. Fuzzer performance results for the NSPK case study

Model size	# Steps	Time	RAM
3 users, 2 nonce, 5 messages, 1 session, 32 steps per run	436	9.6 s	654 MB
4 users, 10 nonce, 16 messages, 2 sessions, 32 steps per run	483	3.0 min	805 MB
5 users, 30 nonce, 50 messages, 4 sessions, 100 steps per run	274	30 min	746 MB
5 users, 36 nonce, 60 messages, 4 sessions, 100 steps per run	486	1.1 h	774 MB

using `AsmetaSMV`, since the mapping cannot manage such a codomain, due to the expressivity limitations of NuSMV. Therefore, the model would have to be flattened, requiring changes to the corresponding signatures and a substantial rewriting of the model to ensure compatibility with the model checker.

5.2   The Dining Philosophers Case Study

To compare the fuzzer with the `AsmetaSMV` translation to a model checker, and to evaluate their performance on a concrete benchmark, we selected the well-known Dining Philosophers problem.

The adopted scheduling strategy randomly selects a philosopher at each step. If the selected philosopher is hungry and both adjacent forks are available, it starts eating. If the philosopher is already eating, it may nondeterministically decide either to stop eating and release the forks or to continue eating. The system starts with all philosophers in a hungry state. The model is available online [1].

Invariant. The property of interest is that the model never reaches a configuration in which *all philosophers are eventually satisfied*, i.e., at least one philosopher remains hungry in every reachable state.

$$\exists p \in Philosophers : \text{isHungry}(p)$$

We therefore aim to falsify the invariant asserting that all philosophers can eventually become non-hungry by identifying a counterexample execution trace.

Hyperproperty. The property of interest over the set of observed runs is that *there exists, on average, a philosopher who consumes more than the others.* We detect a counterexample by requiring that, after a sufficiently large number of runs, there always exists a pair of philosophers such that one has consumed at least 10% more than the other:

$$run > 250 \Rightarrow \exists p_1, p_2 \in Philosophers : \text{consumption}(p_1) > 1.1\,\text{consumption}(p_2)$$

Evaluating Fuzzer Scalability. To assess how the approach scales with the problem size, we conduct an experimental evaluation (see Table 2) restricted to invariant violation detection. We compare the results obtained using the fuzzing approach and those produced by executing the model in NuSMV, employing both BDD-based model checking and bounded model checking with a SAT solver. The results clearly indicate that the problem exhibits exponential growth with respect to the number of philosophers when approached via model checking, whereas it scales linearly when using the fuzzer.

We also evaluated NuSMV using its simulation mode. However, simulation is mainly intended to help users familiarize themselves with a model and gain confidence in its behavior. In particular, it does not automatically stop when an invariant is violated, and therefore, it cannot be effectively used for automated counterexample discovery.

In contrast, generating a trace that automatically exposes the invariant violation with the ASMETA fuzzer only required increasing the number of philosophers and re-running the fuzzer on the modified model for a few seconds. This demonstrates that the proposed fuzzing approach is both simple and scalable, and can effectively complement existing validation and verification techniques.

Table 2. Time and memory scalability: comparison of `AsmetaSMV` model checking and ASMETA model fuzzing on the Dining Philosophers case study

# philosophers	Model checking					Model-fuzzing	
	BDD-based		Bounded SAT-based				
	Time	RAM	Time	RAM	Depth	Time	RAM
7	0.41 s	44 MB	0.78 s	24 MB	18	1.2 s	115 MB
8	6.0 s	66 MB	14 min	75 MB	20	1.3 s	118 MB
9	9.3 s	78 MB	5.9 h	200 MB	23	1.3 s	116 MB
10	1.8 min	300 MB	> 40 h	≥ 540 MB	≥ 25	1.4 s	128 MB
11	3.0 min	630 MB	N/A	N/A	N/A	1.4 s	136 MB
12	28 min	3.4 GB	N/A	N/A	N/A	1.5 s	137 MB
13	49 min	6.7 GB	N/A	N/A	N/A	1.7 s	183 MB
14	3.6 h	27 GB	N/A	N/A	N/A	2.5 s	233 MB
200	N/A	N/A	N/A	N/A	N/A	15.6 s	640 MB
500	N/A	N/A	N/A	N/A	N/A	51.7 s	648 MB
1000	N/A	N/A	N/A	N/A	N/A	2.8 min	667 MB

6   Discussion

The model analysis strategy presented in this paper should be viewed as an additional, integrated approach suitable for use in the early stages of system development. It complements existing techniques and can be applied before more heavyweight analysis methods, such as model checking, are employed, or as an alternative when other techniques cannot be used due to limitations such as state-explosion or the inability of target tools to support all constructs of the source ASMETA model (as in the case of mappings to NuSMV).

Advantages of the Approach. Implementing the fuzzer directly in ASMETA provides several benefits. First, it offers a familiar environment for ASMETA users and avoids reliance on external tools. Second, the native implementation enables greater expressiveness during fuzzing, including the ability to manipulate monitored functions, inspect internal states, and measure hyperproperties. This white-box access is a significant advantage over classical black-box fuzzers.

The approach complements existing ASMETA V&V methods.

Compared with model simulation and scenario-based validation, fuzzing explores a substantially broader space of behaviors, increasing confidence in the model's adherence to its specification. It supports the reproduction of complex environment behaviors, enables the measurement of hyperproperties, and provides a scalable avenue for validating systems too large for traditional methods.

Compared with model-based testing (MBT), model fuzzing shares the fundamental idea of driving a system specification through diverse input sequences to observe and validate its behavior. However, the two approaches differ in their objectives: MBT is primarily aimed at ensuring specification correctness and functional reliability, whereas fuzzing focuses on uncovering crashes, vulnerabilities, and unexpected behaviors. As a result, MBT is typically used for functional validation, while fuzzing is better suitable for assessing security and robustness. Thus, the two approaches are not only compatible but also mutually reinforcing.

Compared with symbolic execution and model checking, fuzzing is lightweight, scalable, and able to execute very large models that are otherwise infeasible to analyze exhaustively. The symbolic executor for ASMETA [17] systematically explores execution paths and can achieve higher coverage than random testing, but it is limited to enumerated and non-dynamic abstract domains, finite quantifiers, function definitions, and macro rules. It also becomes computationally expensive as model complexity grows. Model checking [8] faces similar scalability challenges, as it does not support infinite domains or the ASM domain extension mechanism. Moreover, mapping ASMETA functions into NuSMV variables is not always feasible–e.g., our NSPK model cannot be mapped into an input model for `AsmetaSMV` since many functions have Cartesian product sets as codomain–, and using `AsmetaSMV` is generally impractical for large or highly complex models. However, when considering CTL liveness properties expressed using the F (eventually) operator, exhaustive state space exploration techniques, such as those provided by model checking, remain necessary. More generally, fuzzing can effectively identify counterexamples for properties whose violations admit finite traces, such as those involving the AG (globally) or AU (until) operators, but it cannot establish liveness or existential path properties. Properties based on F, as well as those involving existential quantification such as EG, require reasoning over complete and potentially infinite traces. Consequently, the absence of a satisfying or witnessing trace during fuzzing is inconclusive, since the property may hold but remain unobserved, or it may only manifest in traces beyond those explored by the fuzzer.

In any case, while model checking excels at proving correctness properties and symbolic execution is powerful for detecting concrete bugs, our fuzzing approach offers a cost-effective alternative that scales better on large models and naturally supports the measurement of hyperproperties. Because the fuzzer executes the model concretely, it can also operate on real input traces, avoiding issues such as invariants depending on uninterpreted functions in the initial state. Moreover, the fuzzer performance can be increased by automatically translating the ASMETA model of the fuzzer into C++ with `Asmeta2C++` [12], offering a practical advantage for large-scale experimentation.

Model fuzzing is also particularly valuable when seeking security assessment. Unlike safety analysis, which ensures that the system does not harm the environment, security-oriented analysis checks that hostile or erroneous environments do not compromise the system. The fuzzer can reproduce a wide range of possible environment behaviors through randomized inputs, increasing the chance of exposing vulnerabilities or unexpected corner cases.

Limitations. The limitations of our method coincide with well-known limitations of traditional fuzzers. The approach is inherently non-exhaustive and cannot guarantee full behavioral coverage. Although randomness provides diversity, it may still miss certain behaviors. Moreover, the current implementation does not incorporate coverage-guided or constraint-solving input-generation techniques, such as those used in symbolic fuzzers or concolic testing.

7   Related Work

We now relate our approach to existing work. We do not compare our model fuzzing technique with other analysis methods in ASMETA, as this comparison has already been extensively discussed in Sect. 6. Instead, we focus on similar approaches in the broader area of model testing. Indeed, in contrast to the software domain, where fuzzing has been widely explored, mainly to detect security vulnerabilities and other faults in the code [33,35,38], our idea is to apply fuzzing to formal model itself to validate the model or identify problems in the specification.

The work in [36] proposes a model-based whitebox fuzzing method that uses input models to generate valid randomized files. These models specify data-chunk formats and integrity constraints to guide code fuzzing. The goal, however, is to test the code rather than to fuzz or analyze the model itself, as in our approach.

The study in [5] uses models to guide protocol fuzzing, with their Dolev–Yao model defining the fuzzer's search space. While we also adopt the Dolev–Yao formalism, our focus remains at the specification level rather than the code level.

The work in [37] infers state machines from protocol implementations using code fuzzing. The resulting state-machine models of TLS are then analyzed to uncover inconsistencies. However, the approach is not fully automated: state-machine checking is performed manually, and the inferred models are relatively small. Once again, the primary objective is code validation rather than model analysis.

A contribution similar to ours, which focuses on fuzzing a model rather than the code, was proposed in the context of embedded systems and model-driven design [4, 28]. In the first line of work, a model is derived from the code and then analyzed to detect faults. Their method is based on UML models, whereas our work relies on rigorous formal models. In [28], an executable model constructed with Extended Finite State Machines is first created and then tested through concolic execution. In contrast, our method uses a more expressive state-based formalism, the Abstract State Machines, which allow infinite, dynamic domains and nondeterminism. In addition, our analysis can employ hyperproperties, a feature absent in the previously discussed works.

Our approach is closely related to statistical model checking (SMC) [3], as it relies on the generation and analysis of executions rather than exhaustive state-space exploration. SMC is supported by widely used tools such as PRISM [31], based on probabilistic automata, STORM [29], supporting both discrete- and continuous-time Markov models, UPPAAL [22], based on networks of timed automata, and GreatSPN [10], based on (stochastic) Petri nets for concurrent system modeling.

Nevertheless, our approach differs in terms of the adopted formalism, toolset context, and analysis objective. We rely on Abstract State Machines (ASMs) as the underlying modelling framework, providing a higher-level, more expressive, compact, and user-friendly specification language compared to the input languages typically supported by model checkers. Moreover, ASMETA was originally developed in the context of model specification and validation, rather than as a dedicated model-checking environment. Furthermore, the statistical extensions of mainstream tools such as PRISM, Storm, UPPAAL, and GreatSPN are primarily designed to perform statistical hypothesis testing and/or statistical estimation of trace properties, and do not natively support hyperproperties, which require reasoning over relations among multiple executions. By developing our fuzzer directly within the ASMETA ecosystem, we enable scalable model fuzzing and the validation of hyperproperties through the analysis of sets of executions rather than individual traces.

Despite the availability of several dedicated approaches for the verification of hyperproperties [26, 30], there are still relatively few instruments aimed at non-exhaustive, lightweight, and scalable analysis. Among the existing dedicated tools, RVHyper [24] provides runtime monitoring for temporal hyperproperties by observing the executions of a running system. This approach differs from ours, since we perform hyperproperty checking directly on the formal ASM model executions generated within ASMETA, rather than monitoring an external implementation. Moreover, recent research efforts have investigated the extension of statistical model checking techniques to probabilistic hyperproperties, for instance in the context of real-valued signals [9]. These works further confirm the relevance of execution-based and sampling-based approaches for hyperproperty analysis, while highlighting that scalable tool support is still an open and active research direction.

8 Conclusion

In this work, we explored how the principles of code fuzzing can be effectively transferred to the domain of executable formal models. We presented a fuzzer for Abstract State Machine specifications developed natively in ASMETA, enabling randomized execution of models to reveal unexpected behaviors such as assertion violations, erroneous states, or potential security flaws. The applicability and usefulness of the approach were demonstrated through the analysis of the Needham–Schroeder public-key protocol, a classical case study known for its vulnerabilities. These results indicate that model fuzzing can serve as a practical complement to existing formal analysis techniques, particularly for uncovering subtle behaviors in complex or security-critical specifications.

This work represents a first step toward several research directions.

In future work, we will investigate the automation of embedding a model into the fuzzer, as described in Sect. 4. However, some model-specific instrumentation and fuzzer configuration steps will remain user-defined. These include setting parameters (e.g., maxRun and maxStep), defining termination conditions (e.g., terminatedRun), specifying input-related properties via propList() over generated inputs, and, when required, defining additional signatures and rules for the verification of hyperproperties.

We plan to further investigate the use of model fuzzing as a means of providing security guarantees in domains such as security-oriented IoT protocols and blockchain smart contracts, where model-checking analyses are often challenging and require substantial abstraction or model reduction [18,19]. We also aim to explore its applicability to safety assurance in large and complex systems [7,13].

Given the complementary strengths of fuzzing and symbolic execution [17], a promising direction for future work is combining the two techniques to create a *concolic* testing framework for ASMETA models, analogous to hybrid approaches used in software testing. Such a combination can be useful to increase the path coverage, as done in the more advanced approaches in code fuzzing [27].

We also plan to improve the performance of our fuzzing technique by mapping the ASMETA model of the fuzzer into C++ [12], offering a practical advantage for large-scale experimentation.

Future work may include a systematic investigation of the limits and trade-offs of hyperproperty checking in ASMETA, particularly in terms of expressivity, computational cost, and modeling complexity. This paper introduces the ability to reason over sets of states, leaving a formal assessment of these aspects to subsequent studies.

A ASMETA Fuzzer for Needham Schroeder Protocol

Below is the fuzzer instrumentation used to analyze the Needham–Schroeder protocol. For a complete overview of the ASMETA models, including the Needham–Schroeder model, see [1]

```
asm NeedhamSchroederSpy_Fuzzer

import ../../STDL/StandardLibrary
import ./NeedhamSchroederSpy_signatureAndRules

signature:
 // To measure some observed behavior of the simulated model
 // these are useful for model analysis or to check hyperproperties
 controlled totTerminatedProtocols: Integer
 controlled totStartedProtocols: Integer
 // ------- SIMULATION SIGNATURE --------------
 controlled errorExitCode: Integer
 controlled steps: Integer
 controlled run: Integer
 derived hyperproperty: Boolean
 derived invariant1: Boolean
 derived invariant2: Boolean
 derived invariant3: Boolean
 derived invariant4: Boolean
 derived isRunTerminated: Boolean
 static maxRun: Integer
 static maxStep: Integer

definitions:
 // FUNCTION DEFINITIONS
 function maxRun = 1000
 function maxStep = 32
 function isRunTerminated = (terminatedSession = maxProtocolRuns or steps>=maxStep)
 // Functions for invariants (we translated invariants of simulated model into derived boolean functions)

 // test that even with an attacker, that can introduced random faults, the protocol terminates at least
     70% of the times
 function hyperproperty = (totTerminatedProtocols*100 >= 70*totStartedProtocols)

 // test the model implementation of the protocol
 // groups of honest users shouldn't send the same nonce to different users //maxProtocolRuns = 1
     implies
 function invariant1 = not(exist $s in UserID with isSpy($s) = FALSE and (exist $r1 in UserID with (exist
     $r2 in UserID with $r1 != $r2 and isSpy($r1) = FALSE and isSpy($r2) = FALSE and (exist $n in
     Nonce with (hasSentTo($s,$r1,$n) = TRUE and hasSentTo($s,$r2,$n) = TRUE)))))

 // test both correct model implementation and protocol correctness
 function invariant2 = terminatedSession <= startedSessions

 // test protocol property: check confidentiality when the protocol finished at least one time
 function invariant3 = terminatedSession >= 1 implies not(exist $u1 in UserID with (exist $u2 in UserID
     with (exist $u3 in UserID with ($u1!=$u2 and $u3!=$u1 and $u3!=$u2 and (exist $n1 in Nonce
     with(exist $n2 in Nonce with $n1!=$n2 and knowNonce($u1,$n1)=TRUE and knowNonce($u2,$n1
     )=TRUE and knowNonce($u3,$n1)=TRUE and knowNonce($u1,$n2)=TRUE and knowNonce($u2
     ,$n2)=TRUE and knowNonce($u3,$n2)=TRUE))))))

 // test protocol property: check correctness of the delivery when the protocol end for the first time
 function invariant4 = (terminatedSession = 1 implies (exist $u1 in UserID with (exist $u2 in UserID with
     ($u1 != $u2 and (exist $n1 in Nonce with (exist $n2 in Nonce with ($n1 != $n2 and knowNonce(
     $u1,$n1) = TRUE and knowNonce($u1,$n2) = TRUE and knowNonce($u2,$n1) = TRUE and
     knowNonce($u2,$n2) = TRUE)))))))


 // RULE DEFINITIONS
 rule r_reinitializeSimulatedModel =
```

```
par
 startedSessions := 0
 terminatedSession := 0
 forall $u in UserID with true do
  par
   hasAlreadySent($u) := FALSE
   forall $n in Nonce with true do
    par
     knowNonce($u, $n) := FALSE
     forall $r in UserID with true do hasSentTo($u, $r, $n) := undef
    endpar
  endpar
 forall $n1 in Nonce with true do isNonceArrivedToReceiver($n1) := FALSE
 forall $m in MessageID do
  par
   comunication($m) := (undef, undef)
   hasBeenRead($m) := undef
   messageType($m) := undef
   messageNUK($m) := (undef, undef, undef)
   messageNNK($m) := (undef, undef, undef)
   messageNK($m) := (undef, undef)
  endpar
 steps := 0
endpar

rule r_simulatedMain =
 choose $u in UserID with true do
  if isSpy($u) = TRUE then
   r_behaveRandomly[$u] // r_behaveCorrectly[$u]
  else
   r_behaveCorrectly[$u]
  endif

// MAIN RULE
main rule r_Main =
 // initialize simulated model for the first execution
 if run = -1 then
  par
   r_reinitializeSimulatedModel[]
   run := 1
  endpar
 // stop simulation when detecting one error
 else if errorExitCode != 0 then skip
 // check invariants
 else if run >= 40 and not(hyperproperty) then
  errorExitCode := -1
 else if not(invariant1) then errorExitCode := 1
 else if not(invariant2) then errorExitCode := 2
 else if not(invariant3) then errorExitCode := 3
 else if not(invariant4) then errorExitCode := 4
 else
 // do one transition in the simulated model
  if not(isRunTerminated) then
   par
    steps := steps +1
    r_simulatedMain[]
   endpar
  else
   par
    // save model behavior in global attributes for model analysis or to check hyperproperties
    totTerminatedProtocols := totTerminatedProtocols + terminatedSession
    totStartedProtocols := totStartedProtocols + startedSessions
    // reset the simulated model and simulate again
    if run < maxRun then
     par
      run := run + 1
      r_reinitializeSimulatedModel[]
     endpar
```

```
      endif
     endpar
    endif
  endif endif endif endif endif endif endif

// INITIAL STATE
default init s0:
 // Initialize counters to track simulation statistics for analysis and hyperproperty checks
 function totTerminatedProtocols = 0
 function totStartedProtocols = 0
 // ———————— SIMULATOR INIZIALIZATION ——————————————————
 function steps = 0
 function run = −1
 function errorExitCode = 0
```

Fuzzer model for fuzzing NSPK model

References

1. https://github.com/gabriele-bellini/fuzzing-asmeta-models-artifact-abz26
2. ASMETA (ASM mETAmodeling) toolset. https://asmeta.github.io/
3. Agha, G., Palmskog, K.: A survey of statistical model checking. ACM Trans. Model. Comput. Simul. **28**(1), 6:1–6:39 (2018). https://doi.org/10.1145/3158668
4. Ahmadi, R., Dingel, J.: Concolic testing for models of state-based systems. In: Proceedings of the 2019 27th ACM Joint Meeting on European Software Engineering Conference and Symposium on the Foundations of Software Engineering (2019). https://doi.org/10.1145/3338906.3338908
5. Ammann, M., Hirschi, L., Kremer, S.: DY fuzzing: formal Dolev–Yao models meet cryptographic protocol fuzz testing. In: Proceedings of the 45th IEEE Symposium on Security and Privacy (S&P 2024). IEEE Computer Society Press (2024). https://doi.org/10.1109/SP54263.2024.00096
6. Arcaini, P., Bombarda, A., Bonfanti, S., Gargantini, A., Riccobene, E., Scandurra, P.: The asmeta approach to safety assurance of software systems. In: Raschke, A., Riccobene, E., Schewe, K.-D. (eds.) Logic, Computation and Rigorous Methods. LNCS, vol. 12750, pp. 215–238. Springer, Cham (2021). https://doi.org/10.1007/978-3-030-76020-5_13
7. Arcaini, P., Bonfanti, S., Gargantini, A., Riccobene, E., Scandurra, P.: A journey with ASMETA from requirements to code: application to an automotive system with adaptive features. Int. J. Softw. Tools Technol. Transf. **26**(3), 379–401 (2024). https://doi.org/10.1007/S10009-024-00751-4
8. Arcaini, P., Gargantini, A., Riccobene, E.: AsmetaSMV: a way to link high-level ASM models to low-level NuSMV specifications. In: Frappier, M., Glässer, U., Khurshid, S., Laleau, R., Reeves, S. (eds.) ABZ 2010. LNCS, vol. 5977, pp. 61–74. Springer, Heidelberg (2010). https://doi.org/10.1007/978-3-642-11811-1_6
9. Arora, S., Hansen, R.R., Larsen, K.G., Legay, A., Poulsen, D.B.: Statistical model checking for probabilistic hyperproperties of real-valued signals. In: Legunsen, O., Rosu, G. (eds.) Model Checking Software, pp. 61–78. Springer, Cham (2022). https://doi.org/10.1007/978-3-031-15077-7_4
10. Baarir, S., Beccuti, M., Cerotti, D., De Pierro, M., Donatelli, S., Franceschinis, G.: The GreatSPN tool: recent enhancements. SIGMETRICS Perform. Eval. Rev. **36**(4), 4–9 (2009). https://doi.org/10.1145/1530873.1530876

11. Bombarda, A., Bonfanti, S., Gargantini, A., Riccobene, E., Scandurra, P.: ASMETA tool set for rigorous system design. In: Formal Methods - 26th International Symposium, FM 2024, Milan, Italy, 9–13 September 2024, Proceedings, Part II. LNCS, vol. 14934, pp. 492–517. Springer (2024). https://doi.org/10.1007/978-3-031-71177-0_28
12. Bonfanti, S., Gargantini, A., Mashkoor, A.: Design and validation of a C++ code generator from abstract state machines specifications. J. Softw. Evol. Process. **32**(2) (2020). https://doi.org/10.1002/SMR.2205
13. Bonfanti, S., Riccobene, E., Scandurra, P.: Formal specification and validation of the MVM-adapt system using compositional I/O abstract state machines. Sci. Comput. Program. **244**, 103299 (2025). https://doi.org/10.1016/J.SCICO.2025.103299
14. Börger, E., Gervasi, V.: Structures of Computing - A Guide to Practice-Oriented Theory. Springer, Cham (2024). https://doi.org/10.1007/978-3-031-54358-6
15. Börger, E., Raschke, A.: Modeling Companion for Software Practitioners. Springer, Heidelberg (2018). https://doi.org/10.1007/978-3-662-56641-1
16. Börger, E., Stärk, R.F.: Abstract State Machines. A Method for High-Level System Design and Analysis. Springer, Heidelberg (2003). https://doi.org/10.1007/978-3-642-18216-7
17. Braghin, C., Castillo, G.D., Riccobene, E., Valentini, S.: Using symbolic model execution to detect vulnerabilities of smart contracts. In: Leuschel, M., Ishikawa, F. (eds.) ABZ 2025. LNCS, vol. 15728, pp. 31–51. Springer, Cham (2025). https://doi.org/10.1007/978-3-031-94533-5_3
18. Braghin, C., Lilli, M., Riccobene, E.: A model-based approach for vulnerability analysis of IoT security protocols: the Z-wave case study. Comput. Secur. **127**, 103037 (2023). https://doi.org/10.1016/J.COSE.2022.103037
19. Braghin, C., Riccobene, E., Valentini, S.: Modeling and verification of smart contracts with abstract state machines. In: Proceedings of the 39th ACM/SIGAPP Symposium on Applied Computing, SAC 2024, Avila, Spain, 8–12 April 2024, pp. 1425–1432. ACM (2024). https://doi.org/10.1145/3605098.3636040
20. Cimatti, A., et al.: NuSMV 2: an opensource tool for symbolic model checking. In: International Conference on Computer Aided Verification (2002). https://doi.org/10.1007/3-540-45657-0_29
21. Clarkson, M.R., Schneider, F.B.: Hyperproperties. J. Comput. Secur. **18**(6), 1157–1210 (2010). https://doi.org/10.3233/JCS-2009-0393
22. David, A., Larsen, K.G., Legay, A., Mikucionis, M., Poulsen, D.B.: Uppaal SMC tutorial. Int. J. Softw. Tools Technol. Transf. **17**(4), 397–415 (2015). https://doi.org/10.1007/S10009-014-0361-Y
23. Dolev, D., Yao, A.C.C.: On the security of public key protocols. In: 22nd Annual Symposium on Foundations of Computer Science (SFCS 1981), pp. 350–357 (1981). https://doi.org/10.1109/SFCS.1981.32
24. Finkbeiner, B., Hahn, C., Stenger, M., Tentrup, L.: RVHyper: a runtime verification tool for temporal hyperproperties. In: Beyer, D., Huisman, M. (eds.) TACAS 2018. LNCS, vol. 10806, pp. 194–200. Springer, Cham (2018). https://doi.org/10.1007/978-3-319-89963-3_11
25. Finkbeiner, B., Hahn, C., Stenger, M., Tentrup, L.: Monitoring hyperproperties. Formal Methods Syst. Des. **54**(3), 336–363 (2019). https://doi.org/10.1007/s10703-019-00334-z
26. Finkbeiner, B., Rabe, M.N., Sánchez, C.: Algorithms for model checking Hyper-LTL and HyperCTL*. In: Kroening, D., Păsăreanu, C.S. (eds.) CAV 2015. LNCS,

vol. 9206, pp. 30–48. Springer, Cham (2015). https://doi.org/10.1007/978-3-319-21690-4_3

27. Godefroid, P., Kiezun, A., Levin, M.Y.: Grammar-based whitebox fuzzing. In: Proceedings of the ACM SIGPLAN 2008 Conference on Programming Language Design and Implementation, Tucson, AZ, USA, 7–13 June 2008, pp. 206–215. ACM (2008). https://doi.org/10.1145/1375581.1375607

28. Guglielmo, G.D., Fujita, M., Fummi, F., Pravadelli, G., Soffia, S.: EFSM-based model-driven approach to concolic testing of system-level design. In: 9th IEEE/ACM International Conference on Formal Methods and Models for Codesign, MEMOCODE 2011, Cambridge, UK, 11–13 July 2011, pp. 201–209. IEEE (2011). https://doi.org/10.1109/MEMCOD.2011.5970527

29. Hensel, C., Junges, S., Katoen, J.P., Quatmann, T., Volk, M.: The probabilistic model checker STORM. Int. J. Softw. Tools Technol. Transfer **24**(4), 589–610 (2022). https://doi.org/10.1007/s10009-021-00633-z

30. Hsu, T.-H., Sánchez, C., Bonakdarpour, B.: Bounded model checking for Hyperproperties. In: TACAS 2021. LNCS, vol. 12651, pp. 94–112. Springer, Cham (2021). https://doi.org/10.1007/978-3-030-72016-2_6

31. Kwiatkowska, M., Norman, G., Parker, D.: PRISM 4.0: verification of probabilistic real-time systems. In: Gopalakrishnan, G., Qadeer, S. (eds.) CAV 2011. LNCS, vol. 6806, pp. 585–591. Springer, Heidelberg (2011). https://doi.org/10.1007/978-3-642-22110-1_47

32. Lowe, G.: An attack on the Needham-Schroeder public-key authentication protocol. Inf. Process. Lett. **56**, 131–133 (1995). https://doi.org/10.1016/0020-0190(95)00144-2

33. Manès, V., et al.: The art, science, and engineering of fuzzing: a survey. IEEE Trans. Software Eng. **47**(11), 2312–2331 (2021). https://doi.org/10.1109/TSE.2019.2946563

34. Needham, R.M., Schroeder, M.D.: Using encryption for authentication in large networks of computers. Commun. ACM **21**(12), 993–999 (1978). https://doi.org/10.1145/359657.359659

35. Oehlert, P.: Violating assumptions with fuzzing. IEEE Secur. Priv. **3**(2), 58–62 (2005). https://doi.org/10.1109/MSP.2005.55

36. Pham, V.T., Böhme, M., Roychoudhury, A.: Model-based whitebox fuzzing for program binaries. In: Proceedings of the 31st IEEE/ACM International Conference on Automated Software Engineering, pp. 543–553. Association for Computing Machinery (2016). https://doi.org/10.1145/2970276.2970316

37. de Ruiter, J., Poll, E.: Protocol state fuzzing of TLS implementations. In: Proceedings of the 24th USENIX Security Symposium (USENIX Security 2015), pp. 193–206. USENIX Association (2015). https://www.usenix.org/conference/usenixsecurity15/technical-sessions/presentation/de-ruiter

38. Shen, W.: Fuzzing: state of the art. IEEE Trans. Reliab. **67**(1), 27–45 (2018). https://doi.org/10.1109/TR.2017.2710266

Formal Verification of Healthcare Computer Network Architectures Using Alloy and TLA$^+$

Daniel Daukševič$^{(\boxtimes)}$ (iD) and Linas Laibinis (iD)

Institute of Computer Science, Vilnius University, Vilnius, Lithuania
`daniel.dauksevic@mif.stud.vu.lt` , `linas.laibinis@mif.vu.lt`

Abstract. The healthcare sector is increasingly recognising cybersecurity as an integral part of patient safety. In recent years, healthcare computer networks have been severely affected by numerous large-scale cyberattacks that have exposed fundamental security gaps in network architectures. As a result, governments and regulatory organizations have introduced comprehensive cybersecurity standards and cyberdefense strategies for healthcare infrastructure. In this paper, we develop a security requirements specification for a healthcare computer network and present a combined approach to formally model and verify it using Alloy and TLA$^+$. With Alloy, we analyse the structural constraints, which include network segmentation, the security lattice, and access control rules. In TLA$^+$, we verify temporal correctness properties, with particular emphasis on dynamic reconfiguration, state-based monitoring, and the isolation of critical devices during cyberattacks. By integrating two state-based methods, we demonstrate how both static and dynamic security properties can be analysed within a unified framework, enabling the formal verification of cybersecurity requirements for critical infrastructure.

Keywords: Formal methods · Healthcare cybersecurity · Network segmentation · Dynamic reconfiguration · Alloy · TLA$^+$

1 Introduction

Cybersecurity of healthcare is a major concern of modern society and a matter of national interest. In healthcare computer networks, particularly legacy medical and clinical device systems, patient safety and operational availability have traditionally been prioritized, often at the expense of cybersecurity [5]. In recent years, due to the development of standards and regulations, cybersecurity has been increasingly recognized as an integral part of patient safety.

However, hospitals often create separate subnets yet solely relying on core switching, bypassing internal firewalls and effectively allowing "any-to-any" traffic. Various large-scale cyberattacks in the last decade have demonstrated how

© The Author(s), under exclusive license to Springer Nature Switzerland AG 2026
F. Ishikawa and A. Cunha (Eds.): ABZ 2026, LNCS 16579, pp. 43–61, 2026.
https://doi.org/10.1007/978-3-032-26752-8_3

attackers exploit such topological weaknesses. A notable example is the WannaCry ransomware attack which exposed how vulnerabilities in the network architecture of the United Kingdom's National Health Service, in particular insufficient network segmentation, can lead to widespread operational disruption [20].

Our contributions in this paper are twofold. First, we present a requirements document and its formalized specification for dynamic, resilient healthcare network architectures. This facilitates a formal definition of the involved security concepts, their interrelationships, and the employed mechanisms. Second, we formally model the network using Alloy and TLA$^+$to verify static and dynamic security properties. This allows us to demonstrate that the described network architecture is consistent, attack-resilient, and maintains critical connections under various-scale incident scenarios. Although formal approaches to network segmentation exist [19], and healthcare security has been extensively studied post-WannaCry, to our knowledge, this is the first work that combines structural (Alloy) and temporal (TLA$^+$) verification to prove both architectural correctness and incident response mechanisms for healthcare infrastructures.

The rest of this paper is organized as follows. Section 2 briefly reviews the background and related work. The healtcare network architecture is described in Sect. 3. Section 4 presents a formal system specification and its security properties. The Alloy-based verification of static structural properties is demonstrated in Sect. 5, while Sect. 6 presents TLA$^+$model checking of dynamic behavioral properties. Section 7 concludes the paper with discussion of the approach limitations and future work.

2   Background

According to the 2017 Healthcare Industry Cybersecurity Task Force Report, convened by the U.S. Department of Health and Human Services, out of 151 identified potential risks in the healthcare industry, 68 were related to confidentiality, 30 to availability, 30 to integrity and 23 to patient safety, with 55 percent of the total risks related to the loss of protected health information (PHI) [9]. As healthcare systems process highly sensitive PHI data, they must ensure the confidentiality and integrity of the data while maintaining the availability of safety-critical communications, even under partial compromise resulting from intrusion attacks. In order to meet regulatory requirements for layered organizational and technical security measures, healthcare organizations often adopt a *defense-in-depth* strategy that employs multiple overlapping technical and organizational security layers to mitigate cybersecurity risks [23].

Typically, such multi-layered defense consists of, among others, an administrative layer (e.g. security awareness trainings), an application layer (e.g. vulnerability management systems), and a network security layer (e.g. firewalls and segmentation) [7]. Network segmentation partitions a network into security zones with strictly controlled communication paths, each grouping assets with similar levels of cybersecurity protection requirements determined by risk analysis [6].

This approach follows the principles of Zero Trust Architecture (ZTA), which assumes that zones should not implicitly trust each other [8,27]. Essentially, the network should enforce deny-by-default communication policies between logical network segments (e.g. Virtual Local Area Networks, VLANs) with each access request verified according to the defined access policies [21]. The access privileges are limited to a minimum according to the *least privilege* principle [24].

The importance of securing healthcare networks has been highlighted by numerous large-scale cyberattacks in recent years. In particular, a ransomware cyberattack targeting the Osaka General Medical Center in 2022 caused severe operational disruptions at a hospital treating approximately 1,300 outpatients daily [25]. The attack, which blocked access to electronic medical records and patient management systems, was reportedly carried out via an external connection between the hospital and a third-party vendor. Although network segmentation would not have prevented the initial compromise, it would have allowed significant confinement of the attack surface and limitation of attack propagation, thus minimizing the overall impact on the hospital operations [5]. Similarly, another ransomware attack, which happened in 2024 and was aimed at Change Healthcare, a technology and payments company and an integral part of United States healthcare system, underscored the importance of data recovery strategies, such as robust and tested backups [3]. The aftermath outlines the importance of managing risks rather than seeking absolute security. Therefore, even with a proper segmentation, healthcare network must be prepared for dynamic reconfiguration and response to a potential cyberattack [10].

Formal methods are widely used in critical infrastructures [4]. In healthcare, formal methods are applied primarily to verify the safety and reliability properties of medical devices, such as insulin pumps and pacemakers [14]. In addition, formal methods have been used to ensure data precision in Electronic Health Record (EHR) systems, verifying how such systems store, process, and retrieve patient information [15]. From a cybersecurity perspective, however, existing research has mostly focused on the formal verification of communication protocols and cryptography [2].

3 Network Architecture

In this section, we discuss the core concepts and architecture of a typical healthcare computer network. We begin by introducing an extended hierarchy of security zone trust levels. Next, we define the principal security zones and rank them according to their trust levels. We then describe the data classification. Later, we introduce the data exchange regulations, which determine data exchange between zones according to the defined data sensitivity levels. The section concludes with a description of the overall network architecture.

3.1 Network Segmentation

Healthcare networks are typically segmented into different security zones, with different security-related characteristics. A security zone is defined by its designated trust level. Trust levels (listed below) determine the data sensitivity the zone may process, the access control requirements for device connectivity, and the security policies which are enforced within and across the zones [6,26]:

- *Public Zone* (*PZ*) – a fully open and externally accessible part of the network. With almost no applicable restrictions, it is assumed to be extremely hostile;
- *Public Access Zone* (*PAZ*) – a mediation layer between the *Public Zone* and the internal zones;
- *Operations Zone* (*OZ*) – supports routine internal operational activities of the organization. While not mission-critical, with proper security controls can be suitable for moderate-sensitivity information processing;
- *Restricted Zone* (*RZ*) – maintains critical level services and large repositories of sensitive information. In the context of healthcare, the *Restricted Zone* can be subdivided further into two zones based on their functional roles:
  - *Administration Zone* (*AZ*) – administrative systems and management servers, supporting internal control functions;
  - *Critical Zone* (*CZ*) – hosts life-critical systems, clinical and medical devices.

In healthcare, the network can be separated into nine logical security zones, based on the combination of trust level, functionality, device class, and the sensitivity of data (in the parentheses – the associated trust level) [6]:

- *Guest* (PZ) – a wireless access network for patients and visitors to connect and access *Public* data only;
- *Demilitarized zone* or *DMZ* (PAZ) – a logical subnetwork separating a publicly accessible segment from the internal network through controlled mediation mechanisms (firewalls, switches, and servers). Public data can be shared with Guest, while internal data may be exchanged with the remaining zones;
- *Enterprise* (OZ) – internal business systems, such as Enterprise Resource Planning (ERP), Human Resources (HR) and emails. Process confidential data;
- *Lab* (OZ) – laboratory information systems; process data such as disease diagnosis. Although this data are unquestionably highly sensitive, it is often depersonalized and therefore can be treated as confidential;
- *Core services* (*Core*) (AZ) – highly restricted data administration systems, such as Picture archiving and communication system (PACS), Laboratory Information System (LIS), etc.
- *Database* (AZ) – critical patient data repositories, requires strict access controls and monitoring;
- *Backup* (CZ) – protected replicas of the Database with clinical-related core services. Designed for resilience and recovery;
- *Clinical* (CZ) – clinical information systems, such as Electronic Health Record (EHR) workstations, nursing stations, medication systems;
- *Internet of Medical Things* or *IoMT* (CZ) – a special-purpose network for IoMT devices, such as infusion pumps, implantable defibrillators, telemetry devices, and patient monitoring systems.

The network segmentation model is illustrated in Fig. 1. From the static security analysis perspective, the *Administration* and *Critical* zones are treated equivalently, as they typically process the information of the same, highest, sensitivity. However, when we consider dynamic network reconfiguration scenarios – for example, during a large-scale cyberattack – they should be distinguished. In general, *Critical* zones have a direct impact on patients health and life and therefore require prioritization and more strict protection.

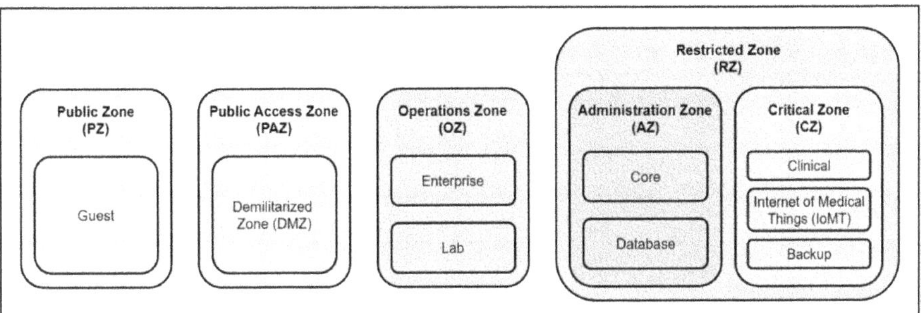

Fig. 1. Healthcare network segmentation model

3.2 Security Enforcement Rules

Not all information shared within the healthcare network is sensitive. We classify data sensitivity relying on the impact-based approach of NIST SP 800-60, which groups information based on potential adverse effects of confidentiality, integrity, or availability breaches (Low, Moderate, High) [22]:

- *Public* – the least sensitive information, e.g. public health statistics. Can be shared openly without significant risk of harm;
- *Internal* – non-public, low-sensitivity information intended for internal use, e.g. routine administrative records. Unauthorized access has minimal operational or organizational impact;
- *Confidential* – sensitive information, e.g. personal data. Unauthorized access has moderate operational or reputational impact;
- *Restricted* – highly sensitive information, e.g. PHI. Unauthorized access can cause severe damage to the patient and operational or legal consequences.

Network segmentation enables direct control of communication between specific security zones. In practice, this is achieved through the combination of various network security controls, such as firewall rules, access control lists, and software-defined networking policies. For formal modeling purposes, we abstract these control mechanisms as *Security Enforcement Rules* (SER). A SER is defined as a directional authorization tuple (*source_zone, destination_zone,* and *maximum_data_sensitivity_level*). SER can be dynamically de- and reactivated, based on the network state. Such abstraction distinguishes a security policy from implementation details, therefore enabling formal verification not bound to a specific network architecture. The full list of all SERs defined in the network is presented in Table 1.

Table 1. Defined SERs in the network

Source Zone	Destination Zone	Max. Data Sensitivity	Example Data Exchange
Guest	DMZ	Public	Patient Portal access request
DMZ	Guest	Public	Appointment information response
DMZ	Enterprise	Public	Email from vendor
Enterprise	DMZ	Internal	Appointment confirmation email
Enterprise	Core	Public	Employee credential authentication
Lab	Core	Confidential	Lab test results
Core	Enterprise	Confidential	Software updates
Core	Lab	Confidential	Software updates
Core	Database	Restricted	Patient record query
Core	Clinical	Restricted	Notification to the doctor's workstation
Database	Core	Restricted	Patient record data
Database	Backup	Restricted	Incremental database backup
Backup	Database	Restricted	Database restoration
Backup	Clinical	Restricted	Emergency patient data access
Clinical	Core	Restricted	Patient review results
Clinical	Backup	Restricted	Emergency patient data update
Clinical	IoMT	Restricted	Infusion pump setting adjustment
IoMT	Clinical	Restricted	Real-time cardiac telemetry

The complete network architecture, containing all the described zones and SERs, is presented in Fig. 2. This model serves as an abstract representation of a widely adopted and commonly pursued network security practice. The color of the zone matches the one in Fig. 1 and represents its trust level classification. The arrows connecting zones represent the *SERs* defined between them, with the firewall icons emphasizing the security controls applied. The *SERs* between *Backup* and *Database* or *Clinical* zones are highlighted; these security enforcement rules are active based on the operational mode (*Idle* or *Reconfiguration*) the *Backup* zone is currently in. When in *Idle* mode, the *Backup* zone maintains only one active *SER* with *Database* to access database records. During compromise of a zone associated with the trust levels *AZ* or *CZ*, the *Backup* zone enters the *Reconfiguration* mode, at the same time activating the *SER* with *Clinical* to support critical devices with required data and services.

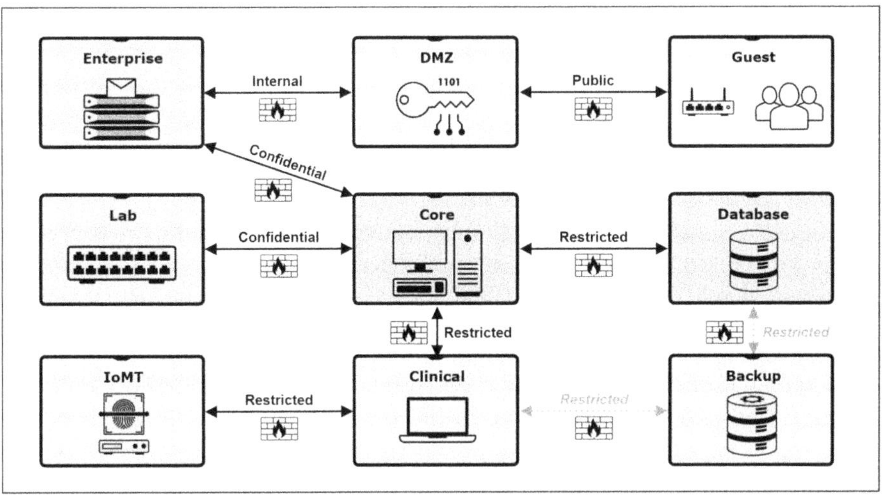

Fig. 2. Healthcare computer network architecture

4   System Requirements and Their Formalization

We will now further investigate the systems described in Sect. 3, guided by the established principles of formal model-based development [1]. We begin by developing the requirements document for such systems, followed by formalizing the principal concepts, relationships, and characteristics based on this document. The derived mathematical definitions will serve as a formal basis for the subsequent modeling and verification of fundamental system properties in Alloy and TLA$^+$, ensuring at the same time traceability with system requirements.

The resulting formal model is an abstraction of the considered computer network, focusing on the formal verification of the logical communication and routing behavior, i.e., the Layer 3 (Network) of the Open Systems Interconnection (OSI) model [11]. Modeling of other layers is omitted because hardware behavior and frame-level details, as well as application-level protocols, are outside the scope of this research.

4.1   Requirements

With key network components defined in the previous section, we have prepared the requirements document containing 39 requirements for network architecture and security enforcement mechanisms [6,27,28,30]. In this paper, we cover a part of it, with the reference to the full document provided in Appendix A.1. The requirements are divided into 2 groups: static (R1 to R21) and dynamic (R22 - R39). The first group covers the structural requirements, such as network segmentation and connections between zones. In particular, it expands on the relationships between security zones by defining multi-hop connectivity. In particular, zones not directly connected by a single SER may still be related through a sequence of SERs, formalized as a *path*:

R14. A path is a non-empty finite sequence of Security Enforcement Rules such that consecutive rules are composable (destination of the first SER equals source of the next SER).

Certain *paths* connecting highest trust level zones are designated as *critical paths*. They must remain available in all network operational modes. *Critical paths* are therefore defined by requirement R20:

R20. The network shall maintain a finite set of critical paths whose availability shall be ensured with defined data sensitivity level under all network operational modes defined in this document.

This requirement is followed by R21, which emphasizes which zones should have paths between them enabled. For example, IoMT and Clinical must maintain bidirectional connectivity (R21.1) regardless of the network compromise state. This connection supports life-critical operations, such as remote medical device control and patient state monitoring. Disrupting them would cause critical patient safety risk, which is the biggest concern of any healthcare network.

The second group of requirements describes the network incident detection and response mechanisms. Requirements R22-R31 define network mode and zone state classification, while R32-R39 specify dynamic reconfiguration scenarios. In particular, R35 describes how the network should respond to a compromise in an AZ zone – denying all communication with PZ, PAZ, and CZ zones, with data exchange with OZ reduced to the *Internal* sensitivity level. SER between *Backup* and *Database* is dropped as *Backup* connects to *Clinical*, isolating the CZ trust level zones to ensure their availability to patient care. Similarly, R36 specifies network actions in case a CZ zone is compromised.

4.2   Formal Definition

We formalize the described requirements using set theory and predicate logic. The reference to the document is provided in Appendix A.2. For presentation clarity, we define a unified model combining both static architecture and dynamic behavior state:

$$\textbf{HCN} = (\textbf{Z}, \textbf{ZL}, \textbf{D}, \textbf{S}, \textbf{inZone}, \textbf{trustLevel}, \textbf{SER}, \textbf{P}, \textbf{CP},$$
$$\textbf{pathZones}, \textbf{pathSensitivity}, \textbf{zoneCompromised},$$
$$\textbf{networkMode}, \textbf{activeSER}, \textbf{backupMode})$$

with the following static components:

- $Z = \{\textit{Guest}, \textit{DMZ}, \textit{Enterprise}, \textit{Lab}, \textit{Core}, \textit{Database}, \textit{Backup}, \textit{Clinical}, \textit{IoMT}\}$
  A finite set of zones;

- $ZL = \{PZ, PAZ, OZ, RZ\}$, where $RZ = \{CZ, RZ\}$
  A finite set of strictly ordered trust levels, where:

$$PZ < PAZ < OZ < RZ(AZ = CZ)$$

  We rely on a successor function $Next$ that returns the higher zone, i.e.
  $Next(PZ) = PAZ$, $Next(PAZ) = OZ$, $Next(OZ) = RZ$, $Next(RZ) = RZ$.
- D is an abstract, non-empty finite set of system devices;
- $S = \{Public, Internal, Confidential, Restricted\}$
  A finite set of strictly ordered data sensitivity levels, where:

$$Public < Internal < Confidential < Restricted;$$

- $inZone : D \rightarrow Z$
  A total function that maps each device to its zone;
- $trustLevel : Z \rightarrow ZL$
  A total function that maps each zone to its security level;
- $SER \subseteq Z \times Z \times S$
  A finite set of Security Enforcement Rules. Additionally, the named projection functions are defined: $src(p)$ denotes the source zone; $dst(p)$ denotes the destination zone; $mds(p)$ denotes the maximum data sensitivity level;
- $P \subseteq seq(SER)$
  A finite set of paths where each $p \in P$ is a sequence of SERs;
- $CP \subseteq P$
  A non-empty finite set of critical paths;
- $pathZones : P \rightarrow \wp(Z)$
  where $pathZones(p) = \{src(p[i])|i \in 1..|p|\} \cup dst(p[|p|])$;
- $pathSensitivity : P \rightarrow S$
  where $pathSensitivity(p) = min\{mds(ser)|ser \in p\}$.

Additionally, the specification includes dynamic system components defining the network state:

- $zoneCompromised : Z \rightarrow BOOLEAN$
  A total function mapping each zone to a true/false value, indicating whether zone is compromised;
- $activeSER \subseteq SER$
  A dynamic subset of the currently established Security Enforcement Rules;
- $networkMode \in \{Secure, Operational, Reconfiguring, Recovering\}$;
  The current network mode;
- $backupMode \in \{Idle, Reconfiguration\}$;
  The current backup mode.

  The requirements document is finalized with definitions of three static (SP) and three dynamic (DP) network properties that should be verified to prove network compliance with the security requirements. They are presented in detail in the next sections.

4.2.1 Static Security Properties

In this section, we discuss static properties about consistency and integrity of security data. The first property **SP1** relates zone trust level enforcement with data sensitivity. Specifically, all zones included in the paths with the highest maximum data sensitivity level (*Restricted*) must have the *Restricted* zone trust level (*RZ*).

SP1. Confidentiality Preservation: *Restricted data shall never reach zones with trust level PZ, PAZ, or OZ.*

$$\mathbf{SP1} \triangleq \forall p \in P : \mathrm{pathSensitivity}(p) = \mathrm{Restricted} \Rightarrow$$
$$\forall z \in \mathrm{pathZones}(p) : \mathrm{trustLevel}(z) \notin \{\mathrm{PZ}, \mathrm{PAZ}, \mathrm{OZ}\}$$

The existence of paths between critical zones of the system, described in R20-R21, is formulated as the **SP2** property.

SP2. Critical Path Existence: *All critical paths defined in R21 shall exist as valid paths in the network.*

$$\mathbf{SP2} \triangleq (\exists p \in CP : src(p[1]) = \mathrm{Clinical} \wedge dst(p[|p|]) = \mathrm{IoMT})$$
$$\wedge (\exists p \in CP : src(p[1]) = \mathrm{IoMT} \wedge dst(p[|p|]) = \mathrm{Clinical})$$
$$\wedge (\exists p \in CP : src(p[1]) = \mathrm{Clinical} \wedge dst(p[|p|]) = \mathrm{Database})$$
$$\wedge (\exists p \in CP : src(p[1]) = \mathrm{Database} \wedge dst(p[|p|]) = \mathrm{Clinical})$$

Third static property **SP3** verifies paths do not violate trust level hierarchy.

SP3. Architectural Integrity: *Every hop in every path shall connect zones whose trust levels are equal or differ by at most one level in total ordering.*

$$\mathbf{SP3} \triangleq \forall p \in P : \forall i \in \{1, \ldots, |p|\} :$$
$$\mathrm{trustLevel}(src(p[i])) = \mathrm{Next}(\mathrm{trustLevel}(dst(p[i])))$$
$$\vee\ \mathrm{trustLevel}(dst(p[i])) = \mathrm{Next}(\mathrm{trustLevel}(src(p[i])))$$
$$\vee\ \mathrm{trustLevel}(src(p[i])) = \mathrm{trustLevel}(dst(p[i]))$$

4.2.2 Dynamic Security Properties

In this section, we discuss the properties constraining the network behavior during compromise of one or multiple security zones. We begin with a dynamic (temporal logic) property **DP1** which checks whether the network eventually starts reconfiguration after at least one of the *Restricted* trust level (either *Administration* or *Critical*) zones was compromised:

DP1. Dynamic Reconfiguration: *Upon detection of compromise in any zone with trust level AZ or CZ, the network shall eventually transition to Reconfiguring mode.*

$$\mathbf{DP1} \triangleq \Box((\exists z \in Z : \text{zoneCompromised}(z) \land \text{trustLevel}(z) \in \{AZ, CZ\})$$
$$\rightarrow \Diamond(\text{networkState} = \text{Reconfiguring}))$$

The property **DP2** verifies that the connections between *IoMT*, *Clinical* and the zones storing and processing data (either *Core* and *Database*, or *Backup*) are available at any point of time.

DP2. Critical Availability: *All critical paths defined in R21 shall exist as valid paths in the network at all times.*

$$\mathbf{DP2} \triangleq \Box([\text{Clinical}, \text{IoMT}, \text{Restricted}] \in \text{activeSER}$$
$$\land \ [\text{IoMT}, \text{Clinical}, \text{Restricted}] \in \text{activeSER}$$
$$\land \ ((([\text{Clinical}, \text{Core}, \text{Restricted}] \in \text{activeSER}$$
$$\land \ [\text{Core}, \text{Database}, \text{Restricted}] \in \text{activeSER}$$
$$\land \ [\text{Database}, \text{Core}, \text{Restricted}] \in \text{activeSER}$$
$$\land \ [\text{Core}, \text{Clinical}, \text{Restricted}] \in \text{activeSER})$$
$$\lor \ ([\text{Clinical}, \text{Backup}, \text{Restricted}] \in \text{activeSER}$$
$$\land \ [\text{Backup}, \text{Clinical}, \text{Restricted}] \in \text{activeSER})))$$

Finally, the dynamic property **DP3** checks the correctness of the *Backup* mode described earlier in this paper. When the *Backup* is in the *Idle* mode, it must have a single established connection with *Database*. If *Backup* is in the *Reconfiguration* mode, it should only be connected to the *Clinical* zone.

DP3. Backup Adaptiveness: *The Backup zone connectivity shall adapt to network operational mode.*

$$\mathbf{DP3} \triangleq \Box((\text{backupMode} = \text{Idle}$$
$$\rightarrow ([\text{Database}, \text{Backup}, \text{Restricted}] \in \text{activeSER}$$
$$\land \ [\text{Backup}, \text{Database}, \text{Restricted}] \in \text{activeSER}$$
$$\land \ [\text{Clinical}, \text{Backup}, \text{Restricted}] \notin \text{activeSER}$$
$$\land \ [\text{Backup}, \text{Clinical}, \text{Restricted}] \notin \text{activeSER}))$$
$$\land \ (\text{backupMode} = \text{Reconfiguration}$$
$$\rightarrow ([\text{Clinical}, \text{Backup}, \text{Restricted}] \in \text{activeSER}$$
$$\land \ [\text{Backup}, \text{Clinical}, \text{Restricted}] \in \text{activeSER}$$
$$\land \ [\text{Database}, \text{Backup}, \text{Restricted}] \notin \text{activeSER}$$
$$\land \ [\text{Backup}, \text{Database}, \text{Restricted}] \notin \text{activeSER})))$$

With the requirements and desired properties formulated, we can formally model the network. The separation of concerns (static from dynamic properties), as well as the potential for state explosion, motivates the adoption of various formal methods to analyze different properties of the same system. In this paper, we use the Alloy formal specification language to model and verify the correctness of the network architecture and its Security Enforcement Rules. To analyze the network behavior and dynamic reconfiguration under a compromise of one or multiple security zones, we will use the TLA$^+$formal specification language.

5 Static Analysis in Alloy

We formally analyze static architectural security properties (SP1-SP3) using Alloy, a formal specification language based on relational first-order logic. It provides an automated framework for modeling and analyzing complex systems with a particular focus on their structure [12]. The analysis is conducted using a propositional satisfiability (SAT) solver to check for consistency and identify potential counterexamples to the specifications [13]. Alloy's scalability and efficiency make it particularly useful for finding inconsistencies in the initial state of the system and proving its static properties [29]. The Alloy framework version used in this paper is Alloy Analyzer (version 6.2.0).

5.1 Formal Modeling

Our Alloy model formalizes the static network architecture, described in previous chapters. The model contains 9 network zones, with 18 SERs specified in R13, and the path composition constraints (specified in R14-R19). The complete specification written in Alloy is provided in Appendix A.3. In Listing 1.1 we provide abstract definitions and instances of some network entities like data sensitivity levels, zone trust levels, zones, and Security Enforcement Rules.

```
abstract sig DataSensitivity {}
one sig Public, Internal, Confidential, Restricted
    extends DataSensitivity {}

abstract sig TrustLevel {}
one sig PZ, PAZ, OZ, RZ extends TrustLevel {}

abstract sig Zone { trustLevel : one TrustLevel }
one sig Core extends Zone{} { trustLevel = RZ }
one sig Clinical extends Zone{} { trustLevel = RZ }

abstract sig SecurityEnforcementRule
{ src : one Zone, dst : one Zone,
 maxSensitivity : one DataSensitivity }

one sig serCoreClinical extends SecurityEnforcementRule{}
{ src = Core and dst = Clinical and maxSensitivity =
    Restricted }
```

Listing 1.1. Formal definitions (signatures) in Alloy

Assertion checking, the primary verification technique in Alloy, is performed within an explicitly defined finite scope of instances. In our model, the signature

Device is constrained during analysis by requiring that each security zone contains at least four devices, while the overall scope is limited to 45 instances of *Device*, as in Listing 1.2 which presents the SP1 modeled in Alloy.

```
assert SP1_Confidentiality
{ all p : Path | pathSensitivity[p] = Restricted implies
   all z : pathZones[p] | z.trustLevel != PZ and
       z.trustLevel != PAZ and z.trustLevel != OZ }

check SP1_Confidentiality for 45 Device
```

Listing 1.2. Confidentiality property (SP1)

Formulation of the properties SP2-SP3 are provided in Listing 1.3 and 1.4.

```
assert SP2_CriticalAvailability
{ (some p : Path | p.src = Clinical and p.dst = Database
    and pathSensitivity[p] = Restricted ) and
 (some p : Path | p.src = Database and p.dst = Clinical
     and pathSensitivity[p] = Restricted ) and
 (some p : Path | p.src = Clinical and p.dst = IoMT and
     pathSensitivity[p] = Restricted ) and
 (some p : Path | p.src = IoMT and p.dst = Clinical and
     pathSensitivity[p] = Restricted )}
```

Listing 1.3. Critical availability property (SP2)

```
assert SP3_ArchitecturalIntegrity
{ all p : Path | all ser : p.hops.elems |
   ser.dst.trustLevel in ser.src.trustLevel.next or
   ser.src.trustLevel in ser.dst.trustLevel.next or
   ser.src.trustLevel = ser.dst.trustLevel}
```

Listing 1.4. Architectural integrity property (SP3)

5.2   Formal Verification

Bounded model checking did not detect counterexamples to the specified properties (Fig. 3). In Alloy, this does not imply the assertions are universally valid – if no valid instances exist within the defined scope, the Analyzer will not identify counterexamples. To complete the proof, we used the *run* command, which explicitly searches for a satisfying instance. The successful identification of an instance confirms that the model is consistent. Therefore, all three static properties are considered to be successfully verified.

The obtained results confirm that our architecture satisfies the formulated security requirements within the analyzed scope. In the following section, we will examine it in the presence of a multi-zone compromise to verify whether the defined dynamic reconfiguration strategies and mechanisms are sufficient to guarantee continuous operation of the critical zones.

```
Executing "Check SP1_Confidentiality for 45 Device"
   Actual scopes: exactly 4 signatures/DataSensitivity, exactly 1 signatures/Public, exactly 1 signatures/Internal
   Solver=glucose Bitwidth=4 MaxSeq=4 SkolemDepth=1 Symmetry=20 Mode=batch
   78453 vars. 3045 primary vars. 260191 clauses. 224ms.
   No counterexample found. Assertion may be valid. 109ms.
Executing "Check SP2_CriticalAvailability for 45 Device"
   Actual scopes: exactly 4 signatures/DataSensitivity, exactly 1 signatures/Public, exactly 1 signatures/Internal
   Solver=glucose Bitwidth=4 MaxSeq=4 SkolemDepth=1 Symmetry=20 Mode=batch
   84340 vars. 3010 primary vars. 279775 clauses. 315ms.
   No counterexample found. Assertion may be valid. 5ms.
Executing "Check SP3_ArchitecturalIntegrity for 45 Device"
   Actual scopes: exactly 4 signatures/DataSensitivity, exactly 1 signatures/Public, exactly 1 signatures/Internal
   Solver=glucose Bitwidth=4 MaxSeq=4 SkolemDepth=1 Symmetry=20 Mode=batch
   77094 vars. 3052 primary vars. 251456 clauses. 217ms.
   No counterexample found. Assertion may be valid. 80ms.
```

Fig. 3. Formal verification of static properties

6 Dynamic Property Analysis in TLA$^+$

We formally verify network dynamic behavior security properties (DP1-DP3) using TLA$^+$, a high-level formal specification language based on Temporal Logic of Actions, a variant of linear-time temporal logic [16]. The language is designed to model programs and systems, in particular distributed and concurrent ones [17]. It is a state-based method, where the system under analysis is described as a state machine [18]. Formal verification of dynamic properties is conducted in TLA$^+$Toolbox TLC Model Checker (version 2.19), allocating to TLC 25GB of physical device memory and assigning 18 worker threads.

6.1 Formal Modeling

Our TLA$^+$model captures the operational behavior of the network under compromise (a cyber incident). It includes compromise detection, zone isolation, dynamic network reconfiguration and recovery procedures defined in R22-R40. The complete TLA$^+$specification is provided via the provided link in Appendix A.4.

Unlike in Alloy, where AZ and CZ are abstracted as RZ, the TLA$^+$model clearly distinguishes these trust levels to capture different isolation strategies (R35-R36). DP1, modeled as a liveness property, verifies that the network eventually reconfigures if at least one AZ or CZ zone is compromised (Listing 1.5).

```
DP1_DynamicReconfiguration ==
    [](((\E z \in Zones : zoneCompromised[z] /\
        ZoneTrustLevel(z) \in {"AZ", "CZ"})
      => <>(NetworkState = "Reconfiguring")))
```

Listing 1.5. Dynamic reconfiguration property (DP1)

The static critical path availability was proven in Alloy – with TLA$^+$, a similar property (DP2) is checked for the dynamic network behavior (Listing 1.6).

```
DP2_CriticalAvailability ==
 /\ [src |-> "Clinical", dst |-> "IoMT", maxSens |->
    "Restricted"] \in activeSER
 /\ [src |-> "IoMT", dst |-> "Clinical", maxSens |->
    "Restricted"] \in activeSER
 /\ \/ (/\ [src |-> "Clinical", dst |-> "Core", maxSens
       |-> "Restricted"] \in activeSER
       /\ [src |-> "Core", dst |-> "Clinical", maxSens
          |-> "Restricted"] \in activeSER
       /\ [src |-> "Core", dst |-> "Database", maxSens
          |-> "Restricted"] \in activeSER
       /\ [src |-> "Database", dst |-> "Core", maxSens
          |-> "Restricted"] \in activeSER)
    \/ (/\ [src |-> "Clinical", dst |-> "Backup", maxSens
          |-> "Restricted"] \in activeSER
       /\ [src |-> "Backup", dst |-> "Clinical", maxSens
          |-> "Restricted"] \in activeSER)
```

Listing 1.6. Critical availability property (DP2)

The correctness of Backup mode execution is verified by property DP3, presented in Listing 1.7.

```
DP3_BackupAdaptiveness ==
 \/ BackupMode = "Idle"
       /\ SER_backupReconfig \ activeSER =
          SER_backupReconfig
       /\ SER_backupIdle \subseteq activeSER
 \/ /\ BackupMode = "Reconfiguration"
       /\ SER_backupReconfig \subseteq activeSER
       /\ SER_backupIdle \ activeSER = SER_backupIdle
```

Listing 1.7. Backup adaptiveness property (DP3)

To reduce the possibility of the state explosion, Device level details were abstracted out. Additionally, a constraint named *StateConstraint* was defined, limiting the number of zones that could be simultaneously compromised as well as reducing the number of checked scenarios to one full network reconfiguration.

6.2   Formal Verification

All dynamic properties were successfully verified (Fig. 4). DP2 and DP3, along with other invariants that checked network mode consistency, isolation application, and absence of deadlocks, were checked during one execution. Model checking took 13 min and found 189 203 824 states.

The dynamic property DP1, which examined the adaptiveness of the *Backup* zone, was checked separately. With the simplified network architecture (*Lab* and

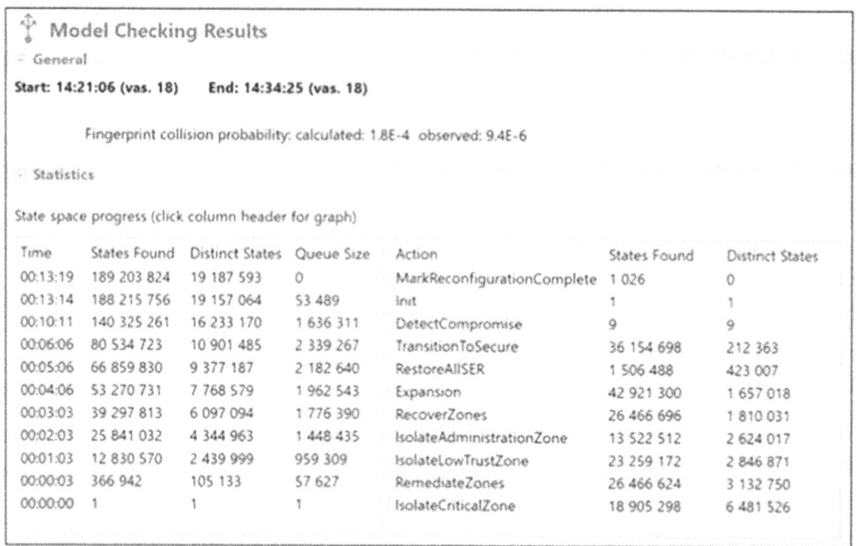

Time	States Found	Distinct States	Queue Size	Action	States Found	Distinct States
00:13:19	189 203 824	19 187 593	0	MarkReconfigurationComplete	1 026	0
00:13:14	188 215 756	19 157 064	53 489	Init	1	1
00:10:11	140 325 261	16 233 170	1 636 311	DetectCompromise	9	9
00:06:06	80 534 723	10 901 485	2 339 267	TransitionToSecure	36 154 698	212 363
00:05:06	66 859 830	9 377 187	2 182 640	RestoreAllSER	1 506 488	423 007
00:04:06	53 270 731	7 768 579	1 962 543	Expansion	42 921 300	1 657 018
00:03:03	39 297 813	6 097 094	1 776 390	RecoverZones	26 466 696	1 810 031
00:02:03	25 841 032	4 344 963	1 448 435	IsolateAdministrationZone	13 522 512	2 624 017
00:01:03	12 830 570	2 439 999	959 309	IsolateLowTrustZone	23 259 172	2 846 871
00:00:03	366 942	105 133	57 627	RemediateZones	26 466 624	3 132 750
00:00:00	1	1	1	IsolateCriticalZone	18 905 298	6 481 526

Fig. 4. Results of dynamic property formal verification

zones with trust level *PZ* or *PAZ* removed; *StateConstraint* cardinality reduced to 2) formal verification explored 23 798 states in 1 h and 15 min, successfully validating the property.

7   Discussion and Conclusions

In this paper, we have presented a study on formal specification, modeling and verification of static and dynamic security properties of resilient healthcare computer network architectures. We have prepared a natural-language requirements document, which we then specified formally. We selected three static and three dynamic network properties to be verified in order to prove network architecture compliance with the security requirements. With Alloy, we analyzed the structural constraints, which include network segmentation, the security lattice, and access control rules. In TLA$^+$, we verified behavior correctness properties, with particular emphasis on dynamic reconfiguration, state-based monitoring, and the isolation of critical devices during a compromise. By integrating two methods we demonstrated how both static and dynamic security properties can be explored within an unified framework.

While the proposed approach demonstrates promising results, it also has certain limitations. System devices were highly abstracted in static analysis and completely removed in dynamic property verification. This was justified by the fact that in the case of large-scale cyberattacks, by the time of detection, the compromise typically expands beyond one device, therefore dynamic reconfiguration mechanisms are implemented on the zone level. More detailed representation of devices could enable modeling specific vulnerabilities (such as outdated software in legacy device) and attacks exploring them. Also, a highly accurate intrusion detection system was considered. In practice, such systems can have significant detection delays and false alarms. This can be addressed by expanding the network failure handling logic, with intermediate modes added between detection of a compromise and the response to it.

In this work, we formalized and verified cybersecurity-related requirements. However, in their essence, a portion of the requirements, such as confidentiality preservation, also can be considered as safety properties. These requirements, expressed as invariants, can be verified using standard safety reasoning techniques. While not all security properties might fall into this category, conceptually safety and security properties are intertwined. A systematic review of how already widely-adopted safety-verification techniques can be reused for security is considered to be a promising direction of future research.

As a future work, we also plan to reduce the abstraction level by more detailed modeling of devices and intrusion detection systems within the network. Expanding the method integration strategy, we consider the inclusion of APALACHE, a symbolic SMT-based checker for TLA^+.

Acknowledgement. This work has been supported by the Lithuanian Research Council under grant No. P-PAD-23-173. The authors greatly thank the reviewers for their helpful and insightful comments.

Appendixes

References

1. Abrial, J.R.: Modeling in Event-B: System and Software Engineering. Cambridge University Press (2010)
2. Ahamad, S.S., Khan Pathan, A.S.: A formally verified authentication protocol in secure framework for mobile healthcare during covid-19-like pandemic. Connect. Sci. **33**(3), 532–554 (2021)
3. American Hospital Association: Change healthcare cyberattack underscores urgent need to strengthen cyber preparedness. Technical Report (2025). https://www.aha.org/system/files/media/file/2025/02/Change-Healthcare-Cyberattack-Underscores-Urgent-Need-to-Strengthen-Cyber-Preparedness.pdf
4. ter Beek, M.H., Larsen, K.G., Ničković, D., Willemse, T.A.: Formal methods and tools for industrial critical systems. Int. J. Softw. Tools Technol. Transfer **24**(3), 325–330 (2022)

5. Bodipudi, A.: Network segmentation of biomedical devices review. J. Eng. Appl. Sci. Technol. **269**(5), 2–7 (2023). SRC/JEAST-386. https://doi.org/10.47363/JEAST/2023

6. Canadian centre for cyber security: network security zoning - design considerations for placement of services within zones (ITSG-38). Technical Report, ITSG-38, Communications Security Establishment Canada (2009). https://www.cyber.gc.ca/en/guidance/network-security-zoning-design-considerations-placement-services-within-zones-itsg-38

7. Fielder, A., Li, T., Hankin, C.: Defense-in-depth vs. critical component defense for industrial control systems (2016)

8. Gambo, M.L., Almulhem, A.: Zero trust architecture: a systematic literature review. J. Netw. Syst. Manage. **34**(1), 25 (2026)

9. Health care industry cybersecurity task force: report on improving cybersecurity in the health care industry. Technical Report, U.S. Department of Health and Human Services (2017). https://healthsectorcouncil.org/wp-content/uploads/2018/06/CYBERSECURITY-TASK-FORCE-REPORT-ON-IMPROVING-CYBERSECURITY-IN-THE-HEALTH-CARE-INDUSTRY.pdf, submitted to the U.S. Congress pursuant to the Cybersecurity Act of 2015

10. HITRUST alliance: letter to the U.S. congress and regulatory bodies on ransomware and cybersecurity risk management. Policy letter / technical report, HITRUST Alliance (2024). https://hitrustalliance.net/hubfs/HITRUST%20Letter%20to%20Congress%20%2824_0606%29_DSN%20Signed.pdf, 6 June 2024

11. ISO/IEC: ISO/IEC 7498-1:1994 information technology – open systems interconnection – basic reference model: the basic model (1994). https://www.iso.org/standard/20269.html

12. Jackson, D.: Software Abstractions: Logic, Language, and Analysis. MIT Press (2012)

13. Jackson, D.: Alloy: a language and tool for exploring software designs. Commun. ACM **62**(9), 66–76 (2019)

14. Jiang, Z., Pajic, M., Moarref, S., Alur, R., Mangharam, R.: Modeling and verification of a dual chamber implantable pacemaker. In: International Conference on Tools and Algorithms for the Construction and Analysis of Systems, pp. 188–203. Springer (2012)

15. Krichen, M.: Formal methods in healthcare: improving safety and reliability. https://encyclopedia.pub/entry/44391 (2023), encyclopedia.pub entry, Accessed January 2026

16. Lamport, L.: The temporal logic of actions. ACM Trans. Program. Lang. Syst. (TOPLAS) **16**(3), 872–923 (1994)

17. Lamport, L.: Specifying Systems, vol. 388. Addison-Wesley Boston, Boston, MA, USA (2002)

18. Merz, S.: The specification language tla+. In: Logics of Specification Languages, pp. 401–451. Springer (2007)

19. Mhaskar, N., Alabbad, M., Khédri, R.: A formal approach to network segmentation. Comput. Secur. **103**, 102162 (2021). https://doi.org/10.1016/j.cose.2020.102162, https://www.sciencedirect.com/science/article/abs/pii/S0167404820304351

20. National audit office: investigation: wannacry cyber attack and the NHS. Report by the Comptroller and Auditor General HC 414, National Audit Office (NAO), London, UK (2017). https://www.nao.org.uk/reports/investigation-wannacry-cyber-attack-and-the-nhs/, ordered by the House of Commons to be printed 25 April 2018. ISBN: 9781786041470

21. National Cyber Security Centre (UK): Introduction to zero trust (2021). https://www.ncsc.gov.uk/collection/zero-trust/introduction. Accessed 19 Feb 2026
22. National Institute of Standards and Technology: Guide for mapping types of information and information systems to security categories. Technical Report, NIST Special Publication 800-60 Revision 1, U.S. Department of Commerce, Gaithersburg, MD (2008). https://nvlpubs.nist.gov/nistpubs/Legacy/SP/nistspecialpublication800-60r1.pdf
23. National Institute of Standards and Technology: Defense-in-depth (nd). https://csrc.nist.gov/glossary/term/defense_in_depth. Accessed 19 Feb 2026
24. National Institute of Standards and Technology: Least privilege (nd). https://csrc.nist.gov/glossary/term/least_privilege. Accessed 19 Feb 2026
25. Osaka General Medical Center: Information security incident investigation report summary (2023). https://www.gh.opho.jp/incident/
26. Rauscher, R., Acharya, R.: A network security architecture to reduce the risk of data leakage for health care organizations. In: 2014 IEEE 16th International Conference on e-Health Networking, Applications and Services (Healthcom), pp. 231–236. IEEE (2014)
27. Rose, S., Borchert, O., Mitchell, S., Connelly, S.: Zero trust architecture. NIST Special Publication 800-207, National Institute of Standards and Technology (2020). https://doi.org/10.6028/NIST.SP.800-207
28. Ross, R.S., Pillitteri, V.Y., et al.: Security and privacy controls for information systems and organizations. NIST Special Publication 800-53 Revision 5, National Institute of Standards and Technology (2020). https://doi.org/10.6028/NIST.SP.800-53r5
29. Team, P.A.: Practical Alloy. https://practicalalloy.github.io/ (2026). Accessed 31 Jan 2026
30. U.S. Department of Health and Human Services: Standards for the protection of electronic protected health information (security rule). 45 C.F.R. Part 160 and Subparts A and C of Part 164 (2003). https://www.ecfr.gov/current/title-45/subtitle-A/subchapter-C/part-164/subpart-C, health Insurance Portability and Accountability Act (HIPAA)

Why Does It Fail? Explanation of Verification Failures

Lars-Henrik Eriksson[✉]

Department of Information Technology, Uppsala University, Uppsala, Sweden
`lhe@it.uu.se`

Abstract. Satisfiability solving is a common technique for formal verification forming the basis of many proof and model checking systems. Failure to show a proof obligation will produce a counterexample or failure trace with typically many thousands or even millions of boolean variables. Interpreting such a counterexample poses a challenge. Even if the individual variables are all understood, it is difficult to form a "big picture" of the situation causing the failure. We consider the case where verification conditions are expressed using concepts from a formal application domain model in a language based on predicate logic or a similar language. We introduce a method to explain verification failures in application domain terms. A measure of the relative relevance of predicates is used to extract the parts of a formula most likely to contribute meaningfully to the explanation. Dependencies between predicates are used to form a branching sequence of successive explanations. These explanations can help a practitioner find faults in the system being verified. The method is demonstrated on examples and compared to other methods.

Keywords: Formal verification · Failure explanation · Model exploration

1   Introduction

Satisfiability (SAT) solving is a fundamental proof technique which is the underlying method of many proof and model checking tools used for formal modelling and verification, notably the Alloy Analyzer [7]. If verification fails, a SAT solving engine will provide a counterexample – a set of facts, such as a combination of inputs and outputs or a trace, which disagrees with the formal specification.

A *formal domain model* [2] is a mathematical description of the environment (application domain) in which a computer system operates. In the *railway domain,* a domain model can describe kinds of entities and their possible relationships such as the physical tracks, signalling systems, train movements etc. [11]. Combining the domain model with data about *concrete* entities and relations, such as the actual tracks, signals etc. of a particular railway [4,5], yields a model of the environment in which a specific computer system operates.

© The Author(s), under exclusive license to Springer Nature Switzerland AG 2026
F. Ishikawa and A. Cunha (Eds.): ABZ 2026, LNCS 16579, pp. 62–69, 2026.
https://doi.org/10.1007/978-3-032-26752-8_4

Using formal domain models, low-level counterexample data can be translated back to high-level concepts. We have developed a method to create explanations of counterexamples using domain models. Compared to other methods, the main innovation is the use of a concept of "interest" to extract the information most likely to give a useful explanation. The method has been implemented and experimentally tested with the verification tool GTO [5, 12].

This short paper gives a summary of the method. A complete description with a fully worked example and a more extensive discussion is given in [6].

2   Finding Explanations

Our formal setting is first-order logic with finite universes (bounded quantification). Verification problems in this setting can be translated into propositional form and solved using SAT solvers. Explanations are always in the context of a particular counterexample (interpretation).

The logic includes *definitions* of the form $p(x_1, \ldots, x_n) \equiv P, n \geq 0$ where the x_i are distinct variables. Logically, definitions are the same as equivalences but provide additional guidance to our explanation algorithm.

Our method proceeds in two alternating phases. One phase gives an explanation of a formula in terms of its parts, while the other phase builds a tree of successive explanations. We will introduce the first phase by examples.

Example 1. Let p be the characteristic predicate of a set and let q represent an interesting property. Assume a universe $\{a, b, c\}$ and an interpretation such that $p(a), q(a), q(c)$ are all true and $p(b), p(c), q(b)$ are all false. That is, the set characterised by p is $\{a\}$ and a and c both have the property.

The formula $\forall x.(p(x) \rightarrow q(x))$ is true under the interpretation. Arguably, $q(a)$ is the most important literal for understanding why the formula is true. Atoms $p(x)$ serve as "filters" to decide for what objects the property is checked and are thus less interesting. As b and c are "filtered out", $q(b)$ and $q(c)$ do not affect the truth value of the formula and are thus also less interesting. We say that the set $\{q(a)\}$ is the explanation of why $\forall x.(p(x) \rightarrow q(x))$ is true. Our algorithm computes that explanation by selecting "interesting" parts of the formula.

Interest is first determined by whether a subformula determines the truth value of the whole formula. Suppose that P is true and Q is false. The explanation of Q is also an explanation of why $P \wedge Q$ is false, as only changing the truth value of Q (to true) will change the truth value of $P \wedge Q$ (from false to true).

If both subformulæ determine the value of the whole formula, an "interest measure", *intr*, on formulæ is used. Suppose that $P \wedge Q$ is true. Changing the truth value of *either* subformula makes it false. If $intr(P) > intr(Q)$, then the explanation of P alone is taken as explanation of why $P \wedge Q$ is true. If instead $intr(P) = intr(Q)$, then the explanations of P and Q together are used.

If the formula $P \wedge Q$ is false, then *both* subformulæ must be changed to make it true. In that case we use the explanation of the subformula with the *least* interest measure. If both subformulæ have the same measure, one explanation is chosen arbitrarily. This seemingly unintuitive choice is motivated below.

These principles are applied recursively. Initial interest measures are applied to predicates and explanation formulæ inherit the measure of their explanation subformulæ. Atoms are negated in explanations if they are false. The explanation function $expl$ and the interest measure function $intr$ are defined together as:

Definition 1 (*expl* **and** *intr*).

$$expl(A) = \begin{cases} \{A\} & \text{when } A \text{ is true} \\ \{\neg A\} & \text{when } A \text{ is false} \end{cases} \Bigg\} \text{ if } A \text{ is an atom}$$
$$intr(A) = \text{(depending on the application)}$$
$$expl(\neg P) = expl(P) \Big\}$$
$$intr(\neg P) = intr(P)$$
$$\left. \begin{array}{l} expl(P \wedge Q) = \\ intr(P \wedge Q) = \end{array} \right\} \text{ according to Table 1}$$
$$\left. \begin{array}{l} expl(P) = expl(rewrite(P)) \\ intr(P) = intr(rewrite(P)) \end{array} \right\} \text{ in other cases, see definition 2}$$

Definition 2 (*rewrite*).

$$rewrite(P_1 \vee \cdots \vee P_n) = \neg(\neg P_1 \wedge \cdots \wedge \neg P_n)$$
$$rewrite(P \rightarrow Q) = \neg(P \wedge \neg Q)$$
$$rewrite(P \leftrightarrow Q) = (P \rightarrow Q) \wedge (Q \rightarrow P)$$
$$rewrite(\forall x.P) = P[c_1/x] \wedge \cdots \wedge P[c_n/x]$$
$$rewrite(\exists x.P) = \neg(\forall x.\neg P)$$

where the c_i are the constants of the universe.

Table 1. Explanations of $\wedge$

P	Q	$intr(P)$ vs. $intr(Q)$	$expl(P \wedge Q)$	$intr(P \wedge Q)$
false	*false*	$<$	$expl(P)$	$intr(P)$
false	*false*	$=$	$expl(P)$ alt. $expl(Q)$	$intr(P)$
false	*false*	$>$	$expl(Q)$	$intr(Q)$
false	*true*		$expl(P)$	$intr(P)$
true	*false*		$expl(Q)$	$intr(Q)$
true	*true*	$<$	$expl(Q)$	$intr(Q)$
true	*true*	$=$	$expl(P) \cup expl(Q)$	$intr(Q)$
true	*true*	$>$	$expl(P)$	$intr(P)$

Considering again the false-false case for $\wedge$, *expl* will successively rewrite the formula $\forall x.(p(x) \rightarrow q(x))$ of Example 1 to a conjunction of (true) formulæ:

$$\neg(p(a) \wedge \neg q(a)) \quad (1)$$
$$\neg(p(b) \wedge \neg q(b)) \quad (2)$$
$$\neg(p(c) \wedge \neg q(c)) \quad (3)$$

The explanations of (1) and (2) are $\{q(a)\}$ and $\{\neg p(b)\}$, respectively. As (1) and (2) are both true and p is less interesting than q, the explanation of their conjunction, $\neg(p(a) \wedge \neg q(a)) \wedge \neg(p(b) \wedge \neg q(b))$ will be $\{q(a)\}$. In (3), both $p(c)$ and $\neg q(c)$ are false, so there are two possibilities. If we use the most interesting one, $\neg q(c)$, for the explanation of (3), the explanation of the conjunction of (1), (2), and (3) – and thus the quantified formula – will be $\{q(a), q(c)\}$ – as $q(a)$ and $q(c)$ are of equal interest. That is not what we intended. If we instead choose the less interesting one, $\neg p(c)$, from (3) it will be discarded when compared to $q(a)$, as both are true. The explanation of the whole formula will then be as intended, $\{q(a)\}$. This case is further discussed in [6].

In the second phase, we attempt to find further explanations of any defined explanation literals. For example, if q is defined by $q(x) \equiv r(x) \vee s(x)$ the definition is used on $q(a)$ to obtain $r(a) \vee s(a)$. The explanation process is then repeated on this new formula. In Example 1, the explanation only included one literal, but generally there can be more than one. In that case we will get a branching structure of explanations – an "explanation tree" – as in Fig. 2.

3   Applied Example

We will outline the process of explanation finding using a fragment of a formal verification problem taken from the railway domain. The methodology used here is described in more detail in [4,5].

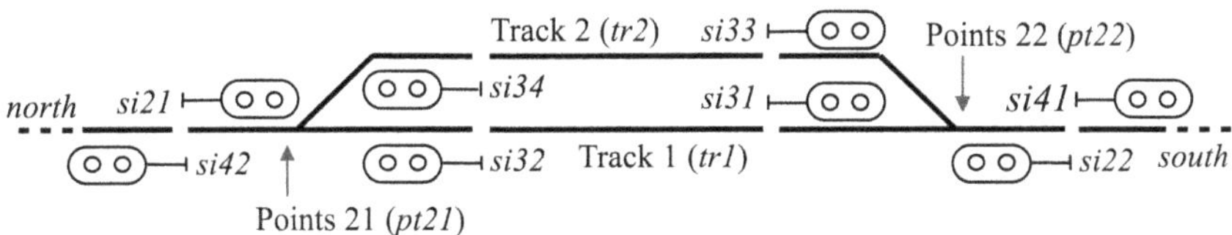

Fig. 1. Railway system

The railway system is divided into *units* (sections) while *signals* control train movements. There are *train routes* – sets of units over which trains move. Train routes start at a signal and extend to the next signal. They are identified by these signals, e.g. *rt2131* designates the train route from signal 21 to signal 31 (Fig. 1).

We will verify that the system controlling signals and points (switches) of the railway – the *interlocking* – sets a signal to display a "proceed" aspect (green light) only when it is safe to do so. Using predicates representing concepts from the domain model, the verification condition is expressed independently of a particular track layout as $\forall s.(proceed(s) \rightarrow \exists r.(entry(s, r) \wedge safe(r)))$, i.e. if a signal shows a "proceed" aspect, then it must lead to a safe route.

The model defines $unoccupied(r) \equiv \forall u.(partof(u, r) \rightarrow \neg occupied(u))$ and $safe(r) \equiv routelocked(r) \wedge pointsok(r) \wedge unoccupied(r) \wedge \neg inconflict(r)$, r and u

being routes and track units, respectively. That is, no train occupies part of a route iff all units in that route are free. Also, a route is safe iff it is reserved for a train (locked), points are set correctly, no other train occupies part of the route and the route does not come in conflict with another (locked) route.

Suppose that an interlocking for the rail system correctly implements the verification condition and that the part controlling signal 21 is modelled by:

$$green21 \equiv lock21 \wedge \neg lock32 \wedge \neg lock34 \wedge tc21 \wedge$$
$$(left21 \wedge tc2 \wedge (\neg lock22 \vee left22) \vee right21 \wedge tc1 \wedge (\neg lock22 \vee right22))$$
$$red21 \equiv \neg green21$$

The propositional symbols $green21$ and $red21$ represent outputs from the interlocking to the signal lights. Other symbols represent states or inputs of the interlocking, being true when a route from a signal is locked (e.g. $lock21$), when a set of points is in a given position (e.g. $left21$) or when a track unit is free of trains (e.g. $tc21$ and $tc1$ are true if points 21 and track 1 are free, respectively).

By adding definitions of predicates describing the layout of the particular railway and connecting abstract concepts to connected to concrete ones, e.g. $occupied(u) \equiv u = tr1 \wedge tc1 \vee u = pt21 \wedge tc21 \vee \ldots$, the verification condition becomes provable from the domain and interlocking models.

We create a fault by dropping $tc1$ from the definition of $green21$ – the check that track 1 is free in route $rt2131$. The verification condition is now falsifiable with a counterexample where $green21$ and $right21$ are true and $tc1$ false.

Before computing the explanation, the interest measure has to be decided on. We use a "syntactic" approach where the user does not have to manually determine interest. Predicates representing input signals to the interlocking – directly pointing to a condition in the actual railway system – are considered most interesting. Then, in descending order, predicates defined to directly depend on input predicates, predicates defined to directly depend only on non-input predicates, and finally defined predicates that do not depend on other predicates.

Applying our method to the counterexample would create the explanation tree in Fig. 2. The tree is cut off at the second occurrence of $green21$, as there already is an explanation for that literal being true.

One explanation of the failure is that signal 21 is showing a "proceed" aspect. Further explanations show that the green light in the signal is turned on and the red light turned off. This is expected, but as the fault would go away if the signal always showed a red light, it is a legitimate – if not very useful – explanation. Another explanation is that the route from signal 21 to signal 31 is not safe. Further explanations show that this is due to the route not being unoccupied, to track 1 being occupied and finally to input signal $tc1$ not being true. As the fault was the removal of the dependency on $tc1$ this is the reason for the failure. One branch remains. Signal 21 is also the starting point of the unsafe train route to signal 33. That turns out to be because points 21 are not set to the left, which is expected as the route takes the right path through the points. This could in principle be a legitimate explanation although in this case not the intended one.

4   Related and Future Work

Most work on explanation of interpretations in terms of a domain models have been done in the context of the Alloy Analyzer [7]. This includes *model exploration* which is technically similar to counterexample explanation. Nelson et al. [10] give an algorithm to find *provenances* – a set of formulæ explaining why a literal is true. In [6], we discuss the relation of provenances to our work.

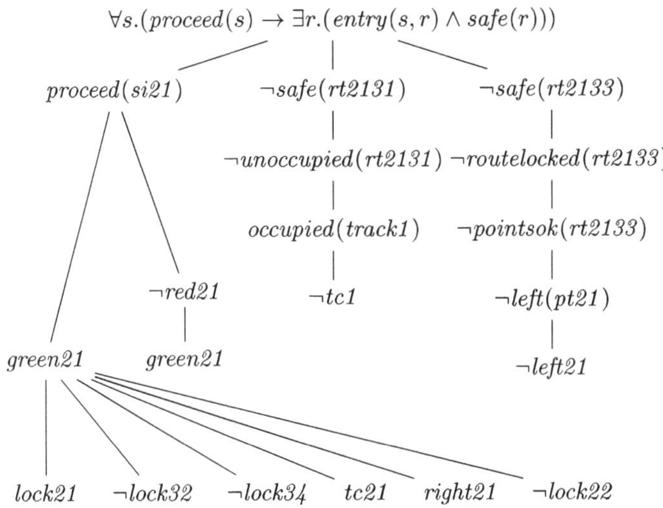

Fig. 2. Explanation tree

Dougherty et.al. [3,13,14] have studied how interpretations which are, in a sense, minimal can help provide explanations. Zheng et.al. [17] describe fault localisation for Alloy models using SAT solving to both find interpretations with a fault and without one. Differences between them are used to pinpoint parts of the model likely to contribute to the failure. Wang et.al. [8,16] use a similar approach, where tests are generated by mutating failing properties. Interpretations using different tests are compared to find parts of the model that likely contribute to the failure. Siegel et.al. [15] pinpoint the parts of verification conditions that contribute to a failure. It has some similarities to our work but without using the high-level descriptions provided by a domain model.

Extending our approach to past-time linear time temporal logic (LTL) [9] seems straightforward. We would have a sequence of counterexamples – a trace. The algorithm would first use the final counterexample and move back in the sequence when encountering the previous-moment operator, $\ominus$. The *since* connective, S, could be handled using the fact that $P\ S\ Q \leftrightarrow P \vee Q \wedge \ominus(P\ S\ Q)$. As past-time and future-time LTL have the same expressibility over finite traces [9], future-time LTL can be handled by translating into past-time LTL.

Handling unbounded quantification would allow explanations of counterexamples generated by SMT solvers [1]. The difficult case is when a universally quantified formula is true. If all instances have uniform explanations, a single explanation could be given. The question is how to determine that. On the other hand, the Alloy Analyzer has been very successful using only finite domains, so maybe an extension to unbounded quantification is not so important.

References

1. Barrett, C., Tinelli, C.: Satisfiability modulo theories. In: Handbook of model checking, pp. 305–343. Springer (2018)
2. Bjørner, D.: Domain modelling: a foundation for software development. In: Theories of Programming and Formal Methods: Essays Dedicated to Jifeng He on the Occasion of His 80th Birthday, pp. 165–210. No. 14080 in Lecture Notes in Computer Science, Springer (2023)
3. Dougherty, D.J.: Model finding for exploration. In: Dougherty, D., Meseguer, J., Mödersheim, S.A., Rowe, P.D. (eds.) Protocols, Strands, and Logic - Essays Dedicated to Joshua Guttman on the Occasion of his 66.66th Birthday. Lecture Notes in Computer Science, vol. 13066, pp. 156–174. Springer (2021). https://doi.org/10.1007/978-3-030-91631-2_9
4. Eriksson, L.H.: Use of domain theories in applied formal methods. Tech. Rep. 2006-029, Uppsala University, Dept. of Information Technology (2006). https://www.diva-portal.org/smash/get/diva2:48912/FULLTEXT01.pdf
5. Eriksson, L.H.: The GTO toolset and method. In: Proceedings of the 6th International Workshop on Automated Verification of Critical Systems (AVoCS 2006). Electronic Notes in Theoretical Computer Science. vol. 185, pp. 77–91. Elsevier (2007). https://doi.org/10.1016/j.entcs.2007.05.030
6. Eriksson, L.H.: Why does it fail? Explanation of verification failures (Full version) (2026). https://arxiv.org/abs/2603.21788
7. Jackson, D.: Alloy: a language and tool for exploring software designs. Commun. ACM **62**(9), 66–76 (2019). https://doi.org/10.1145/3338843
8. Khan, T.A., Sullivan, A., Wang, K.: AlloyFl: a fault localization framework for Alloy. In: Proceedings of the 29th ACM Joint Meeting on European Software Engineering Conference and Symposium on the Foundations of Software Engineering, pp. 1535–1539 (2021)
9. Lichtenstein, O., Pnueli, A., Zuck, L.D.: The glory of the past. In: Parikh, R. (ed.) Logics of Programs, Conference, Brooklyn College, New York, NY, USA, June 17-19, 1985, Proceedings. Lecture Notes in Computer Science, vol. 193, pp. 196–218. Springer (1985). https://doi.org/10.1007/3-540-15648-8_16
10. Nelson, T., Danas, N., Dougherty, D.J., Krishnamurthi, S.: The power of "why" and "why not": enriching scenario exploration with provenance. In: Bodden, E., Schäfer, W., van Deursen, A., Zisman, A. (eds.) Proceedings of the 2017 11th Joint Meeting on Foundations of Software Engineering, ESEC/FSE 2017, pp. 106–116. ACM (2017). https://doi.org/10.1145/3106237.3106272
11. Penicka, M.: Towards a Theory of Railways. Ph.D. thesis, Czech Technical University and Technical University of Denmark (2006)

12. Saadoun, R.: Implementation of Explanatory Algorithm for Logical Models. Bachelor thesis, Uppsala University (2022)
13. Saghafi, S., Danas, R., Dougherty, D.J.: Exploring theories with a model-finding assistant. In: Felty, A.P., Middeldorp, A. (eds.) Automated Deduction - CADE-25 - 25th International Conference on Automated Deduction, Berlin, Germany, August 1-7, 2015, Proceedings. Lecture Notes in Computer Science, vol. 9195, pp. 434–449. Springer (2015). https://doi.org/10.1007/978-3-319-21401-6_30
14. Saghafi, S., Dougherty, D.J.: Razor: Provenance and exploration in model-finding. In: Schulz, S., de Moura, L., Konev, B. (eds.) 4th Workshop on Practical Aspects of Automated Reasoning, PAAR@IJCAR 2014, Vienna, Austria, 2014. EPiC Series in Computing, vol. 31, pp. 76–93. EasyChair (2014). https://doi.org/10.29007/TCVW
15. Siegel, M., Maggiore, A., Pichler, C.: Untwist your brain: efficient debugging and diagnosis of complex assertions. In: Proceedings of the 46th Annual Design Automation Conference. p. 644–647. DAC '09, Association for Computing Machinery, New York, NY, USA (2009). https://doi.org/10.1145/1629911.1630081
16. Wang, K., Sullivan, A., Marinov, D., Khurshid, S.: Fault localization for declarative models in Alloy. In: 2020 IEEE 31st International Symposium on Software Reliability Engineering (ISSRE), pp. 391–402. IEEE (2020)
17. Zheng, G., Nguyen, T., Brida, S.G., Regis, G., Frias, M.F., Aguirre, N., Bagheri, H.: Flack: Counterexample-guided fault localization for Alloy models. In: 2021 IEEE/ACM 43rd International Conference on Software Engineering (ICSE), pp. 637–648. IEEE (2021)

Security-Minded Modelling and Verification of Autonomous Satellite Docking

Juel Hussain[(⊠)], Louise A. Dennis, Clare Dixon, and Marie Farrell

University of Manchester, Manchester, UK
`juel.hussain@postgrad.manchester.ac.uk`

Abstract. Formal verification of autonomous systems is well established for safety and liveness analysis, yet the explicit modelling and verification of adversarial behaviour at the system level remains limited. In particular, attacker behaviour is often encoded implicitly, obscuring the distinction between attacker capability and system response. This paper presents a security-minded, state-based modelling approach in which the system and the attacker are represented as separate transition systems that interact exclusively through shared inputs. This separation preserves semantic clarity, enables compositional reasoning, and supports rigorous security analysis using standard model-checking techniques. The approach is demonstrated on an autonomous space docking system. An attacker transition system is systematically derived from CAPEC-148 (Content Spoofing) and models image-spoofing attacks against a vision-based navigation subsystem. Security countermeasures are modelled as constrained variations of the system transition semantics. Security properties are specified in LTL and verified using the SPIN model checker. The results show that explicit separation of system and attacker transition systems enables the identification of insecure configurations and the formal verification of mitigation effectiveness, providing design-time security assurance for autonomous systems.

Keywords: Autonomous systems · Security verification · LTL

1 Introduction

The increasing reliance on complex, autonomous, and interconnected systems has made security a primary concern throughout the system lifecycle. Modern cyber-physical systems are exposed to threats that arise from implementation defects, design-time assumptions, and architectural decisions. The recognition that security must be addressed early and systematically has motivated the emergence of *security-minded verification*, which integrates security analysis directly

This work is partially supported by a Royal Academy of Engineering Research Fellowship and the CRADLE project under EPSRC grant EP/X02489X/1.

© The Author(s), under exclusive license to Springer Nature Switzerland AG 2026
F. Ishikawa and A. Cunha (Eds.): ABZ 2026, LNCS 16579, pp. 70–88, 2026.
https://doi.org/10.1007/978-3-032-26752-8_5

into formal system modelling [10,16]. Prior work on security-minded verification demonstrated how security concerns can be embedded within the formal verification process for critical systems, including space systems and vehicular protocols [7,10,14,16]. However, attacker behaviour in these approaches is typically represented implicitly through assumptions, guards, or environmental constraints rather than as explicit, compositional models that can be analysed independently of system logic [15]. This limits the ability to reason separately about attacker capabilities, system vulnerabilities, and security countermeasures.

This paper addresses that limitation by introducing an explicit *separation* between attacker and system models, as transition systems (TS), within a security verification framework. The key principle is that attacker and docking transition systems interact exclusively through shared inputs: the attacker controls *when* malicious data is available, while the system TS determines *how* the system responds to whatever inputs it receives. This separation preserves semantic clarity, attacker capabilities remain distinct from system transition logic, while enabling compositional security analysis using standard model-checking techniques.

We demonstrate our approach using on an autonomous satellite docking scenario, a critical application in which vision-based navigation creates opportunities for perception attacks. An attacker TS is derived from CAPEC-148 (Content Spoofing) [18], modelling an adversary injecting falsified camera imagery. The system TS captures the docking mission's operational phases and perception-driven decisions. Security countermeasures [17,19] are modelled as guarded modifications of the system's transition semantics, enabling verification of mitigation effectiveness without altering attacker assumptions. We express and verify security properties using *linear temporal logic* (LTL) and SPIN model checker [11].

- We present a *security-minded verification* workflow that integrates threat modelling with formal verification for autonomous systems. This extends [10, 16] by directly including models of the attacker as composable transition systems derived from CAPEC patterns [18], rather than encoding threats implicitly as assumptions or using STRIDE-based analysis [23] (Sect. 3).
- A *state-based modelling approach* in which attacker and system behaviours are distinct TSs that interact only through inputs, enabling clear separation between adversarial capabilities and system response (Sect. 4.2).
- A demonstration of how threat information from structured catalogues (e.g. CAPEC) can be systematically translated into explicit attacker TSs and introducing corresponding LTL security properties for verification (Sect. 2.1).
- Verification results showing that the compositional approach identifies insecure configurations (where attacks succeed) and confirms mitigation effectiveness (where security properties hold) (Sect. 5.2).

2 Background and Related Work

This section summarises the autonomous satellite docking case study, the formal modelling and verification approach using Promela/SPIN, and the CAPEC threat classification framework used to derive attacker models.

2.1 Formal Modelling and Verification

We model system and attacker behaviour using *transition systems*, the standard formalism for model checking [3].

Definition 1 (Transition System). *A transition system is a tuple $TS = (S, Act, \rightarrow, I, AP, L)$ where S is a finite set of states, Act a set of actions, $\rightarrow \subseteq S \times Act \times S$ a transition relation, $I \subseteq S$ a set of initial states, AP a set of atomic propositions, and $L : S \rightarrow 2^{AP}$ a labelling function.*

We write $s \xrightarrow{\alpha} s'$ to denote $(s, \alpha, s') \in \rightarrow$, meaning action α transitions the system from state s to state s'. We assume S is finite, extensions to infinite state spaces are outside the scope of this paper.

Promela is a specification language for modelling concurrent and reactive systems for verification using the SPIN model checker [11]. Properties are expressed in Linear Temporal Logic (LTL) [20], enabling specification of safety properties (e.g. undesirable states are never reached) and liveness properties (e.g. desired states are eventually reached). The labelling function, L, connects states to atomic propositions. In this work, we demonstrate how security invariants, such as perception integrity and the unreachability of compromised states under adversarial conditions, can be expressed and verified using LTL. When properties are violated, SPIN produces counterexample traces showing how the violation occurs [24].

CAPEC Attack Patterns. The Common Attack Pattern Enumeration and Classification (CAPEC) [18] is a structured repository of adversarial attack patterns providing standardised descriptions of how attacks are performed, prerequisites, and potential impact. Table 1 gives an example of a pattern we will formalise.

Table 1. CAPEC-148 attack pattern details.

CAPEC-ID	Attack Mechanism	Prerequisites
CAPEC-148 (Content Spoofing): An adversary modifies content while preserving apparent source identity.	Deceptive manipulation of content to induce trust in falsified data.	Target fails to protect content integrity; adversary can modify or intercept data.

2.2   Case Study: Autonomous Satellite Docking

Autonomous satellite docking is a safety-, mission- and security-critical capability for on-orbit servicing, refuelling, and resupply missions. Such operations require precise guidance, navigation, and control (GNC), robust relative navigation, and coordinated interaction between a chaser spacecraft and target satellite. These capabilities were demonstrated in the DARPA Orbital Express mission [2], which validated fully autonomous rendezvous, capturing, and servicing in low Earth orbit. Figure 1 shows the rendezvous and docking process phases.

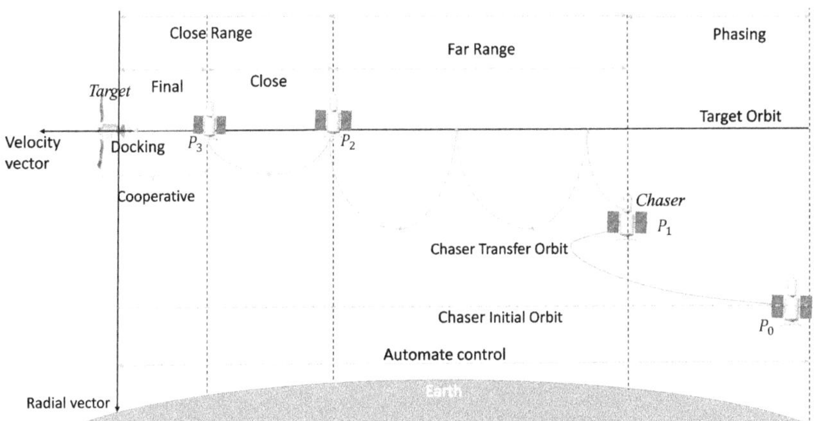

Fig. 1. Autonomous satellite docking scenario [16].

Technical Architecture and Attack Surface. The chaser spacecraft's autonomous operation depends on many interacting subsystems. We will analyse one primary attack surface for our case study, namely the perception subsystem.

Perception Subsystem. The chaser's camera captures images of the target, typically using fiducial markers or known geometric features for pose estimation. The perception pipeline processes raw frames to extract relative position (d), velocity (v), and attitude estimates which feed directly into the guidance logic. An adversary who is capable of injecting falsified imagery (e.g. CAPEC-148) can manipulate the perceived state without triggering sensor faults, causing the guidance system to compute manoeuvres with incorrect situational awareness.

2.3   Related Work

Existing security verification techniques operate within specific domains and abstraction levels. Symbolic protocol analysis (e.g. Tamarin [4] and ProVerif [1]) reasons about cryptographic protocols and message-passing adversaries, while network-level frameworks (e.g. Veriflow [13]) analyse configuration correctness and reachability in large-scale networks. These approaches provide strong guarantees but do not connect structured threat modelling to state-based system models that are suitable for model checking. Another approach uses symbolic model execution over abstract state machines to detect security vulnerabilities in blockchain smart contracts through invariant violations, but state space explosion and extensibility challenges remain [6]. Recent work on refinement of concurrent systems has explored compositional reasoning through thread-local and step-local proof obligations to enable modular verification of system behaviour. Despite the work focusing on refinement correctness rather than security analysis, it shares with our approach, a state-based modelling foundation [21].

Prior work on *security-minded verification* [10,14,16] has argued that security concerns should be embedded within formal verification of safety-critical systems. These works demonstrate how attacker assumptions can be incorporated into verification of space systems and cooperative vehicular protocols. This paper extends security-minded verification, as mentioned earlier, by representing attackers as explicit transition systems derived from structured threat patterns.

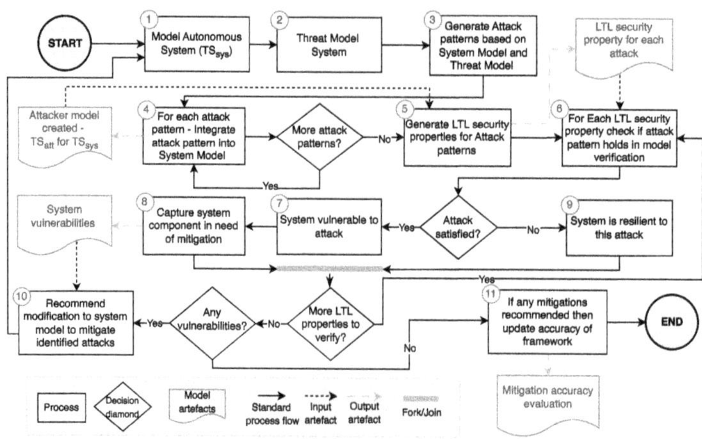

Fig. 2. Security-Minded Verification Methodology, inspired by [16], capturing the generalised workflow that we propose. Processes are indicated by rectangles, diamonds represent decision points with input and output artefacts also shown.

3   Security-Minded Verification Methodology

This paper introduces a structured methodology for *security-minded formal verification* that explicitly integrates threat modelling with system-level formal verification. The methodology is designed to decompose security analysis into a sequence of well-defined modelling and verification steps, enabling systematic reasoning about adversarial behaviour alongside nominal system functionality [10,16]. Figure 2 presents the activity-flow overview of our proposed methodology that is inspired by the security-minded verification approach of [10,16], with the addition of the explicit attacker transition system derived from CAPEC patterns.

We begin the methodology by constructing a model of the nominal system (Step 1), followed by structured threat modelling of the system (Step 2), following [10], as shown in Fig. 2. Based on the identified threats, relevant CAPEC attack patterns are selected and translated into explicit attacker models (Steps 3 and 4). This explicit attacker modelling represents a key extension over prior work, enabling adversarial behaviour to be analysed alongside the system model.

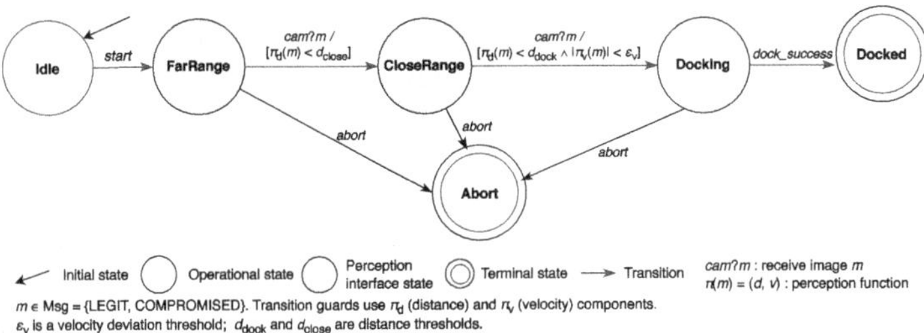

Fig. 3. Modelling system - TS_{sys} for autonomous satellite docking. Circles represent operational states; double circles denote terminal states (Docked, Abort). Shaded circles show the perception interface. Solid arrows are perception-driven or command transitions. Guards in brackets reference the perception function π. Atomic propositions correspond to states (Idle, FarRange, etc.) and are omitted visually for readability.

The system and attacker models are then composed via a shared input interface, enabling formal analysis of attacker influence on system behaviour. Security properties are expressed in LTL (Step 5). These properties are subsequently verified via model checking (Step 6), determining whether the model satisfies the specified security requirements. If a property violation is detected, counterexamples identify the vulnerability (Steps 7 and 8) leading to mitigation controls being incorporated into the system model (Step 10), resulting in a modified secured system model. If properties hold, mitigation is already in place (Step 9). The workflow concludes with mitigation accuracy evaluation (Step 11), supporting iterative optimisation of the security verification process. Subsequent sections detail each stage.

4   System and Attacker Modelling

We begin by defining the system model for autonomous satellite docking following our *Security-Minded Verification Methodology* (Fig. 2). The model exposes the system's attack surface, components, interfaces, and decision points where adversarial actions can influence state transitions.

4.1 Docking Transition System

This corresponds to Step 1 of the methodology in Fig. 2, where we model the operational states of the docking mission using a transition system (Definition 1). The intent is not to reproduce orbital mechanics, but to capture the mission phases and decision logic relevant to security analysis: perception-driven transitions, abort conditions, and docking commitment points captured in Fig. 3.

Definition 2 (Docking Transition System). *The autonomous docking system is a transition system $TS_{sys} = (S, Act_{sys}, \rightarrow_{sys}, I_{sys}, AP_{sys}, L_{sys})$ where:*

- *$S = \{Idle, FarRange, CloseRange, Docking, Docked, Abort\}$ is the set of operational states,*
- *$Act_{sys} = \{start, abort, dock\_success\} \cup \{cam?m \mid m \in Msg\}$ is the set of actions, where $Msg = \{LEGIT, COMPROMISED\}$ represents camera image types and cam?m denotes receiving image m from the camera channel,*
- *$\rightarrow_{sys} \subseteq S \times Act_{sys} \times S$ is the transition relation that is defined in Table 2,*
- *$I_{sys} = \{Idle\}$ is the set of initial states,*
- *$AP_{sys} = \{idle, farrange, closerange, docking, docked, abort, hack\}$ is the set of atomic propositions, and*
- *$L_{sys} : S \rightarrow 2^{AP_{sys}}$ is a labelling function. $L_{sys}(s)$ includes proposition p_s corresponding to state s, and $hack \in L_{sys}(s)$ iff $\phi_{hack}(s)$ (see Sect. 5).*

Table 2 defines the transition relation. Transitions are triggered by control commands (*start, abort, dock_success*) or by camera inputs that satisfy the relevant guard.

During *CloseRange* operations, the system relies on vision-based navigation: camera input is processed by the perception function $\pi : Msg \rightarrow \mathbb{R}_{\geq 0} \times \mathbb{R}$ to extract distance, d, and velocity, v, estimates. For legitimate images, π returns values approximating ground truth. For compromised images (Sect. 4.2), an attacker controls the perceived values, satisfying transition guards with falsified data. This reliance on visual perception creates the attack surface exploited by CAPEC-148 (Table 1). The *Abort* state can be entered from any active state (*FarRange, CloseRange, Docking*) in response to sensor failures or emergency stop conditions. The *Docked* and *Abort* states are terminal.

Attack Surface. The system model in Fig. 3 exposes a single *perception interface* relevant to this work, where external inputs enter the system and can be targeted by adversaries. During close-range operations, camera images drive distance and velocity estimation via the perception function, π. The system trusts that received images accurately represent the environment. Actions of the form *cam?m* consume images from the camera channel, and the guards on transitions from *FarRange* and *CloseRange* depend on the perceived values, $\pi(m)$.

The attacker's objective is to manipulate input images processed by the perception subsystem such that incorrect state estimates are accepted as valid, influencing control decisions during autonomous docking. To operationalise this

Table 2. Transition relation $\rightarrow_{sys}$ for the docking transition system. The perception function $\pi(m) = (d, v)$ extracts distance and velocity estimates from an image, m. The thresholds, d_{close} and d_{dock}, govern phase transitions.

Source	Action	Guard	Target
Idle	*start*	–	*FarRange*
FarRange	*cam?m*	$\pi_d(m) < d_{close}$	*CloseRange*
CloseRange	*cam?m*	$\pi_d(m) < d_{dock} \wedge |\pi_v(m)| < \epsilon_v$	*Docking*
Docking	*dock_success*	–	*Docked*
FarRange	*abort*	–	*Abort*
CloseRange	*abort*	–	*Abort*
Docking	*abort*	–	*Abort*

threat within our formal verification framework, we construct an attacker transition system (Sect. 4.2). This attacker captures the adversary's progression from passive reconnaissance to active spoofing once the required capabilities (ability to inject or intercept sensor data) are obtained.

How CAPEC-148 Manifests in the System Model. Let us recall the docking transition system TS_{sys} (Definition 2). The camera channel can carry both compromised images (*COMPROMISED*) and legitimate images (*LEGIT*). CAPEC-148 manifests when the attacker injects a compromised image that the perception function π processes, yielding falsified, guard satisfying distance and velocity values.

Consider the transition from *FarRange* to *CloseRange* (Table 2):

$$FarRange \xrightarrow{cam?m} CloseRange \text{ when } \pi_d(m) < d_{close}$$

For a legitimate image, $m = LEGIT$, the perception function returns values that approximate the ground truth, and the transition occurs only when the chaser is genuinely within close range. For a compromised image, $m = COMPROMISED$, the attacker controls the output of π, potentially satisfying the guard $\pi_d(m) < d_{close}$ even when the real distance exceeds d_{close}.

Crucially, this transition is not *forced* by the attacker. The attacker does not alter $\rightarrow_{sys}$; instead, it supplies inputs that satisfy existing transition guards under false pretences, causing the system to execute legitimate transitions on illegitimate data. CAPEC-148 therefore targets the *inputs* to transitions, not the transition relation itself. The system's vulnerability lies in trusting the camera channel without verifying content authenticity.

4.2 Attacker Transition System

This stage corresponds to Steps 2–4 of the methodology in Fig. 2. Following threat modelling (Step 2), relevant CAPEC attack patterns are identified and

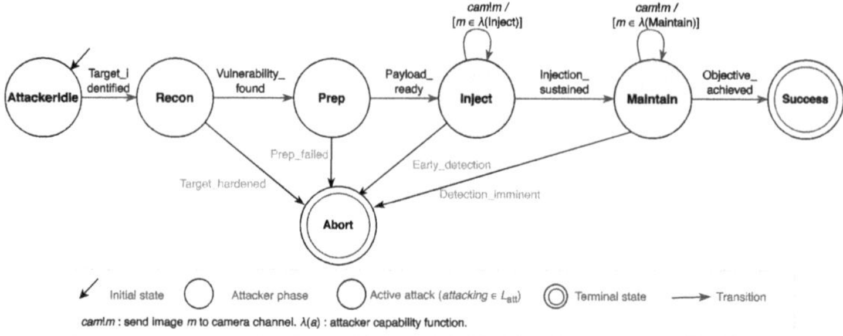

Fig. 4. Attacker transition system TS_{att} derived from CAPEC-148 (Content Spoofing) attack lifecycle. Circles represent attacker phases; double circles denote terminal states (Success, Abort). Transitions are labelled with conditions; channel actions, cam!m, denote sending an image, m, to the camera channel. Self-loops on Inject and Maintain indicate repeated spoofed image injection ($m \in \lambda(a) = LEGIT, COMPROMISED$). Shaded states indicate active attack phases ($attacking \in L_{att}(a)$).

translated into an explicit attacker transition system (Steps 3–4), enabling adversarial behaviour to be analysed independently of the nominal system model. We model the attacker using the CAPEC-148 attack pattern in Fig. 4.

The attacker progresses through states that mirror the CAPEC-148 attack lifecycle: starting with AttackerIdle to identify target to Recon (reconnaissance - identifying the target and assessing its vulnerabilities) and Prep (preparation - constructing the spoofed payload), before entering active injection phases where compromised images are injected. The attacker then either maintains the attack (continuing to inject spoofed data), evades detection, or achieves success (the system has been irreversibly compromised). The shaded states in Figs. 4 and 3 highlight the shared perception interface and the states that are impacted.

Definition 3 (Attacker Transition System). *The attacker is modelled as a transition system* $TS_{att} = (A, Act_{att}, \rightarrow_{att}, I_{att}, AP_{att}, L_{att})$ *where:*

- *$A = \{AttackerIdle, Recon, Prep, Inject, Maintain, Abort, Success\}$ is the set of attacker states,*
- *$Act_{att} = \{\tau\} \cup \{cam!m \mid m \in Msg\}$ is the set of actions. τ denotes internal transitions and cam!m denotes sending image m to the camera channel,*
- *$\rightarrow_{att} \subseteq A \times Act_{att} \times A$ is the transition relation captured in Fig. 4,*
- *$I_{att} = \{AttackerIdle\}$ is the set of initial states,*
- *$AP_{att} = \{attacking, att\_success\}$ is the set of atomic propositions, and*
- *$L_{att} : A \rightarrow 2^{AP_{att}}$ is the labelling function where $attacking \in L_{att}(a)$ iff $a \in \{Inject, Maintain\}$, and $att\_success \in L_{att}(a)$ iff $a = Success$.*

Definition 4 (Attacker Capability Function). *The capability function $\lambda : A \rightarrow 2^{Msg}$ defines which message types the attacker can produce in each state:*

$$\lambda(a) = \begin{cases} \{LEGIT, COMPROMISED\} & \text{if } a \in \{Inject, Maintain\} \\ \{LEGIT\} & \text{otherwise} \end{cases}$$

The attacker can inject compromised images only during the Injection and Maintaining phases. In other phases, only legitimate images are produced, modelling the environment's normal behaviour when no attack is active. The attacker transition system determines *when* spoofing capabilities are available and *what* can be injected; it never encodes system control logic or mission outcomes.

4.3 Composition via Buffered Channel

This section formalises the composition of TS_{sys} and TS_{att}. This corresponds to Step 4 of the methodology in Fig. 2, where the system and attacker transition systems are formally composed via a shared input interface. This composition produces the global transition system used for subsequent security property specification and verification.

Definition 5 (Composed Transition System). *The system and attacker interact through a shared camera channel cam with capacity, $cap(cam) = 1$, and message set, $Msg = \{LEGIT, COMPROMISED\}$. The channel state is $\mathcal{B} \in \{\bot\} \cup Msg$, where $\bot$ denotes the empty buffer. The composition of system and attacker via the channel, cam, is the transition system*

$$TS = TS_{sys} \parallel_{cam} TS_{att} = (Q, Act, \rightarrow, I, AP, L)$$

where

- *$Q = S \times A$ is the global state space,*
- *$I = I_{sys} \times I_{att} = \{\langle Idle, AttackerIdle \rangle\}$ is the set of initial states,*
- *$Act = Act_{sys} \cup Act_{att}$,*
- *$AP = AP_{sys} \cup AP_{att}$, and*
- *$L(\langle s, a \rangle) = L_{sys}(s) \cup L_{att}(a)$.*

The system and attacker communicate via a bounded channel, *cam*, with capacity $cap(cam) = 1$. The channel acts as a synchronisation mechanism: the attacker sends messages ($cam!m$) that the system receives ($cam?m$). The transition relation $\rightarrow$ permits the following rules:

Rule 1. Attacker Send: $\langle s, a \rangle \xrightarrow{cam!m} \langle s, a' \rangle$ when $a \xrightarrow{\tau}_{att} a'$ and $m \in \lambda(a')$.

Rule 2. System Receive: $\langle s, a \rangle \xrightarrow{cam?m} \langle s', a \rangle$ when $s \xrightarrow{cam?m}_{sys} s'$.

Rule 3. System Internal: $\langle s, a \rangle \xrightarrow{\alpha} \langle s', a \rangle$

   when $s \xrightarrow{\alpha}_{sys} s'$ and $\alpha \notin \{cam!m, cam?m \mid m \in Msg\}$.

Rule 4. Attacker Internal: $\langle s, a \rangle \xrightarrow{\tau} \langle s, a' \rangle$ when $a \xrightarrow{\tau}_{att} a'$.

Where τ denotes internal (non-observable) transitions, as defined in the attacker action set in Definition 3. α is an action not of the form cam!m or cam?m, i.e., α is a non-channel action such as start, abort, dock_success, or τ.

The following theorem establishes that this composition preserves the separation between attacker and system state.

Theorem 1 (Input-Mediated Interaction). *In the composed transition system* $TS = TS_{sys} \parallel_{cam} TS_{att}$:

1. *Every transition that modifies the system state s is governed by $\rightarrow_{sys}$.*
2. *The attacker can influence s only via messages placed on cam, which the system may receive and process according to $\rightarrow_{sys}$.*

Proof. By exhaustive case analysis on the four composition rules (Definition 5). **Rule 1** (Attacker Send) and **Rule 4** (Attacker Internal) produce transitions of the form $\langle s, a \rangle \rightarrow \langle s, a' \rangle$; the system component is unchanged, establishing that no attacker transition directly modifies s. The remaining rules, **Rule 2** (System Receive) and **Rule 3** (System Internal), both require $s \xrightarrow{\alpha}_{sys} s'$ for the system state to change, confirming claim (1). For claim (2), suppose that s changes and the cause is attacker-influenced. **Rule 3** is independent of the attacker by construction, so the change must occur via **Rule 2**, which requires $cam?m$, a message the attacker previously placed on the channel via **Rule 1**.

Theorem 1 enables modular analysis: attacker capabilities can be assessed by examining λ independently of system internals, and system resilience can be evaluated by analysing how $\rightarrow_{sys}$ responds to messages in Msg, including $COMPROMISED$. This will be shown in Sect. 4.4, where security countermeasures can be incorporated by modifying only the system's transition semantics while leaving the attacker model unchanged.

4.4 Security Countermeasure for Securing System

This section corresponds to Steps 7–10 of the methodology in Fig. 2, where verification results are analysed to determine whether vulnerabilities exist, affected system components are identified, and mitigation strategies are derived and incorporated into the system model. A security countermeasure is a mechanism that mitigates a security risk [23]. Here, it is a formally modelled defensive mechanism that monitors system inputs and constrains transition behaviour if spoofing is suspected. In CAPEC-148, the attacker can produce compromised images. The countermeasure ensures that such inputs do not induce unsafe state transitions.

Definition 6 (Compromise Predicate). *The compromise predicate, ϕ_{hack} : $S \rightarrow \mathbb{B}$, indicates whether the system has been compromised due to spoofed inputs:*

$$\phi_{hack}(s) = true \quad \textit{iff} \quad dist(s) \geq HACK\_DIST$$

where $dist(s)$ is the accumulated navigation error and $HACK\_DIST$ is the threshold beyond which mission recovery is impossible.

Definition 7 (Detection Predicate). *The detection predicate detect : $Msg \times H \rightarrow \mathbb{B}$ determines whether a received message appears to be spoofed, where H represents detection history (e.g., a sliding window of recent frames):*

$$detect(m, h) \iff |\pi_d(m) - \hat{d}| > \epsilon_d \ \lor \ |\pi_v(m) - \hat{v}| > \epsilon_v \ \lor \ \neg consistent(m, h)$$

where $\hat{d}, \hat{v}$ are the predicted distance and velocity values derived from recent navigation history, ϵ_d, ϵ_v are the maximum tolerable deviation thresholds for distance and velocity respectively, and consistent(m, h) checks physical consistency with recent frame history.

Definition 8 (Secured Docking Transition System). *Given a detection predicate detect, the secured transition system extends TS_{sys} with an Alert state:*

$$TS_{sys}^{sec} = (S \cup \{Alert\}, Act_{sys}, \rightarrow_{sys}^{sec}, I, AP_{sys} \cup \{alert\}, L_{sys}^{sec})$$

where the secured transition relation modifies camera receive transitions:

$$s \xrightarrow{cam?m}{}_{sys}^{sec} s' \triangleq \begin{cases} s \xrightarrow{cam?m} Alert & \text{if } detect(m, h) \\ s \xrightarrow{cam?m}{}_{sys} s' & otherwise \end{cases}$$

When spoofing is detected, the system transitions to the Alert state.

Table 3. Mapping formal concepts and Promela implementation.

Formal Concept	Promela Realisation
Attacker capability λ	Implicit: `Attacker()` sends only `COMPROMISED_IMAGE`
Channel *cam*	`chan camera_channel = [1] of {mtype}`
Attacker send $(cam!m)$	`camera_channel!COMPROMISED_IMAGE`
System receive $(cam?m)$	`camera_channel?img`
Detection predicate *detect*	`validate_image_secure(img)` inline
Compromise predicate ϕ_{hack}	`(dist >= HACK_DIST)`
Composed state (s, a, β)	SPIN's global state space
Non-determinism	`if :: ... :: skip fi`

Definition 9 (Secured Composition). *The secured composed system is:*

$$TS^{sec} = TS_{sys}^{sec} \parallel_{cam} TS_{att}$$

This composition preserves the attacker transition system unchanged while modifying only the system's response to potentially spoofed inputs.

Verification compares TS (without mitigation) and TS^{sec} (with mitigation). Properties that fail on TS but hold on TS^{sec} demonstrate mitigation effectiveness while confirming that the attacker model captures genuine vulnerabilities.

5   Promela Implementation and Verification

This corresponds to Steps 4–6 of the methodology in Fig. 2, where the formal composition (Definition 5) is implemented for verification with SPIN [11]. Table 3 summarises the correspondence between formal concepts and its implementation.

82   J. Hussain et al.

Process Structure. We model three concurrent processes. `System()` models the docking transition system TS_{sys}, processing images from `camera_channel` and moving through mission states. `Camera()` models the legitimate environment, producing `NORMAL_IMAGE` and `TARGET_DETECTED` frames. `Attacker()` models the attacker TS_{att}, which injects `COMPROMISED_IMAGE` frames with non-deterministic timing. `Camera()` and `Attacker()` send to the shared `camera_channel`, modelling the attacker's ability to inject spoofed images and legitimate sensor data.

Labelling Function. L (Definitions 2 and 3) is encoded in Promela using boolean variables whose valuations determine which propositions hold in each state.

Variable	Formal Meaning
`hack_state`	$hack \in L_{sys}(s)$: true when $\phi_{hack}(s)$, i.e., `dist >= HACK_DIST` (200 units)
`attack_occurred`	$attacking \in L_{att}(a)$: set true on first successful injection
`compromised_processed`	Spoofed image passed validation & influenced navigation
`mission_success`	System reached `MISSION_COMPLETE` state
`mission_failure`	System reached `MISSION_FAILED` or HACK state
`validation_result`	Result of detection predicate: `VALID` or `DROPPED`

Abstraction Relationship. The formal model (Definition 2) abstracts our Promela implementation, which uses a more detailed state space for realistic mission modelling and introduces the `HACK` state to represent the compromise condition $\phi_{hack}(s) = true$ (formal model treats hack as a proposition that labels existing states), reachable when accumulated navigation error from processing spoofed images exceeds the recovery threshold. Therefore, the `HACK` state is an implementation-level representation of the formal compromise predicate ϕ_{hack}.

Security Control. The countermeasure (Definition 8) is implemented as sliding window validation over recent camera frames. Listing 1.1 shows the core validation logic implementing the detection predicate *detect* (Definition 7).

Attacker Process and Mechanism. Listing 1.2 shows the attacker process which implements TS_{att}, injecting `COMPROMISED_IMAGE` frames via the shared camera channel according to the attacker transition relation. When security is disabled (`SECURITY_CONTROL_ENABLED = 0`) and a `COMPROMISED_IMAGE` passes validation, the system erroneously processes the spoofed perception data. In *CloseRange*, which corresponds to the label `VISUAL_SERVO` in Promela implementation of TS_{sys}, a compromised image triggers `move_away(dist)` procedure, simulating the effect of falsified pose estimates causing incorrect manoeuvres. When `dist >= HACK_DIST` (200 units), the system transitions to the `HACK` state, setting `hack_state = true` and `compromised_processed = true`. This models irreversible mission compromise: the satellite has drifted beyond recovery distance due to accumulated navigation error from spoofed perception.

Listing 1.1. Sliding window validation implementing *detect* (Definition 7). Compromised images are dropped if they deviate from history or exceed the threshold.

```
inline validate_image_secure(img) {
  if
  :: (img == COMPROMISED_IMAGE) ->
      compromised_count = compromised_count + 1;
      if
      :: (window_0 != COMPROMISED_IMAGE) ->
          validation_result = DROPPED  /* Previous was normal - sudden deviation */
      :: (window_0 == COMPROMISED_IMAGE &&
         compromised_count >= COMPROMISED_THRESHOLD) ->
          validation_result = DROPPED  /* Threshold exceeded */
      :: else ->
          validation_result = DROPPED  /* Default safe */
      fi
  :: (img != COMPROMISED_IMAGE) ->
      compromised_count = 0; validation_result = VALID
  fi;
  window_2 = window_1; window_1 = window_0; window_0 = img /* Slide the window */
}
```

Listing 1.2. Attacker process implementing TS_{att}. The attacker injects spoofed images via the shared channel with non-deterministic timing.

```
proctype Attacker() {
  byte attack_count = 0;
  byte max_attacks = 15;
  (system_ready);  /* Wait for system initialisation */
  do
  :: (mission_success || mission_failure) -> break
  :: (attack_count >= max_attacks) -> break
  :: (!mission_success && !mission_failure) ->
      if
      :: camera_channel!COMPROMISED_IMAGE ->
          attack_occurred = true;
          attack_count = attack_count + 1
      :: skip  /* Non-deterministic: injection may fail */
      fi
  od
}
```

Comparative Verification Configuration. Two configurations are used:

- **Without mitigation** (`SECURITY_CONTROL_ENABLED = 0`): Corresponds to the unsecured composition $TS = TS_{sys} \parallel_{cam} TS_{att}$ (Definition 5). All images pass validation, enabling verification that the attacker model captures genuine vulnerabilities.
- **With mitigation** (`SECURITY_CONTROL_ENABLED = 1`): Corresponds to the secured composition $TS^{sec} = TS^{sec}_{sys} \parallel_{cam} TS_{att}$ (Definition 9). The detection predicate filters spoofed inputs, enabling verification of mitigations.

Properties that fail on TS but hold on TS^{sec} demonstrate both that the attack model is realistic and that the countermeasure is effective. The complete Promela model is available in the project repository [12].

5.1   Security Properties in LTL

This corresponds to Step 5 of the methodology in Fig. 2, where security properties are formally specified in LTL based on the identified attack patterns and security requirements. The labelling functions L_{sys} (Definition 2) and L_{att} (Definition 3) ground LTL properties in the composed state space. For a global execution state (s, a, β), where $(s, a) \in Q$ and β is the channel buffer state, proposition p holds iff $p \in L(q) = L_{sys}(s) \cup L_{att}(a)$. Table 4 lists the LTL properties used to validate both vulnerability and mitigation effectiveness. Safety properties ensure compromise states remain unreachable, causality properties confirm attacks are responsible for violations, and liveness guarantees mission termination.

Table 4. LTL security properties for autonomous docking verification. Propositions are grounded via the labelling function, L (Definitions 2 and 3).

Property	Informal Meaning	LTL Formula
Safety Properties		
safety_no_hack	System never reaches compromised state	$\square \neg hack\_state$
security_blocks_processing	Compromised images are never processed	$\square \neg compromised\_processed$
no_success_and_hack	Success and compromise are mutually exclusive	$\square \neg(mission\_success \wedge hack\_state)$
Causality Properties		
hack_requires_attack	Compromise requires prior attack	$\square(hack\_state \rightarrow attack\_occurred)$
processed_leads_to_hack	Processing spoofed images leads to compromise	$\square(compromised\_processed \rightarrow \Diamond hack\_state)$
dropped_blocks_hack	Dropping spoofed image prevents immediate compromise	$\square((validation\_result = \texttt{DROPPED}) \rightarrow \bigcirc \neg hack\_state)$
Liveness Properties		
mission_terminates	Mission eventually completes	$\Diamond(mission\_success \vee mission\_failure)$

The `dropped_blocks_hack` property captures the direct causal relationship between the validation control dropping a frame and prevention of compromise in the immediately following step. The `hack_requires_attack` property confirms that the `HACK` state is reachable only through the modelled attack vector, not spontaneously.

The properties are verified under both configurations of `SECURITY_CONTROL_ENABLED`. Properties expected to *fail* without mitigation (e.g., `safety_no_hack`) confirm that the attack model captures genuine vulnerabilities. Properties expected to *pass* with mitigation confirm countermeasure effectiveness. This dual verification provides evidence that the formal model is neither trivially secure nor trivially vulnerable.

5.2   Results

This corresponds to Steps 6–11 of our methodology (Fig. 2), where formal verification is used to determine if the specified security properties hold, and vulnerabilities are identified through counterexample analysis when violations occur.

Table 5. SPIN verification results for image validation

Configuration	Property	Interpretation	Result
Without Image Validation (`SECURITY_CONTROL_ENABLED=0`)			
	`safety_no_hack`	Compromised state unreachable	**FAIL**
	`security_blocks_processing`	Spoofed images not processed	**FAIL**
	`processed_leads_to_hack`	Processing leads to compromise	**PASS**
	`mission_terminates`	Mission completes	**PASS**
With Image Validation (`SECURITY_CONTROL_ENABLED=1`)			
	`safety_no_hack`	Compromised state unreachable	**PASS**
	`security_blocks_processing`	Spoofed images not processed	**PASS**
	`dropped_blocks_hack`	Dropping spoof prevents compromise	**PASS**
	`mission_terminates`	Mission completes	**PASS**

Table 5 summarises the verification outcomes of LTL properties using SPIN. Without image validation, SPIN identifies counterexamples in which the attacker successfully injects `COMPROMISED_IMAGE` frames that are processed by the navigation system, ultimately driving the chaser into the `HACK` state. The failure of `safety_no_hack` confirms the system's vulnerability, while the success of `processed_leads_to_hack` confirms that the attack mechanism functions as modelled; processing spoofed images does indeed lead to compromise. The counterexample trace identifies the `VISUAL_SERVO` state as the vulnerability point where unvalidated camera inputs influence navigation, leading to irreversible mission compromise. This demonstrates that a security countermeasure must be placed in the `VISUAL_SERVO` component to validate frames before they influence satellite trajectory control.

When image validation is enabled (security countermeasure introduced), all safety properties hold. The `security_blocks_processing` property confirms that no spoofed image is ever processed, as the sliding window validation drops all anomalous frames before they can influence navigation decisions. Consequently, `safety_no_hack` holds: the `HACK` state becomes unreachable across all explored executions. The `dropped_blocks_hack` property further confirms the causal link between the validation control's drop action and the prevention of compromise.

These results demonstrate that the proposed image validation control effectively mitigates CAPEC-148 content spoofing attacks within the verified state space, providing formal assurance that the security property $\Box(\neg hack\_state)$ holds under adversarial conditions.

6   Discussion

We have presented our security-minded verification workflow, shown in Fig. 2, that extends prior work [10,16] by integrating CAPEC-derived attacker models with formal verification. We explicitly represent both the nominal docking system and adversarial behaviour as separate transition systems, derived from operational mission logic and CAPEC patterns respectively, and formally compose them via a shared input channel. This workflow enables attacker capabilities to be analysed independently of the system logic while preserving a formal basis for reasoning about attack–defence interactions. This traceability ensures that vulnerabilities that are identified during verification can be directly linked to threat modelling assumptions and attacker capabilities, thus providing design-time security assurance. The verification results (Sect. 5) confirmed that with the security countermeasure in place for CAPEC-148 spoofing, all of the formalised safety properties, including $\Box \neg hack\_state$, hold across all of the explored executions, providing formal evidence of mitigation effectiveness. Furthermore, our approach leverages mature verification tools (Promela/SPIN), reducing implementation overhead. Our formal models are available in our repository [12].

However, our methodology also has its limitations. The abstract docking model provides logical guarantees over the modelled system behaviour rather than guarantees over the real-world spacecraft dynamics. The effectiveness of our approach depends on the completeness and accuracy of the associated threat modelling. Our current evaluation focuses on camera spoofing (CAPEC-148), rather than broader aspects including protocol manipulation or flooding/availability attacks. The CAPEC to formalised properties mapping still requires expert judgement and state space explosion remains a scalability concern as model complexity grows. Furthermore, the verified properties are trace properties that are expressible in standard LTL. Relational security guarantees such as non-interference and observational determinism are hyperproperties in the sense of Clarkson and Schneider [9] and cannot be expressed over a single execution trace. Extending our approach to support hyperproperties is left as future work.

Future Work. We will explore more attack patterns in different use cases to analyse the generalisability and reusability of our approach in different domains and sectors. We will also examine other threat modelling techniques such as attack trees [22], and investigate richer state-based formalisms such as ASM models [5] that allow more expressive modelling of data structures and parametric attack behaviours. Moreover, extending our framework to support hyperproperty specification and verification (e.g. via HyperLTL [8]) would enable other kinds of guarantees, including non-interference properties, attacker-agnostic hypersafety guarantees that hold across variations in attacker strategy beyond the specific CAPEC-148 model, and cross-execution mission assurance properties.

References

1. Aizatulin, M., Gordon, A.D., Jürjens, J.: Extracting and verifying cryptographic models from C protocol code by symbolic execution. In: Proceedings of the 18th ACM Conference on Computer and Communications Security (CCS), pp. 331–340. ACM (2011)
2. Akin, D.L., Scheeres, D.J., Whittaker, W.L.: Orbital express demonstration manipulator system (OEDMS): autonomous rendezvous and on-orbit servicing. In: Proceedings of the IEEE Aerospace Conference. IEEE (2008)

3. Baier, C., Katoen, J.P.: Principles of Model Checking. MIT Press, Cambridge (2008)
4. Basin, D., Dreier, J., Hirschi, L., Radomirovic, S., Sasse, R., Stettler, V.: Tamarin Prover Manual. ETH Zurich (2018)
5. Börger, E.: The abstract state machines method for high-level system design and analysis. In: Formal Methods: State of the Art and New Directions, pp. 79–116. Springer (2009)
6. Braghin, C., Del Castillo, G., Riccobene, E., Valentini, S.: Using symbolic model execution to detect vulnerabilities of smart contracts. In: Leuschel, M., Ishikawa, F. (eds.) Rigorous State-Based Methods, pp. 31–51. Springer, Cham (2026)
7. Cardoso, R., et al.: Verification for Space Robotics. IET Cyber-Physical Systems: Theory & Applications (2024)
8. Clarkson, M.R., Finkbeiner, B., Koleini, M., Micinski, K.K., Rabe, M.N., Sánchez, C.: Temporal logics for hyperproperties. In: Principles of Security and Trust, pp. 265–284. Springer, Heidelberg (2014)
9. Clarkson, M.R., Schneider, F.B.: Hyperproperties. J. Comput. Secur. **18**(6), 1157–1210 (2010)
10. Farrell, M., et al.: Security-minded verification of cooperative awareness messages. IEEE Trans. Dependable Secure Comput. **21**(4), 4048–4065 (2024). https://doi.org/10.1109/TDSC.2023.3345543
11. Holzmann, G.J.: The SPIN Model Checker: Primer and Reference Manual. Addison-Wesley, Boston (2003)
12. Hussain, J.: Autonomous Satellite Docking - Security Verification Promela Code (2025). https://github.com/juelhussain/autosecver-docking. Accessed 2026
13. Khurshid, A., Zou, X., Zhou, W., Caesar, M., Godfrey, P.B.: VeriFlow: verifying network-wide invariants in real time. In: Proceedings of the 10th USENIX Symposium on Networked Systems Design and Implementation (NSDI), pp. 15–27. USENIX (2013)
14. Luckcuck, M., Farrell, M., Dennis, L., Dixon, C., Fisher, M.: Formal specification and verification of autonomous robotic systems: a survey. ACM Comput. Surv. **52**(5), 1–41 (2019). https://doi.org/10.1145/3342355
15. Malik, R., Mohajerani, S., Fabian, M.: A survey on compositional algorithms for verification and synthesis in supervisory control. Discret. Event Dyn. Syst. **33**(3), 279–340 (2023). https://doi.org/10.1007/s10626-023-00378-8
16. Maple, C., et al.: Security-minded verification of space systems. In: Proceedings of the IEEE Aerospace Conference. IEEE (2020). https://doi.org/10.1109/AERO47225.2020.9172563
17. Merkow, M.S., Raghavan, L.: Secure and Resilient Software: Requirements, Test Cases, and Testing Methods. CRC Press (2012)
18. MITRE Corporation: Common Attack Pattern Enumeration and Classification (CAPEC). https://capec.mitre.org. Accessed 2026
19. MITRE Corporation: MITRE ATT&CK Framework: Adversarial Tactics, Techniques, and Common Knowledge. https://attack.mitre.org. Accessed 2026
20. Pnueli, A.: The temporal logic of programs. In: 18th Annual Symposium on Foundations of Computer Science (SFCS 1977), pp. 46–57 (1977). https://doi.org/10.1109/SFCS.1977.32
21. Schellhorn, G., Bodenmüller, S., Reif, W.: Thread-local, step-local proof obligations for refinement of state-based concurrent systems. In: Glässer, U., Creissac Campos, J., Méry, D., Palanque, P. (eds.) ABZ 2023. LNCS, vol. 14010, pp. 70–87. Springer, Cham (2023). https://doi.org/10.1007/978-3-031-33163-3_6

22. Schneier, B.: Attack Trees (1999). https://www.schneier.com/academic/archives/1999/12/attack_trees.html. Accessed 2026
23. Shostack, A.: Threat Modeling: Designing for Security. Wiley (2014)
24. Taylor, R.G., Foster, M., North, S.: An automated framework for verifying or refuting trace properties of extended finite state machines. Int. J. Softw. Tools Technol. Transf. **24**(6), 949–972 (2022). https://doi.org/10.1007/s10009-022-00666-y

Verifying Properties of State-Based Models Using Constraint Programming

Victoria Johnson[1], Pedro Ribeiro[2], Simon Foster[2],
Peter Nightingale[2(✉)], and Felix Ulrich-Oltean[2]

[1] University of Sheffield, Sheffield, UK
v.johnson@sheffield.ac.uk
[2] Department of Computer Science, University of York, York, UK
{pedro.ribeiro,simon.foster,peter.nightingale,
felix.ulrich-oltean}@york.ac.uk

Abstract. We explore the application of Constraint Programming (CP) tools to modelling state-based systems and verifying their properties. This includes finding execution traces leading to a particular state, and proving deadlock-freedom up to a given bound on the number of transitions. We present three distinct case studies. The first formulates a railway signal in the Essence CP modelling language, demonstrating use of Essence types and operators to model states, transitions, and invariants, in a system with a single finite-state automaton. The second case study is based on Dining Philosophers, and demonstrates effective CP modelling of a system with a large number of automata, synchronised on transitions. The third case study is part of the Alpha Algorithm, an example from swarm robotics. It introduces a clock, and has transitions with guards that refer to the clock. It also has triggers, representing sensor inputs, and non-deterministic waits, demonstrating that these concepts can be represented in a CP model. Finally we demonstrate that the CP approach is complementary to a model checking approach using FDR4. In many cases the CP approach can scale substantially better than the model checker, despite the CP toolchain being general-purpose, i.e. not explicitly designed for verifying properties of state-based models.

1 Introduction

Automating the verification of state-based systems in notations like Z [33,34] and RoboChart [22] state machines requires that we can exhaustively analyse the state spaces for scenarios that violate the safety requirements. This can be achieved using model checkers like FDR [11] and SPIN [15], which enumerate a labelled transition system, and then use this to search for properties of interest. Model checking is fully automated, but suffers from the state-explosion problem. In contrast, theorem proving also allows verification that overcomes state-explosion through an implicit encoding of the transition relation using symbolic logic, but usually requires manual intervention, such as finding invariants. A middle alternative is the use of Contraint Programming (CP). Like theorem proving,

© The Author(s), under exclusive license to Springer Nature Switzerland AG 2026
F. Ishikawa and A. Cunha (Eds.): ABZ 2026, LNCS 16579, pp. 89–107, 2026.
https://doi.org/10.1007/978-3-032-26752-8_6

CP uses symbolic logic, and so allows a large number of states to be considered efficiently without enumerating all the states, but at the same time has a high level of automation as in model checking.

In this paper, we consider how CP can be harnessed as a method for verifying state-based languages, such as RoboChart state machines. Since constraint solvers avoid searching every possible state with efficient algorithms, our hypothesis is that we can use them as a more efficient complementary technique to model checking. We therefore evaluate CP as a technique for modelling and verifying a variety of state-based languages, encompassing diverse paradigms such as non-determinism, concurrency, and real-time.

We encode the transition system of a state-based model as a matrix in the Essence language [10], and then formulate a property of interest as a constraint problem. In particular, we can use CP to search for deadlocking states by formulating the existence of a deadlock as a constraint problem, and similarly for the violation of an invariant. If a deadlocking or erroneous state exists then the Savile Row tool can locate a trace of a maximum given length that shows this.

We apply this technique to three case studies: a railway signal [20], the dining philosophers problem, and the Alpha Algorithm [5] for swarms. The final case study uses the RoboChart language, and applies a systematic translation including timed transitions. For the latter two case studies, we perform a side-by-side comparison with FDR, and evaluate our findings. Our early results demonstrate that, subject to a time horizon on the model, CP can achieve greater scalability than model checking, and so provides a useful complementary technique.

The structure of our paper in as follows. In Sect. 2 we introduce the background for our paper: Constraint Programming and RoboChart. In Sect. 3, we introduce our approach by encoding a Dwarf railway signal model in the Essence language. In Sect. 4 we present a systematic encoding from state machines into Essence, which is used by the two case studies. In Sect. 5 we model the dining philosophers problem. In Sect. 6 we introduce the encoding of the Alpha Algorithm. In Sect. 7 we outline the results of our experiments. In Sect. 8 we highlight related work, and in Sect. 9 we conclude.

2   Background

The earliest forms of state machines appear in the foundational theories of computation, namely in the form of Moore [23] and Mealy [21] machines that make an explicit distinction between inputs and outputs. Harel's statecharts [14] expanded on those ideas by associating trigger events, conditions, and actions with transitions. A condition is specified by a predicate, over some state variables, that guards a transition's applicability. Other related formalisms, such as, Extended Finite State Machines (EFSMs) [7] and UML support a similar style of specification. This is in contrast with the simple notion of events between edges of a graph, as captured by Labelled Transition Systems (LTS), for example, at the core of operational [29] accounts of reactive systems.

RoboChart. One of our case studies is based on a RoboChart [22] model. RoboChart is a Domain-Specific Language (DSL) for the design of timed reactive control software. It supports a model-driven engineering approach to development, focusing on high-level system design. Its component model provides for the definition of self-contained behavioural components based on state machines that are platform-independent. The core notation is based on that of UML statecharts, however, it avoids some of the concepts that can make formal reasoning challenging, such as inter-level transitions. Distinctively, in RoboChart, state machines provide primitives for specifying time budgets and deadlines and have a formal semantics given in *tock*-CSP [2,29], a discrete-timed process algebra with support for verification using the model checker FDR [11].

Constraint Programming. Constraint Programming (CP) [30] is a paradigm for representing and solving combinatorial problems. In CP, a problem is modelled (represented) as a set of decision variables, a set of constraints on subsets of the decision variables, and an optional optimisation function. CP draws on techniques from artificial intelligence and operations research to develop effective general-purpose solvers for combinatorial problems, as well as tools that support the modelling process. CP modelling tools typically read in a modelling language and reformulate it to produce output for a chosen solver or class of solvers. Modelling tools automate the often tedious process of translating constraints for a particular solver, while also reformulating the model to improve solver performance. Prominent examples include OPL [32] and MiniZinc [25].

In this work we use two modelling languages: Essence [10] and the simpler lower-level language Essence Prime. Essence includes several types of decision variables that Essence Prime does not (sets, multisets, functions, partitions, relations, and variable-length sequences). They both have decision variable matrices (containing elements of any type in the language), integers, and Booleans. We use Essence when we need set variables and Essence Prime otherwise. When using Essence, we use the automated modelling tool Conjure [1] 2.6.0 to refine it to Essence Prime. In both cases we use Savile Row [26] 1.11.1 to translate Essence Prime into SAT (using default SAT encoding settings) and solve with the SAT solver Kissat [3] 3.1.1 or Google OR-Tools CP-SAT [27] 9.11.

3   A State-Based Model in Essence: Dwarf Signal

In this section we give an example to illustrate the use of a CP modelling language to verify properties of a state-based model. A Dwarf Signal is a type of railway signal used in places where track-side space is limited. It has three lamps, as shown in Fig. 1. Their implementation is based on the old semaphore signalling system in which a bar (arm) was raised and lowered into vertical, horizontal and diagonal positions. Clearly, railway signals need to be safe and reliable in their implementation, and so the Dwarf Signal has been given a precise specification [20]. The signal has three lamps, which can be lit or unlit, and are displayed in different configurations to give instructions to train drivers.

Fig. 1. A Dwarf Signal

The three lamps are named $L1 - L3$, as illustrated, and a signal configuration is a subset of $Signal = \mathbb{P}\{L1, L2, L3\}$. Different configurations of a signal can be written using set notation, for instance the signal in Fig. 1 is in $\{L1, L2\}$, which means *stop*. The signal has a total of four "proper states," which are the well-defined commands a signal can convey to a driver:

$$dark = \{\} \quad stop = \{L1, L2\} \quad warning = \{L1, L3\} \quad drive = \{L2, L3\}$$

The controller of the dwarf signal transitions between proper states by lighting and extinguishing the three lamps one at a time. The state variables include

- *currentState* : *Signal*, which gives the current configuration;
- *desiredProperState* : $\{dark, stop, warning, drive\}$, with the next proper state;
- *turnOn, turnOff* : $\mathbb{P}\{L1, L2, L3\}$, which gives the lights that need to be respectively lit or extinguished to reach the desired proper state.

The system is specified with three operations: $TurnOn(l)$, which turns a lamp $l \in \{L1, L2, L3\}$ on, $TurnOff(l)$, which turns a lamp off, and $SetNewProperState(s)$, which requests that the signal transitions to a new proper state. We can encode this system in Essence as follows.

Decision Variables. As described in Sect. 2, CP modelling languages provide decision variables of various types including integers, booleans, sets of integers, and in some cases more complex types such as relations and functions. However they do not provide a built-in way to define states with transitions from one state to another. Therefore states and transitions must be modelled in the language. The state of the Dwarf Signal can simply be a set of integers drawn from $\{1 \ldots 3\}$. Its evolution over time can be represented as a time-indexed array of sets of integers, as follows. The `horizon` is the final time step.

```
find currentState : matrix[int(1..horizon)] of set of int(1..3)
```

In the declaration above, the `find` keyword indicates that `currentState` is a matrix of decision variables, whose values are unknown in advance and will be decided by the constraint solver.

We have chosen to use the Essence language in this case because it supports the required types of decision variables. Alongside `currentState` we define the following time-indexed arrays representing traces of the other state variables.

```
find lastProperState : matrix[int(1..horizon)]
    of set of int(1..3)
find turnOff : matrix[int(1..horizon)] of set of int(1..3)
find turnOn : matrix[int(1..horizon)] of set of int(1..3)
find desiredProperState : matrix[int(1..horizon)]
    of set of int(1..3)
```

We now need to model the three operations of the Dwarf Signal. For each timestep except the last, we define a decision variable for the chosen operation and two other variables representing operation parameters (which may or may not be required, depending on the chosen operation). The operations are numbered $0, 1, 2$, corresponding to *TurnOff*, *TurnOn* and *SetNewProperState*.

```
find action : matrix [ int(1..horizon-1) ] of int(0..2)
find actionLampId : matrix [ int(1..horizon-1) ] of int(1..3)
find newDesiredState : matrix [ int(1..horizon-1) ]
    of set of int(1..3)
```

Constraints. Having defined the decision variables, we need to connect one timestep to the next with constraints. Essence includes common operators that can be used to write constraints for each of its abstract types (set, multiset, variable-length sequence, function, relation, partition). Here, we are using sets, and Essence provides union, intersection, set difference, and cardinality among others. The following constraints implement the *TurnOn* operation (action 1).

```
1   forAll t : int(1..horizon-1).
2     action[t]=1 -> and([
3       actionLampId[t] in turnOn[t],
4       lastProperState[t+1]=lastProperState[t],
5       turnOff[t+1]=turnOff[t],
6       turnOn[t+1]=turnOn[t]-{actionLampId[t]},
7       currentState[t+1]=currentState[t]
8       union {actionLampId[t]},
9       desiredProperState[t+1]=desiredProperState[t]
10      ]),
```

The first and second lines ensure that the constraints are applied for each timestep where operation 1 is chosen. Line 3 represents a precondition, which states that the lamp chosen to turn on must be in the set `turnOn`. Lines 4–8 update (or carry forward unchanged) the value in each state matrix from timestep `t` to `t+1`. The other two actions are implemented similarly.

The initial state of the dwarf signal is set to *stop* as follows.

```
currentState[1]={1,2},          lastProperState[1]={1,2},
turnOff[1]={},                  turnOn[1]={},
desiredProperState[1]={1,2},
```

Finally, decision variables representing action parameters (`actionLampId` and `newDesiredState`) are set to a default value when they are not needed. For the *turnOn* and *turnOff* operations, only `actionLampId` is needed, while the *setNewProperState* action requires only `newDesiredState`.

Invariants. We can check whether it is possible to violate an invariant within a given time horizon. The simple **NeverShowAll** invariant states that we should never have all lamps on simultaneously, formally $currentState \neq \{L1, L2, L3\}$. We write the negation (!) of the invariant in order to find a counterexample trace, if one exists. Representing **NeverShowAll**, the following constraint states that it is *not* the case that the invariant holds for all time steps. In other words, there must exist (in a counterexample trace) a timestep when the invariant is violated. The constraint solver will either find a trace or report that none exist.

```
!forAll t: int(1..horizon) . currentState[t]!={1,2,3},
```

Solving the model with this constraint and a horizon of 5 produced the following trace for `currentState`, indicating an invariant violation: `[{1, 2}, {1, 2},` `{1, 2, 3}, {1, 3}, {1, 3}; int(1..5)]`. In the third state all three lights are on, which is due to insufficient preconditions on the *TurnOn* operation. A solution is to extinguish the required lamps prior to lighting others.

Invariants can refer to multiple time steps, and any of the state variables. The **MaxOneLampChange** invariant requires that at most one lamp changes state from one timestep to the next. Using the set operators available in Essence, **MaxOneLampChange** can be expressed as follows:

```
!forAll t: int(2..horizon).
  exists l : int(1..3). (
    currentState[t] = currentState[t-1] union {l} \/
    currentState[t-1] = currentState[t] union {l} \/
    currentState[t-1]=currentState[t]
  ),
```

Once again the invariant is negated: the constraint solver will search for a counterexample trace where the invariant is violated at any timestep t within the horizon. Solving the model with **MaxOneLampChange** and a horizon of 100 produced no solutions (**MaxOneLampChange** was not disproven).

The **ForbidStopToDrive** invariant requires that the signal never transitions from *stop* to *drive* without another proper state in between. The invariant does not mention the current state, but instead uses the last proper state, and the desired proper state at timestep t. It is modelled as follows.

```
!forAll t: int(1..horizon) .
  lastProperState[t]=stop -> desiredProperState[t]!=drive,
```

Solving the model with **ForbidStopToDrive** and a horizon of 5 produces the following trace for `currentState`, showing an invariant violation: `[{1, 2},` `{1, 2}, {1, 2, 3}, {2, 3}, {2, 3}; int(1..5)]`. There is a transition straight from *stop* to *drive* due to a missing precondition on *SetNewProperState*.

In this extended example we have shown that a simple state-based model with set variables can be represented naturally in Essence, and that a CP toolchain can be straightforwardly used to check invariants. Counterexample traces produced by the constraint solver can then be used to improve the system so that the desired invariants hold. In the next section we move from a simple state-based model to state machines with guarded transitions and other features.

4   Encoding State Machines into CP

In this section we describe how we encode finite state automata into CP in a general way, while also prioritising constraint solver performance. We encode both states and transitions as integers, and implement transitions using a type of constraint that allows us to list the transitions explicitly. The approach taken in this section is somewhat different from the Dwarf Signal example in Sect. 3, where the transitions (turning a lamp on or off, setting a new desired state) correspond to common set operations. In general we cannot assume that state-based models will conform to the operations available in a high-level modelling language such as Essence.

Following Quimper and Walsh's decomposition of the regular language constraint [28], we model state machines in CP using integer decision variables for both states and transitions. State variables, denoted S[p,k] for automaton p at time step k, and defined within a set of possible states, encode the state of the automaton at time step k. Transition variables T[p,k] encode the transition from step k to k+1. The validity of a transition is enforced using a table constraint. Table constraints are used to ensure that for every timestep k, the tuple (S[p,k], T[p,k], S[p,k+1]) corresponds to a row in the transition table provided by the user. Finally, to encode the initial state, we assign S[p,1] to a constant for each automaton p. The model fragment below shows the CP model of the Philosopher state machine from Sect. 5 (where philTT is the transition table: one row for each transition specifying the origin state, transition number, and subsequent state).

```
find Sp: matrix[int(1..nP), int(1..horizon)] of int(1..4)
find Tp: matrix[int(1..nP), int(1..horizon - 1)] of int(1..8)
....
forAll k: int(1..horizon - 1). forAll p: int(1..nP).
    table([Sp[p, k], Tp[p, k], Sp[p, k + 1]], philTT),
forAll i: int(1..nP). Sp[i, 1] = 1,
```

4.1   Modelling Guarded Transitions

In some kinds of state models, transitions may be guarded by arbitrarily complex expressions referencing external timers, states, variables, or other elements. To encode this in CP, the conditions for a transition are separated into two boolean matrices: guard and trigger. guard[p,k,t] represents the internal conditions that must be true for transition t to be available. trigger[p,k,t] represents external events or inputs required for the transition. For a transition t to be taken at time step k, both the guard and trigger must be true:

```
T[p,k]=t -> (guard[p,k,t] /\ trigger[p,k,t]),
```

4.2   Maximal Progress Assumption and Time Transitions

For both our case studies we have *time transitions* (i.e. transitions that do not change the state of the automaton but allow one unit of time to pass). The maximal progress assumption requires that an automaton does not idle if it can act at any given timestep, i.e. it cannot use a time transition if any other transition is possible. We add constraints to enforce the maximal progress assumption: if a transition `t2` is available (its guard and trigger are both true), the time transition `t1` is disallowed. Here, the set of transitions that are time transitions are called `TimeT`, and the set of all other transitions are called `NonTimeT`.

4.3   Modelling Properties to Check

It is possible to represent various interesting properties in CP in a general way, allowing us to check them (to the horizon) using CP tools. In this section we give representations of deadlock freedom, reachability, and divergence freedom.

The simplest form of deadlock occurs if the system reaches a state where the only available transitions (for which the guard is *true*) for all automata are time transitions. It suffices to constrain a subset of the guards to be *false* at the horizon. An example can be found in the Dining Philosophers model (Sect. 5).

For state-based models that contain clocks, guards can become *true* simply by time passing without any other changes to the state. To model this scenario we define a *deadlock horizon* `h2`, and we consider the system to be deadlocked if all guards are *false* (except the guards of time transitions) for all automata, for any sequence of `h2` consecutive time steps. An example of this kind of deadlock detection can be found in the Alpha Algorithm model in Sect. 6.

State reachability ensures that specific states can be visited within the horizon. This can be expressed as follows (where `i` is a state and `p` is a finite state automaton): **exists** `k:` **int**`(1..horizon)`. `S[p,k]=i`

Divergence freedom in general ensures the system does not enter an infinite loop of internal actions without producing observable outputs. This could be, for example, remaining within a subset of the states. Given a pair of states `s1` and `s2`, we can test whether the system can visit `s1`, then `s2`, then `s1` again as follows, for some automaton p.

```
exists k,a,b : int(1..horizon).
   S[p,k]=s1 /\ S[p,k+a]=s2 /\ S[p,k+a+b]=s1,
```

5   Case Study 1: Dining Philosophers

The Dining Philosophers problem deals with synchronisation of resource allocation and management. In the problem, there are `nP` philosophers and forks, arranged alternating in a circle. The states of the philosophers are thinking, hungry (and searching for forks), and eating. Each philosopher is only permitted to eat if they have picked up the forks on both their left and right sides. For this particular implementation, the philosophers have four states: (1) thinking;

(2) hungry and holding no forks; (3) hungry and holding the left fork; and (4) holding both forks and eating. Transitions must always happen "forwards" – philosophers may proceed from state `i` to `i+1` but never `i` to `i-1`. Transition from state 4 to state 1 is permitted as well. All states have a time transition. A philosopher may only pick up the forks on either side if they not already held by another philosopher. The state diagram for the philosophers is shown in Fig. 2a.

Similarly, the forks have three states: (1) not held; (2) held by the philosopher on the left; (3) held by the philosopher on the right. The forks are able to transition from (1) to (2), and (1) to (3) freely, but must transition through state 1 when being transferred from one philosopher to the other. The state diagram for the forks is shown in Fig. 2b. The state decision variables for the philosophers and forks are denoted `Sp` and `Sf` respectively, while the transition decision variables are denoted `Tp` and `Tf`. In addition we have the horizon and the number of philosophers/forks as parameters.

The automata are synchronised on transitions, and we express this with the following constraints, where `p_right = (p - 2)%nP + 1`:

```
Tp[p,k]=2 <-> Tf[p,k]=3,          Tp[p,k]=3 <-> Tf[p_right,k]=1,
Tp[p,k]=4 <-> Tf[p_right,k]=2,  Tp[p,k]=4 <-> Tf[p,k]=4
```

For example, philosopher p's transition 2 (pick up the fork on the left) can only happen if the fork on the left is being picked up by the philosopher to its right (the first constraint above). The initial conditions are that all philosophers are in state 1 (thinking), and all forks are in state 1 (not held).

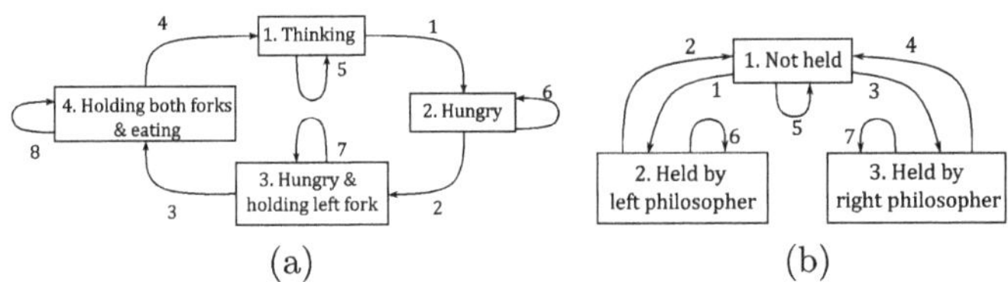

Fig. 2. State diagrams for (a) the philosophers, and (b) the forks.

We use deadlock-freedom as an example of a property that would be desirable to verify. Deadlock occurs if each philosopher holds the fork to their left simultaneously, preventing any other philosopher from making a transition (other than time transitions). The deadlock detection method discussed in Sect. 4.3 is used, with guards indicating if a transition is possible for both the philosophers and the forks. If the system is deadlocked, all guards of transitions that are not time transitions (`philNotTimeT` and `forkNotTimeT`) at the horizon are *false*, as described in Sect. 4.3. We have the following constraint expressing deadlock for all philosophers and forks simultaneously.

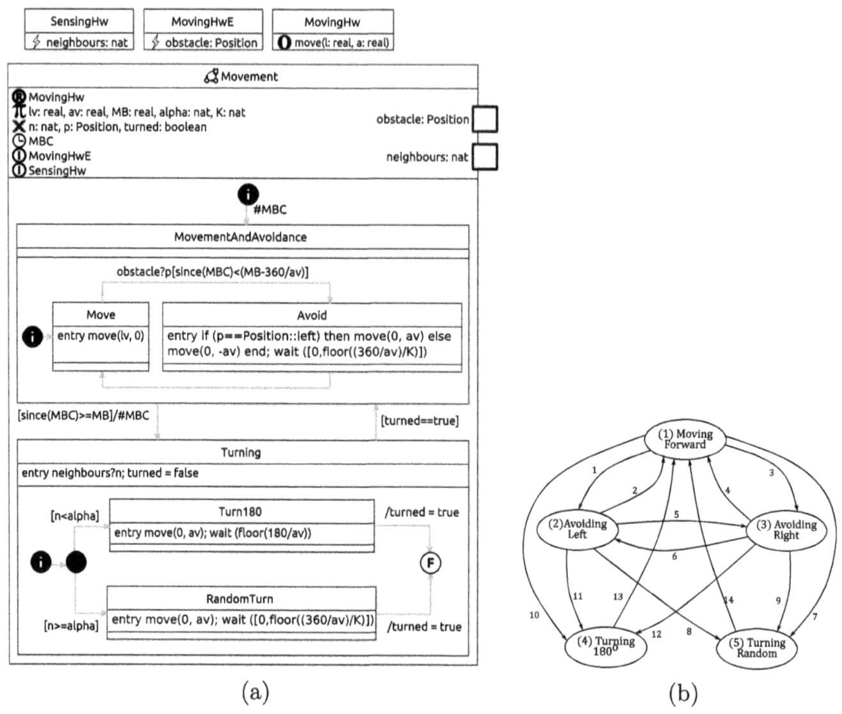

Fig. 3. (a) RoboChart state machine Movement; (b) The finite state diagram representing Movement. The time transitions are not included here for brevity.

```
forAll p: int(1..nP).
    (forAll t : philNonTimeT. !guard_p[p, horizon-1, t]) /\
    (forAll t : forkNonTimeT. !guard_f[p, horizon-1, t]),
```

6   Case Study 2: Alpha Algorithm

The Alpha Algorithm [5] is a swarm robotics algorithm designed to disperse robots when the swarm density becomes too high. In this case study, a single robot is modelled within a swarm. There are two behaviours of a robot acting under the Alpha Algorithm, which we model here via two interacting RoboChart state machines: a Movement machine, that determines the physical movement of the robot, such as moving, turning, and reacting to the density of the swarm; and a Communication machine (omitted), that determines the communications of a robot with its neighbours. In this case study, we consider only the Movement machine (⚙), reproduced in Fig. 3a , as we explain next.

The contents in the top box of Movement in Fig. 3a define the machine's context. It (ℝ) requires an interface MovingHW that defines an operation (**O**) of the robot called move with two parameters of type real for linear and angular velocity, and uses (ⓘ) the interfaces MovingHwE and SensingHw, that define (typed) input events (⚡) obstacle, of an enumerated type Position with possible values left or right, and neighbours of the natural type. Using these events the machine can receive information about the relative position of obstacles and the number of neighbouring robots currently detected. In addition, we declare (π) constants, (✖) variables, and a (⊘) clock MBC.

The constants lv and av are used for setting the linear and angular velocity, while MB is used to decide how long to perform MovementAndAvoidance, alpha is the threshold of the alpha algorithm, and K is a constant that controls the time interval allowed for turns. The variables n and p are used to store values received via the events neighbours and obstacle, respectively, while turned is an auxiliary variable that aids with the control flow specification for state Turning.

The control flow of the machine Movement starts in the initial junction (indicated by ●), whose outgoing transition (#) resets the clock MBC and identifies the starting state of the control flow. In Movement, that state is the composite state MovementAndAvoidance, whose control flow also starts from its initial junction and therefore state Move. In Move, there is an entry action, where the operation move is called with values lv and 0. Here, we assume that move is an operation provided by the robot's embedded software that is always available, and so the call takes no time. After completing the entry action, state Move and MovementAndAvoidance become active, so any outgoing transitions, if enabled, can interrupt their execution. For example, the transition from Move to Avoid can be triggered by the event obstacle when the condition since(MBC)<(MB-360/av) is true, where since(MBC) is the time elapsed since the last reset of clock MBC. If triggered, the value communicated via obstacle is assigned to the variable p, leading to state Avoid. In Avoid, there is an entry action, where if the obstacle is positioned on the left, then move is called with zero linear velocity but positive angular velocity av, and otherwise negative angular velocity -av, and afterwards there is a non-deterministic delay (wait) between 0 and floor((360/av)/K) time units. The transition back to Move has no trigger or condition, so it must be taken as soon as Avoid finishes its entry action to ensure maximal progress.

Similarly, in MovementAndAvoidance, after entering states Move or Avoid, the transition to Turning, guarded by since(MBC)>=MB, must be taken as soon as it is enabled to ensure maximal progress. If it is enabled at the same time as a transition between Move and Avoid, then the choice over which transition is taken is nondeterministic. So, in Turning we use the auxiliary variable turned to eliminate this kind of nondeterminism. In its entry action, we have, first of all, an input communication on neighbours and then the assignment of false to turned. In the control flow of Turning, there is a junction, with mutually exclusive conditions: if n<alpha then control transitions to Turn180, and otherwise to RandomTurn. The behaviour of their entry actions is similar in that both call move(0,av), however, the subsequent waiting period is floor(180/av) in the first case, and otherwise is a nondeterministic delay between 0 and floor((360/av)/K) time units in Random-Turn, similarly to that in state Avoid. Once the entry action completes, control transitions to a final state, with the action on the transitions setting turned to

true, thus enabling the transition from Turning to MovementAndAvoidance. This concludes our discussion of the Movement state machine.

Figure 3b shows a flattened version of Movement as a state transition diagram used as starting point for our encoding in CP. Figure 3b was modelled in Essence Prime using the encoding framework from Sect. 4. The implementation includes user-defined parameters that define the physical limits and thresholds of the system, and decision variables that track the robot's state from the first timestep to the horizon. Parameters include the number of simulation timesteps (horizon), alpha and av (both described above).

The main decision variables are: the sequence of states (Smov), transitions (Tmov), and guard and trigger for each transition at each step (as described in Sect. 4). The maximal progress assumption is included, as are time transitions. To encode the timed elements of the Alpha Algorithm, we define variables to track MBC (named MBC), the time taken at each simulation step (timings), and the total elapsed time (cumulTime) for each step. The value of MBC is carried forward unchanged at each step unless the clock is reset (in which case MBC is constrained to be equal to cumulTime). The timings variables are constrained according to the wait instructions in the RoboChart model (defaulting to 1 if there is no wait for the current state). The cumulTime variables simply accumulate timings for each step.

We also define decision variables for the random turn duration lambda (with domain $\{0 \dots 72\}$ in our experiments) and the number of robots detected in the vicinity (nDet with domain $\{0, \text{alpha} - 1, \text{alpha}, \text{alpha} + 1\}$) at each step. If the robot is in a random turning state, the turning time is proportional to lambda. However, if the robot is performing a 180-degree turn, the duration is fixed based on the angular velocity. The value of nDet affects the guards on some of the transitions, as described below. Finally we define sensor $\in \{-1, 0, 1\}$ for each step, corresponding to obstacle with values Position::left, none, or Position::right in the RoboChart model. The sensor variables are used in triggers for transitions that enter the Avoid states.

For each simulation step k and each transition t, we translate the guards and triggers in RoboChart to constraints on guard[k,t] and trigger[k,t]. As an example, consider transition 1 (from state (1) Moving Forward to (2) Avoiding Left). Transition 1 is available when the automaton is in state 1, and the elapsed time since MBC was last reset is less than a constant. Transition 1 is triggered if the sensor returns a value, and the value is 1 (corresponding to Position::right). The guard and trigger at step k are constrained as follows:

```
guard[k, 1] <-> (Smov[k]=1 /\ (cumulTime[k]-MBC[k] < MB-360/av))
trigger[k, 1] <-> (sensor[k] = 1)
```

Note how the external event (a sensor reading) is captured in the trigger, and internal conditions in the guard.

We model timed deadlock as follows (where time_t is the set of time transitions for the automaton), following the approach described in Sect. 4. Recall that h2 is a parameter: the deadlock horizon. For the system to be considered deadlocked, a set of guards must be false for h2 consecutive steps.

```
exists t: int(1..horizon-h2+1). forAll transition: int(1..nTm).
   (!(transition in time_t)) ->
       forAll t2 : int(t..t+h2-1). !guard[t2, transition],
```

Table 1. Results of verifying deadlock freedom of dining philosophers with FDR4, without using partial order reduction, and CP. Complexity is reported in terms of states and transitions visited, and the time taken to find a counter-example. CP time consists of SR (Savile Row) time and time spent by the backend solver.

Phil.	FDR4			CP Toolchain	
	States	Transitions	Time (s)	SR Time (s)	Solv Time (s)
2	17	59	1.27	0.20	0.00
4	389	2,533	1.34	0.30	0.00
6	9,656	92,527	2.11	0.42	0.01
8	236,996	3,000,560	2.75	0.59	0.01
10	6,067,403	95,176,648	4.05	0.79	0.02
11	30,198,167	519,705,897	8.77	0.90	0.03
12	150,317,646	2,816,473,446	33.83	1.06	0.01
13	761,791,638	15,418,186,708	191.86	1.10	0.04
14	3,822,052,236	83,132,411,124	1218.44	1.17	0.04
15	19,203,016,180	446,657,002,703	7510.32	1.36	0.05

7   Experimental Results

We compare the performance of our approach to verification, based on our CP encoding, versus model checking with FDR4 [11] of comparable CSP models for our case studies. For the Alpha Algorithm, its *tock*-CSP semantics can be automatically calculated using RoboTool[1], while for the Dining Philosophers we construct an untimed CSP model that encodes the state diagram in Fig. 2.

Experiments were carried out on a server with two AMD EPYC 7501 processors and 2 TB of RAM. In some cases experiments were parallelised but processes were never contending for CPU cores or RAM. Model and parameter files are available: https://github.com/pwn1/abz26-experiments.

FDR4 allows verifying properties via refinement [24]. Briefly, FDR calculates the operational semantics of a CSP process explicitly as a LTS. So, an untimed deadlock manifests as a state in the LTS that refuses every possible interaction, whereas a timed deadlock occurs when, despite maximal progress, *tock* becomes the only possible interaction indefinitely. In contrast with CP, FDR4 does not require a time horizon, exploring the LTS in a breadth-first-search manner.

---

[1] https://robostar.cs.york.ac.uk/robotool.

The results of checking the Dining Philosophers model for deadlocks are summarised in Tables 1 and 2. Table 1 shows the results for FDR4 using its default settings, with the number of states and transitions visited and the time taken, and for the CP toolchain, as the number of philosophers grows. We used the -O0 option for Savile Row 1.11.1 to reduce the time spent performing pre-solving optimisations. The backend solver was Kissat 3.1.1, and the horizon was 1.5 times the number of philosophers. We observe that the model is not deadlock free. FDR4 shows exponential growth in time, whereas the CP approach is nearly constant up to 15 philosophers.

Table 2. Results of verifying deadlock freedom of dining philosophers with FDR4 using partial order reduction and CP. Complexity is reported in terms of states and transitions visited, and the time taken to find a counter-example.

Phil.	FDR4			CP Toolchain	
	States	Transitions	Time (s)	SR Time (s)	Solv Time (s)
10	37	81	0.95	0.79	0.02
20	85	194	1.30	2.10	0.06
40	165	380	2.47	6.87	0.17
80	290	659	6.71	22.59	0.89
100	404	902	10.35	35.47	1.37
200	803	1,782	84.12	162.87	6.16
400	1,631	3,684	1041.58	825.17	28.19
800	3,305	7,567	14,940.89	4605.43	134.22
1000	4,071	9,153	35,734.29	7953.44	226.84

In Table 2 we show another set of results for the Dining Philosophers model, but this time using FDR4's support for partial order reduction [12] that can tackle a larger number of philosophers. With up to 300 philosophers, FDR4 completes the check faster than CP, with smaller complexity than before (Table 1), but for larger values the verification time grows faster than for CP, with FDR spending most of the time on computing the reduction prior to verification.

For the Alpha Algorithm, we fix the values of the RoboChart model constants as $av = 5$, $lv = 1$, $alpha = 8$ and $K = 1$, and define the discrete domains of the model types as follows: $nat = \{0, alpha - 1, alpha, alpha + 1\}$, $real = \{0, -av, av, -lv, lv\}$, so that all states in Turning are reachable. Moreover, we introduce a constant D, that we vary for our experiments, and define MB as $(360/av) + D$, using integer division. We also let clock MBC take discrete values from 0 to MB+1, inclusive, ensuring that state Turning is reachable.

For the CP model of the Alpha Algorithm, we set parameters to the same values as in the RoboChart model. We also set horizon to be 110, and h2 (the deadlock horizon) to 100 (i.e. to be considered deadlocked, the relevant guards must be false for 100 consecutive steps, taking 100 time units). We also include a parameter D that takes the same value and has the same effect as D in the RoboChart model. In this case we use Savile Row 1.11.1 with default settings, and Google OR-Tools 9.11 as the backend solver.

Table 3 shows the results of checking the machine Movement for timed deadlocks with both FDR4 and CP. We observe that FDR4 is unable to use partial order reduction for this model. Our results show that CP performs better than FDR4 for all values of D considered, indicating that CP can play a role in verification of liveness properties, such as, timed deadlock freedom. On the other hand, CP can only identify violations up to a given horizon.

Table 3. Results of verifying timed deadlock freedom of the alpha algorithm using FDR4 and CP, varying the parameter D to vary the size of the state space.

D	FDR4			CP Toolchain	
	States	Transitions	Time (s)	SR Time (s)	Solv Time (s)
0	2,269,830	5,033,595	169.16	14.92	0.00
10	10,448,306	24,728,591	430.64	54.60	0.00
20	10,761,506	25,464,151	442.91	29.61	0.00
40	11,387,906	26,935,271	460.04	32.24	0.00
80	12,640,706	29,877,511	515.94	32.29	0.00
100	13,267,106	31,348,631	538.25	32.47	0.00
200	16,399,106	38,704,231	662.64	36.16	0.00
400	22,663,106	53,415,431	892.84	41.24	0.00
800	35,191,106	82,837,831	1394.00	56.45	0.00
1000	41,455,106	97,549,031	1634.13	63.87	0.00

8   Related Work

Our work is essentially a form of bounded model checking (BMC). BMC is a key application area for SAT solvers, to verify hardware [4, Ch.18] and software [4, Ch.20]. In BMC, a formula is constructed representing a bounded-length counterexample trace of a given property. The formula is then solved (typically using a SAT solver), either producing a counterexample trace or a proof that no such trace exists (assuming correctness of the encoding). BMC can revisit states, so it can in some cases be less efficient than conventional unbounded model checking.

CP has been applied to verification problems, including bounded program verification. For example, CPBPV [8] (constraint programming for bounded program verification) verifies a given computer program with respect to a formal specification. The framework uses constraint stores which are incrementally updated according to non-deterministic symbolic execution. CPBPV is able to explore execution paths of a bounded length; it avoids spurious execution paths, pruning them early when the constraint store becomes inconsistent. By employing a sequence of solvers in sequence (including MIP and CP solvers), starting with faster and less generalised ones, CPBPV is able to verify programs many times faster than previous bounded-length CP-based approaches. Delzanno and Podelski [9] implicitly represent the set of reachable states as a constraint store in constraint logic programming (CLP), iteratively extending the set by applying the transition function until the least fixpoint is reached. Their approach is not BMC, and does not construct traces. Similarly, CLPS-B [6] uses CLP constraint stores to represent sets of concrete states implicitly. CLPS-B enables animation of B specifications, which is akin to BMC.

Hallerstede and Leuschel [13] extend ProB with a specialised constraint solver for finding deadlock states (and other similar tasks), where a deadlock state satisfies all axioms and invariants, but falsifies all guards. In contrast to our approach, this form of constraint-based deadlock checking does not construct a trace, so the deadlock state may not be reachable from the initial state.

Krings and Leuschel's symbolic model checking [17] is very closely related to our work. They propose a BMC method for B and Event-B models that uses a constraint solver (in ProB), as well as inductive proof methods related to BMC that are complete (i.e. unbounded). Recently the ProB constraint solver has been integrated with SAT to extend its reach [19]. APALACHE [16,18] is a symbolic model checker (avoiding explicit enumeration of states) for the TLA$^+$ language. It uses the SMT solver Z3 and can generate BMC formulas that have a similar high-level structure to our CP models. Alloy 6 [31] now has mutable state variables. Actions can be expressed in first-order logic, and the Alloy Analyzer can generate BMC formulas in SAT as one of its verification methods.

9   Conclusions

We have explored the formulation of state-based models in CP, encompassing multiple finite-state automata (synchronised on transitions), clocks and timed transitions, non-determinism, and external events acting as triggers. We present a systematic and automatable translation from state-based models to CP. CP also offers a rich language for stating properties to verify. The CP approach could possibly be more general than traditional model-checking because properties can refer to any element of the state at any time step, and make unlimited use of the logic and arithmetic offered by a CP modelling language. The CP models have a time horizon, and so any verification outcomes (such as deadlock freedom) only apply within the time horizon. However, we found that a CP toolchain (i.e. the modelling tool Savile Row with the SAT solver Kissat or CP solver OR-Tools) can scale substantially better than FDR4 in some cases, particularly when partial order reduction does not apply.

As part of our future work, we intend to investigate complete verification of properties with CP. If the horizon is sufficiently large (for example, to ensure that all states of the system can be reached within the horizon), then a given property can be fully verified. Automatically obtaining a suitable value for the horizon is challenging but we can draw on existing work in bounded model checking. Also, we intend to automate the translation to CP, and translation of solutions (traces) back to the original state-based model, in order to avoid errors and improve comprehensibility.

Acknowledgments. RoboChart icons have been made by Sarfraz Shoukat, Freepik, Google, Icomoon and Madebyoliver from www.flaticon.com, and are licensed CC 3.0 BY. This work was supported by EPSRC grant EP/W001977/1.

References

1. Akgün, O., Frisch, A.M., Gent, I.P., Jefferson, C., Miguel, I., Nightingale, P.: Conjure: automatic generation of constraint models from problem specifications. Artif. Intell. **310**, 103751 (2022). https://doi.org/10.1016/j.artint.2022.103751
2. Baxter, J., Ribeiro, P., Cavalcanti, A.: Sound reasoning in tock-CSP. Acta Informatica **59**, 125–162 (2022). https://doi.org/10.1007/s00236-020-00394-3
3. Biere, A., Fleury, M.: Gimsatul, IsaSAT and Kissat entering the SAT Competition 2022. In: Proceedings of SAT Competition 2022 - Solver and Benchmark Descriptions. Department of Computer Science Series of Publications B, vol. B-2022-1, pp. 10–11. University of Helsinki (2022). https://hdl.handle.net/10138/359079
4. Biere, A., Heule, M., van Maaren, H., Walsh, T. (eds.): Handbook of Satisfiability. IOS Press (2021)
5. Bjerknes, J.D., Winfield, A.F.T.: On fault tolerance and scalability of swarm robotic systems. In: Martinoli, A., et al., (eds.) Distributed Autonomous Robotic Systems - The 10th International Symposium, DARS 2010, Lausanne, Switzerland, 1–3 November 2010. Springer Tracts in Advanced Robotics, vol. 83, pp. 431–444. Springer, Heidelberg (2010). https://doi.org/10.1007/978-3-642-32723-0_31
6. Bouquet, F., Legeard, B., Peureux, F.: CLPS-B - a constraint solver for B. In: Katoen, J.P., Stevens, P. (eds.) Proceedings TACAS'02. LNCS, vol. 2280, pp. 188–204. Springer-Verlag (2002)
7. Cheng, K., Krishnakumar, A.S.: Automatic functional test generation using the extended finite state machine model. In: Dunlop, A.E. (ed.) Proceedings of the 30th Design Automation Conference, Dallas, Texas, USA, 14–18 June 1993, pp. 86–91. ACM Press (1993). https://doi.org/10.1145/157485.164585
8. Collavizza, H., Rueher, M., Van Hentenryck, P.: CPBPV: a constraint-programming framework for bounded program verification. Constraints **15**(2), 238–264 (2010). https://doi.org/10.1007/s10601-009-9089-9
9. Delzanno, G., Podelski, A.: Constraint-based deductive model checking. STTT **3**(3), 250–270 (2001)
10. Frisch, A.M., Harvey, W., Jefferson, C., Martínez-Hernández, B., Miguel, I.: Essence: a constraint language for specifying combinatorial problems. Constraints **13**(3), 268–306 (2008). https://doi.org/10.1007/s10601-008-9047-y
11. Gibson-Robinson, T., Armstrong, P., Boulgakov, A., Roscoe, A.: FDR3 – A Modern Refinement Checker for CSP. In: Ábrahám, E., Havelund, K. (eds.) Proceedings TACAS'14. LNCS, vol. 8413, pp. 187–201 (2014)

12. Gibson-Robinson, T., Hansen, H., Roscoe, A.W., Wang, X.: Practical partial order reduction for CSP. In: NASA Formal Methods - 7th International Symposium, NFM 2015, Pasadena, CA, USA, 27–29 April 2015, Proceedings. Lecture Notes in Computer Science, vol. 9058, pp. 188–203. Springer, Heidelberg (2015). https://doi.org/10.1007/978-3-319-17524-9_14
13. Hallerstede, S., Leuschel, M.: Constraint-based deadlock checking of high-level specifications. Theory Pract. Log. Program. **11**(4–5), 767–782 (2011)
14. Harel, D.: Statecharts: a visual formalism for complex systems. Sci. Comput. Program. **8**(3), 231–274 (1987). https://doi.org/10.1016/0167-6423(87)90035-9
15. Holzmann, G.J.: The model checker SPIN. IEEE Trans. Softw. Eng. **23**(5), 279–295 (1997). https://doi.org/10.1109/32.588521
16. Konnov, I., Kukovec, J., Tran, T.: TLA+ model checking made symbolic. Proc. ACM Program. Lang. **3**(OOPSLA), 123:1–123:30 (2019). https://doi.org/10.1145/3360549
17. Krings, S., Leuschel, M.: Proof assisted bounded and unbounded symbolic model checking of software and system models. Sci. Comput. Program. **158**, 41–63 (2018). https://doi.org/10.1016/j.scico.2017.08.013
18. Kukovec, J., Tran, T., Konnov, I.: Extracting symbolic transitions from TLA$^+$ specifications. In: Abstract State Machines, Alloy, B, TLA, VDM, and Z - 6th International Conference, ABZ 2018, Southampton, UK, 5–8 June 2018, Proceedings, pp. 89–104 (2018). https://doi.org/10.1007/978-3-319-91271-4_7
19. Leuschel, M.: B2SAT: a bare-metal reduction of B to SAT. In: International Symposium on Formal Methods, pp. 122–139. Springer, Heidelberg (2024)
20. McEwan, A., Woodcock, J.: A refinement based approach to calculating a fault-tolerant railway signal device. In: Proceedings of the 18th IFIP World Computer Congress, Topical Day on Verified Software. Springer, Heidelberg (2004)
21. Mealy, G.H.: A method for synthesizing sequential circuits. Bell Syst. Tech. J. **34**(5), 1045–1079 (1955). https://doi.org/10.1002/j.1538-7305.1955.tb03788.x
22. Miyazawa, A., Ribeiro, P., Li, W., Cavalcanti, A., Timmis, J., Woodcock, J.: RoboChart: modelling and verification of the functional behaviour of robotic applications. Softw. Syst. Model. **18**, 1–53 (2019). https://doi.org/10.1007/s10270-018-00710-z
23. Moore, E.F., et al.: Gedanken-experiments on sequential machines. Automata Stud. **34**, 129–153 (1956)
24. Murray, T.C.: On the limits of refinement-testing for model-checking CSP. Formal Aspects Comput. **25**(2), 219–256 (2013). https://doi.org/10.1007/S00165-011-0183-6
25. Nethercote, N., Stuckey, P.J., Becket, R., Brand, S., Duck, G.J., Tack, G.: MiniZinc: towards a standard CP modelling language. In: Proceedings of 13th International Conference on Principles and Practice of Constraint Programming CP-2007, pp. 529–543 (2007)
26. Nightingale, P., Özgür Akgün, Gent, I.P., Jefferson, C., Miguel, I., Spracklen, P.: Automatically improving constraint models in Savile Row. Artif. Intell. **251**, 35–61 (2017). https://doi.org/10.1016/j.artint.2017.07.001
27. Perron, L., Didier, F.: OR-Tools CP-SAT, version 9.11 (2024). https://developers.google.com/optimization/cp/cp_solver/
28. Quimper, C.G., Walsh, T.: Global grammar constraints. In: International Conference on Principles and Practice of Constraint Programming, pp. 751–755. Springer, Heidelberg (2006)
29. Roscoe, A.W.: Understanding Concurrent Systems. Texts in Computer Science. Springer, Heidelberg (2011)

30. Rossi, F., Van Beek, P., Walsh, T.: Handbook of Constraint Programming. Elsevier (2006)
31. Sinha, S., Kang, E.: Formal modeling and analysis of Apache Kafka in Alloy 6. In: Proceedings of ABZ 2024, pp. 25–42 (2024). https://doi.org/10.1007/978-3-031-63790-2_2
32. Van Hentenryck, P.: The OPL Optimization Programming Language. MIT Press, Cambridge (1999)
33. Woodcock, J.C.P., Davies, J.: Using Z - Specification, Refinement, and Proof. Prentice-Hall, Upper Saddle River (1996)
34. Yan, F., Foster, S., Habli, I.: Automated compositional verification for robotic state machines using Isabelle/HOL. In: Aït-Ameur, Y., Khendek, F., Méry, D. (eds.) 27th International Conference on Engineering of Complex Computer Systems, ICECCS, pp. 167–176. IEEE (2023). https://doi.org/10.1109/ICECCS59891.2023.00029

Formal Modelling and Analysis of the O-RAN O2 Interface in Alloy: Implications for NTN Deployment

Sean McLaren[1(✉)], Tsutomu Kobayashi[2], Leon Wong[3], and Paul Harvey[1]

[1] University of Glasgow, Glasgow, UK
`2893505m@student.gla.ac.uk`, `paul.harvey@glasgow.ac.uk`
[2] Japan Aerospace Exploration Agency, Tokyo, Japan
`kobayashi.tsutomu@jaxa.jp`
[3] Rakuten Mobile, Inc., Tokyo, Japan
`leon.wong@rakuten.com`

Abstract. Open Radio Access Networks (O-RAN) aims to transition telecommunication networks from vendor-specific hardware to open, virtualised control architectures. As interest grows in deploying O-RAN in non-terrestrial networks (NTNs), understanding the robustness of its protocol specifications becomes critical.

This paper reports on the formal modelling of the stable O2 O-RAN interface specification using the Alloy modelling language. We encode ten representative operational scenarios from the O2 specification and formalise safety and feasibility properties relevant to deployment constraints. Bounded model checking reveals several classes of specification weaknesses, including underconstrained pre/post conditions, ambiguous sequencing of protocol steps, and conflicting simultaneous triggers that permit inconsistent system states or violate intended progress conditions.

Keywords: Open Radio Access Networks · Alloy · Non-Terrestrial Networks

1 Introduction

Correct operation of telecommunication networks is both operationally critical and, in many jurisdictions, a legal requirement [8]. To increase flexibility and reduce costs associated with proprietary hardware and vendor lock-in, operators are transitioning from vertically integrated network appliances to open, software-defined ecosystems in which standardised components interact via well-defined interfaces. The Open Radio Access Network (O-RAN) specification [25] defines a modular architecture of components and interfaces intended to enable inter-operable, multi-vendor RAN deployments. Developed by the O-RAN Alliance, a

This work was supported by EPSRC grant EP/X5257161/1.

© The Author(s), under exclusive license to Springer Nature Switzerland AG 2026
F. Ishikawa and A. Cunha (Eds.): ABZ 2026, LNCS 16579, pp. 108–125, 2026.
https://doi.org/10.1007/978-3-032-26752-8_7

consortium of international operators and vendors, the specification has already underpinned several compliant terrestrial deployments [25].

Building on this terrestrial success, O-RAN has been proposed as a candidate architecture for non-terrestrial network (NTN) deployments. Existing NTN systems are typically customised and proprietary, limiting interoperability and third-party participation [16], both of which have been central to innovation in terrestrial networks. However, NTN environments impose significantly stronger resilience requirements due to limited physical accessibility, high latency, and the cost of intervention. In such contexts, reliable software-based operation is essential. At the same time, recent studies have reported issues in O-RAN implementations [26,31], motivating a rigorous assessment of the specification itself rather than its implementations alone.

In this paper, we formally model aspects of the O-RAN specification in Alloy to assess its robustness for NTN deployment. All Alloy models are available online[1]. Aligned to the proposed regenerative NTN architecture [23], we focus on the O-RAN's O2 interface, a stable and foundational interface responsible for cloud-based infrastructure provisioning, and model ten representative operational scenarios. While prior work has applied formal methods to O-RAN applications (see Sect. 2), to the best of our knowledge, this is the first study to formally verify the normative behavioural specification of an O-RAN interface itself. Our analysis reveals specification ambiguities, incomplete treatment of error conditions, violated feasibility properties, and potential race conditions, challenging the robustness of O-RAN for deployment in NTN environments.

2 Background

2.1 O-RAN

Open Radio Access Network [22] is designed to address technical and non-technical challenges in traditional telecommunication systems. At its core, O-RAN is built on two fundamental principles: *vendor-agnostic interoperability* and *open architecture*. The vendor-agnostic nature of O-RAN is achieved through the definition of open interfaces for different tasks, such as RAN control via the E2 or A1 interfaces, or infrastructure provisioning via the O1, O2 interfaces, see Fig. 1. These open interfaces enable communication between components from different vendors [22]. The intention is that network operators are no longer limited by proprietary ecosystems, and are able to mix and match hardware and software components to suit their needs [21].

Central to O-RAN's architecture are the RAN Intelligent Controllers (RIC). There are two variants: the Near-Real-Time RAN Intelligent Controller (Near-RT RIC) and the Non-Real-Time RAN Intelligent Controller (Non-RT RIC) [17]. The Near-RT RIC is intended to support control operations with a timescale of ten milliseconds to one second, enabling time-sensitive control through modular applications called *xApps* [22]. The Non-RT RIC focuses on long-term network optimisation and analytics, leveraging *rApps* for policy and decision making [18].

---

[1] https://github.com/SMcL248/FVTS_Alloy.

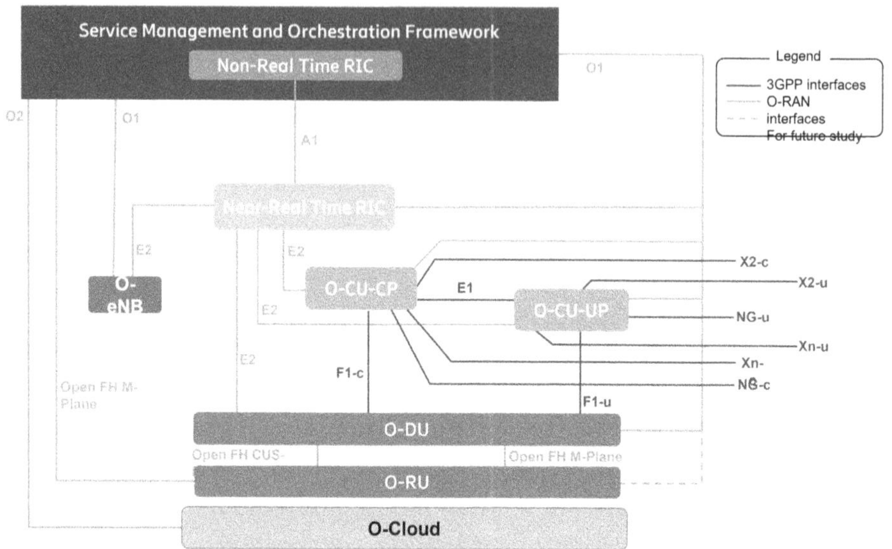

Fig. 1. O-RAN Architecture [19]

The Service Management and Orchestration (SMO) provides centralised management, orchestration, and automation functions. The SMO is responsible for lifecycle management, policy control, performance monitoring, and coordination of network functions (NFs) deployed on distributed infrastructure. It interfaces with the O-Cloud, which supplies the virtualised compute, storage, and networking resources required to host O-RAN components. O-Cloud abstracts the underlying physical infrastructure and exposes managed resources through standardised interfaces, including the O2 interface examined in this work.

2.2 Formal Modelling and Analysis in Alloy

Alloy [9] is a lightweight formal modelling language based on first-order relational logic, supported by the Alloy Analyzer [29] for automated bounded analysis. Models are expressed declaratively using *signatures* (types), *relations*, and *logical constraints*, enabling concise specification of structural properties and temporal properties. The Analyzer translates models into propositional logic and uses SAT solvers to generate instances of the model and perform bounded model checking. Alloy 6 has enhanced support for modelling and analysis of dynamic behaviour and state transitions within this relational framework.

Alloy has been used to formalise abstractions derived from informal or natural-language specifications, particularly in distributed systems and protocol design [32]. Its bounded model checking approach supports early detection of inconsistencies, underspecification, and unintended interactions, consistent with the "small scope hypothesis," which suggests that many specification errors manifest in small instances [10]. Overall, Alloy provides a rigorous yet accessible environment for analysing coordination logic and communication protocols, balancing expressiveness with automated verification support. An example of how Alloy was used to model the O2 interface state transition can be seen in Listing 1.2.

2.3 Formal Verification in Telecommunications

Formal analysis of communication protocols has a long history, including model checking and state exploration techniques [2,12]. Model checking has been successfully applied to detect deadlocks, race conditions, and feasibility violations in distributed and networked systems [7,11].

In telecommunications, formal methods have been applied to analyse signalling protocols and distributed coordination logic derived from natural-language standards [4,13]. Such efforts often uncover ambiguities and conflicting behaviours not evident during manual review. Our work aligns with this tradition by treating the O-RAN O2 specification as a behavioural artefact subject to formal interpretation and validation. Recent works have also begun to explore how AI tools (e.g. large language models) can support use of formal methods by non-experts in telecommunication networks [30].

2.4 Formal Modelling in O-RAN

Several recent works have explored applying formal methods to O-RAN, however, they have focused on the third-party applications (xApp, rApp) that *use* interfaces, as opposed to the normative behaviour of the O-RAN interfaces themselves. Exemplar O-RAN applications include PRISM-based analysis of resource allocation [15], threat analysis [28], or energy-efficient service availability [14].

To the best of our knowledge, our work is the first to formally model and verify the normative behavioural semantics of an O-RAN interface, see Sect. 4.

3 O-RAN Operational Scenarios to Model

In the O-RAN specification, the seven key interfaces (A1, O1, O2, E2, Open Fronthaul, Xn, and F1), describe over 300 potential operational scenarios to model across all interfaces. Given space limitations, we focus on the O2 interface. We now describe the O2 interface and the modelled operational scenarios.

3.1 The O-RAN O2 Interface

The O2 interface connects the Service Management and Orchestration (SMO) framework to the underlying cloud infrastructure and is responsible for infrastructure resource management, virtual network function lifecycle management,

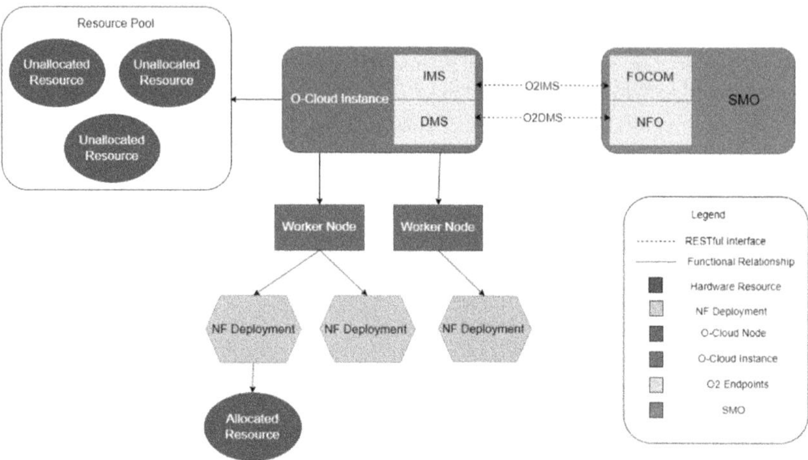

Fig. 2. O-Cloud overview showing the Infrastructure Management Services (IMS) and Deployment Management Services (DMS) which communicate with the SMO via the O2 interface. O-Cloud uses Worker Nodes to host Network Function (NF) Deployments. Resources can be scaled in and out of resource pool to increase functional capacity of NF Deployments.

and orchestration of O-Cloud resources. Considering NTN environments, compute platforms may be satellite-borne, intermittently connected, resource-constrained, or geographically distributed. This makes the correctness of infrastructure orchestration mission-critical: Failures in lifecycle operations, state synchronisation, or resource allocation can have amplified consequences due to long propagation delays, limited physical access, and constrained recovery options. By contrast, interfaces such as E2 or A1 primarily govern RAN control and optimisation logic, which, while important, presuppose a stable and correctly managed infrastructure substrate. Verifying O2 procedures therefore targets the foundational control plane governing deployment, scaling, healing, and configuration consistency across heterogeneous and latency-sensitive environments.

The O2 interface was one of the first O-RAN interfaces to be documented, giving it stability, and has several mappings to other standardised telecommunication architectures and frameworks (ETSI NFV MANO [5], ETSI ZSM [6], and 3GPP [1]), and open source projects (ONAP [24], Kubernetes [3]).

3.2   Operational Scenarios of the O2 Interface

The O-RAN specification describes 55 operational scenarios of the O2 interface. Given space limitations, we focus on those most commonly found or used. The following summarises the selected operational scenarios and their associated clause in the O-RAN specification [20], with Fig. 2 giving an overview of the components, roles, and relations:

Hardware Infrastructure Scaling Post-deployment (clause 3.1.5) describes the addition of a new worker compute node to a previously installed O-Cloud and related to clause 3.1.5 [20]. It involves a worker Node interacting with the IMS of a given O-Cloud to request a *software image*, which allows the Node to *boot*. Once booted, the O-Cloud Node has been effectively added to the O-Cloud. Subsequentially, the SMO should trigger an inventory update to retrieve an up-to-date list of available resources.

Network Function Lifecycle (clause 3.2.1, 3.2.2, 3.2.3, 3.2.4, 3.2.5). The lifecycles of Network Functions (NFs) are defined through 5 operational scenarios. NF Deployments can be instantiated (clause 3.2.1) or terminated in the O-Cloud (clause 3.2.5). The O-Cloud can alter the processing power of NF via scaling. NF Deployments can have further resources allocated to it via scale out (clause 3.2.2), and have resources deallocated through scale in (clause 3.2.3). A software modification (clause 3.2.4) procedure is also detailed. This operation follows a *replace-and-build* approach. This consists of a NF with the new software version being instantiated, and depending on the status of this NF, the new or existing NF is terminated. Each of these use cases are initiated by request via the O2 interface, and generate SMO responses.

Network Slices (clause 3.10.1, 3.10.2). Network slices may be created (clause 3.10.1) and destroyed (clause 3.10.2) over multiple O-Cloud instances. Such slices consist of NF Deployments which may or may not need to be instantiated as part of the slice creation. For each O-Cloud in the slice, a unique ID (VLAN-ID) is used to mark appropriate NFs. Such VLAN-IDs are requested from the given O-Cloud, and must be locally unique. The deletion of a network slice will include the termiantion of specified NFs and the deallocation of VLAN-IDs in each O-Cloud included in the network slice.

O-Cloud Node Clusters (clause 3.11.2.3, 3.11.3.2). The creation and deletion of O-Cloud Node Clusters are described in the specification. Clusters are groupings of O-Cloud resources that are used to deploy workloads. To create a Cluster, a request is sent the O-Cloud. Upon receiving a request, an O-Cloud Node Cluster ID shall be generated and used to book required resources. When all resources are successfully booked, they are allocated and the Cluster is created. This then generates an SMO response. Upon failure, it is stated that all actions should be rolled back. In deletion, all booking IDs are removed and resources are deallocated. Similarly to creation, an SMO response is generated and the system is told to roll-back upon error.

4   Formalising the O2 Interface in Alloy

We now describe the process of formally modelling the described O2 operational scenarios in Alloy, as well as verification of safety and feasibility.

Listing 1.1. Model structure of NF Deployment Instantiation

```
1  sig Node {var deployment: set NF}
2  sig NF {}
3  sig Request {
4      target: one oCloud,
5      payload: one NF,
6      var underlying_error: lone Response,
7      var processed: lone Response
8  }
9  sig oCloud { dms: one DMS, var nodes: set Node}
10 sig DMS {cloud: one oCloud, var requests: set Request}
11 one sig SMO {var responses: set Request->Response}
12 enum Response{SUCCESS, ERROR}
```

4.1 Modelling the O2 Interface in Alloy

In the O-RAN specification, each operational scenario has a defined goal, participating actors, preconditions, starting conditions, prescribed steps and actions, end conditions, exception flows, and post-conditions [20].

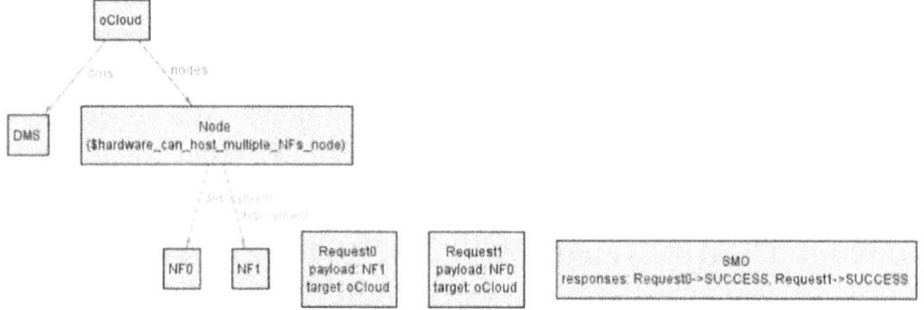

Fig. 3. Alloy Visualisation of Listing 1.1

We represent O2 components and interactions in Alloy using signatures and predicates, respectively. Each Alloy signature contains a list of fields that allow for mappings between O2 components. Listing 1.1 shows the structure of the NF Deployment Instantiation protocol, with Fig. 3 showing this visually. From the specification, the SMO sends requests to the DMS. O-Cloud Worker Nodes are represented by the Node signature, and network functions are represented by the NF signature. An O-Cloud instance is represented by the oCloud signature, and must be associated with a DMS signature. We represent request objects using the Request signature. Requests contain an NF for instantiation, a target O-Cloud, and a status which is represented by the Response enumerate type. The lone keyword enforces that a field contains at most one mapping, while the one keyword enforces that a field contains exactly one mapping. The -> operator defines the relations between signatures in fields.

Listing 1.2. Predicate that sends a NF Deployment Instiation request to a DMS

```
pred initiate_deployment(r:Request){
  historically r not in r.target.dms.requests and
            some r.targets.nodes //guard conditions
  requests'= requests + r.target.dms->r //effect condition
  //frame conditions
  deployment' = deployment and nodes' = nodes and
      responses' = responses and err' = err and processed'
      = processed
}
```

Listing 1.3. Predicate that simulates the NF instatiation process

```
pred sim_error(r:Request, c:oCloud){
  r in c.dms.requests and no r.error//guard
  error' = error + r->SUCCESS or error' = error + r->ERROR
  // code to update frame conditions, as in Listing 1.2
}
```

O2 sequence steps are represented in Alloy predicates, as shown in Listing 1.2. Such predicates define how the system may transition from one state to another. They are broken down into guard, effect, and frame conditions. Effect conditions specify which mutable fields change, while frame conditions ensure that mutable fields that should not change remain unaltered. Guard conditions must be satisfied for the predicate to take effect, and most closely represent O-RAN preconditions. Listing 1.2 shows a predicate representing a request being sent to a DMS. Here, the guard condition is that there must exist a worker Node that the NF can be instantiated on.

Listing 1.3 shows the transition associated with instantiating an NF Deployment. For this step, the specification only states that resources are allocated. We abstract the allocation, returning the success or failure of the instantiation. We include an error possibility is to show that NF instantiation may not be successful, as in real life.

Fact statements were written to force the solver down specific traces to explore possible real world states. That is, these statements set conditions that cannot be violated. Facts can take the form of initial conditions, as shown in Listing 1.4, or fairness conditions. Fairness conditions force system progression, preventing solver-generated counterexamples where the system *stutters* indefinitely.

4.2   Analysing Feasibility and Safety

Our analysis of the O2 interface consists of verification of feasibility (there exist cases where something good happens) and safety (something bad never hap-

Listing 1.4. Initial conditions in NF Deployment Instantiation

```
fact init {
    all c : oCloud | some c.nodes
    all node : Node | no node.deployment
    all r : Request |
        no r.underlying_error and
        no r.processed and
        r.payload not in Node.deployment
    no SMO.responses
    all d : DMS | no d.requests
}
```

Listing 1.5. Safety assertion in NF Deployment Instantiation

```
assert response_implies_added_node {
  always (all r : Request | (r->SUCCESS in SMO.responses)
      implies (once r.payload not in Node.deployment) and r
      .payload in Node.deployment)
}
```

pens in every case). To check feasibility, we instructed the Alloy analyser to find traces (instances) in which the target property holds. To verify safety, we instructed the Alloy analyser to perform bounded model checking. Due to Alloy's bounded analysis, results are necessarily scope-dependent. Increasing the number of atoms per signature or extending the trace length increases confidence in the conclusions.

Safety assertions were used to detect the existence of undesirable behaviour. These capture invariants that must always hold across all instances, such as consistency between SMO and O-Cloud state representations, absence of conflicting lifecycle transitions, and preservation of resource allocation constraints. For example, in the NF Deployment Instantiation protocol (Listing 1.5), we specify that a success response in the SMO's inbox implies that the corresponding NF was previously not instantiated and is now instantiated. This ensures that responses are only generated following successful completion of the associated deployment procedure. The solver then searches for traces that violate this invariant; absence of a counterexample indicates that the invariant holds under the given scope.

Feasibility assertions were written to establish the existence of valid behaviour and intended progress conditions. These properties express that certain desirable outcomes are achievable within the model. Listing 1.6 presents a property that should be feasible for the NF Deployment Instantiation protocol. For example, it is expected that an O-Cloud Worker Node may be able to host more than one NF instance. To evaluate feasibility, a fact statement that

Listing 1.6. Property that should be feasible in NF Deployment Instantiation

```
fact hardware_can_host_multiple_NFs_fact {
    eventually (some node : Node | (some disj a,b : NF | (
        a+b) in node.deployment))
}
```

states that the expected behaviour eventually occurs is created. If the enclosed behaviour is valid under the model, we expect a valid trace to be generated that demonstrates the expected behaviour. If the solver produces no such trace, the intended behaviour is therefore not achievable within the given scope.

Across the analysed scenarios, safety properties ensured that O2 components do not enter deployment without completion of the corresponding protocol, that responses are only generated upon legitimate completion, and that error statuses are consistent with request outcomes. Feasibility properties examined whether worker nodes can host multiple NF instantiations were permitted, whether a single NF can be instantiated across multiple nodes, whether failure messages are propagated back to the SMO, and whether concurrent requests targeting the same O2 component may both succeed. Together, these properties reflect the dual requirement in NTN contexts to prevent unsafe configurations while ensuring forward progress despite delay, concurrency, or disruption.

5   Results

We now discuss the results of the analysis described in Sect. 4.2. We also report problems we found through modelling the O2 interface.

5.1   Feasibility

Hardware Scaling Post-deployment (clause 3.1.5). We attempted to confirm that multiple O-Cloud Nodes may be deployed in a single O-Cloud instance, and single O-Cloud Nodes may be shared between O-Cloud instances. For each of these conditions, the analyser successfully generated traces that satisfy it. In this case, there is ambiguity in the O-RAN specification. For example, despite being against best practice [27], it is unclear whether shared Nodes between O-Cloud instances is expected behaviour. Also, the hardware scaling preconditions do not state that the targeted O-Cloud Node should not be previously deployed.

Another feasibility we checked is whether O-Cloud Node boot failure stalls progression. For example, we stated an assertion that boot failure implies that the request remains in the IMS inbox. Checking this assertion did not produce a counterexample, implying that boot failure is not recoverable under the model; the expected behaviour (a configuration attempt associated with a failed boot is completed) never occurs. To further highlight this invalid behaviour, a fairness condition was introduced that forces all hardware scaling operations to complete. Upon asserting that boot failures cannot exist under this constraint, no counterexample was found. That is, for hardware scaling to complete, the Node must always successfully boot.

NF Deployment Instantiation (clause 3.2.1). It is commonly accepted that worker Nodes possess the ability to host multiple NF instantiations, or that a single NF Deployment may be instantiated among multiple nodes [5]. We check this ability in Alloy. This includes that a request failure does not prevent the corresponding NF from later instantiation, or that two requests of the same NF may both yield successful outcomes. The analyser generated traces for each of these behaviours, showing they are permitted in the model, as expected.

Conversely, graceful error handling on instantiation was not observed. The analyser failed to generate a trace in which the SMO receives an error response during instantiation. Hence, this expected behaviour can never occur in the model.

NF Deployment Scaling (clause 3.2.2, 3.2.3). Another feasibility assertion explored is that deallocated resources can be reused. We successfully obtained a trace showing that an allocated resource is removed due to a scale in request and subsequently reallocated during a separate scale out operation. Furthermore, we checked that NF Deployments have the ability to make use of multiple resources. This returned a trace where two successive scale out requests allocate resources to the same NF Deployment.

An ambiguity in the specification concerns whether a single resource can be allocated to multiple NFs. The specification states only that resources are allocated as required, and does not mention whether currently allocated hardware resources can also be used for scaling. Best practice states that isolation is preferable to hardware sharing [27], however, in an NTN context, where resources are limited [23], shared may be required. To understand resource allocation during scaling behaviour in the specification, a resource pool was implemented in the NF Deployment scaling model to represent unused resources that are available for deployment. If a scale out request is received, then a resource from the pool is allocated to the target NF. We attempted to show that resource sharing between NF Deployments is feasible. However, no trace is returned, meaning that resource sharing is not possible assuming best practise, which can only scale out using *unallocated* resources from the pool.

NF Deployment Software Modification (clause 3.2.4). For software modification, the existence of failure and success responses is checked as feasibility properties. We successfully produced traces in which both response types are observed in the SMO. Hence, complete success and failure pathways exist.

It is also checked that both the desired and existing NF may be deployed on different hardware of the same O-Cloud instance. This produced a valid trace in which this property is realised. Hence, the new NF need not be deployed upon the same hardware as the NF for replacing.

NF Deployment Termination (clause 3.2.5). Two feasibility conditions were tested to validate the suitability of the termination model. For each of two SMO response types, the analyser returned traces in which the SMO response is generated. This implies that both termination success and failure pathways are reachable under the model.

Network Slices (clause 3.10.1, 3.10.2). For Cluster creation (clause 3.10.1), it is stated in the specification that network slices may span multiple O-Cloud instances. Hence, this property was tested using a feasibility assertion. As expected, a trace is produced showing that a slice may be associated with multiple O-Clouds.

Furthermore, we checked that the failure to create a network slice does not necessarily imply that all associated NFs are not instantiated. The analyser successfully returned traces, showing that previously deployed NFs remain unaffected by creation failures.

For network slice deletion (clause 3.10.2), a returned trace illustrated the existence if complete success and error pathways, showing appropriate SMO responses.

O-Cloud Node Clusters (clause 3.11.2.3, 3.11.3.2). For O-Cloud Node Cluster creation (clause 3.11.2.3) and deletion (clause 3.11.3.2) operations, we successfully generated traces showing that both error and success responses can be sent to the SMO in these use cases. All requests, no matter success or failure, can result in an SMO response. Hence, errors are handled gracefully in the model, as expected.

For the creation use case specifically, it was checked that multiple O-Cloud Node Clusters may be created on a single O-Cloud instance. This produced a trace implying that such a property occurs as expected. The possibility of multiple clusters existing in a O-Cloud instance is an important property for checking that cluster IDs are locally unique within O-Clouds, and that clusters have disjoint resources as discussed later in Sect. 5.2.

5.2   Safety

Hardware Scaling Post-deployment (clause 3.1.5). As per the specification, explored properties included that O-Cloud Nodes only boot due to an ongoing scaling request, deployed Nodes must have successfully booted, and that a successful boot implies eventual Node deployment using Alloy `facts` to mitigate stutter. Each assertion did not produce counterexamples, and thus, O-Cloud Node configuration does not occur without a corresponding scale request.

NF Deployment Instantiation (clause 3.2.1). In the NF Deployment instantiation model, various safety assertions were examined. For example, if a request is completed, then an SMO response must be generated. Conversely, if an SMO response is received, the corresponding NF must have been successfully instantiated. Neither of these assertions yield counterexamples. This implies that NFs cannot be instantiated without it being directly requested, and that responses cannot be sent to the SMO without the completion of the corresponding request. An assertion stating that NFs cannot be instantiated on undeployed Nodes was also written. This provided no counter examples, and thus, NFs can only be instantiated upon deployed Nodes, as expected.

Upon altering the model so that the allocation of resources is included, a safety condition was created to ensure that resources are only allocated to NFs that are successfully instantiated. This assertion unexpectedly revealed a counterexample in which an NF instantiation request has failed, but a required resource has been allocated. This is depicted in Fig. 4. As there is no roll-back mechanism in the spec, this demonstrates a resource leak upon error.

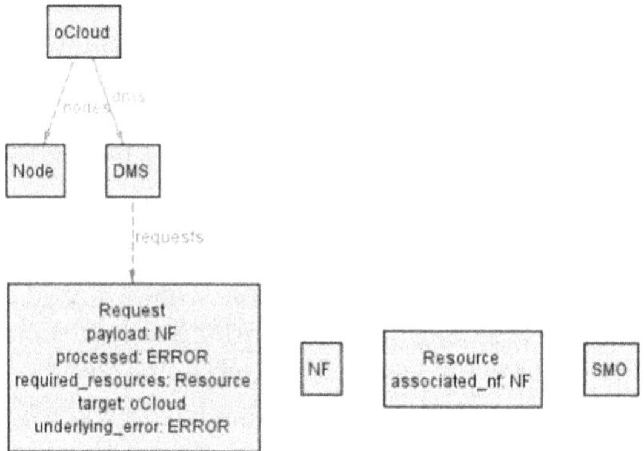

Fig. 4. Unhandled Error Condition: resources were allocated but the overall NF instation request failed (clause 3.2.1).

Network Function Scaling (clause 3.2.2, 3.2.3). For NF deployment scaling, we specified assertions requiring that resource allocation occurs only if a successful scale-out request targeting the same NF deployment previously appeared in the trace; no counterexamples were found. The dual property was verified for deallocation, ensuring resources are released only following a successful scale-in request, again yielding no counterexamples. Together, these results show that resources cannot move between pools and NF deployments without an explicit request. We further verified that any request leaving a DMS returns a final status to the SMO, confirming that requests cannot be silently discarded before completion. Finally, by constraining traces to include failed scaling operations with corresponding SMO responses, we identified a counterexample in which allocation fails but an error response is eventually returned. This demonstrates that failures do not block overall system progression.

NF Deployment Software Modification (clause 3.2.4). Safety assertions were checked on the software modification operation. This included that all SMO responses correspond to a preceding operation, that the completion of requests imply SMO responses, that the termination of the new NF implies an unsuccessful operation, the termination of the existing NF implies a successful operation, that all terminated NFs have there resources deallocated, and that if both the desired and existing NF are concurrently instantiated, then they must both exist within the same O-Cloud. Each of these assertions produced no counterexamples, implying that SMO responses can only be generated via request completion, there are no partially allocated resources and that the correct NF is always terminated during software modifications.

NF Deployment Termination (clause 3.2.5). Several safety conditions were written to confirm the absence of unwanted states due to NF Deployment termination. This includes that success responses imply only occur if the appropriate NF has been terminated as well as that error responses imply that the corresponding NF remains instantiated. It was also tested that the termination of an NF implies the deallocation of all appropriate resources. Each of these assertions did not produce counterexamples. This shows that certain unwanted behaviours are forbidden under the model. This includes that responses are only generated upon operation success or failure, and that resources do not remain partially allocated.

Network Slices (clause 3.10.1, 3.10.2). For slice creation (clause 3.10.1), it was checked that success responses imply that all required NF have been instantiated. This revealed no counterexample, as expected. Also, it was verified that upon creation failure the slice has no associated VLAN IDs. No counterexamples were produced, meaning VLAN ID clean up is always successful, as expected.

A safety assertion was written to verify that partial slices may only exist during slice deletion (clause 3.10.2). That is, if a network slice exists but an NF that should be included in the slice has since been terminated, then there must be an on-going deletion attempt. This assertion unexpectedly produces a counterexample which is visualised in Fig. 5. The `ids` relation in the `Slice` atom contains a mapping to an O-Cloud and VLAN-ID, implying that this slice is currently deployed. The preceding trace that generated this counterexample attempted to delete this slice, but an error prevents this deletion as implied by the response in the `SMO` atom. However, before the error occurred, the deletion of the slice had already started, and the `NF` atom was terminated. Hence, there now exists a network slice which is no longer slated for deletion, but an NF which should be associated with the slice is no longer deployed.

O-Cloud Node Clusters (clause 3.11.2.3, 3.11.3.2). For O-Cloud Node Cluster creation (clause 3.11.2.3), various assertions were used to test safety properties. This includes that no two Clusters may share the same resource, all successfully created clusters contain at least one resource, no two Clusters in a single O-Cloud instance may share the same cluster ID, and that resources that reside in the same O-Cloud but different Clusters must be booked with distinct IDs. Each of these assertions produced no counterexamples. Thus, it has been shown that the inverse of these properties, which are invalid behaviours, never occur. For O-Cloud Node Cluster Deletion (clause 3.11.3.2), similar safety asser-

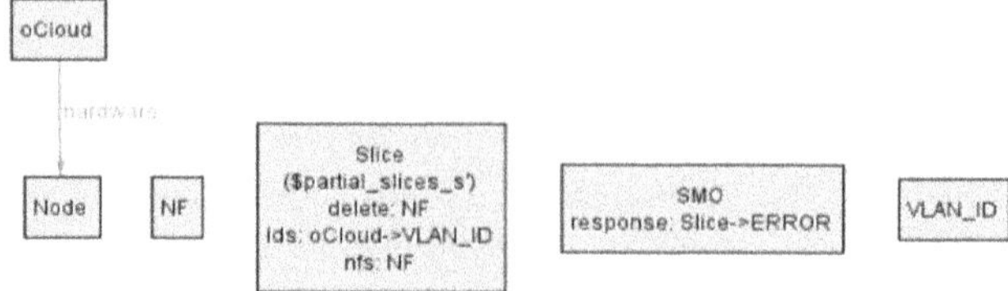

Fig. 5. Output of safety assertion violation for network slice deletion (clause 3.10.1). As a counterexample is generated, it has been shown that slices may exist but not have all required NFs instantiated. This is unexpected behaviour.

tions were checked. This includes that all deletion requests deemed successful imply that the corresponding cluster no longer exists as well as the fact that all Clusters remain non-empty and disjoint when in deployment.

5.3   Race Conditions

The O-RAN documentation does not prescribe a normative protocol for concurrent access. Instead, it offers illustrative examples of implementation approaches that could be used to achieve safe concurrent operation (e.g. semaphore flags, transaction tokens). This leaves specification conformance open to interpretation. An initial exploration of race conditions in Alloy found an example in hardware scaling post deployment (clause 3.1.5), however, given the absence of normative constraints, we cannot classify this as specification violation.

5.4   Lack of Error Conditions

Throughout the model process, it was observed that multiple sequences (clauses 3.1.5, 3.2.1) have insufficient error descriptions. As discussed in Sect. 5.1, there are no valid traces in which an error message is propagated back to the SMO. This is due to the complete lack of error specification in these sequences. As no exceptions are given, it is not well-defined how the system handles error. Hence, the system idles and instantiation requests remain unfinished indefinitely. It is also unclear how the O-Cloud should *clean-up* resources allocated during an NF instantiation (clause 3.2.1) that has failed to complete. As shown in Sect. 5.1, this lack of roll-back procedure causes resources to remain allocated to NFs that are not currently deployed. This is not a desirable state. In Sect. 5.2, it is shown that there exists traces in which network slices exist, but not all required NFs are instantiated. This again is due to the lack of roll-back procedures. While the specification states that error may occur during network slice deletion (clause 3.10.1), it is not stated that the slice must be restored to its initial configuration. This allows for the unwanted state in which a network slice exists, but not all of its required NFs are deployed. As undesirable states are reachable under the error conditions set out by the specification, it must be the case that such error conditions are not satisfactory to maintain valid behaviour.

5.5 Summary

Through analysis of the O-RAN O2 interface specification description and Alloy modelling, we have identified several issues with the robustness and correctness of the O2 interface. A combination of feasibility assertion violations (Sect. 5.1) and safety assertion violations (Sect. 5.2), show that the specification contains ambiguities in error specification. As a consequence of these ambiguities, simulated errors cause models to enter unwanted states, as discussed in Sect. 5.4. It was directly observed that errors in clauses 3.1.5 and 3.2.1 of the O2 specification cause requests to indefinitely idle and prevent responses from being generated. In addition, the lack of roll-back/clean up procedures in clauses 3.2.1 and 3.10.2 allow for resources to be left in partially allocated states.

These findings suggest that the specification would benefit from clearer normative concurrency semantics, explicit pre/post conditions, and a canonical lifecycle state model to reduce ambiguity and unintended non-determinism, especially in NTN deployment contexts.

6 Conclusions

To understand the robustness of the open radio access network (O-RAN) specification for use in non-terrestrial network environments, we use Alloy to formally model the O2 interface. While others have explored formal verification of O-RAN, this work has focused on the control applications that use the specification, as opposed to modelling the normative specification itself. We choose Alloy as it enables incremental specification for the hundreds of O-RAN use cases. Through Alloy modelling of ten use cases, we observed that multiple use cases did not contain sufficient error specification. The lack of any error conditions causes models to indefinitely stutter, never completing requests that have been deemed unsuccessful. Furthermore, the lack of clean-up procedures allow for partially allocated resources. These issues challenge the correctness and robustness of the O2 interface specification for use in NTN deployments.

References

1. 3GPP: Management and orchestration; Architecture framework. Technical Specification V15.3.0, ETSI (2020). https://bit.ly/3MNGOXJ
2. Clarke, E.M.: Model checking. In: International Conference on Foundations of Software Technology and Theoretical Computer Science, pp. 54–56. Springer (1997)
3. Cloud Native Computing Foundation: Kubernetes – production-grade container orchestration (2026). https://www.kubernetes.io/. Accessed 15 Feb 2026
4. Cremers, C., Dehnel-Wild, M.: Component-based formal analysis of 5G-AKA: channel assumptions and session confusion. In: Network and Distributed System Security Symposium (NDSS). Internet Society (2019)
5. ETSI: Network Functions Virtualisation (NFV) Release 4; Management and Orchestration; Architectural framework. Group Specification GS NFV 006, European Telecommunications Standards Institute (ETSI) (2022). https://bit.ly/4tXpXmf

6. ETSI ISG ZSM: Zero-touch network and Service Management (ZSM); Reference Architecture. Group Specification GS ZSM 002, European Telecommunications Standards Institute (2019). https://bit.ly/4kKKGpa

7. Gotmanov, A., Chatterjee, S., Kishinevsky, M.: Verifying deadlock-freedom of communication fabrics. In: International Workshop on Verification, Model Checking, and Abstract Interpretation, pp. 214–231. Springer (2011)

8. ITU-T: Network reliability in public telecommunication data networks. ITU-T Recommendation Y.2614 (2011). https://www.eolss.net/sample-chapters/C05/E6-108-13-00.pdf

9. Jackson, D.: Alloy: a lightweight object modelling notation. ACM Trans. Softw. Eng. Methodol. (TOSEM) **11**(2), 256–290 (2002)

10. Jackson, D.: Software Abstractions: Logic, Language, and Analysis. MIT Press (2012)

11. Kaveh, N.: Using model checking to detect deadlocks in distributed object systems. In: Engineering Distributed Objects: Second International Workshop, EDO 2000 Davis, CA, USA, 2–3 November 2000, Revised Papers, pp. 116–128. Springer (2001)

12. Leathrum, J., Morsi, R., Leathrum, T.: Formal verification of communication protocols. In: IASTED Eighth International Conference on Parallel and Distributed Computing and Systems. Citeseer (1996)

13. Li, Z., Xiao, M., Xu, R.: Formal analysis of signal protocol based on logic of events theory. Sci. Rep. **14**(1), 20606 (2024)

14. Metere, R., et al.: Towards achieving energy efficiency and service availability in 6G O-RAN via formal verification. In: Czekster, R.M., Milazzo, P. (eds.) From Data to Models and Back, pp. 137–157. Springer, Cham (2025)

15. Mumtaz, T., Muhammad, S., Bouali, F.: Formal verification- and AI/ML-assisted radio resource allocation for open RAN compliant 5G/6G networks. IEEE Access **13**, 96198–96212 (2025). https://doi.org/10.1109/ACCESS.2025.3575021

16. Nguyen, C.T., et al.: Emerging technologies for 6G non-terrestrial-networks: from academia to industrial applications. IEEE Open J. Commun. Soc. **5**, 3852–3885 (2024). https://doi.org/10.1109/OJCOMS.2024.3418574

17. Niknam, S., Roy, A., Dhillon, H.S., et al.: Intelligent O-RAN for Beyond 5G and 6G Wireless Networks. arXiv preprint arXiv:2005.08374 (2020). https://arxiv.org/abs/2005.08374

18. O-RAN Alliance: O-RAN Minimum Viable Plan and the Acceleration towards Commercialization. https://bit.ly/4rWbIw3. Accessed 08 Jan 2025

19. O-RAN Alliance: O-RAN Software Community (SC) Documentation. https://docs.o-ran-sc.org/en/j-release/index.html. Accessed 15 Feb 2026

20. O-RAN Alliance: O-RAN Use Cases. https://specifications.o-ran.org/specifications. Accessed 22 Mar 2026

21. O-RAN Alliance: O-RAN Use Cases and Deployment Scenarios. https://bit.ly/4qFZ2YY. Accessed 08 Jan 2025

22. O-RAN Alliance: O-RAN White Papers and Resources. https://www.o-ran.org/o-ran-resources. Accessed 08 Jan 2025

23. O-RAN Alliance White Paper Contributors: Deployments of o-ran-based non-terrestrial networks. White Paper O-RAN.WP.IEFG.O-RAN_NTN, O-RAN ALLIANCE (2025). https://bit.ly/4aVybn5. Accessed 05 Feb 2025

24. ONAP Project: Open Network Automation Platform. https://www.onap.org/

25. Polese, M., et al.: Open RAN: a concise overview. IEEE Commun. Mag. (2024). https://doi.org/10.1109/MCOM.005.2300467. https://ieeexplore.ieee.org/document/10601697/

26. Rodgers, P., Harvey, P.: The xApp store: a framework for xApp onboarding and deployment in O-RAN. In: 2025 IEEE 45th International Conference on Distributed Computing Systems Workshops (ICDCSW), pp. 647–652 (2025). https://doi.org/10.1109/ICDCSW63273.2025.00121
27. StarlingX Project: O-RAN Specification Compliant O2 Interfaces (2022). https://bit.ly/4ar6ssY, starlingX stx-8.0 Approved Specification, Story 2010278
28. Thimmaraju, K., Shaik, A., Flück, S., Mora, P.J.F., Werling, C., Seifert, J.P.: Security testing the O-RAN near-real time RIC & A1 interface. In: Proceedings of the 17th ACM Conference on Security and Privacy in Wireless and Mobile Networks, pp. 277–287 (2024)
29. Wang, W., Wang, K., Zhang, M., Khurshid, S.: Learning to optimize the alloy analyzer. In: 2019 12th IEEE Conference on Software Testing, Validation and Verification (ICST), pp. 228–239 (2019). https://doi.org/10.1109/ICST.2019.00031
30. Wray, T., Wang, Y.: 5G specifications formal verification with over-the-air validation: prompting is all you need. In: MILCOM 2024 - 2024 IEEE Military Communications Conference (MILCOM), pp. 412–418 (2024). https://doi.org/10.1109/MILCOM61039.2024.10773849
31. Yang, T., Rashid, S.M.M., Ranjbar, A., Tan, G., Hussain, S.R.: ORANalyst: systematic testing framework for open RAN implementations. In: 33rd USENIX Security Symposium (USENIX Security 2024), pp. 1921–1938. USENIX Association, Philadelphia, PA (2024). https://www.usenix.org/conference/usenixsecurity24/presentation/yang-tianchang
32. Zave, P.: Using lightweight modeling to understand chord. SIGCOMM Comput. Commun. Rev. **42**(2), 49–57 (2012). https://doi.org/10.1145/2185376.2185383

A Method for Testing Partial-Order Reduction Theories in Alloy

Mara Miulescu$^{(\boxtimes)}$ and Thomas Neele

Eindhoven University of Technology, Eindhoven, The Netherlands
`{m.c.miulescu,t.s.neele}@tue.nl`

Abstract. Partial-order reduction (POR) is a technique for tackling the state-space explosion problem in model checking. The search space can be significantly reduced by disabling certain events at the state level. Recent research has brought to light issues in the theory behind several POR approaches. In this work, we demonstrate a method for rigorously testing the soundness of POR theories using Alloy, a SAT-based formal specification tool. We apply this method to several POR theories and formalisms. To explain the modelling challenges that we faced, we show two Alloy models in detail. In our experiments, Alloy manages to produce counterexamples to all theorems that we know to be flawed. This indicates that our ideas are viable for preventing comparable issues in the future development of POR methods.

Keywords: Partial-order reduction · Parity games · Alloy

1 Introduction

In model checking, *partial-order reduction* (POR) theory studies methods for tackling the state-space explosion problem that occurs in the context of verifying (interleaving) concurrent systems. The common intuition behind most POR approaches is that many interleavings can be considered equivalent, and it suffices to explore only one interleaving per equivalence class. This can greatly reduce the amount of effort required for verification. Though a mature field, with notable techniques introduced by Valmari [32], Peled [27] and Godefroid [13], POR theory remains difficult to understand because of its complexity. A proper understanding of any formal theory is essential for judging its correctness.

Recently, a number of correctness issues [22, 24, 30] (five in total) were uncovered in various POR theories. It thus turns out that the complexity of POR theory indeed impacts it correctness, and traditional pen and paper methods are not sufficient for reliably developing such theory. Therefore, we devise a methodology for modelling and rigorously testing POR theories using an *automated theorem prover* (ATP). Inspired by [30], we use the Alloy analyser [16]. In our setting, a *POR theory* comprises (i) a formalism (some form of transition system), (ii) a set of conditions under which reduction may be applied, and (iii) a theorem that states what properties are preserved in the reduced system

© The Author(s), under exclusive license to Springer Nature Switzerland AG 2026
F. Ishikawa and A. Cunha (Eds.): ABZ 2026, LNCS 16579, pp. 126–144, 2026.
https://doi.org/10.1007/978-3-032-26752-8_8

(usually a behavioural equivalence such as *stutter-trace equivalence*). Accordingly, the generic implementation comprises a model of transition systems and, to enable modelling the reduction conditions and behavioural equivalence, an approach for handling quantifications over paths. Such higher-order quantifications are not directly supported by Alloy. We validate our idea by applying it to the aforementioned flawed theories and show that Alloy can reproduce all the issues automatically. Our contributions are[1]:

- A generic Alloy model of transition systems and related concepts. We show how to model paths so that it is possible to write quantifiers over them. This is essential to modelling most POR theories.
- We show in detail how this can be applied to the *stubborn set* methods for *labelled-state transition systems* [33,34] (repaired in [22]) and *parity games* [23] (repaired in [24]). These ideas carry over straightforwardly to other flawed theories we have modelled (but do not discuss in detail here): *ample sets* for labelled Kripke structures [1] (found by [21]) and stubborn sets for reachability games [4] (found by [25], repaired in [5]).
- We run a SAT solver on each of the models and show that counterexamples can be found fully automatically for all of the known flawed theories. Moreover, testing the models of repaired theories reveals no new counterexamples up to the bounds that we set. The models are available online[2].

Considering the variety of theories we implemented as well as the results we obtained from our experiments, we believe our approach is a viable tool for testing the soundness of POR theories.

Related Work. Correctness issues have been surfacing in the field of formal theories for a long time. An early account of errors in published set theory results dates back to 1979 by De Millo *et al.* [10]. They argue that a proof is only a step in the direction of confidence, stating: "the point is not that mathematicians make mistakes; that goes without saying. The point is that mathematicians' errors are corrected, not by formal symbolic logic, but by other mathematicians".

In the field of POR, a multitude of issues have been found. First, the combination of *on-the-fly* partial-order reduction and nested-depth first search [27,28] proved to be incompatible by default and needed amending [14]. A formalisation in Isabelle/HOL (an interactive theorem prover) of the same on-the-fly approach by Brunner and Lammich [7] revealed that one supporting lemma is not correct, although they were not able to assess correctness of the main theorem. Finally, Siegel [30] was able to produce a counterexample to the theorem using Alloy. Siegel's formalisation is limited to ample sets for Büchi automata. To capture more powerful theories (in particular those involving stubborn sets or games), our Alloy models add support for non-deterministic transition systems and quantification over paths and strategies.

---

[1] This paper is based on the MSc thesis of the first author [20].
[2] See https://doi.org/10.5281/zenodo.19134774 for the reproduction artifact.

Interestingly, at an earlier point Chou and Peled [8] formalised the correctness proofs of the *offline* algorithm of [27] in HOL, but did not find any issues. Later, other issues were found [22,24] in methods for labelled transition systems, Kripke structures, parity games, reachability games.

In other areas within formal methods, issues have been found in various places, including in a derivation system for consistent consequence for Boolean equation systems [9], in an antichain algorithm for failures refinement [18], in an algorithm for computing simulation preorder [12] and in a unifying framework for timed automata [17].

Overview. First, in Sect. 2 we introduce the background of our work, including relevant Alloy formalisations. We expand on this in Sects. 3 and 4, discussing our Alloy formalisation of POR. Finally, we present our experiments in Sect. 5 and conclude in Sect. 6.

2   Preliminaries

This section introduces the background concepts used in the remainder of the paper, in particular the Alloy language and labelled-state transition systems.

Alloy. Alloy is an open source language and an automated theorem prover [16]. Given a specification and a property to be verified within a given set of bounds, it creates a *Boolean satisfiability* (SAT) [3] problem. Our approach boils down to transforming the question "is this theory sound?" into a SAT problem: "is there an instance that shows the theory is unsound?". We refer to such an instance as a *counterexample*.

We now give a non-exhaustive overview of the semantics and syntax of the Alloy language, which is a first-order *relational* logic. The Alloy *universe* consists of *atoms*, and we determine the size of the universe by setting *bounds*. Alloy searches for an *instance* that meets the specification for the given bounds. An instance is an assignment of values to *expressions*. We use the notation $[\![e]\!]$ to refer to the set of values of an expression `e`. Expressions may be of type Boolean (also called *formulas*), relational, or integer. Formulas can be combined with the standard operations $\neg, \vee, \wedge, \leftrightarrow, \rightarrow$ (`not`, `or`, `and`, `iff`, and `implies` in Alloy). Logical implication can be followed by the keyword `else` to capture the case where $[\![e]\!]$ is `false`. Universal and existential quantifiers work as expected (respectively: `all x:T | e` and `some x:T | e`). Additionally we can express: there exists exactly one `x`, or there is no `x` (respective operators are `one` and `no`). We sometimes use the keyword `disj` inside quantifications. For instance, we write `all disj x, y: X` to quantify over disjoint $[\![x]\!]$ and $[\![y]\!]$. Operations that we frequently use on relations are transpose, transitive closure, reflexive transitive closure, set union, set difference, set intersection, join, cartesian product (`~e`, `^e`, `*e`, `e+e`, `e-e`, `e&e`, `e.e`, `e->e` in Alloy for some expression `e`). We use `in` to check set membership (e.g., `x in T`). A model in Alloy consists of declarations of *signatures, relations, functions, predicates, facts, assertions,* and *commands*.

Signatures define the types in an Alloy formalism. Their declaration can be preceded by keywords, like `abstract` and `one`, which indicate how many atoms of this type will be in the universe (no atoms and exactly one, respectively). Signatures may be extended with the `extends` keyword; for instance, we can write `sig A {}` and `sig B extends A {}`. We declare *fields* inside of a signature to model relations over that signature. To indicate multiplicities for fields we use `lone`, `one`, and `set`. For example, `sig A { r: lone B }` introduces a relation $r \subseteq A \times B$ containing, for each atom $a \in A$ at most one pair (a, b) for $b \in B$. The default behavior of r (if we omit the multiplicity) is to relate each atom a to some atom b. Relations can also be defined outside of signatures, by using `let` followed by a set comprehension or by declaring a (parameterised) function. Predicates are functions that evaluate to `true` or `false`. We may also use `let` to declare local variables inside of functions and predicates. We use facts to enforce that certain predicates, or simply expressions, hold true in the model. Assertions are statements containing the predicates to be checked. The commands for testing in Alloy are `run` and `check`, where the latter is used to find counterexamples for assertions. Both commands require setting bounds (upper or exact) for each signature, which is fundamental to how the Alloy analyser works.

Labelled-State Transition Systems. Transition systems are commonly chosen in literature to formally reason about the behaviour of concurrent systems. Recall that a POR theory consists of (i) a formalism (some form of transition system), (ii) a set of conditions under which reduction may be applied, and (iii) a theorem that states what properties are preserved in the reduced system. The POR theories we consider reason about state *and* transition labels, hence we use a formalism containing both as the basis for our methodology. All definitions introduced in this section live in a parameterised Alloy module. When modelling a POR theory, we always start by extending this module. We will often show snippets of Alloy code next to the corresponding definitions.

Definition 1 (Labelled-state transition system). *A labelled-state transition system (LSTS) is a tuple* $(S, \hat{s}, \mathcal{L}, \mathcal{A}, T, L)$, *where:*

- S *is a finite set of states,*
- $\hat{s} \in S$ *is the initial state,*
- $\mathcal{L}$ *is a set of state labels,*
- $\mathcal{A}$ *is a set of actions,*
- $T \subseteq S \times \mathcal{A} \times S$ *is the transition relation,*
- $L : S \to \mathcal{L}$ *is a state labelling.*

```
module lib/lsts [Label, A]

abstract sig AState {
  label: set Label
}

sig Transition {
  src: one AState,
  label: one A,
  dest: one AState
}

let T = {
  s: AState, a: A, s": AState |
    some t: Transition | t.src = s and t.label
    = a and t.dest = s"
}
```

We introduce a signature for transitions in order to treat these as individual atoms. This is necessary for our encoding of paths. Note that we overload the field `label`. For transitions, the label captures the action executed by that transition, whereas for states this corresponds to a subset of $\mathcal{L}$. We use a set comprehension to build the transition relation `T` in Alloy. If $(s, a, s') \in T$, then we also write $s \xrightarrow{a} s'$. We overload this notation to capture the *successor* relation $\rightarrow = \{(s, s') \in S \times S \mid \exists\, a \in \mathcal{A}.\ s \xrightarrow{a} s'\}$. We assume in our models that an LSTS is rooted at $\hat{s}$, i.e., all states can be reached from the initial state. This is specified using the reflexive transitive closure $\rightarrow^*$. Whenever $s \xrightarrow{a} s'$, we say that a is *enabled* in state s and denote this $a \in enabled(s)$.

Notice that the module `lib/lsts[Label, A]` defines signatures for S, L, and T, whereas $\mathcal{L}$ and $\mathcal{A}$ are parameters. This choice makes the approach generic enough to accommodate different formalisms. We can view e.g. parity and reachability games as LSTSs that differ in how their states and transitions are labelled.

Higher-Order Relations. By design, Alloy does not support universal quantification over higher-order relations. This poses a challenge when modelling POR, because higher-order evaluation is required to encode most POR theories. As we will see in Sects. 3 and 4), we often need to impose conditions on all *paths*. In an LSTS, a path is a finite or infinite sequence of transitions $s_0 \xrightarrow{a_1} s_1 \xrightarrow{a_2} \dots$. Alloy provides a utility for modelling sequences of atoms as a relation. Writing `seq Transition` produces all relations over `seq/Int->Transition`, where the values of `seq/Int` range from 0 to a bound that we set. Nevertheless, sequences are second-order relations, meaning that Alloy does not support quantifications such as `all path: seq Transition`. We tried to resolve this by using Alloy* [19], which is an extension of Alloy with support for higher-order logic. However, its performance proved insufficient to obtain meaningful results in our experiments. For these reasons, we introduce a signature that enables us to quantify over paths, i.e., `all path: Path`. This signature and the relevant predicates are included in the `lib/lsts` module.

Path has three fields to exactly identify where it starts, where it ends, and the sequence of transitions that it represents. Empty paths play a role in our encoding, therefore we define a relation to easily find those paths with no transitions (`P_e`). A *valid* path follows the transition relation, and its start and end must coincide with the start and end of its associated transition sequence. We capture this in the predicates `valid_paths` and `valid_trseq`, where `first`, `last`, and `inds` are defined in the `seq` module.

```
sig Path {
    start: one AState,
    end: one AState,
    tr: seq Transition
}
let P_e = { p: Path | no p.tr }

pred valid_paths {
    all p: P_e | p.start = p.end
    all p: Path - P_e {
      p.start = p.tr.first.src
      p.end = p.tr.last.dest
    }
    all p: Path | valid_trseq[p.tr]
}
pred valid_trseq[tr: seq Transition] {
    all i: tr.inds | let t1 = tr[i], t2 =
↪    tr[add[i,1]] |
    (some t1 and some t2) => t1.dest = t2.src
}
```

A subtlety of this approach is that just defining a path signature does not mean that *all* paths of the system will actually be explored in the analysis.

Fig. 1. A deadlock.

Fig. 2. A lasso.

Fig. 3. An ignored path.

Instead, we need to use *generator axioms* to populate the set of paths (we refer to [15, Section 5.3] for more details about the need for such axioms in Alloy). The generator axiom `all_paths_exist` builds paths inductively.

For each state $s \in S$, there must exist one empty path containing s. For every path p and every transition t, if appending t to p yields a *valid* path, that path must also exist.

```
pred all_paths_exist {
    all s: AState | one p: Path | p.start = s
 ↪   and p.end = s and no p.tr

    all p: Path, t: Transition |
        valid_path[p,t] => some q: Path | q.tr =
 ↪   p.tr.add[t] }
```

Above, `valid_path[p,t]` first checks whether the sequence represented by t appended to `p.tr` still follows the transition relation. Additionally, we cannot generate all paths because we consider LSTSs with infinite behaviour, i.e., with loops. Because we are in a bounded setting, we unfold each loop only once. To keep the bound on paths low and the formalisation manageable in complexity, we choose to only generate *deadlocking* paths (Fig. 1) and *lassos* (Fig. 2). We do this below by adding an extra condition to the predicate `valid_path`. The function `stateset` returns, in no particular order, the states occurring on a path. The last line of `valid_path` checks that `tr"` = `p.tr.add[t]` has the right shape.

Either `tr"` is a deadlock: its last state has no enabled actions, and furthermore there are no state repetitions. Otherwise, it is a lasso: the last state of the path also occurs earlier in the path and no other states are repeated.

```
fun stateset[p: Path] : set AState {
    p.start + p.tr.dest.elems }
pred valid_path [p: Path, t: Transition] {
    ...
    add[#(tr".inds),1] = #(stateset[p] +
 ↪   t.dest) or (add[#(p.tr.inds),1] =
 ↪   #stateset[p] and t.dest in stateset[p])
 ↪   }
```

We claim that this restricted setting is sufficient for modelling POR conditions. In particular, our generator does not populate `Path` with paths shaped like the one in Fig. 3. However, it does lead to an under-approximation of path-based behavioural equivalences. We will discuss the consequence of this in Sect. 5.

Reduced Labelled-State Transition Systems. Above, we provided a generic formalism for encoding POR theories in Alloy. We continue with another concept common to all theories: the *reduced* formalism. At a most basic level, the approach of POR, when performing state-space exploration in some state s, is to pick one or more outgoing transitions of s (based on the action labels) and ignore the others. If parts of the state space now become unreachable, we have effectively reduced the number of states to explore. This is captured in the *reduction function* and the *reduced LSTS*.

Definition 2. *Given an LSTS* $TS = (S, \hat{s}, \mathcal{L}, \mathcal{A}, T, L)$ *and a reduction function* $r : S \rightarrow 2^{\mathcal{A}}$, *the reduced LSTS is defined as* $TS_r = (S_r, \hat{s}, \mathcal{L}, \mathcal{A}, T_r, L_r)$, *where* L_r *is the restriction of* L *on* S_r, *and* S_r *and* T_r *are defined as the smallest sets satisfying* $S_r = \{\hat{s}\} \cup \{s' \in S \mid \exists s \in S_r, a \in r(s).(s, a, s') \in T_r\}$ *and* $T_r = \{(s, a, s') \in S_r \times \mathcal{A} \times S_r \mid a \in r(s)\}$.

To encode TS_r in Alloy, we extend TS by adding a field `r` to the signature `AState`. This field captures, for each state, the actions which will remain enabled in that state in TS_r. We extend our notation of transitions to reduced LSTSs such that $s \xrightarrow{a}_r s'$ iff $(s, a, s') \in T_r$ (`succ_r` models $\rightarrow_r$).

```
module lib/lsts [Label, A]

abstract sig AState {
  label: set Label,
  r: set A
}
...

let succ_r = {
  s, s": AState | some a: s.r | s->a->s" in
    T }
```

Notice how this approach "embeds" the reduced LSTS in the full LSTS, meaning that S_r, T_r, and L_r can simply be computed based on r.

3   Modelling POR for Labelled-State Transition Systems

Formalising POR in Alloy involves creating a model that (i) defines signatures for $\mathcal{L}$ and $\mathcal{A}$, (ii) imports the module `lib/lsts [Label, A]`, possibly extending the base signatures with fields or new signatures for the chosen formalism, (iii) defines a predicate for each reduction condition, and (iv) encodes the correctness theorem. Because steps (iii) and (iv) tend to vary with each theory, they cannot be generalised as easily as the LSTS. For this reason, this section demonstrates our method by encoding a specific POR variant: stubborn sets for LSTS.

We write `open lib/lsts [AP, Action]` to import the base module and specify that states are labelled with atomic propositions, and transitions, with actions. To help encode the equivalence relation between TS and TS_r later, we assume that states have exactly one label. The signature `Init` corresponds to $\hat{s}$.

```
module stubborn_lsts

open lib/lsts [AP, Action] as lsts

sig AP {}

sig Action {}

sig State extends AState {}{
  one label
}

one sig Init extends State {}
```

The generic nature of a reduction function allows also nonsensical reductions such as $r(s) = \emptyset$ for all s. Intuitively, the goal of POR is that from every class of equivalent interleavings, at least one is preserved. To achieve this, we need to impose some conditions on r: here, we present the *stubborn set* method. This method was originally presented in [33,34] and repaired in [22] by strengthening a condition called **D1**. We first define *key actions* and *(in)visible* actions.

<table>
<tr>
<td>

An action a is *key* for $r(s)$ in s iff a is enabled in s' on all paths $s \xrightarrow{a_1...a_n} s'$ where $a_1 \notin r(s), \ldots, a_n \notin r(s)$. In this definition $n = 0$ is allowed, thus a is also required to be enabled in s.

</td>
<td>

```
fun enabled[s: AState]: set A { s.T.AState }

pred key_action[a: Action, s: State] {
  let reach = { t,t": State | some b: Action
   - s.r | t->b->t" in T } |
    all s": s.*reach |
      a in enabled[s"]
}
```

</td>
</tr>
</table>

In Fig. 4, a is a key action in $\hat{s}$ because it is enabled in $\hat{s}$ and in all states that can be reached from $\hat{s}$ by performing actions that are not in $r(\hat{s})$.

<table>
<tr>
<td>

An action a is part of a set $\mathcal{I}$ of invisible actions if, but not necessarily only if, $s \xrightarrow{a} s'$ implies that $L(s) = L(s')$ for all $s, s' \in S$. When $a \notin \mathcal{I}$, we say that a is visible.

</td>
<td>

```
let Viz = {
  a: Action | some t: Transition |
    t.label = a and not t.src.label =
     t.dest.label
}

let Inv = Action - Viz
```

</td>
</tr>
</table>

In Fig. 4, action a is allowed to be in $\mathcal{I}$ because it always occurs between states having the same label. However, b is visible because it "changes" the labels, for instance $L(\hat{s}) \neq L(s_2)$.

The reduction r is called a *stubborn set* iff r satisfies the conditions **D1**, **D2w**, **V**, **I**, **L** in every state s. The particular variant that we consider here is called a weak stubborn set in [34]. We now introduce each condition and its corresponding predicate in Alloy. **D1** ensures that the actions that are selected for the stubborn set do not disable other paths. For instance, $r(\hat{s})$ does not disable b in Fig. 4 as witnessed by $\hat{s} \xrightarrow{ab} s_2$. Its Alloy predicate first finds the non-empty paths p of shape $s \xrightarrow{a_1...a_n} s_n \xrightarrow{a} s'_n$. Then, it requires that every p has a *commuting* path: the actions occur in the same order as in p (except for a). Below, recall that `P_e` is the set of empty paths. We can quantify over sequences of transitions because we use an existential quantifier.

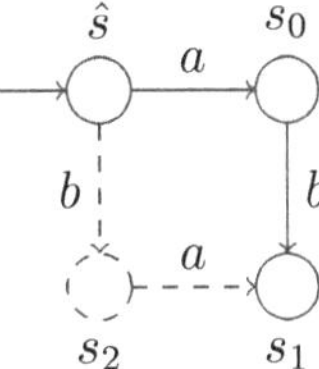

Fig. 4. An LSTS where $r(\hat{s}) = \{a\}$ and $r(s) = \mathcal{A}$ for all other states. Dashed states and transitions are not in T_r and S_r, thus they are eliminated by the reduction.

D1 *For all* $s_1, \ldots, s_n, s'_n$ *and all* $a \in r(s)$ *and* $a_1 \ldots, a_n \notin r(s)$, *if* $s \xrightarrow{a_1} s_1 \xrightarrow{a_2} \ldots \xrightarrow{a_n} s_n \xrightarrow{a} s'_n$, *then there are* $s', s'_1, \ldots, s'_{n-1}$ *such that* $s \xrightarrow{a} s' \xrightarrow{a_1} s'_1 \xrightarrow{a_2} \ldots \xrightarrow{a_n} s'_n$.

```
pred D1 { all s: State, a: s.r |
  let P = { p: start.s - P_e | (no
↪  p.tr.label.elems & s.r) and a in
↪  enabled[p.end] } |
  all p: P |
  some t": seq Transition | (
  valid_trseq[t"]
  and t".first.label = a
  and t".first.src = s
  and t".last.dest = a.(p.end.T)
  and t".rest.label = p.tr.label
}
```

The repaired condition, which we refer to as **D1'**, has an additional requirement on those $a \in r(s)$ that are invisible to prevent the so-called *inconsistent labelling problem* [22].

D1' *... Furthermore, if* a *is invisible, then* $s_i \xrightarrow{a} s'_i$ *for every* $1 \leq i < n$.

```
pred D1" {
  ... and (a in Inv => all i: p.tr.inds |
↪  p.tr[i].dest->a->t"[add[i,1]].dest in
↪  T)}
```

Condition **D2w** ensures that the reduction does not introduce new deadlocks. By selecting key actions, we guarantee that something will happen in the future.

D2w *If* $enabled(s) \neq \emptyset$, *then* $r(s)$ *contains a key action in* s.

```
pred D2w { all s: State | some enabled[s]
↪  implies some a: s.r | key_action[a,s] }
```

Condition **V** ensures that the commuting paths in **D1** have the same sequence of visible actions.

V *If* $r(s)$ *contains an enabled visible action, then it contains all visible actions.*

```
pred V { all s: State | some enabled[s] &
↪  s.r & Viz implies Viz in s.r }
```

Condition **I** guarantees that invisible actions will eventually be performed.

I *If an invisible action is enabled in* s, *then* $r(s)$ *contains an invisible key action.*

```
pred I { all s: State |
  let key = { a: s.r | key_action[a,s] } |
  some enabled[s] & Inv implies some Inv &
↪  key }
```

Condition **L** prevents the *ignoring problem* [11,32], which happens when a visible action is infinitely often not chosen for the stubborn set. Here `P_r = {p: Path | all t: p.tr.elems | t.label in t.src.r}` selects paths that exist in the reduced LSTS.

<table>
<tr>
<td>

L *For every visible action a, every cycle in the reduced LSTS contains a state s' such that $a \in r(s')$.*

</td>
<td>

```
pred L { let cycles = P_r & lassos |
  all a: Viz, p: cycles |
    some s: stateset[p] | a in s.r }
```

</td>
</tr>
</table>

The goal of the reduction is to preserve *stutter equivalent* paths. The *trace* of a path $p = \hat{s} \rightarrow s_0 \rightarrow \ldots$ is the sequence of state labels observed on p, $L(\hat{s})L(s_0)\ldots$. Two paths are stutter equivalent iff they are either both finite (deadlock) or both infinite (lasso), and their traces are equal modulo *stuttering*, i.e., we drop consecutive label repetitions. We sketch the approach of the predicate `stutter_eq`. Checking two deadlocking paths is straightforward: we eliminate repetitions of labels and compare the resulting stutter-free traces. For two lassos this is more involved: it requires distinguishing the initial part of the lasso and the repetitive part before normalising them. Normalisation helps to identify lassos that enter the loop at a different place (e.g., $a(ba)^\omega$ becomes $(ab)^\omega$) or that show a different number of unrollings (e.g., $ab(ab)^\omega$ becomes $(ab)^\omega$).

A path is *initial* when it starts in the initial state. A path is *complete* if it is deadlocking or a lasso (set `P_c = {p: Path | no p.end.enabled or is_lasso[p]}`, where predicate `is_lasso[p]` models the definition from Sect. 2). Complete reduced paths contain only stubborn actions labels (`P_c_r = {p: Path | (no p.end.enabled & p.end.r or is_lasso[p]) and all t: p.tr.elems | t.label in t.src.r}`). We relate an LSTS to its reduced LSTS by checking that every path in the full system has an equivalent in the reduced system. This correctness condition is captured in the following flawed theorem.

Theorem 1. *[33, Theorem 2] For every labelled-state transition system TS, given a stubborn set r (under conditions $\boldsymbol{D1}$–$\boldsymbol{L}$), it holds that for every complete initial path p in TS, there is a complete initial path q in TS_r such that p and q are stutter equivalent.*

```
pred correctness {
  all p: start.Init & P_c | some q: start.Init & P_c_r |
↪   stutter_eq[p,q] }
```

4   Modelling POR for Parity Games

We continue by extending the model from the previous section to the POR method of stubborn sets for *parity games* [23,24]. Parity games are a versatile framework for encoding various decision problems, including deciding whether an LSTS satisfies a given temporal property (e.g. an LTL or μ-calculus formula). A parity game extends an LSTS: states are now owned by a *player* ("even" $\Diamond$ or "odd" $\Box$) and furthermore labelled with a *priority*, a natural number.

Definition 3 (Parity game). *A parity game is an LSTS* $(S, \hat{s}, \mathbb{N} \times \{\lozenge, \square\}, \mathcal{A}, T, L)$*, where:*

- $\mathbb{N}$ *is the set of natural numbers,*

- $\{\lozenge, \square\}$ *represents the two players.*

```
open lib/lsts[Int, Action]

sig Action {}
one sig Even {}
one sig Odd {}
sig State extends AState {
  player: one { Even + Odd }
}{
  label > 0 and label < 4
  one label
}
one sig Init extends State {}
```

Compared to the generally accepted definition of parity games, we added actions on the transitions, which is required for our POR theory. Note that the Alloy formalisation of L deviates from the definition because of a limitation of Alloy where a binary relation (in this case, the set $\mathbb{N} \times \{\lozenge, \square\}$) may not be used as a module argument. While in our theory each state is labelled with a pair (*priority, player*), in practice we use `s.label` to denote the priority, and `s.player` for the player owning s. We restrict the priority to values from $\{1, 2, 3\}$, as that suffices for the small examples we consider. Let $S_\lozenge$ denote the set of states owned by player $\lozenge$, i.e., $S_\lozenge = \{s \in S \mid \mathcal{P}(s) = \lozenge\}$. This set is $\{\hat{s}, s_1\}$ in Fig. 5.

During the game, players move a token from one state to the next: the owner of the state where the token currently resides may choose along which outgoing transition to move the token. This yields an infinite or finite (in case the token ends up in a state without successors) path that the token has traversed. An infinite path $\pi = s_0 \xrightarrow{a_1} s_1 \xrightarrow{a_2} \ldots$ is won by player $\lozenge$ iff the least priority that occurs infinitely often along π is even. A finite path $s_0 \xrightarrow{a_1} \ldots \xrightarrow{a_n} s_n$ is won by player $\lozenge$ iff $\mathcal{P}(s_n) = \square$. Otherwise, these paths are won by $\square$. A *strategy* for a player p is a function $\sigma : S_p \to S$ such that, for all $s \in S_p$, $\sigma(s)$ is a successor of s (i.e. $s \to \sigma(s))^3$. A path $\pi = s_0 \xrightarrow{a_1} s_1 \xrightarrow{a_2} \ldots$ is *consistent* with a strategy

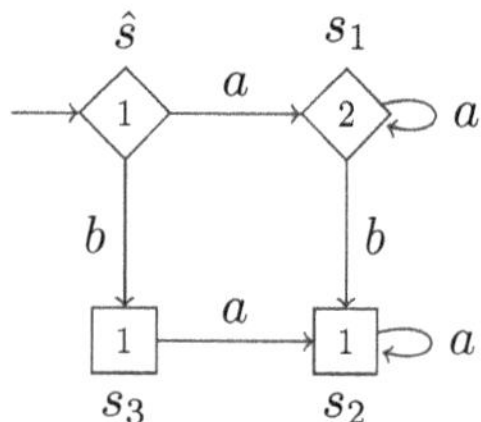

Fig. 5. A four-state parity game. Priorities are inscribed in the states.

σ iff $\sigma(s_i) = s_{i+1}$ for all i such that $\sigma(s_i)$ is defined. Finally, a strategy σ is *winning* for player p in a state s iff all complete paths that start from s and are consistent with σ are won by player p. A state s is won by p iff there is a winning strategy for p in s. These concepts are modelled in Alloy as follows. In predicate `win_state` (and the analogous `r_win_state` for reduced games), we select the relevant paths by intersecting the set of paths starting in s (`start.s`) with the set of complete paths (`P_c`). Note that `win_path` and `win_state` concern player $\lozenge$.

---

^{3} We use Zielonka's theorem about *positional determinacy* [35] (either $\lozenge$ or $\square$ wins in any state s) to forego histories and only reason about *memoryless* strategies.

```
pred win_path [pi: Path] {                pred win_state [s: State] {
  some pi                                   some st: Strategy {
  is_lasso[pi] implies not                    all p: start.s & P_c |
↪ odd_priority[min_priority[pi]] else         consistent[p, st.move] implies
↪ pi.end.player = Odd }                   ↪ win_path[p] } }
```

In Fig. 5, $\Diamond$ can win state s_1 by choosing to never move the token from s_1, and similarly it can win the initial state by always moving the token to s_1. However, $\Diamond$ has no winning strategy for the other states, because the token is trapped in an infinite repetition of an odd priority.

Similar to paths, strategies must be modelled as atoms. So, we introduce a strategy signature and an accompanying generator axiom. We do not need to model strategies for $\Box$, since any results for $\Diamond$ carry over by duality. Thus, strategies in Alloy look like `sig Strategy { move: S_e -> S }`, where `S_e` is $S_\Diamond$ and `move` models σ.

The generator `all_strategies_exist` below has two steps. First, we require the existence of some σ such that $\sigma(s) = s'$ for every transition $s \rightarrow s'$. For example, for the parity game in Fig. 5, this generates $\sigma_1(\hat{s}) = s_1$, $\sigma_1(s_1) = s_1$ and $\sigma_2(\hat{s}) = s_3$, $\sigma_2(s_1) = s_2$. This is insufficient: a strategy where $\hat{s}$ moves to s_1 and s_1 to s_2 is missing, among others. Thus, we also ensure the presence of all combinations of strategies generated in the first step by comparing them pairwise and calculating their differences.

```
pred all_strategies_exist {
  all s: S_e, s": s.succ | some st: Strategy | s.(st.move) = s"
  all disj s1, s2: Strategy {
    let diff1 = s2.move - s1.move | all s: diff1.State | some s3: Strategy |
      s.(s3.move) = s.diff1 and all t: S_e-s | t.(s3.move) = t.(s2.move)
    let diff2 = s1.move - s2.move | all s: diff2.State | some s3: Strategy |
      s.(s3.move) = s.diff2 and all t: S_e-s | t.(s3.move) = t.(s2.move) } }
```

On top of the conditions **D1'–L** presented in Sect. 3, stubborn sets for parity games require adding condition **P** [24]. This is necessary for preserving the winning player by taking into account that control of the token may move between the players.

P *If there is an action $a \in r(s)$ and a state t such that $s \xrightarrow{a} t$ and $\mathcal{P}(s) \neq \mathcal{P}(t)$, then $r(s) = \mathcal{A}$.*

```
pred P { all s: State |
  (some a: s.r, t: State | s->a->t in T and
↪ not s.player = t.player)
  implies s.r = Action }
```

The goal of the reduction is to preserve the winning states of each player. We restate the flawed theorem and give the Alloy predicate that captures the preservation of winners. By duality and positional determinacy, the predicates `win_state` and `r_win_state` only need to check $\Diamond$'s strategies.

Theorem 2. *[23, Theorem 1] For every parity game PG, given a stubborn set r (under conditions **D1'-L**), it holds that for every state s in the reduced game PG_r, the winner of s in PG_r is equal to the winner of s in PG.*

```
pred correctness {all s: State | win_state[s] iff r_win_state[s]}
```

5   Testing POR in Alloy

This section covers our approach to testing POR theories in Alloy. We discuss our experimental set-up, considerations for defining the size of the experiments, and the results. We modelled all the above theory, as well as the theories of [1,4] and their repaired version where available [5]. These additional models do not contain new constructs compared to what was presented above. We focused on two types of tests, (1) reproducing counterexamples to flawed theories from the literature [21,25], and (2) checking for the absence of counterexamples for the corrected theories. We also replicated an Alloy model of another POR technique [27,28] with corrections [30]. We used Alloy 6.2.0 with Kissat 4.0.3 [2] as an external SAT solver. All tests were run five times on an Intel Xeon Gold 6136 with a timeout of 48 hours.

We list some factors for setting experiment bounds. Kodkod [31] is the engine responsible for the translation between the Alloy language and CNF. It requires that n^k is smaller than the maximum integer value in Java, where n is the size of the Alloy universe and k is the arity of a relation in our model. Our formalisations model relations of arity 5: conditions **D1** and **D1'** for LSTS and parity games, and **W** for reachability games. Thus the size of the universe can be at most 73. Furthermore, the `seq` bound has to coincide with the S bound. Recall our assumption that each state is reachable from $\hat{s}$. Then the longest possible path is a lasso of length $|S|$, which is encoded as an Alloy sequence of length $|S|$. The bound of T should also accommodate this. The *Path* scope has a lower bound of $|S| + |T|$ because we generate at least the empty path for each state and a path containing each transition. Due to the generator axiom, the upper bound must be high enough to allow all possible paths. In our experiments we often overestimated this bound, to avoid the model being trivially UNSAT. For games, $\mathcal{L}$ has bound 3 since we always draw the label from a set of three values.

To reduce the runtime needed for larger instances, we prune the search space using *symmetry breaking*. By default, the atoms belonging to signatures are unordered, meaning that any satisfying assignment is part of an equivalence class of assignments obtained by permuting the atoms. Alloy always tries to eliminate symmetries internally, but this built-in mechanism might not perform optimally unless we explicitly order our signatures. To impose an order, we import the built-in `ordering` module (by writing `open util/ordering[sig] as ord_sig` in the same file that defines that signature). This module creates a lexicographic order [29] on the signature and it enforces a predicate that holds true only for the lexically smallest element. However, it also forces the signatures to be exactly bounded by the number we set, instead of upper-bounded. In practice, `ordering` creates relations `First` and `Next` for the considered signature, which helps expose the symmetries to the solver. We always apply the ordering to the sets S and $\mathcal{A}$ and (where applicable) to $\mathcal{L}$. In a separate run, we also apply it to T (specifically to `sig Transition`, not `fun T`), *Path* and *Strategy*. For some theories, a lexicographic ordering cannot be imposed on $\mathcal{L}$ due to a name clash: the `ordering` functions `next` and `last` clash with our encoding of parity games, where Alloy's integer module used for $\mathcal{L}$ also defines a function `next`. It also

Table 1. Testing set-up, size of the generated CNF, and average running time

Theory	Bound							Symm. breaking				CNF		SAT	Time
	seq	S	$\mathcal{A}$	$\mathcal{L}$	T	Path	Strat	$\mathcal{L}$	T	Path	Strat	#var	#clause		
LSTS [33]	5	5	2	2	9	24	-	-			-	671 500	2 186 341	✓	53 m
								-	✓	✓	-	604 430	2 028 322	-	t-o
PG [23]	5	5	4	3	9	26	6	-				1 111 592	3 351 940	✓	43 m
								-	✓	✓	✓	1 008 957	3 094 087	-	t-o
RG [4]	4	4	2	3	4	10	1	✓				76 603	181 450	✓	3 s
								✓	✓	✓	✓	62 258	152 413	✓	6 s
LKS [1]	4	4	2	1	3	8	-	✓			-	18 550	43 815	✓	0.1 s
								✓	✓	✓	-	15 718	38 420	✓	0.1 s
LSTS✓[22]	5	5	2	2	9	24	-	-			-	722 133	2 282 564	✓	11 h 48 m
								-	✓	✓	-	655 063	2 124 545	-	t-o
PG✓[24]	4	4	3	3	6	17	4	-				256 757	692 198	✗	1 h 54 m
								-	✓	✓	✓	227 567	624 244	-	t-o
	5	5	4	3	9	26	6	-				1 111 902	3 352 376	-	t-o
								-	✓	✓	✓	1 009 267	3 094 523	-	t-o
RG✓[5]	4	4	2	3	4	10	1	✓				76 465	181 216	✗	6 s
								✓	✓	✓	✓	62 140	152 199	✗	2 m
PA✓[30]	4	4	4	2	5	1	-	✓			-	18 761	36 364	✗	0.1 s
								✓	✓		-	17 740	34 634	✗	0.1 s

clashes with our LSTS model, because we use the `seq` function `last`. Therefore, we do not import `ordering` on $\mathcal{L}$ for those models.

Table 1 summarises our results. We refer here to each theory by abbreviating the name of its formalism: labelled-state transition system (LSTS), parity game (PG), reachability game (RG), labelled Kripke structure (LKS), product automaton (PA). The first four rows in the "Theory" column concern tests of type (1) and the last four, tests of type (2). In the column "Bound" we list the most important signature bounds, and we indicate with a dash when the Alloy encoding does not use that signature. Each row is then divided in two, where the top corresponds to a run with only some symmetry breaking, and the bottom, to a run with symmetry breaking on all signatures. The next column shows whether a lexicographic order was applied for that particular test. Here we again use dashes when the signatures are not used in the encoding. Since we always apply it to S and $\mathcal{A}$, we omit this in the table. The column "CNF" shows the size of each generated CNF formula in terms of variables and clauses. The "SAT" column shows whether the formula is satisfiable or unsatisfiable. For type (1) tests we wish for SAT, which means that a counterexample exists. Conversely, for type (2) tests we wish for the opposite. Finally, the last column contains the running time averaged over the five runs (a timeout is denoted "t-o").

Alloy found every counterexample from the literature for the flawed theories, or at least one that comes close to it. We first discuss the result for stubborn sets for labelled-state transition systems in detail, and then briefly address the others. Figure 6 shows the counterexample that we set out to reproduce, and Fig. 7, the Alloy counterexample for the following specification.

```
pred test {
  D1 and D2w and I and V and L
  some Init.r
  some enabled[Init] - Init.r
  some enabled[Init] & Init.r }
```

```
check lsts {
    test => correctness
} for 5 seq, 5 State, 2 Action, 2 AP, 9
↪   Transition, 24 Path
```

To avoid generating instances where the conditions are trivially satisfied, in the last three lines of predicate `test` we require that there is some reduction in the initial state. In the `check` command, `correctness` corresponds to Theorem 1.

The LSTS in Fig. 7 captures both the full and the reduced system: the dashed states and transitions are exactly those which are unreachable in the reduced LSTS. The gray-coloured states $\hat{s}, s_0, s_3$ are labelled with $\{l\}$ and the others unlabelled, and we have two actions $\mathcal{A} = \{a, b\}$, with $\mathcal{I} = \{a\}$. The stubborn set is $r(\hat{s}) = \{a\}$ and $r(s) = \mathcal{A}$ for all other $s \in S$, i.e., we only reduce in the initial state. We now explain why this is a valid counterexample by arguing that r satisfies the reduction conditions, while the correctness theorem is violated. Condition **D1** holds because $r(\hat{s})$ does not disable b: the path $\hat{s} \xrightarrow{b} s_2 \xrightarrow{a} s_1$ commutes with $\hat{s} \xrightarrow{a} s_0 \xrightarrow{b} s_1$, and similarly $\hat{s} \xrightarrow{b} s_2 \xrightarrow{b} s_3 \xrightarrow{a} s_0$ commutes with $\hat{s} \xrightarrow{a} s_0 \xrightarrow{b} s_0 \xrightarrow{b} s_0$. Action a is key in $\hat{s}$, thus **D2w** holds. **V** is satisfied because the visible action b occurs in the same order on the commuting paths considered in **D1**. **I** holds as $a \in r(\hat{s})$ is an invisible key action in $\hat{s}$. **L** is satisfied because the only cycle in the reduced LSTS is in state s_0, where no reduction is applied. Thus, the stubborn set is sound but the trace $\{l\}\emptyset\{l\}\{l\}\emptyset$ from the full LSTS (to find this trace in Alloy, we open the instance in the evaluator and write `correctness_p.tr._trace`) has no stutter-free equivalent in the reduced LSTS. This new, Alloy-generated LSTS is exactly half the size of the original counterexample. Although the manually-constructed counterexample is larger, it may offer more insight because it was built "backwards" from the proof of the unsound theorem. Moreover, it is easier to understand because it is deterministic. On the other hand, Alloy found a counterexample in under an hour without access to the proof, while the flaw lay undiscovered for close to three decades.

For parity games we found an equivalent, slightly simpler counterexample to [23, Theorem 1] than the literature counterexample [24, Fig. 2(d)]. For reachability games we managed to generate the exact counterexample from [22, Fig. 12(b)] which violates [4, Theorem 3.6]. Lastly, for labelled Kripke structures we found a similar counterexample to the one in the literature [22, Fig. 12(a)] where [1, Theorem 6.5] is violated.

In the second type of experiment we check that the CNF generated from the corrected theory is unsatisfiable. For example, for LSTS this means using the same predicate `test`, except that on the first line we replace D1 by D1". We test each theory with the same bounds as for the previous experiments. For

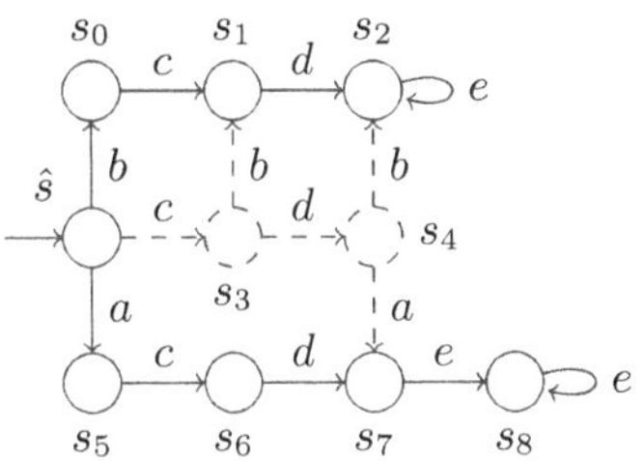

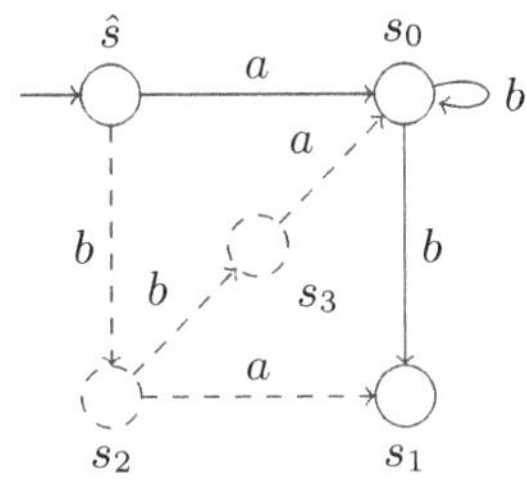

Fig. 6. An LSTS from the literature that violates [33, Theorem 2].

Fig. 7. An Alloy LSTS that violates [33, Theorem 2].

reachability games, we find no counterexamples and terminate in a matter of seconds. For labelled-state transition systems, Alloy found an *invalid* counterexample (Fig. 8). We call a counterexample invalid when we can manually verify that it does not actually violate the checked assertion. In this case, the stubborn set satisfies the conditions and the correctness theorem actually holds. This is a consequence of the way we modelled paths: the path $\hat{s} \xrightarrow{a} s_0 \xrightarrow{b} s_2 \xrightarrow{b} s_0 \xrightarrow{a} s_1$ is shaped like the path in Fig. 3 due to the repetition of s_0. Thus it is not contained in the signature `Path`. Thus it is missed in the computation of stutter equivalence, and, according to our model, the reduction yields a system that is not stutter equivalent to the full LSTS. To resolve this, an alternative approach would be to take each path in the full LSTS and reorder its actions to compute a matching path in the reduced LSTS. After all, partial-order reduction exploits exactly those interleavings where the actions can be reordered. We leave this for future work.

For parity games, the bounds of our first experiment result in timeouts. Therefore, we also checked the corrections up to a lower set of bounds derived from [24, Fig. 2(c)]. Lastly, we modelled ample sets applied to product automata [27,28]. We adapted Siegel's existing Alloy model [30] to our framework, including the proposed corrections, and checked correctness up to the bound of the original counterexample. Compared to the other theories, which required higher-order constructions for paths and/or strategies, ample sets for product automata can be formalised without generating paths, making the model simpler and faster.

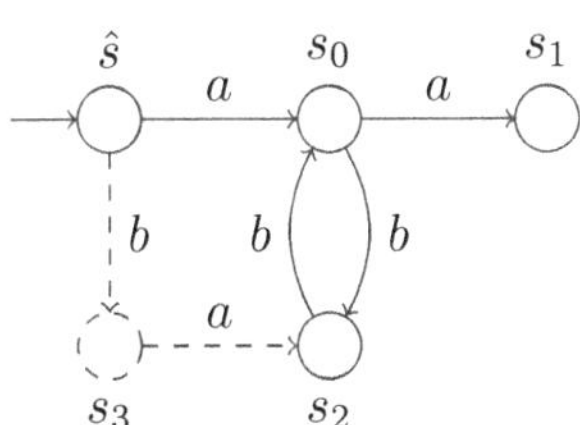

Fig. 8. An invalid counterexample to the repaired theory of stubborn sets for LSTS [22].

It is clear from Table 1 that the experiments timed out or took longer to terminate when we enforced orderings on T, *Path*, and *Strategy*. We have also experimentally found that enabling this one-by-one still impacts the runtime negatively. Given that the CNF always becomes strictly smaller with this optimisation, it is counter-intuitive for the performance to be worse. A possible explanation could be that, in our models, the individual atoms of those signatures are not used meaningfully; we are only interested in their fields. We therefore speculate that applying an ordering predicate in this case is not beneficial in any way.

6 Conclusion

We presented a method for reducing errors in formal theories, specifically partial-order reduction. We can conclude from our results that modelling theories in Alloy is a step in that direction. Our experience is that our approach is significantly less time-intensive than using proof assistants, and that it also provides useful support for troubleshooting and making repairs.

In further research, we intend to improve our formalisation of paths and stutter equivalence as discussed above. The LSTS module could be extended with generalisations of commonly-used definitions, like key actions, (in)visible actions, and strategies. Furthermore, we would like to investigate how Alloy records [6] could improve the efficiency of our implementation of generated signatures. It would also be interesting to see whether applying optimisations at the SAT-solving stage could help in obtaining correctness results for higher bounds, in particular for parity games. A different direction would be to use this methodology to model complex algorithms, such as bisimilarity reduction [26].

Acknowledgments. T. Neele is supported by NWO grant VI.Veni.232.224.

References

1. Beneš, N., et al.: Partial order reduction for state/event LTL with application to component-interaction automata. Sci. Comput. Program. **76**(10), 877–890 (2011). https://doi.org/10.1016/J.SCICO.2010.02.008
2. Biere, A., Fazekas, K., Fleury, M., Heisinger, M.: CaDiCaL, Kissat, Paracooba, Plingeling and Treengeling: entering the SAT competition 2020. In: SAT Competition 2020, pp. 50–53 (2020)
3. Biere, A., Heule, M., van Maaren, H., Walsh, T. (eds.): Handbook of Satisfiability - Second Edition. IOS Press (2021). https://doi.org/10.3233/FAIA336
4. Bønneland, F.M., Jensen, P.G., Larsen, K.G., Muñiz, M., Srba, J.: Partial order reduction for reachability games. In: CONCUR. LIPIcs, vol. 140, pp. 23:1–23:15. Schloss Dagstuhl (2019). https://doi.org/10.4230/LIPICS.CONCUR.2019.23
5. Bønneland, F.M., Jensen, P.G., Larsen, K.G., Muñiz, M., Srba, J.: Stubborn set reduction for two-player reachability games. Log. Methods Comput. Sci. **17**(1) (2021). https://doi.org/10.23638/LMCS-17(1:21)2021
6. Brunel, J., Chemouil, D., Cunha, A., Macedo, N.: Adding records to alloy. In: Glässer, U., Creissac Campos, J., Méry, D., Palanque, P. (eds.) ABZ 2023. LNCS, vol. 14010, pp. 212–219. Springer, Cham (2023). https://doi.org/10.1007/978-3-031-33163-3_16

7. Brunner, J., Lammich, P.: Formal verification of an executable LTL model checker with partial order reduction. J. Autom. Reason. **60**(1), 3–21 (2018). https://doi.org/10.1007/S10817-017-9418-4
8. Chou, C., Peled, D.A.: Formal verification of a partial-order reduction technique for model checking. J. Autom. Reason. **23**(3–4), 265–298 (1999). https://doi.org/10.1023/A:1006225515062
9. van Delft, M., Geuvers, H., Willemse, T.A.C.: A formalisation of consistent consequence for boolean equation systems. In: Ayala-Rincón, M., Muñoz, C.A. (eds.) ITP 2017. LNCS, vol. 10499, pp. 462–478. Springer, Cham (2017). https://doi.org/10.1007/978-3-319-66107-0_29
10. DeMillo, R.A., Lipton, R.J., Perlis, A.J.: Social processes and proofs of theorems and programs. Commun. ACM **22**(5), 271–280 (1979). https://doi.org/10.1145/359104.359106
11. Evangelista, S., Pajault, C.: Solving the ignoring problem for partial order reduction. Int. J. Softw. Tools Technol. Transf. **12**(2), 155–170 (2010). https://doi.org/10.1007/S10009-010-0137-Y
12. van Glabbeek, R., Ploeger, B.: Correcting a space-efficient simulation algorithm. In: Gupta, A., Malik, S. (eds.) CAV 2008. LNCS, vol. 5123, pp. 517–529. Springer, Heidelberg (2008). https://doi.org/10.1007/978-3-540-70545-1_49
13. Godefroid, P.: Partial-Order Methods for the Verification of Concurrent Systems - An Approach to the State-Explosion Problem. LNCS, vol. 1032. Springer (1996). https://doi.org/10.1007/3-540-60761-7
14. Holzmann, G.J., Peled, D.A., Yannakakis, M.: On nested depth first search. In: The Spin Verification System. DIMACS Series, vol. 32, pp. 23–31. DIMACS/AMS (1996). https://doi.org/10.1090/DIMACS/032/03
15. Jackson, D.: Software Abstractions: Logic, Language, and Analysis. The MIT Press (2012)
16. Jackson, D.: Alloy: a language and tool for exploring software designs. Commun. ACM **62**(9), 66–76 (2019). https://doi.org/10.1145/3338843
17. Keiren, J.J.A., Fontana, P., Cleaveland, R.: Corrections to "a menagerie of timed automata". ACM Comput. Surv. **50**(3), 42:1–42:8 (2017). https://doi.org/10.1145/3078809
18. Laveaux, M., Groote, J.F., Willemse, T.A.C.: Correct and efficient antichain algorithms for refinement checking. Log. Methods Comput. Sci. **17**(1) (2021). https://doi.org/10.23638/LMCS-17(1:8)2021
19. Milicevic, A., Near, J.P., Kang, E., Jackson, D.: Alloy*: a general-purpose higher-order relational constraint solver. Formal Methods Syst. Des. **55**(1), 1–32 (2019). https://doi.org/10.1007/S10703-016-0267-2
20. Miulescu, M.: Computer-Assisted Verification of Partial-Order Reduction Methods. Master's thesis, Eindhoven University of Technology (2025)
21. Neele, T., Valmari, A., Willemse, T.A.C.: The inconsistent labelling problem of stutter-preserving partial-order reduction. In: FoSSaCS 2020. LNCS, vol. 12077, pp. 482–501. Springer, Cham (2020). https://doi.org/10.1007/978-3-030-45231-5_25
22. Neele, T., Valmari, A., Willemse, T.A.C.: A detailed account of the inconsistent labelling problem of stutter-preserving partial-order reduction. Log. Methods Comput. Sci. **17**(3) (2021). https://doi.org/10.46298/LMCS-17(3:8)2021
23. Neele, T., Willemse, T.A.C., Wesselink, W.: Partial-order reduction for parity games with an application on parameterised boolean equation systems. In: TACAS 2020. LNCS, vol. 12079, pp. 307–324. Springer, Cham (2020). https://doi.org/10.1007/978-3-030-45237-7_19

24. Neele, T., Willemse, T.A.C., Wesselink, W., Valmari, A.: Partial-order reduction for parity games and parameterised Boolean equation systems. Int. J. Softw. Tools Technol. Transf. **24**(5), 735–756 (2022). https://doi.org/10.1007/S10009-022-00672-0
25. Neele, T.S.: Reductions for parity games and model checking. Ph.D. thesis, Technische Universiteit Eindhoven (2020)
26. Paige, R., Tarjan, R.E.: Three partition refinement algorithms. SIAM J. Comput. **16**(6), 973–989 (1987). https://doi.org/10.1137/0216062
27. Peled, D.: Combining partial order reductions with on-the-fly model-checking. In: Dill, D.L. (ed.) CAV 1994. LNCS, vol. 818, pp. 377–390. Springer, Heidelberg (1994). https://doi.org/10.1007/3-540-58179-0_69
28. Peled, D.A.: Combining partial order reductions with on-the-fly model-checking. Formal Methods Syst. Des. **8**(1), 39–64 (1996). https://doi.org/10.1007/BF00121262
29. Shlyakhter, I.: Generating effective symmetry-breaking predicates for search problems. Electron. Notes Discret. Math. **9**, 19–35 (2001). https://doi.org/10.1016/S1571-0653(04)00311-7
30. Siegel, S.F.: What's wrong with on-the-fly partial order reduction. In: Dillig, I., Tasiran, S. (eds.) CAV 2019. LNCS, vol. 11562, pp. 478–495. Springer, Cham (2019). https://doi.org/10.1007/978-3-030-25543-5_27
31. Torlak, E., Jackson, D.: Kodkod: a relational model finder. In: Grumberg, O., Huth, M. (eds.) TACAS 2007. LNCS, vol. 4424, pp. 632–647. Springer, Heidelberg (2007). https://doi.org/10.1007/978-3-540-71209-1_49
32. Valmari, A.: Stubborn sets for reduced state space generation. In: Rozenberg, G. (ed.) ICATPN 1989. LNCS, vol. 483, pp. 491–515. Springer, Heidelberg (1991). https://doi.org/10.1007/3-540-53863-1_36
33. Valmari, A.: A stubborn attack on state explosion. Formal Methods Syst. Des. **1**(4), 297–322 (1992). https://doi.org/10.1007/BF00709154
34. Valmari, A., Hansen, H.: Stubborn set intuition explained. Trans. Petri Nets Other Model. Concurr. **12**, 140–165 (2017)
35. Zielonka, W.: Infinite games on finitely coloured graphs with applications to automata on infinite trees. Theor. Comput. Sci. **200**(1–2), 135–183 (1998). https://doi.org/10.1016/S0304-3975(98)00009-7

Specification and Analysis of Ethical Requirements in Autonomous Systems Using Abstract State Machines

Patrizia Scandurra[1]([✉]) , Martina De Sanctis[2] , Gianluca Filippone[2] ,
Paola Inverardi[2] , Raffaela Mirandola[3] , and Sara Pettinari[2]

[1] University of Bergamo, Bergamo, Italy
`patrizia.scandurra@unibg.it`
[2] Gran Sasso Science Institute, L'Aquila, Italy
`{martina.desanctis,gianluca.filippone,paola.inverardi,`
`sara.pettinari}@gssi.it`
[3] Karlsruhe Institute of Technology, Karlsruhe, Germany
`raffaela.mirandola@kit.edu`

Abstract. Autonomous systems are increasingly required to comply with ethical norms and human values, motivating the need for rigorous methods to specify and analyze ethical requirements. Social, Legal, Ethical, Empathetic, and Cultural (SLEEC) rules provide a structured means to encode such requirements; however, ensuring their correctness and well-formedness calls for formal specification and systematic, tool-supported analysis.

This paper presents an approach based on Abstract State Machines (ASMs) and the ASMETA tool set for the formal specification and well-formedness analysis of SLEEC requirements. We formally define the semantics of the SLEEC domain-specific language, enabling systematic validation of SLEEC models through conflicts and redundancies detection. Moreover, we extend the core *when–then–unless* structure of a SLEEC rule with response delays and with a clause *unless–until* to support the temporary suspension of a rule. The validated ASMETA-based SLEEC model is directly executable and can be readily adopted as a runtime model to support the subsequent phase, namely the operationalization of ethical requirements in autonomous systems.

Keywords: Normative ethics · SLEEC rules · Autonomous Systems · Abstract State Machines · ASMETA

1 Introduction

Ethical oversight and carefully designed regulatory frameworks are essential to ensure that autonomous systems behave responsibly, operate transparently, and align with human values [12]. As AI-based and robotic systems are increasingly adopted, concerns are intensifying regarding the potential risks arising from

© The Author(s), under exclusive license to Springer Nature Switzerland AG 2026
F. Ishikawa and A. Cunha (Eds.): ABZ 2026, LNCS 16579, pp. 145–164, 2026.
https://doi.org/10.1007/978-3-032-26752-8_9

their decisions and behaviors [12]. Within this context, autonomous agents are expected to act transparently and in compliance with established ethical norms, guidelines, and principles [21,26], while potentially adapting their behavior in an ethically appropriate manner to different users and situational contexts. Along these lines, Townsend et al. [24] introduced a methodology for eliciting *social, legal, ethical, empathetic, and cultural (SLEEC) rules* in autonomous systems. This requirement elicitation process aims to iteratively derive SLEEC rules relevant to the system domain, stakeholders, and operational context, and aligned with both system capabilities and ethical values. The process begins with the identification of high-level ethical norms and principles applicable to the target domain, drawing on established moral and normative frameworks (e.g., *benevolence, non-maleficence, autonomy, justice*). These principles are then mapped to system capabilities in order to identify ethical touch points and formulate initial *base rules*. The resulting rules are reviewed with domain experts and stakeholders to uncover additional SLEEC concerns and potential conflicts. Rules are iteratively refined by introducing *hedge clauses* or additional rules to address newly identified issues. This process continues until all concerns are resolved and a stable, consistent, and conflict-free SLEEC rule set is obtained. In order to support interdisciplinary stakeholders in specifying and analyzing whether SLEEC requirements are well formed, a formal method for the specification and validation of SLEEC rules is essential [15,27].

Building on this premise, this paper explores Abstract State Machines (ASMs) [7] and the ASMETA tool set [5] to formally specify and validate SLEEC requirements. ASMs offer several advantages: (1) they offer a precise system specification at any desired level of abstraction, depending on the stakeholder's needs and technical level; (2) the pseudo-code-like format of transition rules makes them easy for practitioners to understand and suitable for high-level programming; (3) being executable models, they can be co-executed alongside target system implementations. ASMs have been used for the formal specification and validation of functional requirements derived from use case models [22]. Moreover, ASMs and ASMETA V&V techniques (including model animation, validation, verification, and review) [5] have proven effective for reasoning about computation consistency and conflict analysis in decentralized, multiple interacting MAPE-K loop architectures for Self-Adaptive Systems [1,2].

We therefore argue that ASMs and ASMETA can contribute to ensuring the correctness, consistency (via conflict detection), and minimality (no rule redundancy) of a SLEEC requirements specification too. Additionally, while the existing work in the literature focuses primarily on the elicitation, formalization, validation, and verification of SLEEC rules (see works [13,15,18,20,25,27], to name a few), there is still a lack of contributions addressing their *operationalization* at later stages, such as implementation and testing, that remain largely unexplored [23]. Specifically, we refer to approaches that translate ethical principles into concrete designs and implementations capable of guiding the runtime behavior of autonomous systems. ASMs are well suited to be adopted as *formal models at runtime* [3,9] through the ASMETA runtime simulator [6]. This latter aspect is fundamental for the operationalization of SLEEC requirements, a stage complementing their elicitation and formal analysis, as pursued in our recent approach *SLEEC@run.time* [11].

This paper focuses on two main contributions. First, we present a formal approach based on ASMs and ASMETA for SLEEC requirement specification and well-formedness analysis, illustrated through a running example. In particular, we formally define the semantics of the domain-specific language (DSL) SLEEC [15,27], providing a precise and unambiguous interpretation of its constructs. This formalization enables the rigorous specification, validation, and analysis of SLEEC rules, supporting the detection of inconsistencies and ill-formed requirements in a systematic and tool-supported manner. Second, we extend the core *when–then–unless* structure of SLEEC rules – which supports only hedge clauses for *substitution* and *blocking* of the base rule – by introducing delays and a new *unless–until* hedge clause. This extension enables the temporary suspension of a rule until a specified resuming condition holds.

This paper is organized as follows. Section 2 reviews related work. Background concepts on SLEEC DSL, running example, ASMs, and ASMETA are presented in Sect. 3. Section 4 defines the SLEEC DSL semantics and its formalization in ASM, including extensions for response delays and rule suspension. Section 5 presents the formal analysis of the SLEEC rule set for the running example. Finally, Sect. 6 discusses additional case studies and concludes the paper.

2   Related Work

Prior work has explored several approaches for formalizing SLEEC requirements. Yaman et al. introduced the SLEEC-TK toolkit [15,27], which provides a DSL for specifying SLEEC rules and tools based on the process algebra tock-CSP [20] for validating SLEEC rule sets and verifying the conformance of a tock-CSP encoded agent model w.r.t. a set of valid SLEEC rules. Kolyakov et al. [13,18] introduced LEGOS-SLEEC, a tool that assists interdisciplinary stakeholders in defining normative requirements as SLEEC rules and in checking and debugging their consistency using First-Order Logic (FOL) with relational objects. Troquard et al. [25] showed how natural-language SLEEC rules can be converted into classical logic to enable automated normative reasoning. Mirani et al. [19] proposed encoding SLEEC rules in Datalog, a declarative logic programming language, to enable scalable computation of obligations.

Our approach is complementary to these previous works. ASMs [7] is an executable formalism and has proven effective for reasoning about consistency and conflict analysis in decentralized, multiple interacting MAPE-K loop architectures [1,2], and for automated requirements specification and validation from use case models [22]. More specifically, in our approach the set of elicited SLEEC rules is formally specified in ASM[1] and subsequently analyzed using ASMETA V&V techniques (including model-based validation and model review) [5]. This formal analysis ensures correctness, consistency, and minimality of the SLEEC rules specification. Moreover, ASMs are well suited to be adopted as formal models at runtime [6]. This latter aspect is fundamental for the implementation and operationalization of SLEEC requirements, complementing their elicitation and formal analysis. The resulting SLEEC model is thus both formally validated and directly executable, constituting a *SLEEC runtime model*, ready-to-use in runtime approaches for ethics operationalization and assurance, like in the *SLEEC@run.time* enforcement process we presented in [11].

3   Background

This section introduces the SLEEC DSL and provides an overview of ASMs and the ASMETA framework.

3.1   The SLEEC Domain-Specific Language

The SLEEC DSL [15,27] provides a notation for specifying SLEEC rules in natural language, intended for use by non-technical stakeholders. SLEEC rules are typically elicited by a group of SLEEC experts, built as a collaborative engagement of ethicists, philosophers, lawyers, and other domain experts [24]. SLEEC rules are defined with respect to the capabilities of the autonomous system, the application domain, and the stakeholders involved. SLEEC rules complement the functional requirements of an autonomous system to reflect socially recognized values and norms[2].

Running Example. To illustrate our approach, throughout the paper we adopt the firefighter uncrewed aerial vehicle (UAV) example from [27]. The firefighter UAV is aimed to help tackle fires by interacting with human firefighters, bystanders and teleoperators. Its main tasks include: detecting a potential warehouse fire using a thermal camera, localizing it via a depth camera and reporting it by sending video footage of the surveyed building to teleoperators, and deploying onboard water spraying to contain it until human firefighters arrive.

In addition to these functional requirements, the firefighter UAV must address SLEEC concerns arising from interactions with humans (ethical requirements). For instance, an onboard loudspeaker alarm may raise social issues if triggered near people, and transmitting video footage to teleoperators may introduce legal or ethical privacy concerns when bystanders are present.

---

[1] ASMs supports the use of *defeasible logic*; rule defeaters are specified in terms of nested if-then-else statements with short-circuit priority of logic programming as showed in [25].

[2] Note that SLEEC rules do not encode individual user preferences or personal moral judgments.

SLEEC DSL Constructs. Listing 1.1 shows an example of a SLEEC DSL model for the firefighter UAV [27]. The core SLEEC DSL concepts are definitions and rules (see definition and rule blocks in Listing 1.1). Definitions introduce *events* and *measures* that capture system capabilities and interactions with the environment, including humans. Events denote atomic interactions, either inputs or outputs. For example, Listing 1.1 includes the input event *BatteryCritical*, indicating that the battery level is critical, and the input event *CameraStart*, which denotes a teleoperator command to activate the camera and start recording. The output event *GoHome* instead represents a navigation capability that enables the UAV to return to its home location. Measures represent information captured by sensing the environment and the system itself and expressed through typed values (e.g., Boolean, numeric, or ordinal scale). For example, Listing 1.1 declares measures for the temperature of the air, the wind speed level, and the boolean value *personNearby* to indicate whether, using its cameras and associated vision software, the firefighter UAV has detected the presence of a person. Constants are also allowed, such as the constant *ALARM_DEADLINE* in Listing 1.1 to set a time budget for the alarm to sound.

Listing 1.1. SLEEC DSL model for the Firefighter UAV (from [27])

```
def_start
        event BatteryCritical
        event CameraStart
        event SoundAlarm
        event GoHome
        measure personNearby : boolean
        measure temperature : numeric
        measure windSpeed : scale ( light , moderate , strong )
        constant ALARMDEADLINE = 30
def_end

rule_start
        //legal, social
        Rule1 when CameraStart and personNearby then SoundAlarm
        //legal, ethical
        Rule2 when CameraStart and personNearby then SoundAlarm within 2 seconds
        //legal
        Rule3 when SoundAlarm then not GoHome within 5 minutes
        //empathetic
        Rule4 when CameraStart then SoundAlarm
                unless personNearby then GoHome
                unless temperature > 35
rule_end
```

A SLEEC rule specifies how an autonomous system reacts to changes in its context and is expressed in the SLEEC DSL according to the following schema:

$$
\begin{aligned}
&\texttt{when } C_0 \texttt{ then } O_0 \\
&\texttt{unless } C_1 \texttt{ then } O_1 \ \text{①} \\
&\texttt{unless } C_2 \texttt{ then } O_2 \ \text{②}
\end{aligned}
\tag{1}
$$

A SLEEC rule is made up of a single *default rule* or *base rule* (rule *when–then* in (1)) possibly followed by one or more *hedge clauses* (rules *unless–then* in (1)) [24]. The default rule specifies an event (C_0) whose occurrence indicates the need to satisfy the constraints defined in the response (obligation O_0) [28]. According to *defeasible logic* [8,16], the default rule can be defeated or overridden by the hedge clauses triggered by "defeating conditions" (C_1 and C_2). Each hedge clause specifies a condition in which the original response (O_0) should be preempted, and there is an obligation to execute another response. Hence, hedge clauses are evaluated in a top-down manner, with the last one taking priority over the others. Intuitively: the clause ① would be evaluated first, followed by the evaluation of clause ②. Assuming that $C_0 \wedge C_1$ are verified while C_2 is evaluated to false, then the clause ① would be activated and O_1 must be fulfilled. Whereas, if $C_0 \wedge C_1 \wedge C_2$ is evaluated to true, then the clause ② would be activated and O_2 must be fulfilled. C_2 is the last condition that evaluates to true.

Listing 1.1 shows a representative set of SLEEC rules. For example, in rule *Rule4*, *CameraStart* normally leads to *SoundAlarm* (default rule) for triggering a loudspeaker alarm on board of the UAV. However, there are two hedge clauses. If *personNearby* is true, then the rule requires the UAV to go home so as to avoid the anti-social action of sounding an alarm near a person, likely a human firefighter. This is, however, defeated by the last hedge clause: if the measured temperature is greater than 35 °C (that is interpreted as evidence of a nearby fire), no normative response applies. SLEEC DSL supports also the definition of time constraints (construct *within*) for required responses (e.g., for the response *SoundAlarm* in *Rule2* of Listing 1.1), and of alternative responses when a deadline is not met (construct *otherwise*) [27].

The language expressiveness makes the rule semantics non-trivial in the presence of many SLEEC rules with multiple hedge clauses, as their simultaneous execution may lead to unexpected interactions.

3.2   Overview of ASMs and ASMETA

Abstract State Machines (ASMs) [7] are a formal method for modeling computation that uses first-order structures as their states to work with more complex, richly structured states. Dynamic functions (i.e., functions changing during computation) are further classified as: *monitored* (only read, as input events provided by the environment), *controlled* (read and written by the machine), and *out* (only written by the machine, as output events).

The basic transition rule of an ASM is the *update* rule (basic unit of rules construction) of form: **if** *condition* **then** *Updates* where *Updates* is a set of simultaneous assignments $f(t_1, \ldots, t_n) := v$, being f an n-ary dynamic function, t_i terms, and v the value of $f(t_1, \ldots, t_n)$ in the next state. Transition rules have different constructors depending on the update structure they express, e.g., guarded updates (*if-then-else*, *switch-case*), parallel updates (*par*), non-determinism (*choose*), unrestricted synchronous parallelism (*for-all*), etc. An ASM *computation* (or *run*) is a finite or infinite sequence of states starting from an initial state, where each subsequent state is produced by executing the transition rules, typically in parallel, as invoked by a unique *main rule* (the entry execution point).

ASMETA [5] is a set of methods and tools based on ASMs to support the specification, validation, and verification of discrete event systems' behavior. ASMETA provides techniques and tools (integrated within the Eclipse-based IDE or available as standalone tools with a command-line interface or via a web API) for V&V [4,6]. ASMETA also supports a simulation engine, *AsmetaS@run.time*, that is a runtime version of the ASMETA simulation engine for executing an ASM alongside a target system to monitor and enforce correctness properties in dynamic environments [4,6].

4   Semantics of SLEEC Requirements in ASMs

This section defines the semantics of SLEEC DSL using ASMs[3]. Moreover, we propose and formalize an extension of the core *when–then–unless* structure to allow also response delays and the temporary suspension of a SLEEC rule.

4.1   Events and Measures

An ASM representing the SLEEC requirements for a considered autonomous system maintains and changes a state of knowledge about the system and its environment. Before introducing the ASM-based specification of events and measures of the SLEEC DSL, we state two important assumptions concerning the runtime co-execution semantics of the model with the system and the treatment of events.

Assumption on Runtime Ethical Control. We assume that the ASM SLEEC model is deployed within a MAPE-K (Monitor-Analyze-Plan-Execute over a shared Knowledge) [17] control loop, tightly coupled to the autonomous system and acting as an ethical controller for it as in the SLEEC@run.time approach [11]. The autonomous system provides the *probe* interface corresponding to the SLEEC input events and measures, and the *actuator* interface matching SLEEC output events. At each MAPE-K cycle, the *Monitor* component supplies input events to the ASM runtime model, which executes one run step and produces normative prescriptions that are then forwarded to the *Planner/Executor* for enactment on the autonomous system.

Assumption on Events. A SLEEC rule distinguishes between conditions C_i, defined over sensed variables (measures) and input events, and obligations O_i, which prescribe actions (output events or normative responses) that the system must perform according to its capabilities (e.g., sounding an alarm, returning

---

[3] We adopt the semantic framework for metamodel-based languages proposed in [14], using *semantic mapping* to relate SLEEC DSL concepts to ASM modeling constructs.

home). This distinction enables a direct mapping to the probe/actuator interface of the target autonomous system. Accordingly, unlike the SLEEC DSL, in ASM we explicitly differentiate between input and output events. Consequently, when an event e appears in a SLEEC DSL model both as a trigger or defeating condition (i.e., an input event) and as a response (i.e., an output event) – e.g., *SoundAlarm* in Listing 1.1 – we introduce in ASM a monitored function e_{in} (e.g., `alarmSounding` and `CameraStarted`) and a capability object e_{out} (e.g., `soundAlarm` and `startCamera`), where the latter denotes the obligation for the system to eventually act. We assume that e_{in} is sensed as true whenever the target system is executing the action corresponding to e_{out}.

Based on these assumptions, input events and measures of SLEEC DSL are represented by ASM monitored functions, which are refreshed at each ASM run step. Output events of SLEEC DSL, instead, are the prescribed obligations for the system as ethical response. These are denoted in ASM by the output function *outObligation* : *CapabilityID* → *Boolean* representing the obligation(s) to actuate on the system as ethical control action, chosen from an enumerated set of IDs for capabilities (elements of the abstract domain *Capability*) of the autonomous system, till the next observation and decision.

Example. Listing 1.2 shows an excerpt of the ASM SLEEC model for the firefighter UAV using the ASMETA language AsmetaL. It corresponds to the SLEEC DSL model reported in Listing 1.1. The ASM SLEEC model is edited in a textual `.asm` file and structured into five main sections:

- `import`: Imports external definitions, including the SLEEClibrary (line 2) which provides the SLEEC rule constructor (as discussed later in the text).
- `signature`: Declares domains and functions for representing system knowledge (e.g., input events, measures, capabilities) (lines 3–29). Functions are categorized as `static` (e.g., the capabilities, lines 24–28) or `dynamic`, with dynamic `monitored` functions for inputs events and measures (lines 19–22) and dynamic `out` functions for the output events (lines 15–16).
- `definitions`: Contains domains and static function definitions, transition rules, and invariants (first-order formulas that must hold in all states). For example, the invariant `inv_1` expresses mutual exclusion between the obligations *GoHome* and *SoundAlarm*.
- `main rule`: Defines the entry point for computation at each run step. It may invoke other transition rules by name[4]. A run step executes all enabled rules directly or indirectly called from the main rule (SLEEC rules, in our case).
- `default init`: Initializes dynamic domains and controlled/out functions declared in the `signature`.

The complete AsmetaL specification of the SLEEC requirements for the firefighter UAV is available in our online repository [10], together with all related models and analysis artifacts.

---

[4] A named rule is defined as `r_rule(`*params*`)` and invoked as `r_rule[`*params*`]`.

Listing 1.2. Simplified excerpt of a SLEEC model in AsmetaL for the firefighter UAV

```
1    asm firefighter
2    import ../libraries/SLEECLibrary
3    signature:
4    //scenario-independent domains
5    abstract domain Capability
6    enum domain TCType = {AFTER, WITHIN}
7    enum domain TimerUnit={NANOSEC, MILLISEC, SEC, MINUTE, HOUR}
8    ...
9    //scenario-specific domains
10   domain Temperature subsetof Integer
11   enum domain WindScale = {LIGHT,MODERATE,STRONG}
12   enum domain CapabilityID ={SOUNDALARM,GOHOME,STARTCAMERA,DONOTHING}
13
14   //scenario-independent functions
15   out outObligation: CapabilityID -> Boolean
16   out outConstraint: CapabilityID -> Prod(TCType,Integer,TimerUnit,CapabilityID) //time constraint, if any
17   ...
18   //scenario-specific functions
19   monitored batteryCritical: Boolean
20   monitored personNearby: Boolean
21   monitored temperature: Temperature
22   monitored alarmSounding: Boolean
23   ...
24   static goHome: Capability
25   static soundAlarm: Capability
26   static startCamera: Capability
27   static alarm_deadline: Integer
28   static id: Capability -> CapabilityID
29   ...
30   definitions:
31   domain Temperature = {-5:90} //discrete, finite range for thermal sensors to allow model checking
32   function alarm_deadline = 30 //30 seconds (default value)
33   ...
34   rule r_skip = skip // named rule for no ASM state change (no prescribed obligation)
35   rule r_notGoHomeWithinFiveMinutes = r_setObligation[goHome,false,WITHIN,5,MINUTE,DONOTHING]
36   rule r_soundAlarm = r_setObligation[soundAlarm]
37   rule r_soundAlarmWithinTwoSeconds = r_setObligation[soundAlarm,WITHIN,2,SEC,DONOTHING]
38   ...
39   //SLEEC rules
40    //legal, social
41   rule r_Rule1 = if cameraStarted and personNearby then r_soundAlarm[] endif
42
43    //legal, ethical
44   rule r_Rule2 = if cameraStarted and personNearby then r_soundAlarmWithinTwoSeconds[] endif
45
46    //legal
47   rule r_Rule3 = if alarmSounding then r_notGoHomeWithinFiveMinutes[] endif
48
49    //emphatatic
50   rule r_Rule4 =
51   r_SLEEC[cameraStarted,<<r_soundAlarm>>,personNearby,<<r_goHome>>,temperature > 35,<<r_skip>>]
52
53   invariant inv_1 over outObligation =
54       not (outObligation(GOHOME) and outObligation(SOUNDALARM)) //never both true
55   ...
56   main rule r_Main =
57       seq
58           r_Reset[] //reset of out locations to undef value
59           par r_Rule1[] ... r_Rule4[] endpar
60       endseq
61
62   default init s0: function outObligation($idc in CapabilityID) = undef
63   ...
```

4.2   SLEEC rules - rule Substitution and Blocking

To correctly capture the operational semantics of a SLEEC rule in ASM, we build on the previous work [25], which translates SLEEC rules (and the underlying defeasible logic) into classical logic. Essentially, SLEEC rule defeaters are encoded as nested `if-then-else` statements, following the short-circuit evaluation and priority semantics of programming logic, as described in [25]. Specifically, to represent the SLEEC rule computation pattern, we introduce a rule schema (i.e., syntactic sugar). Using the ASMETA language (AsmetaL), such a schema is realized as a named, parameterized rule, `r_SLEEC`, whose formal parameters consist of boolean and rule variables:

```
//SLEEC rule constructor for 3 conditions
rule r_SLEEC($c0 in Boolean, $o0 in Rule, $c1 in Boolean, $o1 in Rule, $c2 in Boolean, $o2 in Rule) =
  if $c0 and not $c1 then $o0
  else if $c0 and $c1 and not $c2 then $o1
  else if $c0 and $c1 and $c2 then $o2 endif endif endif
```

In the rule r_SLEEC, the boolean variable c0 is the triggering condition c0, the boolean variable c1 and c2 are the defeating conditions, the rule o0 corresponds to the default obligation, and the rules o1 and o2 correspond to the defeating obligations. Such rules oi $i = 0 \ldots 2$ are actually aimed at deciding the value of the output function $outObligation : CapabilityID \rightarrow Boolean$ representing the obligations to actuate on the system as ethical control actions, chosen from an enumerated set of capabilities IDs of the autonomous system, till the next observation and decision. The *true* value is assigned to the capabilities to enforce on the system as obligations, while the *false* value denotes that the capability is to forbid, possibly for a time period (like the SLEEC DSL rule *Rule3* in Listing 1.1).

Example. Listing 1.2 contains examples of SLEEC rules corresponding to the namesake rules in SLEEC DSL in Listing 1.1. Rules `r_Rule1`,`r_Rule2`, and `r_Rule3` are defined as conditional rules, while rule `r_Rule4` applies the `r_SLEEC` rule schema. In this last rule, the conditions and the rules for setting obligations are passed as arguments; when executed, the conditions of the clauses are evaluated, and the rule of the enabled clause is invoked[5]. In principle, all SLEEC rules are executed simultaneously within the ASM main rule by means of the `par` rule.

For the semantics of time constraints, i.e. deadlines for responses and required alternative responses in the case of a timeout, we make the following assumption.

Assumption on Time Constraints. Since in SLEEC DSL time constraints are associated with output events (rather than input events), we assume that they apply to the executor, i.e., the target system, and not to the SLEEC model acting as the ethical controller. We assume that the system's actuator interface

---

[5] In AsmetaL, the syntax `«ruleName»` is a special term denoting a transition rule where a term is expected (e.g., as actual parameter in a rule invocation). Its interpretation results, therefore, in a transition rule.

and the underlying runtime platform allow for a task execution manager capable of correctly implementing such time constraints. For instance, a timeout can be managed by a *timed task*, which is commonly supported by most runtime environments and robotic platforms.

Based on this assumption, we introduced the output function $outConstraint :$ $CapabilityID \rightarrow TCType \times Integer \times TimerUnit \times CapabilityID$ representing the time constraint, if any, associated with an obligation. For example, in the rule `r_soundAlarmWithinTwoSeconds` in Listing 1.2, the utility rule `r_setObligation` assigns to the capability `soundAlarm` the tuple (`WITHIN,2,SEC,DONOTHING`) corresponding to the deadline `within` 2 s and no alternative action (do nothing) in case of timeout. In the next Sect. 4.3, we enhance the SLEEC DSL by introducing also *delays* as time constraints. As in SLEEC DSL, the time unit is provided based on the context under consideration. In ASM, it is represented by the enumeration domain `TimerUnit` shown in Listing 1.2 (line 7).

We now reflect on two semantic aspects of a SLEEC rule, namely *substitution* and *blocking*. In a SLEEC rule, the default rule can be altered via defeaters in two main ways:

- *Substitution:* a defeater overrides the default response and prescribes a different action. Syntactically:

    `when` C_0 `then` O_0
    `unless` C_1 `then` O_1

This is the typical hedge clause. When the defeater condition C_1 holds, O_0 is replaced by an alternative normative outcome O_1.
- *Blocking:* a defeater disables the default rule without prescribing any action. Syntactically:

    `when` C_0 `then` O_0
    `unless` C_1

When condition C_1 holds, the rule yields *no normative response* (i.e., O_0 does not apply and nothing replaces it). For example, the last hedge clause of rule `Rule4` in Listing 1.1) provides no normative response when its condition holds. In ASM, this blocking semantics is naturally captured by the rule *skip* for no action (see the `r_skip` rule parameter in the SLEEC rule `r_Rule4` of Listing 1.1).

In the next Sect. 4.3, we enhance the SLEEC DSL by introducing a third case, *suspension*, to temporarily disable the default rule under a transient condition (e.g., in case of resource limitations).

4.3   Enhancing SLEEC Rules with Delays and Rule Suspension

We here introduce and formalize two enhancements to the SLEEC DSL, namely delays and temporary rule suspension.

SLEEC Rule with Delays. SLEEC DSL allows for the specification rules that impose time constraints: deadlines (within t time units) for responses and required alternative responses (otherwise) in the case of a timeout.

We here extend the concept of time constraint for responses (see the definition of the enumeration domain TCType in Listing 1.1, line 6, denoting the two types of time constraint) for a response by adding *delays*: AFTER t time units. They can be implemented by the target system (the executor) as sleep commands, for example, which are very common in all runtime environments. The well-known semantics is: wait for t time units before executing the prescribed obligation.

SLEEC Rule Suspension. SLEEC DSL supports only substitution and blocking with the core *when-then-unless* structure. We here introduce a new hedge clause *unless-until* to temporarily disable a SLEEC rule under a defeater condition C_s, until a given resuming condition C_r holds. Syntactically:

```
when C₀ then O₀
unless C_s until C_r
```

Suspension is a form of blocking over time under a transient situation ($C_s \wedge \neg C_r$); the defeater condition is expected to be temporary (e.g., low battery) and the rule is expect to come back (e.g., when battery is recharged).

Example. Consider the following SLEEC rule:

```
when CameraStart then SoundAlarm
unless batteryLow until batteryCharged
```

when the suspension condition *batteryLow* holds, the default rule (*CameraStart* $\rightarrow$ *SoundAlarm*) is temporarily disabled until the resuming condition *batteryCharged* holds. While the battery is low, *SoundAlarm* is not actuated. Once the battery is recharged, the SLEEC rule becomes applicable again. In other words, the default rule is not canceled, but temporarily suspended.

In most runtime environments, execution of a task can be deferred until a given condition holds. For example, they typically support commands for conditional or event-driven task execution: `wait_until(condition); execute(task)`. However, in this case, the responsibility for suspending the SLEEC rule lies with the ethical controller (namely the ASM SLEEC model), and not with the target system.

The ASM encoding of SLEEC rules with suspension is realized by the following rule constructor:

```
//SLEEC rule constructor with a suspension clause
rule r_SLEEC_S($c0 in Boolean, $o0 in Rule, $cs in Boolean, $cr in Boolean) =
   if $c0 and (not $cs or $cr) then $o0
   else if $c0 and $cs and not $cr then skip
   endif endif
```

It encodes in AsmetaL a simple SLEEC rule semantics where the default outcome O_0 is applied whenever the rule is enabled (C_0) and the suspension is *not* active (i.e., $\neg C_s \vee C_r$). If the suspension condition $C_s \wedge \neg C_r$ holds, the rule produces no normative response (`skip`), and becomes applicable again as soon as C_r is satisfied.

Example. The previous SLEEC rule with suspension is encoded in AsmetaL as follows::

r_SLEEC_S[cameraStarted, <<r_soundAlarm>>, batteryLow, fullyCharged]

The following rule constructor encodes in AsmetaL a SLEEC rule made of a default clause, a substitution clause, and a suspension clause. It captures a prioritized SLEEC semantics in which (i) a substitution clause takes precedence over the default outcome, and (ii) a suspension clause *disables both* the default and the substitution while it holds. Concretely, when C_0 is true and the suspension condition $C_s \wedge \neg C_r$ holds, the rule yields no normative response (`skip`). Otherwise (i.e., when $\neg C_s \vee C_r$), the rule applies the substitution outcome O_1 if C_1 holds, and the default outcome O_0 if C_1 does not hold.

```
//SLEEC rule constructor with substitution and suspension
rule r_SLEEC_S($c0 in Boolean, $o0 in Rule, $c1 in Boolean, $o1 in Rule,
                $cs in Boolean, $cr in Boolean) =
  if $c0 and not $c1 and (not $cs or $cr) then $o0
  else if $c0 and $c1 and (not $cs or $cr) then $o1
  else if $c0 and $cs and not $cr then skip
  endif endif endif
```

More complex rule schemes for mixing default, block, substitution, and suspension clauses can be introduced straightforwardly.

5   Well-Formedness Analysis of SLEEC Rules Using ASMETA

Once the set of elicited SLEEC rules have been formally specified in ASM (possibly using a model compiler from SLEEC requirements to the ASMETA language to automate the encoding), they can be analyzed using the ASMETA V&V techniques [5] to check for their well-formedness. When defining SLEEC rules, in fact, rule redundancies and conflicts can emerge, especially when rules are provided by stakeholders with different backgrounds and involve multiple defeaters.

Intuitively, two rules are in conflict if their alphabets of output events (i.e., the set of all events used in the response of a SLEEC rule) do not overlap. If the rules have no such overlap, the obligations they prescribe cannot interfere with each other. If the alphabets of two rules overlap and their responses do not differ, one of the rules may be redundant and be a weaker restriction. While redundant rules may improve stakeholder understanding, they are unnecessary and should be re-examined. Conflicting rules, by contrast, prevent compliant implementations and therefore must be detected and resolved.

To address these issues in SLEEC rules, we primarily rely on simulation/ animation-based *model validation*, especially the random mode. We also used the verification-based *model review* technique to check the overall quality of the model by statically capturing typical modeling errors, including inconsistent updates or dead specification parts (e.g., functions that are never used or rules that are never triggered) due to overspecification or incompleteness. Through the aforementioned built-in consistency analysis techniques provided by ASMETA, we were able to detect the same conflicts and redundancies reported in [27] for the firefighter UAV case study. The results of this analysis are discussed in detail in the following sections. Models and artifacts of this analysis are available in our online repository [10].

5.1   Well-Formedness via Model Validation

The first analysis a designer can perform on a SLEEC model with ASMETA is *simulation-based model validation*, which enables early interaction with the model and the detection of trivial errors. The simulator supports both *random* and *interactive* modes. In random mode, values for monitored functions are automatically selected from their codomains; to ease the simulation of SLEEC models, we specified the number of steps (e.g. 100, for a massive simulation) to be executed. Graphical animation of simulation results is also supported through the animator for both random and interactive simualtion, offering a compact view of state changes in an ASM run.

A built-in *inconsistent updates checker* (in both the simulator and animator) detects inconsistent function updates, i.e. a function being inconsistently updated to different values by different rules. This checking mechanism is useful to capture both conflicts and redundancies in a SLEEC rule set.

To detect SLEEC rule conflicts, we use the simulator/animator to check that the ASM update set does not contain inconsistent updates, i.e., simultaneous assignments of different values to the same output function `outObligation(id($c))` for a capability c issued by different SLEEC rules.

Example: Rule Conflicts. Figure 1 shows the output of the interactive animation of the firefighter SLEEC model using the ASMETA model animator AsmetaA. The animator's tabular view makes it easy to follow the computation evolution (the ASM run). If an invariant is violated or function updates become inconsistent, the animation is halted and a notification is displayed. In our case, it clearly reveals an inconsistent update on `outObligation(GOHOME)`, which is updated to false and true when SLEEC rules 2–4 run simultaneously and the user inputs consist of all input events being true and a temperature of 23, i.e., below the threshold of 35. The inconsistency arises because `r_Rule3` and `r_Rule4` in Listing 1.2 are both triggered and select the same capability, `goHome`. However, `r_Rule3` assigns it the value `false` (with the intention of disabling it for five minutes), while `r_Rule4` assigns it the value `true` to actuate it with no time constraint.

Fig. 1. Animation example with conflict rule detection for the firefighter SLEEC model.

Most conflicts in the firefighter SLEEC model were initially discovered via random animation with a high number of run steps. Once a conflict was detected, the failing input combination was re-animated in an interactive manner for detailed inspection. Moreover, after animation, the tool allows exporting the model run as a scenario written in the language Avalla, so that it can be executed whenever desired using the tool AsmetaV for scenario-based validation [5].

To detect redundant rules, we check that no multiple updates to the output function `outConstraint(id($c))` occur within the same run step for a given capability `$c`. Such a situation would indicate that multiple SLEEC rules, possibly with overlapping conditions, assign different time constraints to the same activated/deactivated obligation (i.e., the rules do not conflict on the obligation), thus revealing redundancy.

Example: Redundant Rules. Similarly to conflict detection, both the ASMETA simulator and animator can be used. Figure 2 shows the ASMETA output console during the interactive simulation of the firefighter SLEEC model. It detects an inconsistent update on `outConstraint(SOUNDALARM))` when all SLEEC rules 1–4 run with the input events `cameraStarted` and `personNearby` set to true. Specifically, the simulator reports the error message INCONSISTENT UPDATE FOUND !!! : location outConstraint(SOUNDALARM) updated to undef != (WITHIN,2,SEC,DONOTHING). This inconsistency is caused by the SLEEC rules `r_Rule1` and `r_Rule2` in Listing 1.2. Both rules are triggered by the same input events and select the same capability, `soundAlarm`. However, `r_Rule1` does not assign any time constraint (i.e., it sets it to `undef`), whereas `r_Rule2` assigns a deadline of 2 s. This is a clear indication that `r_Rule1` is weaker, and can be eliminated.

```
Asmeta console
Running interactively  firefighter.asm
INITIAL STATE:Capability={doNothing,goHome,soundAlarm,startCamera}
Insert a boolean constant for cameraStarted:
true
Insert a boolean constant for personNearby:
true
INCONSISTENT UPDATE FOUND !!! : location outConstraint(SOUNDALARM)
 updated to undef != (WITHIN,2,SEC,DONOTHING)
FINAL STATE: Capability={doNothing,goHome,soundAlarm,startCamera}
run terminated
```

Fig. 2. Simulation run with redundant rules for the firefighter SLEEC model.

All simulation techniques include *invariant checking*, useful in the early stages of model development. SLEEC designers can define model invariants to make the rules more restrictive, and run the SLEEC model with critical inputs to check correctness. For example, they can introduce invariants for *semantic conflicts*: semantically incompatible responses, even if their prescribing rules are not formally conflicting.

Example: Semantic Conflicts. In cases where multiple SLEEC rules do not conflict at the level of obligations, but nevertheless produce responses that should not be enacted together from a semantic perspective (e.g., goHome may forbid soundAlarm, and vice versa), an ASM model invariant can be introduced to capture such incompatibilities. For example, invariant inv_1 in Listing 1.2 enforces the mutual exclusivity of the goHome and soundAlarm obligations, preventing their simultaneous activation. This invariant is violated, for example, by rules r_Rule2 and r_Rule4 when the input events cameraStarted and personNearby are true and temperature is below the threshold of 35. Violations of this invariant allow the identification of SLEEC rules that incorrectly permit the simultaneous activation of these obligations. Once such SLEEC rules have been determined, they are to be reconsidered by domain experts.

5.2   Well-Formedness via Model Review

SLEEC rule issues can be uncovered more systematically by model checking. Specifically, a static *model review* technique, supported by the ASMETA tool AsmetaMA, can be used to verify application-independent properties, called *meta-properties*, related to consistency, completeness, and minimality of an ASMETA model. The tool checks the presence of seven types of errors by specifying suitable meta-properties in CTL and verifying them using the model checker AsmetaSMV. For SLEEC rules, we found useful the meta-property *MP1: No inconsistent update is ever performed* that checks the presence of inconsistent updates (conflicts and redundancies), and *MP7: every monitored location is read* to check for unnecessary input values.

Example. Figure 3 shows a fragment of the AsmetaMA report for the verification of meta-properties MP1 and MP7. It shows the same rule conflict example reported in Sect. 5.1 for the firefighter SLEEC model when rules 2–4 run. It also shows that measures `batteryCritical` and `windSpeed` are never used.

```
AsmetaMA console
MP1: No inconsistent update is ever performed
Location outConstraint(GOHOME) is updated to values TCTYPE_UNDEF and WITHIN when are satisfied simultaneously the conditions
        (TRUE & (!(cameraStarted & !(personNearby)) & ((cameraStarted & personNearby) & !(temperature > 35))) & TRUE)
        and
        (TRUE & alarmSounding & TRUE).
Location outObligation(GOHOME) is updated to values FALSE and TRUE when are satisfied simultaneously the conditions
        (TRUE & alarmSounding)
        and
        (TRUE & (!(cameraStarted & !(personNearby)) & ((cameraStarted & personNearby) & !(temperature > 35)))).
Location outOtherwiseObligation(GOHOME) is updated to values CAPABILITY_UNDEF and DONOTHING when are satisfied simultaneously
        the conditions
        (TRUE & (!(cameraStarted & !(personNearby)) & ((cameraStarted & personNearby) & !(temperature > 35))) & TRUE & TRUE)
        and
        (TRUE & alarmSounding & TRUE & TRUE).
Location outTimeBudget(GOHOME) is updated to values -2147483647 and 5 when are satisfied simultaneously the conditions
        (TRUE & (!(cameraStarted & !(personNearby)) & ((cameraStarted & personNearby) & !(temperature > 35))) & TRUE & TRUE)
        and
        (TRUE & alarmSounding & TRUE & TRUE).
Location outTimeUnit(GOHOME) is updated to values TIMERUNIT_UNDEF and MINUTE when are satisfied simultaneously the conditions
        (TRUE & (!(cameraStarted & !(personNearby)) & ((cameraStarted & personNearby) & !(temperature > 35))) & TRUE & TRUE)
        and
        (TRUE & alarmSounding & TRUE & TRUE).

MP7: a location could be removed
Monitored location batteryCritical is never used. It could be removed.
Monitored location windSpeed is never used. It could be removed.
```

Fig. 3. Model review excerpt for the firefighter SLEEC model.

6   Conclusion

The SLEEC DSL language supports defeasible reasoning via chains of potentially nested clauses, which allow normative rules to be modified in light of additional information obtained from input events and measures. In this paper, we showed how SLEEC rules can be formally specified in ASM and encoded in the ASMETA language for their well-formedness checking (to detect conflicting and redundant rules). To further validate the approach on a larger and more complex setting, we applied the formalization approach to a second case study, the *Robotic Assistive-Dressing* (RAD) system [27], which is tasked with assisting a physically impaired user in daily dressing activities. Its SLEEC model is medium-to-large in scale and includes approximately 57 events and measures, and 21 rules, each with up to 7 hedge clauses. The ASM SLEEC model of this second case study is also available in our online repository [10]. As the size of the SLEEC model increases, validation through simulation becomes the only viable solution due to the state space explosion problem affecting model checking, unless modularization or model slicing techniques are introduced.

To demonstrate the feasibility of using an ASMETA SLEEC model within the ethic controller of the *SLEEC@run.time* [11] approach, we also developed a proof-of-concept[6] for the firefighter scenario, and additional ones are under development.

---

[6] https://gssi-robotics.github.io/sleec-at-runtime/.

Defining and enforcing ethical requirements in autonomous systems requires multidisciplinary collaboration. Issues related to the elicitation, formal consistency analysis, and operationalization of these requirements and their integration into existing software requirements engineering processes remain largely open.

Acknowledgments. This work has been partially funded by (a) the MUR (Italy) Department of Excellence 2023–2027, (b) the PRIN project P2022RSW5W - RoboChor: Robot Choreography, (c) the PRIN project 2022JKA4SL - HALO: etHicalaware AdjustabLe autOnomous systems, (d) the Helmholtz Association (HGF) with the KiKIT project, (e) the HGF Grant 46.23 (Engineering Secure Systems), and (f) the PRIN 2022 PNRR project SAFEST: truSt Assurance of digital twins For mEdical cyber-phySical sysTems (G53D23002770006 and F53D23004230006).

References

1. Arcaini, P., Mirandola, R., Riccobene, E., Scandurra, P.: Msl: a pattern language for engineering self-adaptive systems. J. Syst. Softw. **164**, 110558 (2020). https://doi.org/10.1016/j.jss.2020.110558
2. Arcaini, P., Riccobene, E., Scandurra, P.: Modeling and analyzing MAPE-K feedback loops for self-adaptation. In: Inverardi, P., Schmerl, B.R. (eds.) 10th IEEE/ACM International Symposium on Software Engineering for Adaptive and Self-Managing Systems, SEAMS 2015, pp. 13–23. IEEE Computer Society (2015). https://doi.org/10.1109/SEAMS.2015.10
3. Bencomo, N., Götz, S., Song, H.: Models@run.time: a guided tour of the state of the art and research challenges. Softw. Syst. Model. **18**(5), 3049–3082 (2019). https://doi.org/10.1007/s10270-018-00712-x
4. Bombarda, A., Bonfanti, S., Gargantini, A., Pellegrinelli, N., Scandurra, P.: Safety enforcement for autonomous driving on a simulated highway using asmeta models@run.time. In: Leuschel, M., Ishikawa, F. (eds.) Rigorous State-Based Methods - 11th International Conference, ABZ 2025. LNCS, vol. 15728, pp. 212–230. Springer (2025). https://doi.org/10.1007/978-3-031-94533-5_13
5. Bombarda, A., Bonfanti, S., Gargantini, A., Riccobene, E., Scandurra, P.: ASMETA tool set for rigorous system design. In: Formal Methods - 26th International Symposium, FM 2024, Milan, Italy, 9–13 September 2024, Proceedings, Part II. LNCS, vol. 14934, pp. 492–517. Springer (2024). https://doi.org/10.1007/978-3-031-71177-0_28
6. Bonfanti, S., Riccobene, E., Scandurra, P.: A component framework for the runtime enforcement of safety properties. J. Syst. Softw. **198**, 111605 (2023). https://doi.org/10.1016/J.JSS.2022.111605
7. Börger, E., Stärk, R.: Abstract State Machines. Springer, Heidelberg (2003). https://doi.org/10.1007/978-3-642-18216-7
8. Brunero, J.: Reasons and defeasible reasoning. Philos. Q. **72**(1), 41–64 (2022)
9. Calinescu, R., Kikuchi, S.: Formal methods @ runtime. In: Calinescu, R., Jackson, E. (eds.) Foundations of Computer Software. Modeling, Development, and Verification of Adaptive Systems, pp. 122–135. Springer, Heidelberg (2011)
10. De Sanctis, M., Filippone, G., Inverardi, P., Mirandola, R., Pettinari, S., Scandurra, P.: Online model artifact repository for Specification and Analysis of Ethical Requirements using ASMs (2026). https://github.com/foselab/ethical-requirements-asm, https://github.com/foselab/ethical-requirements-asm

11. De Sanctis, M., Filippone, G., Inverardi, P., Mirandola, R., Pettinari, S., Scandurra, P.: A process to enforce ethical requirements of autonomous systems at runtime. In: 21st IEEE/ACM Symposium on Software Engineering for Adaptive and Self-Managing Systems, SEAMS@ICSE 2026. IEEE (2026). https://doi.org/10.1145/3788550.3794876

12. Dignum, V.: Responsible AI and autonomous agents: Governance, ethics, and sustainable innovation. In: Proceedings of the 24th International Conference on Autonomous Agents and Multiagent Systems, AAMAS 2025, pp. 1–2. ACM (2025). https://doi.org/10.5555/3709347.3743508

13. Feng, N., Marsso, L., Chechik, M.: Diagnosis via proofs of unsatisfiability for first-order logic with relational objects. In: Filkov, V., Ray, B., Zhou, M. (eds.) Proceedings of the 39th IEEE/ACM International Conference on Automated Software Engineering, ASE 2024, Sacramento, CA, USA, October 27 - November 1, 2024, pp. 1521–1532. ACM (2024). https://doi.org/10.1145/3691620.3695522

14. Gargantini, A., Riccobene, E., Scandurra, P.: A semantic framework for metamodel-based languages. Autom. Softw. Eng. **16**(3–4), 415–454 (2009). https://doi.org/10.1007/S10515-009-0053-0

15. Getir Yaman, S., Ribeiro, P., Burholt, C., Jones, M., Cavalcanti, A., Calinescu, R.: Toolkit for specification, validation and verification of social, legal, ethical, empathetic and cultural requirements for autonomous agents. Sci. Comput. Program. **236**, 103118 (2024). https://doi.org/10.1016/j.scico.2024.103118

16. Horty, J.F.: Reasons as Defaults. Oxford University Press (2012)

17. Kephart, J.O., Chess, D.M.: The vision of autonomic computing. Computer **36**(1) (2003)

18. Kolyakov, K., Marsso, L., Feng, N., Quan, J., Chechik, M.: Legos-sleec: tool for formalizing and analyzing normative requirements. In: International Conference on Software Engineering: Companion Proceedings (ICSE-C), pp. 33–36. IEEE (2025)

19. Mirani, M., Raimondi, F., Troquard, N.: Towards efficient norm-aware robots' decision making using datalog (short paper). In: Workshop on Bias, Ethical AI, Explainability and the role of Logic and Logic Programming co-located with the 23rd International Conference of the Italian Association for Artificial Intelligence (AIxIA 2024). CEUR Workshop Proceedings, vol. 3881, pp. 50–59. CEUR-WS.org (2024). https://ceur-ws.org/Vol-3881/paper6.pdf

20. Miyazawa, A., Ribeiro, P., Li, W., Cavalcanti, A., Timmis, J., Woodcock, J.: RoboChart: modelling and verification of the functional behaviour of robotic applications. Softw. Syst. Model. **18**(5), 3097–3149 (2019). https://doi.org/10.1007/s10270-018-00710-z

21. Radanliev, P.: Ai ethics: integrating transparency, fairness, and privacy in ai development. Appl. Artif. Intell. **39**(1) (2025). https://doi.org/10.1080/08839514.2025.2463722

22. Scandurra, P., Arnoldi, A., Yue, T., Dolci, M.: Functional requirements validation by transforming use case models into abstract state machines. In: Proceedings of the 27th Annual ACM Symposium on Applied Computing, SAC 2012, pp. 1063–1068. ACM (2012). https://doi.org/10.1145/2245276.2231942

23. Shahin, M., Hussain, W., Nurwidyantoro, A., Perera, H., Shams, R., Grundy, J., Whittle, J.: Operationalizing human values in software engineering: a survey. IEEE Access **10**, 75269–75295 (2022)

24. Townsend, B., Paterson, C., Arvind, T.T., Nemirovsky, G., Calinescu, R., Cavalcanti, A., Habli, I., Thomas, A.: From pluralistic normative principles to autonomous-agent rules. Mind. Mach. **32**(4), 683–715 (2022). https://doi.org/10.1007/s11023-022-09614-w

25. Troquard, N., De Sanctis, M., Inverardi, P., Pelliccione, P., Scoccia, G.L.: Social, legal, ethical, empathetic, and cultural rules: compilation and reasoning. Proc. AAAI Conf. Artif. Intell. **38**(20), 22385–22392 (2024). https://doi.org/10.1609/aaai.v38i20.30245
26. UNESCO: Recommendation on the ethics of artificial intelligence (2022). https://www.unesco.org/en/artificial-intelligence/recommendation-ethics
27. Yaman, S., Ribeiro, P., Cavalcanti, A., Calinescu, R., Paterson, C., Townsend, B.: Specification, validation and verification of social, legal, ethical, empathetic and cultural requirements for autonomous agents. J. Syst. Softw. **220**, 112229 (2025). https://doi.org/10.1016/j.jss.2024.112229
28. Yaman, S.G., Burholt, C., Jones, M., Calinescu, R., Cavalcanti, A.: Specification and validation of normative rules for autonomous agents. In: International Conference on Fundamental Approaches to Software Engineering, pp. 241–248. Springer, Cham (2023)

A Spectabular Model of an Automotive Adaptive Exterior Light System

Emil Sekerinski[(✉)] [iD]

McMaster University, Hamilton, ON, Canada
`emil@mcmaster.ca`

Abstract. Spectabular is a model-based specification and analysis tool supporting tabular specifications. These allow specifications to be written naturally by considering cases and to be checked for totality, disjointness, definedness, possibility, and necessity. Tabular specifications are intended to be read and checked by domain experts. Spectabular is used to model and analyze the adaptive exterior light automotive case study proposed for ABZ'20.

Keywords: Tabular expressions · Tabular verification · Interactive Notebooks · SMT Solver · Case Study

1 Introduction

The input/output behaviour of programs, in particular control systems, exhibits "discontinuities" in the sense of "equivalence classes." Tabular expressions describe such discontinuities explicitly and naturally. The structure of tables provides an intuitive way to check whether "all cases have been covered properly." Like with Dijkstra's guarded commands, all conditions are explicit; there is no "else." The usefulness of different kinds of tabular expressions for software development has been shown by [1, 6–8, 15, 17, 20]. Parnas proposes ten kinds of tables and argues how they can serve to check the soundness of requirements [20, 21]; they have been further unified and generalized [10, 11].

Of the tables Parnas proposes, here we use predicate and vector tables; they are visual representations of predicates in disjunctive normal form [23] and are intended to be read and checked by domain experts.

In Spectabular, the top and left table headers can be arbitrary predicates, like in Parnas tables [24]. Timing is orthogonal to the tabular format by an integer variable. By comparison, Matlab/Simulink tables [25] have fixed columns with precondition, duration, postcondition, and action, and rows are numbered requirements; timing is part of the tabular structure. Spectabular can check tabular specifications for totality, disjointness, definedness, possibility, and necessity. Since tables are predicates, they can be used to construct other predicates. This way, large specifications can be split into manageable tables. Tables can be used to express a model or its properties. Spectabular preserves the structure of tables

© The Author(s), under exclusive license to Springer Nature Switzerland AG 2026
F. Ishikawa and A. Cunha (Eds.): ABZ 2026, LNCS 16579, pp. 165–179, 2026.
https://doi.org/10.1007/978-3-032-26752-8_10

and uses it to decompose proofs, following [23]. By contrast, PVS defines tables as nested conditionals [19].

Spectabular is a Jupyter-based interactive notebook environment for tabular requirements specifications, currently in development[1]. Jupyter notebooks promote *interactive literate programming* by allowing programs to be written with human comprehension in mind rather than execution [13]: *code cells* with program pieces and *markdown cells* with formatted prose are interleaved. Prose and program cells have an equal visual status. As the program fragments and their explanations are adjacent, they are easier to keep in sync. Code cells can be executed, and their output, whether textual or graphical, is inserted into the notebook. In Spectabular, the code cells can have table definitions that are "executed" and displayed. Jupyter notebooks are commonly used for data science. Notebooks are executed from top to bottom to generate all output: they support reproducible research [12]. Spectabular supports literate tabular requirement specifications, related to how [5] supports literate B specifications. The approach is that a table is followed by interpreting each column for justifying it, followed by cross-checking each table by interpreting each row.

The structure of interactive notebooks allows models to be explored, e.g., by gradually proposing more elaborate models or discussing alternatives; the author exploited this extensively for this case study. Spectabular uses the Python kernel of Jupyter and the Z3 SMT solver through its Python binding [4]. Thus, Python is the meta-language in which tabular specifications are constructed and analyzed. Using Python allows, in principle, libraries for visualization and animation to be used, though this is not explored in this work. Familiarity with Python and the mathematical language of Z3 is required.

This paper treats the Adaptive Exterior Light and Speed Control System [9,22] of the industrial case studies of the ABZ conference series[2], as it is particularly suitable for tabular specifications. This work focuses on the functionality of the signalling and hazard lights. Compared to other treatments [2,3,14,16,18], the Spectabular model aims to be readable and checkable by domain experts. All these treatments have elaborate modularizations, combined with refinement in ASMETA, classical B, and Event-B. Here, there is no modularization or abstraction. Alloy and Pro B support checking LTL temporal logic formulae. Spectabular does not support temporal logic. In [14], first an implementation is developed and then verified. As no abstraction is involved, the tabular specifications here are close to an implementation, although Spectabular does not support code generation.

2   Working with Spectabular

The following two cells declare integer, boolean, real, and enumeration variables, as well as some vectors; as Bool, Int, Enum, etc., are Python functions, newly introduced Z3 and Spectabular variables must be quoted:

---

[1] https://gitlab.cas.mcmaster.ca/spectabular.
[2] https://abz-conf.org/case-studies/.

```
Bool('a'); Bool('b'); Bool('c'); Bool('d'); Bool('e')
Int('x'); Int('y'); Int('z'); Real('r')
Enum('light', 'Red', 'Yellow', 'Green')
BoolVector('av', 3); IntVector('xv', 3); RealVector('rv', 3)
```

The following cell defines a *predicate table* and displays it. The meaning of a table is given by *flattening* it:

```
t = \
    Table([a, b],
        [c, e, ~e],
        [d, ~e, e]); t
```

	a	b
c	e	¬e
d	¬e	e

```
flatten(t)
```

c ∧ a ∧ e ∨ c ∧ b ∧ ¬e ∨ d ∧ a ∧ e ∨ d ∧ b ∧ ¬e ∨ c ∧ a ∧ ¬e ∨ c ∧ b ∧ e ∨ d ∧ a ∧ ¬e ∨ d ∧ b ∧ e

As tables are more readable when displayed, their textual definition can be shortened to the first line, as in the rest of this paper. When a table is defined, it is automatically analyzed for the totality and disjointness of its headers. The header above is neither total nor disjoint. In this case, counterexamples are provided:

```
assert not t.toptotal and not t.topdisjoint
```

```
t.toptotalcounterexample
```

[b = False, a = False]

```
t.topdisjointcounterexample
```

[b = True, a = True]

If a header is total, it is visually separated from the body with double lines:

```
t = \ •••
```

	a	¬a ∨ b
c	e	¬e
d	¬e	e

```
assert t.toptotal and not t.topdisjoint
```

If a header is disjoint, the corresponding columns or rows are separated by thick lines:

```
t = \ •••
```

	a	¬a ∧ b
c	e	¬e
d	¬e	e


```
assert not t.toptotal and t.topdisjoint
```

It is possible that Z3, as any other decision procedure, cannot determine totality or disjointness. In this case, dotted lines are instead displayed.

A *relation table* uses unprimed variables for the initial values and primed variables for the final values of the variables. Here is a one-dimensional relation table:

```
t = \ •••
```

$$\frac{a \quad\ \ |\quad \neg a}{x' + y \geq 3 \ |\ x' = x}$$

```
assert t.normal
```

A table is in *normal form* if primed variables appear only in its body, as in the above table.

Negation, conjunction, disjunction, equality, and inequality are written in Z3 and Spectabular as ~, &, |, =, != and are displayed as $\neg$, $\wedge$, $\vee$, $=$, $\neq$. Spectabular allows these to be used for tables and adds >> for implication and << for consequence:

```
t, u = \ •••
```

```
t & u
```

$$\left(\frac{\begin{array}{c|c|c} & a & b \\ \hline a & d & \neg d \\ \hline c & \neg d & d \end{array}}{}\right) \wedge \left(\frac{\begin{array}{c|c|c} & a & b \\ \hline a & e & \neg e \\ \hline c & \neg e & e \end{array}}{}\right)$$

Unlike Python Boolean operators, Z3 and Spectabular do not evaluate them. Tabular expressions must be explicitly evaluated. In this example, a table is checked to satisfy a property:

```
t = \ •••
```

$$\frac{a \ |\ \neg a}{b \ |\ c}$$

```
t >> (a >> b)
```

$$\left(\frac{a \ |\ \neg a}{b \ |\ c}\right) \Rightarrow (a \Rightarrow b)$$

```
assert valid(_)
```

The underscore (_) refers to the output of the previous cell.

A *vector table* is a two-dimensional table with variables (or, in general, expressions) in the left header:

```
t = VectorTable((a, b),
        (x', x + y, x - y),
        (y', y - x, y + x)); t
```

$$\frac{\begin{array}{c|c|c} & a & b \\ \hline x' = & x+y & x-y \\ \hline y' = & y-x & y+x \end{array}}{}$$

The above vector table is equivalent to the following one-dimensional table:

```
u = \ •••
```

a	b
$x' = x + y \wedge y' = y - x$	$x' = x - y \wedge y' = y + x$

Headers can be arbitrarily nested:

```
t = \ •••
```

	a	¬a	
		b	¬b
$x' =$	$x + 1$	$y - 1$	$y + 1$
$y' =$	y	$x + y$	x

The meaning of a nested header is given by conjoining the super-header to each of the sub-headers. The above table is equivalent to the following one:

```
u = \ •••
```

	a	¬a ∧ b	¬a ∧ ¬b
$x' =$	$x + 1$	$y - 1$	$y + 1$
$y' =$	y	$x + y$	x

Timed events are expressed using the implicitly defined variable time, a non-negative integer of time units. The following example demonstrates how to schedule a timed event in 10 time units and how to cancel it. The Python function Timer(timeout, handler) generates a ticker that increments time and at time = timeout, executes handler. If the event is not due, all variables are preserved, due' = due below.

```
Int('due')

scheduletimedevent = \ •••
```

due' = time + 10

```
canceltimedevent = \ •••
```

due' = -1

```
timedevent = Timer(time == due, due' == time + 5); timedevent
```

Tabular relations can be analyzed with three operators. The *domain* operator characterizes those initial states for which a final state is possible by existentially quantifying all primed variables:

```
t = \ •••
```

$$\frac{a \mid b}{c' \mid \neg c'}$$

```
Dom(t)
```

$$\Delta\left(\frac{a \mid b}{c' \mid \neg c'}\right)$$

```
flatten(_)
```

$$\exists c' : a \land c' \lor b \land \neg c'$$

```
assert valid(Dom(t) == a | b)
```

The *possibility* operator $\langle P \rangle\, c$ characterizes all initial states from which P terminates and possibly leads to a state satisfying c: it is the precondition under which the states of c are reachable. Here is an example in which the relation is a tabular expression and the postcondition is a plain expression:

```
Possible(t, c)
```

$$\left\langle \frac{a \mid b}{c' \mid \neg c'} \right\rangle c$$

```
flatten(_)
```

$$\exists c' : (a \land c' \lor b \land \neg c') \land c'$$

```
assert valid(a >> _)
```

The postcondition must not have primed variables. All primed variables of the relation are primed in the postcondition and existentially quantified.

The *necessity* operator $[P]\, c$ characterizes all initial states from which P necessarily leads to a state satisfying c, if P is defined. That is, it is the precondition under which no state outside of c can be reached:

```
Necessary(t, c)
```

$$\left[\frac{a \mid b}{c' \mid \neg c'} \right] c$$

```
flatten(_)
```

$$\forall c' : a \land c' \lor b \land \neg c' \Rightarrow c'$$

```
assert valid((a & ~b) >> _)
```

This states that under the precondition $a \land \neg b$, the relation t necessitates the postcondition c.

3   Modelling the Exterior Light System

The specification document lists all sensors and actuators [9]. These are modelled verbatim. No attempt is made to abstract from them. This way, domain experts can read and check the formalized specification. Controller variables are introduced only for timing and to track history when that influences controller actions.

The specification document is a monolithic description of the required behaviour. Although different hardware components are involved, the specification document abstracts from the distribution aspects. The specification here mimics that in not being modularized; when operations become too large to display comfortably, they are partitioned and composed using logical operators.

Only propositional logic is used. There is no "language" with a specific syntax that needs to be mastered, except for Python as the meta-language. This makes it easier for domain experts to read and check the formalized specification.

- First, the sensors and actuators are identified, the controller variables are determined, and invariants are identified.
- Each external event and the sole timer event are defined by tables. These are first interpreted vertically for justification and then cross-checked horizontally to confirm their adequacy. These interpretations are documented.
- Each event is mechanically checked to preserve the invariant. This is the only formalized analysis.

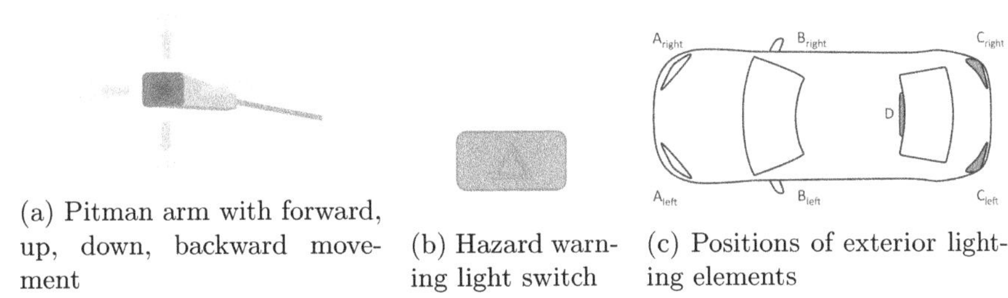

(a) Pitman arm with forward, up, down, backward movement

(b) Hazard warning light switch

(c) Positions of exterior lighting elements

Fig. 1. Driver controls and positions of exterior lighting elements [9].

4 Sensors, Actuators, and Invariants

There are two kinds of sensors: driver controls from the instrument panel and vehicle sensors. The driver controls relevant here are the pitman arm and the hazard warning switch, Fig. 1(a) and (b). The following is adopted from [9]:

> By moving [the pitman arm] up or down: Temporary or permanent activation of the direction indicator to the left or right. The temporary activation (so-called tip-blinking) happens by a deflection of about 5° (Downward5, Upward5), the permanent activation by about 7° deflection (Downward7, Upward7). The engagement ends either by manually bringing the pitman back to neutral position or automatically by a mechanical reset mechanism if the steering wheel has been turned more than 10°.

The Hazard Warning Light Switch, hazardWarningSwitchOn [...] is a simple toggle switch which turns on the corresponding function when pushed (value True) and turns it off when pushed again (value False).

This leads to the following declarations:

```
Enum('pitmanArmUD', 'Downward7', 'Downward5', 'UDNeutral', 'Upward5', 'Upward7')
Bool('hazardWarningSwitchOn')
```

Regarding actuators, [9] states:

Figure 1(c) schematically shows the possible positions A (front), B (exterior mirror), C (rear), and D (rear center) of exterior lighting elements of a vehicle. The direction indicator (blinker) (A, B, C) is controlled via the signals blinkLeft and blinkRight.

The value range of blinkLeft and blinkRight is 0–100%:

This leads to the following declarations and invariant:

```
Int('blinkLeft'); Int('blinkRight')

INV1 = \ •••
```

blinkLeft ≥ 0 ∧ blinkLeft ≤ 100 ∧ blinkRight ≥ 0 ∧ blinkRight ≤ 100

Here are the requirements pertaining to the controller state [9]:

ELS-1 Direction blinking left: When moving the pitman arm in position "turn left", the vehicle flashes all left direction indicators (front left, exterior mirror left, rear left) synchronously with pulse ratio bright to dark 1:1 and a frequency of $1.0\text{Hz} \pm 0.1\text{Hz}$.

ELS-2 Tip-blinking left: If the driver moves the pitman arm for less than 0.5 s in position "Tip-blinking left", all left direction indicators (see Req. ELS-1) should flash for three flashing cycles.

ELS-3 If the driver activates the pitman arm in another direction or activates the hazard warning light switch during the three flashing cycles of the tip-blinking, the tip-blinking cycle must be stopped and the requested flashing cycle must be started (i.e. direction blinking, tip-blinking, or hazard warning light).

ELS-4 If the driver holds the pitman arm for more than 0.5 s in position "tip-blinking left", flashing cycles are initiated for all direction indicators on the left (see Req. ELS-1) until the pitman arm leaves the position "tip-blinking left".

ELS-5 Direction blinking right and tip-blinking right: Analogous to the left side (see Req. ELS-1 to Req. ELS-4).

ELS-7 If the driver activates the pitman arm during the three flashing cycles of tip-blinking for the same direction again, only the current flashing cycle is completed, and then the new command is processed (either three flashing cycles due to tip-blinking or constant direction blinking).

We note that the behaviour is dependent on the history: if the signalling lights are off and the pitman arm is in neutral, if tip-blinking was started, it has to continue to the left or right. For suggests introducing a variable, blinking: to generalize, Left and Right mean that tip-blinking or directional blinking are active. For uniformity, Hazard means that both left and right lights are engaged. We also note that in order to determine if 0.5 s have passed in the tip-blinking position, we need to introduce a variable, tipTime, measuring time in milliseconds. As the lights are turned off and on after 1 sec, flashTimer is introduced. To count the number of remaining flashes, *flashCyles* is introduced; if it is -1, flashing continued indefinitely:

```
Enum('blinking', 'No', 'Left', 'Right', 'Hazard')
Int('tipTime')
Int('flashTimer')
Int('flashCycles')

INV2 = \ •••
```

flashCycles ≥ -1 ∧ flashCycles ≤ 3

The plausibility of the formalization is checked by the following invariants:

```
INV3 = \ •••
```

blinkLeft > 0 ∨ blinkRight > 0 ⇒ flashTimer > time

```
INV4 = \ •••
```

(flashCycles = 0 ⇒ blinking = No) ∧ (flashCycles = -1 ⇒ blinking ≠ No)

```
INV5 = \ •••
```

blinking ≠ No ⇒ flashCycles ≠ 0

If the left or right signalling lights are on, a timer must be set. If there are no remaining flash cycles, blinking must be off, and if there are infinitely many remaining flash cycles, blinking cannot be off. If blinking is enabled, there must be remaining flash cycles.

5   Controller Operations

A relevant change in sensor values triggers an event (interrupt) that causes the corresponding operation to be executed.

Pitman Arm Up and Down. The specification for the case where the hazard warning light switch is not pressed is split into three tables. The interpretation of the first one follows:

`pitmanArmUpDownNoHazard1 = \ •••`

	pitmanArmUD = Downward7	pitmanArmUD = Downward5		
		flashCycles > 0	flashCycles = 0	flashCycles = -1
blinking' =	Left	Left	Left	Left
tipTime' =	-1	time	time	-1
flashTimer' =	flashTimer	flashTimer	time + 1000	flashTimer
flashCycles' =	-1	-1	-1	-1
blinkLeft' =	blinkLeft	blinkLeft	100	blinkLeft
blinkRight' =	blinkRight	0	blinkRight	blinkRight

`pitmanArmUpDownNoHazard2 = \ •••`

	pitmanArmUD = UDNeutral	
	tipTime < 0 ∨ time ≥ tipTime + 500	tipTime ≥ 0 ∧ time < tipTime + 500
blinking' =	No	blinking
tipTime' =	-1	-1
flashTimer' =	flashTimer	flashTimer
flashCycles' =	0	3
blinkLeft' =	blinkLeft	blinkLeft
blinkRight' =	blinkRight	blinkRight

`pitmanArmUpDownNoHazard3 = \ •••`

	pitmanArmUD = Upward5			pitmanArmUD = Upward7
	flashCycles > 0	flashCycles = 0	flashCycles = -1	
blinking' =	Right	Right	Right	Right
tipTime' =	time	time	-1	-1
flashTimer' =	flashTimer	time + 1000	flashTimer	flashTimer
flashCycles' =	-1	-1	-1	-1
blinkLeft' =	0	blinkLeft	blinkLeft	blinkLeft
blinkRight' =	blinkRight	100	blinkRight	blinkRight

Vertical reading (for justification):

(1) Suppose the pitman arm is moved to the left direction blinking position, pitmanArmUD = Downward7; we assume that it has passed the Downward5 position when moving from UDNeutral. The blinking mode and the remaining flash cycles are kept at left and infinity, blinking' = Left and flashCycles' = -1, the flash timer and the state of the left and right signalling lights are preserved so as not to interrupt the current flashing cycle, flashTimer' = flashTimer, blinkLeft' = blinkLeft, and blinkRight' = blinkRight; if the right signalling lights are on, blinkRight > 0, they will be turned off at the next flash timer event. The tip blink time is reset, tipTime' = -1.

(2) When the pitman arm is moved to the left tip blinking position, pitmanArmUD = Downward5, the blinking mode is set, blinking' = Left, and the number of the remaining flash cycles is set to infinity, flashCycles' = -1.

(2.1) If there are remaining flash cycles from previous tip blinking, flashCycles > 0, the current state of the left and right signalling lights is preserved, blinkLeft' = blinkLeft and blinkRight' = blinkRight so as not to interrupt the current blinking cycle, the start of the current tip blinking time is recorded, tipTime' = time, and the timer for flashing is preserved, flash-Timer' = flashTimer.

(2.2) If there are no remaining flash cycles from tip blinking or directional blinking, flashCycles = 0, a new flashing cycle starts: the start of the tip blinking time is recorded, tipTime' = time, and the flashing timer is set, flashTimer' = time + 1000.

(2.3) If flashing continues from directional blinking, flashCycles = -1, the pitman arm was in Downward7: the tip blinking time is not recorded, tipTime' = -1, and the timer for flashing is preserved so as not to interrupt the current cycle, flashTimer' = flashTimer.

Horizontal reading (for confirmation):

blinking' : The blinking mode is set to Left when the pitman arm is moved to the left directional blinking position, pitmanArmUD = Downward7, or to the left tip blinking position, pitmanArmUD = Downward5, and set to Right when it is moved to the right tip blinking position, pitmanArmUD = Upward5 or the right directional blinking position, pitmanArmUD = Upward7. When the pitman arm is moved to neutral position, pitmanArmUD = UDNeutral, the blinking mode is set to No if there was no previous tipping (at Downward5 or Upward5), i.e., the tip time is not set, tipTime < 0, or if tipping was longer than .5 s, time ≥ tipTime + 500. Otherwise, if the tip time was set, tipTime ≥ 0 and tipping took less than .5 s, time < tipTime + 500, the blinking mode retains its value, Left or Right (the table does not cover Hazard mode).

tipTime' : The tip time is not set (set to -1) when the pitman arm is moved to left or right directional blinking or to neutral position, pitmanArmUD = Downward7, pitmanArmUD = Upward7, or pitmanArmUD = UDNeutral. When the pitman arm is moved to the left or right tip blinking position, pitmanArmUD = Downward5 or pitmanArmUD = Upward5, the tip time is set to the current time if there are flash cycles left from previous tip blinking, flashCycles > 0, or no more flashing is scheduled, flashCycles = 0. Otherwise, if there is indefinite flashing from the previous directional blinking, flashCycles = -1, the tip time is not set (set to -1).

The three tables are combined by disjunction:

```
pitmanArmUpDownNoHazard = pitmanArmUpDownNoHazard1 | pitmanArmUpDownNoHazard3 | \
    pitmanArmUpDownNoHazard3
```

If the hazard warning light switch is pressed, moving the pitman arm does not have any effect. The values of all variables are preserved:

```
pitmanArmUpDownHazard = \ •••
```

blinkLeft' = blinkLeft ∧ blinkRight' = blinkRight ∧ blinking' = blinking ∧ tipTime' = tipTime ∧ flashTimer' = flashTimer ∧ flashCycles' = flashCycles

The hazard and non-hazard operations for pitman arm movement are combined into a single one, expressed as a table with a table as an element:

```
pitmanArmUpDownEvent = \ •••
```

hazardWarningSwitchOn	¬hazardWarningSwitchOn
pitmanArmUpDownHazard	pitmanArmUpDownNoHazard

Hazard Warning Light Switch. A table for handling the event of pressing and releasing the hazard warning light switch is developed similarly; for brevity, it is not included here.

Flash Timer. The timer is engaged in tip-blinking, directional blinking, and hazard blinking. Here is the specfication, without interpretation:

```
flashTimerEvent1 = \ •••
```

	blinking = No	blinking = Left			
		blinkLeft > 0			blinkLeft = 0
		flashCycles > 1	flashCycles = 1	flashCycles ≤ 0	
blinking' =	No	Left	No	blinking	Left
flashTimer' =	-1	time + 1000	-1	flashTimer	time + 1000
flashCycles' =	0	flashCycles - 1	0	flashCycles	flashCycles
blinkLeft' =	0	0	0	0	100
blinkRight' =	0	0	0	0	0

```
flashTimerEvent2 = \ •••
```

	blinking = Right			
	blinkRight > 0			blinkRight = 0
	flashCycles > 1	flashCycles = 1	flashCycles ≤ 0	
blinking' =	Right	No	blinking	Right
flashTimer' =	time + 1000	-1	flashTimer	time + 1000
flashCycles' =	flashCycles - 1	0	flashCycles	flashCycles
blinkLeft' =	0	0	0	0
blinkRight' =	0	0	0	100

```
flashTimerEvent3 = \ •••
```

	blinking = Hazard	
	blinkLeft > 0 ∨ blinkRight > 0	blinkLeft = 0 ∧ blinkRight = 0
blinking' =	Hazard	Hazard
flashTimer' =	time + 1000	time + 1000
flashCycles' =	-1	-1
blinkLeft' =	0	100
blinkRight' =	0	100

Then, flashTimerEvent is defined as the disjunction of the above three tables and used for the timer:

```
timerEvent = Timer(time == flashTimer, flashTimerEvent)
```

6   Checking Invariants

The joint invariant is defined as the conjunction of all invariants. For pitman-
ArmUpDownEvent, invariant preservation is checked by:

```
INV = INV1 & INV2 & INV3 & INV4 & INV5
```

```
Correct("INV", pitmanArmUpDownEvent, "INV")
```

$$\text{INV} \left\{ \frac{\text{hazardWarningSwitchOn}}{\text{pitmanArmUpDownHazard}} \middle| \frac{\neg\text{hazardWarningSwitchOn}}{\text{pitmanArmUpDownNoHazard}} \right\} \text{INV}$$

Invariant preservation of hazardWarningLightSwitchEvent and flashTimerEvent
is checked similarly. Each of the checks takes less then 50 ms and appears instan-
taneous.

7   Discussion

The development resulted in two tables for pitmanArmUpDownEvent, one table
for hazardWarningLightSwitchEvent, and one for flashTimerEvent. Three tables
are so large that they have to be split (manually) for printing. However, large
tables are preferred on the screen. We intend to support the extraction of table
columns for printing.

Since Spectabular automatically analyses the disjointness and totality of
headers, we note that all tables are disjoint, meaning that all specifications are
deterministic, but none are total. For example, tables make a case analysis of
flashCycles, which ranges from -1 to 3; these tables are only "total" when the
invariant is considered.

The size of the tables is sensitive to the number of variables and the number
of their values. Tables work best if they are kept to a minimum.

The experience is that all design errors were found when reading the tables
vertically for justification and re-reading them horizontally for confirmation, and
writing the interpretations. Checking invariants was useful for detecting editing
errors when copying table entries for left signalling to entries for right signalling.

The first attempt with flat headers resulted in very large tables. However,
when writing nested headers, there is often a choice of what to put in the top-
level header and what in the subheaders. The notebook format was handy, as
several solutions were explored.

The developed specification includes only the signalling lights and hazard
lights. While we believe the approach scales to the full problem, it would be
insightful to confirm that.

The formalization does not include a model of the environment. For example,
the pitman arm can generate transitions only in a specific order, e.g., from
UDNeutral to Downward5 to Downward7, but not directly to Downward7. This
was assumed when writing the table. A formalization of the environment would
allow additional analysis.

The premise of this line of work is that having self-explanatory tables, a formalization in terms of the problem domain without abstraction, using plain

mathematics without a dedicated language, and leaving out modularization allows the specification to be read and checked by domain experts; it would be intriguing to experience that.

Acknowledgments. We acknowledge the support of the Natural Sciences and Engineering Research Council of Canada [project number RGPIN-2024-06779].

References

1. Abraham, R.: Evaluating generalized tabular expressions in software documentation. CRL Report 346, McMaster University (1997)
2. Arcaini, P., Bonfanti, S., Gargantini, A., Riccobene, E., Scandurra, P.: A journey with ASMETA from requirements to code: application to an automotive system with adaptive features. Int. J. Softw. Tools Technol. Transfer **26**(3), 379–401 (2024). https://doi.org/10.1007/s10009-024-00751-4
3. Cunha, A., Macedo, N., Liu, C.: Validating multiple variants of an automotive light system with Alloy 6. Int. J. Softw. Tools Technol. Transfer **26**(3), 365–377 (2024). https://doi.org/10.1007/s10009-024-00752-3
4. de Moura, L., Bjørner, N.: Z3: an efficient SMT solver. In: Ramakrishnan, C.R., Rehof, J. (eds.) TACAS 2008. LNCS, vol. 4963, pp. 337–340. Springer, Heidelberg (2008). https://doi.org/10.1007/978-3-540-78800-3_24
5. Geleßus, D., Leuschel, M.: ProB and Jupyter for logic, set theory, theoretical computer science and formal methods. In: Raschke, A., Méry, D., Houdek, F. (eds.) ABZ 2020. LNCS, vol. 12071, pp. 248–254. Springer, Cham (2020). https://doi.org/10.1007/978-3-030-48077-6_19
6. Heimdahl, M.P.E., Leveson, N.G.: Completeness and consistency in hierarchical state-based requirements. IEEE Trans. Software Eng. **22**(6), 363–377 (1996). https://doi.org/10.1109/32.508311
7. Heitmeyer, C.L., Jeffords, R.D., Labaw, B.G.: Automated consistency checking of requirements specifications. ACM Trans. Softw. Eng. Methodol. **5**(3), 231–261 (1996). https://doi.org/10.1145/234426.234431
8. Heninger, K.L.: Specifying software requirements for complex systems: new techniques and their application. IEEE Trans. Software Eng. **6**(1), 2–13 (1980). https://doi.org/10.1109/TSE.1980.230208
9. Houdek, F., Raschke, A.: Adaptive exterior light and speed control system. In: Raschke, A., Méry, D., Houdek, F. (eds.) ABZ 2020. LNCS, vol. 12071, pp. 281–301. Springer, Cham (2020). https://doi.org/10.1007/978-3-030-48077-6_24
10. Janicki, R.: Towards a formal semantics of Parnas tables. In: 17th International Conference on Software Engineering, Seattle, Washington, USA, pp. 231–240. ACM Press (1995)
11. Janicki, R., Khedri, R.: On a formal semantics of tabular expressions. Sci. Comput. Program. **39**(2–3), 189–213 (2001)
12. Kluyver, T., et al.: Jupyter Notebooks-a publishing format for reproducible computational workflows. In: Loizides, F., Schmidt, B. (eds.) Positioning and Power in Academic Publishing: Players, Agents and Agendas, pp. 87–90. IOS Press (2016). https://doi.org/10.3233/978-1-61499-649-1-87
13. Knuth, D.E.: Literate programming. Comput. J. **27**(2), 97–111 (1984). https://doi.org/10.1093/comjnl/27.2.97

14. Krings, S., Körner, P., Dunkelau, J., Rutenkolk, K.: A verified low-level implementation and visualization of the adaptive exterior light and speed control system. Int. J. Softw. Tools Technol. Transfer **26**(3), 403–419 (2024). https://doi.org/10.1007/s10009-024-00750-5

15. Lawford, M., McDougall, J., Froebel, P., Moum, G.: Practical application of functional and relational methods for the specification and verification of safety critical software. In: Rus, T. (ed.) AMAST 2000. LNCS, vol. 1816, pp. 73–88. Springer, Heidelberg (2000). https://doi.org/10.1007/3-540-45499-3_8

16. Leuschel, M., Mutz, M., Werth, M.: Modelling and validating an automotive system in Classical B and Event-B. In: Raschke, A., Méry, D., Houdek, F. (eds.) ABZ 2020. LNCS, vol. 12071, pp. 335–350. Springer, Cham (2020). https://doi.org/10.1007/978-3-030-48077-6_27

17. Leveson, N.G., Heimdahl, M.P.E., Hildreth, H., Reese, J.D.: Requirements specification for process-control systems. IEEE Trans. Software Eng. **20**(9), 684–707 (1994). https://doi.org/10.1109/32.317428

18. Mammar, A., Frappier, M., Laleau, R.: An Event-B model of an automotive adaptive exterior light system. Int. J. Softw. Tools Technol. Transfer **26**(3), 331–346 (2024). https://doi.org/10.1007/s10009-024-00748-z

19. Owre, S., Rushby, J., Shankar, N.: Integration in PVS: tables, types, and model checking. In: Brinksma, E. (ed.) TACAS 1997. LNCS, vol. 1217, pp. 366–383. Springer, Heidelberg (1997). https://doi.org/10.1007/BFb0035400

20. Parnas, D.L.: Tabular representation of relations. CRL Report 260, McMaster University (Oct 1992)

21. Parnas, D.L.: Some theorems we should prove. In: Joyce, J.J., Seger, C.-J.H. (eds.) HUG 1993. LNCS, vol. 780, pp. 155–162. Springer, Heidelberg (1994). https://doi.org/10.1007/3-540-57826-9_132

22. Raschke, A., Méry, D.: An automotive case study. Int. J. Softw. Tools Technol. Transfer **26**(3), 327–330 (2024). https://doi.org/10.1007/s10009-024-00753-2

23. Sekerinski, E.: Exploring Tabular Verification and Refinement. Formal Aspects Comput. **15**(2), 215–236 (2003). https://doi.org/10.1007/s00165-003-0010-9

24. Sekerinski, E.: Spectabular: interactive tabular requirements specifications. In: Rodrigues, G.N., Menghi, C. (eds.) IEEE/ACM 14th International Conference on Formal Methods in Software Engineering (FormaliSE '26) (2026, in press). https://doi.org/10.1145/3793656.3793693

25. The MathWorks, Inc.: Requirements table (2022). https://www.mathworks.com/help/slrequirements/ref/requirementstable.html

Identifying Design Flaws in a Lock-Free Task Pool with TLA+

Vasil Dyadov[iD], Alexander Kogtenkov[iD], and Ilya Shchepetkov[(✉)][iD]

Kaspersky Lab, Moscow, Russia
`ilya.shchepetkov@17451k.space`

Abstract. Lock-free data structures are notoriously difficult to design and implement correctly. The absence of critical sections protected by synchronization primitives makes reasoning much harder, often leading to almost unreproducible bugs and subtle errors. All of these can be systematically addressed using formal methods. We use TLA+, a state-based formal method especially suitable for working with concurrency, to verify SALSA, a scalable and low synchronization NUMA-aware algorithm for producer-consumer pools. The task pool was considered as part of a redesign phase of inter-process communication in a microkernel-based operating system under development. During this work, we uncovered numerous issues with the algorithm, from small typos in the pseudocode to significant design flaws. The work was completed in two person-months and resulted in a decision to abandon this task pool in favor of a more traditional lock-free queue. This potentially saved us many more months of development and debugging and advanced formal verification use within the company.

Keywords: formal verification · lock-free queue · concurrency · TLA+

1 Introduction

High-assurance systems achieve their goals with appropriate design and technology principles. In our case of a secure operating system KasperskyOS, the microkernel design reduces the attack surface compared to monolithic kernels, and lock-free structures for the central mechanism, inter-process communication (IPC), guarantee desired performance. Among the research questions are the pros and cons of different algorithms for message queues, including SALSA [12], a scalable and low synchronization NUMA-aware algorithm for producer-consumer pools.

SALSA is a lock-free algorithm that relies on hardware atomic instructions to keep its operations thread safe. Compared to more traditional lock-based algorithms with critical sections, lock-free ones guarantee progress (no deadlocks and stalling) and enable higher performance in high-contention scenarios [3,8]. However, they are significantly harder to design and reason about [4,11], which

© The Author(s), under exclusive license to Springer Nature Switzerland AG 2026
F. Ishikawa and A. Cunha (Eds.): ABZ 2026, LNCS 16579, pp. 180–190, 2026.
https://doi.org/10.1007/978-3-032-26752-8_11

often leads to subtle bugs. As a preventive measure to avoid these issues, we employed formal methods.

This paper presents the process and results of a formal verification of SALSA with TLA+ [20]. Contributions of our work include the following:

- A detailed TLA+ specification that accurately captures the concurrent behavior of the SALSA task pool.
- A brief review of the risks associated with formalization and their possible mitigation.
- A collection of invariants that should be preserved at any time during the algorithm execution.
- Demonstration of the suitability of the TLA+ formalism for verification of lock-free queues in the industrial setting.
- Discovery of significant flaws in the algorithm that were not previously publicly described.

The paper is organized as follows: the reasoning behind choosing TLA+ (Sect. 2), an overview of SALSA (Sect. 3), the formal specification (Sect. 4), analysis of the results and the discovered issues (Sect. 5), discussion of the findings (Sect. 6), the related work (Sect. 7), and the conclusion (Sect. 8).

2   Choosing TLA+

The following requirements influenced the choice of the verification tool: the verification project should remain practical and achieve results in a time frame of no more than two months; the produced artifacts should be understandable by developers without a steep learning curve. The latter one facilitates the ownership transfer of the produced specification and its future maintenance and improvement by the developer team.

To reduce risk, we excluded methods that we had no previous experience with. This left us with the Isabelle/HOL proof assistant [24], Alloy [17], Event-B [1], and TLA+ [20]. Isabelle/HOL contains layers of specialized logic and tooling that differ significantly from standard software engineering workflows, making it very hard to introduce developers into. Alloy is a great choice for structural modeling and has a sufficiently simple language, but it struggles with very long execution traces that arise due to possible interleavings within concurrent algorithms. The Event-B language is not tailored towards the specification of concurrent executions expressed as a sequential algorithm, though it can be done using control variables. This would be unintuitive for the developers; and the process of proving the correctness of the model in this case would probably require the use of refinement [1,2], which is yet another potential barrier.

TLA+ is a high-level formal specification language designed to model and to verify complex systems, especially distributed and concurrent ones [21]. Using it, a verification engineer can model threads, simulate all possible interleavings between them, quickly iterate, and debug issues by using the available tools and inspecting reported reports or error traces. On top of it, the PlusCal language [22], which can be automatically transpiled into raw TLA+, greatly simplifies the specification of concurrent executions and is more easily understandable by developers, because it looks like a pseudocode.

There are different ways to find errors in TLA+ specifications or to prove their absence. The primary tool is the TLC model checker [29]. It can exhaustively explore all reachable states of a specification to find a state where invariants or temporal properties are violated. If such is found, TLC outputs an error trace that shows a shortest path from an initial state to the error one. Other tools include Apalache [19], a bounded symbolic model checker, capable of exploring infinite state space but usually no longer than 6–12 steps from an initial state. And finally, TLAPS [9] is used to write and to mechanically verify formal proofs of a system's correctness.

PlusCal is best used for specifying shared-memory concurrent algorithms and is reportedly more approachable by engineers, since it feels closer to a traditional programming language rather than to a sophisticated math [23]. The language introduces labels to define an atomic "step" of an algorithm:

- Everything between two labels is executed as a single atomic action.
- Context switches (interleaving) can occur only at labels.
- TLC checks invariants and explores different states only at labels.

3   Overview of SALSA

SALSA is a non-blocking **producer-consumer** task pool that offers high throughput and supports the writing of policies to achieve load balancing and cache locality. Load balancing is further improved through **stealing**, which allows one consumer to take **tasks** that were originally assigned to another. To make this process efficient, tasks are grouped into larger units of fixed size called **chunks**. Stealing an entire chunk significantly reduces overhead compared to stealing individual tasks one by one.

To support stealing, chunks store information about their **owner**, who is one of the consumers. Each chunk may be encapsulated within a **node** containing an integer index field (**idx**); its purpose is to track the last taken task in that chunk. With the index, the owner can claim tasks sequentially without interfering with other consumers. Stealing a chunk involves creating a new encapsulating node with a separate index, which protects from possible reading collisions between the original and new owners.

Initially, a chunk does not contain any tasks. Each producer chooses a consumer to work with, chooses a chunk owned by that consumer, adds new tasks to it until it is full, and then repeats the process. Consumers retrieve tasks and replace the corresponding chunk entries with the **TAKEN** entry.

Each consumer has its own task pool represented by several **chunk lists** and a single **chunk pool** (see Fig. 1). Contrary to the name, each chunk list is a linked list of nodes, which may or may not point to chunks. Consumers can freely retrieve tasks from all their local chunk lists.

When working with a particular consumer task pool, each producer can insert tasks only to a single chunk list fully reserved for its use. This eliminates synchronization between multiple producers.

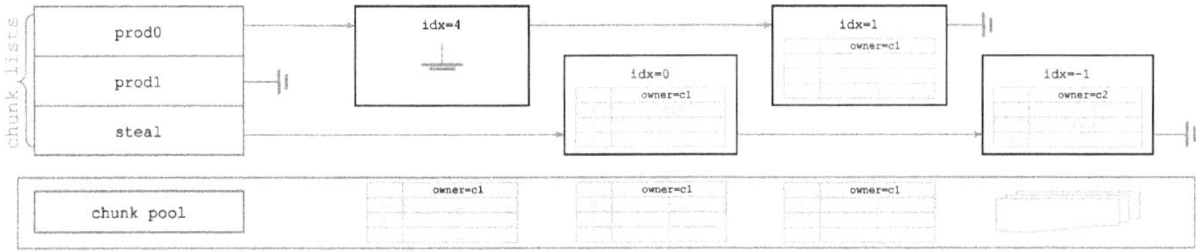

Fig. 1. Architecture of a representative task pool for an individual consumer. Each consumer maintains a dedicated chunk list for every producer in the system, an additional list for stealing tasks, and a pool of free chunks. Each entry in the chunk lists includes an **owner** field to identify the consumer that currently has the right to take tasks from this chunk.

Chunk pools are collections of spare chunks that facilitate efficient memory usage. Fully consumed chunks are stored in the chunk pool by a consumer and are retrieved by a producer when a new chunk is required for new tasks.

The stealing process is the most complicated part of the whole algorithm, as it tries to strike a balance between correctness of synchronization and efficiency by design.

4   Specification in TLA+

Working with TLA+ includes the following logical steps:

1. Formalization of the algorithm.
2. Definition of the properties to be checked.
3. Configuration and evaluation by the tool.
4. Analysis of the results; implementation of any changes if necessary.

This section describes the first two steps, and the next section discusses the evaluation and results.

We chose PlusCal to verify SALSA and specified the algorithm as closely as possible, describing the slight deviations and the reasoning behind them in the comments. The translation from the informal pseudocode to PlusCal was fairly straightforward. The difficult part was to set the correct atomicity zones using labels (see the example in Fig. 2) and come up with invariants. Too granular placement of the labels can lead to redundant interleaving checks: for example, several writings to local process variables can be safely grouped together under common labels, since they can not interfere with the execution of other processes.

We check the following categories of properties in lock-free algorithms:

Pseudocode	Simplified PlusCal

```1: Function checkLast(Node n):```
```2:   if(n.idx + 1 = CHUNK_SIZE) then```
```3:   n.c ← ⊥;```
```4:   return chunk to chunkPool;```
```5:   currentNode ← ⊥;```
	```1: procedure checkLast(n)```
	```2: variable chunk = NULL;```
	```3: if nodes[n].idx + 1 = CHUNK_SIZE then```
	```4: chunk := nodes[n].c;```
	```5: nodes[n].c := NULL;```
	```6: if chunk /= NULL then```
	```7: scPools[self].chunkPool := Append(```
	```8: scPools[self].chunkPool, chunk);```
	```9: end if;```
	```10: scPools[self].currentNodeId := NULL;```
	```11: end if;```

Fig. 2. Translation example for the `checkLast()` procedure from algorithmic pseudocode to PlusCal. The procedure is executed by a consumer; all variables, except for the procedure argument `Node n`, are global. Colors denote atomicity zones defined via PlusCal labels (absent in the example). Some syntax details are omitted for clarity.

- *Linearizability*, a strong correctness condition that helps to reason about the system [15].
- *Lock-freedom* confirms that there is always a thread that makes progress.
- *Absence of ABA problems* or correctness of proposed mitigations.
- *Functional correctness* guarantees that the algorithm never produces a wrong result or enters an invalid state.
- *Structural correctness* covers invariants of the underlying data structures, including type correctness.

Orthogonally to the above, we add an additional layer—*memory models*—to take into account specific hardware behavior with memory access. There is a recent report on the formalization of a weak ARM memory model in TLA+ [28]. Internally, we employ ARM and x86-TSO memory models with TLA+ specifications.

Shortly after starting adding invariants and checking the specification of SALSA with TLC, we began receiving issue reports with error traces. After analysis, we found that some of the initial invariants turned out to be too strict and the reports were actually false positives, so we removed them from the specification. However, we categorized other reports as true positives, representing critical issues (see Sect. 5) in the SALSA algorithm. We had been attempting to fix them and ultimately failed; we believe that it may be impossible to do so without fundamentally affecting the reported performance characteristics. Also, having failed to prove existing invariants, we stopped adding new ones. In the end, our specification contains only invariants that describe functional and structural correctness, as well as the absence of runtime errors.

The TLA+ specification of SALSA is available online under MIT license[1]. It includes 850 lines of invariants and PlusCal code; the PlusCal part translates into about 1,250 lines of TLA+.

---

[1] https://codeberg.org/17451k/salsa-spec.

5 Evaluation of the Model and Discovered Issues

Model checkers usually report one error at a time because they halt upon encountering an inconsistency. Stopping early prevents a cascade of misleading, secondary errors caused by the initial violation, reducing false positives. It makes it difficult to find several issues without first fixing the existing ones, but we did our best to manually check the error traces and to confirm that the occurrence of each reported error does not depend on another one.

With the above in mind, we found the following problems in the published version of the algorithm:

1. **Task loss, use-after-free.** The algorithm does not explain in detail what happens to a chunk when it is returned to a chunk pool. We assume that it is re-initialized, since one of the purposes of its existence is memory reuse, and other possible interpretations lead to even more significant errors. However, verification shows that re-initialization causes a broken state in several places and, most importantly, task loss. Example of the latter:
   - The system runs 2 concurrent consumers, C1 and C2.
   - C1 initiates `takeTask(Node n)` function and increases the index `n.idx++` to tell the world that it is going to take a task from `n`.
   - C2 steals the chunk and finishes taking the rest of the tasks from it. C2 returns an empty chunk to a chunk pool, where it is reinitialized.
   - Except that it was not empty: consumption of one task by C1 was not finished. This results in the use-after-free error down the line.
2. **Index out of bounds.** This happens when a `Consumer` takes a task from a chunk that it just stole:
   - Assuming that the stolen chunk is full except for one last task, this last task will be successfully consumed at the end of the `steal()` function (lines 106–111 of the algorithm [12]).
   - The algorithm here has a mistake: the `checkLast()` call occurs before the node index increases, and thus the call fails to detect that the chunk is now fully consumed.
   - This leads to a runtime error in `takeTask()`, when the `Consumer` tries to access a task at index `n.idx+1`, which just became out of bounds.
3. **Unexpected value.** When there are no available tasks anywhere and only a single chunk is present, two consumers may end up stealing this chunk from each other continuously in a loop. During this process, one consumer may try to insert the node into its `STEAL` chunk list that already contains the copy of this node, causing duplicates. It is unlikely to cause any safety issues, but leads to excess memory or CPU usage required to handle this behavior.
4. **Invalid state.** It is possible to execute the "take last task" part of the algorithm twice. This leads to two consumers having the same chunk in their chunk pools, which in turn results in producers adding tasks to the same chunk concurrently without any synchronization.
   - Assume that there is an almost fully consumed chunk owned by C1 with only two tasks.

- C2 starts the stealing process, but stops in the middle.
- C1 notices that its chunk is stolen, takes the *last task*, and goes away. Note that during this procedure, the `currentNode` variable becomes empty, but the node itself is still in the chunk list of C1.
- C1 executes the second part of `consume()` function (see lines 68–71). It selects the same node with the stolen task and calls `takeTask()`.
- C1 notices for the second time that the chunk is stolen and again takes one *last task* from it. If the chunk is fully consumed, C1 returns it to its own chunk pool.
- C2 finishes the stealing process, notices that one task was consumed by C1 and adjusts the index in its own node to reflect it.
- C2 tries to take the next task and receives `TAKEN` instead. As it should not be possible at this stage, there are no checks to detect it, so `takeTask()` returns `TAKEN` as a valid task to the consumer.
- C2 finishes working with the chunk and returns it to its own chunk pool, which combined with previous actions of C1 registers the same chunk in two different chunk pools, causing a potential conflict between producers.

All the issues we found on the following configuration: single producer; two consumers; no more than two chunks, two nodes, and two tasks per chunk. On a 16 core Ryzen 5950x CPU, each TLC execution took only a couple of seconds until an invariant violation. Most of the error traces were around one hundred steps of execution. Since we did not reach checking of temporal properties, RAM usage was minimal.

6   Discussion

We identified the following risks that may affect the validity of the findings:

1. Misinterpretation of the SALSA paper and the pseudocode.
2. Possible divergence between the pseudocode and the specification.
3. Mistakes during error trace analysis, wrong conclusion.
4. Wrong configuration of the specification.
5. Issues that are known, documented, or fixed.

To mitigate the first three risks, the specification and the error traces were independently audited by a separate person from our team; no issues affecting the results were found. As far as we can tell, all the discovered errors arise when consumers try to steal chunks from each other via `steal()` function and are located within inter-consumer synchronization code. Producers do not interact with each other at all, and it seems that there are no bugs in the logic of production and consumption of tasks without stealing. We attempted to confirm this observation by turning off stealing in our model. Such a configuration successfully passes all our invariants, as incomplete as they may be. However, the simplified algorithm is hardly useful and does not guarantee the declared performance properties.

Although all reported issues were found on a specific set of the specification parameters, we extended our analysis to other possible configurations that were larger in scope. These configurations were subject to state-space explosion, making exhaustive model checking computationally expensive. Nevertheless, additional checks replicated the same failure patterns, suggesting that the identified issues are not artifacts of a restricted scope and that the chosen smaller configuration can represent the algorithm's general behavior.

We attempted to find other publications or reports that mention SALSA; none discussed its use in production or potential issues. An extended technical report [13] by the same authors describes SALSA with slight deviations in the pseudocode. We tried to formalize it as well, but quickly encountered similar issues, and decided to focus solely on the conference version.

Unfortunately, neither regular nor extended description provides a link to the source code used in benchmarks, so we were unable to compare the specification with the implementation.

A thorough discussion with the SALSA authors would be beneficial to further validate and explore our findings.

7   Related Work

There are quite a few works related to the formal verification of lock-free algorithms using interactive theorem provers. Carbonneaux et al. applied the Rocq prover (formerly named Coq [5]) and the implementation of concurrent separation logic called Iris [18] to verify two queue data structures used for inter-process communication in their microkernel [7]. The same techniques were also applied to verify a concurrent queue from Meta's Folly library [27]. Doherty et al. describe a semi-automated verification of an optimized version of Michael and Scott's lock-free FIFO queue via forward and backward simulations [10]. Tofan et al. presented KIV [25] proofs that cover memory safety, ABA prevention, and preservation of linearizability and lock-freedom for a lock-free stack with safe memory reclamation [26]. The formally proved properties are quite similar to what we check (Sect. 4). But while theorem provers provide general and unbounded correctness guarantees, model checkers, such as TLC used in our work, focus on automatic bug detection in finite instances and bounded configurations, freeing developers from manual construction of mathematical proofs.

TLA+ also has an extensive history of usage for specification and verification of non-blocking algorithms. Hackett et al. describe a methodology for validating concurrent implementations against high-level TLA+ specifications [14]. It is evaluated on a state-of-the-art lock-free data structure from the research community and a lock-free queue featuring aggressive performance optimizations. Their approach is capable of finding known bugs injected into the systems under test and helped discover two previously unknown bugs. Hurault and Quéinnec used TLA+ and TLAPS to prove the correctness and completeness of a wait-free concurrent algorithm used to rename processes [16].

Amazon Web Services has integrated formal methods [23] into the engineering workflow to verify the correctness of their most critical distributed systems, including lock-free data structures. They reported significant benefits of using TLA+, most notably the ability to discover subtle high-severity bugs and to verify aggressive performance optimizations. According to the publication, engineers were able to learn TLA+ from scratch and to get useful results in two to three weeks. Recently though, their focus shifted from TLA+ to P [6]: a high-level state machine based programming language also capable to formally model and validate distributed systems.

8   Conclusion

It is almost inevitable to encounter minor inaccuracies and errors while reading descriptions of lock-free algorithms, though this can be generalized to any other system as well. In articles describing queues, it is customary to provide a simple textual proof of their correctness. In our experience, such proofs are incomplete and insufficient, yet almost no one performs formal verification of their submissions. This is particularly dangerous because any inaccuracy, let alone a design flaw, can lead to serious consequences when using a queue in practice. Formal methods enable finding and fixing such problems at an early stage of development, where the cost of error is not yet prohibitive.

In this work, we applied the TLA+ formal specification language to evaluate the SALSA algorithm within the context of a microkernel redesign. A key factor was the use of the TLC model checker, which provided a fully automated verification approach that helped us finish the work in just two person-months. The analysis exposed several issues, including design flaws that undermined the algorithm's reliability in concurrent environments. This early detection of flaws likely preempted months of costly debugging and potential system failures during later development stages.

References

1. Abrial, J.R.: Modeling in Event-B: system and software engineering. Cambridge Univ. Press (2010). https://doi.org/10.1017/CBO9781139195881
2. Abrial, J.R., Hallerstede, S.: Refinement, decomposition, and instantiation of discrete models: application to Event-B. Fund. Inform. **77**(1–2), 1–28 (Jan2007)
3. Alistarh, D., Censor-Hillel, K., Shavit, N.: Are lock-free concurrent algorithms practically wait-free? J. ACM (JACM) **63**(4) (2016). https://doi.org/10.1145/2903136
4. Ben-David, N., Blelloch, G.E., Wei, Y.: Lock-free locks revisited. In: Proceedings of the 27th ACM SIGPLAN Symposium on Principles and Practice of Parallel Programming, pp. 278–293. PPoPP '22, Association for Computing Machinery, New York (2022). https://doi.org/10.1145/3503221.3508433
5. Bertot, Y., Castéran, P.: Interactive theorem proving and program development. Springer (2004). https://doi.org/10.1007/978-3-662-07964-5
6. Brooker, M., Desai, A.: Systems correctness practices at Amazon Web Services. Commun. ACM **68**(6), 38–42 (2025). https://doi.org/10.1145/3729175

7. Carbonneaux, Q., Zilberstein, N., Klee, C., O'Hearn, P.W., Zappa Nardelli, F.: Applying formal verification to microkernel IPC at meta. In: Proceedings of the 11th ACM SIGPLAN International Conference on Certified Programs and Proofs, pp. 116–129. ACM, Philadelphia (2022). https://doi.org/10.1145/3497775.3503681

8. Cong, G., Bader, D.: Lock-free parallel algorithms: an experimental study. In: Bougé, L., Prasanna, V.K. (eds.) High Performance Computing - HiPC 2004, pp. 516–527. Springer, Heidelberg (2005). https://doi.org/10.1007/978-3-540-30474-6_54

9. Cousineau, D., Doligez, D., Lamport, L., Merz, S., Ricketts, D., Vanzetto, H.: TLA+ Proofs. In: Giannakopoulou, D., Méry, D. (eds.) FM 2012: Formal Methods, pp. 147–154. Springer, Heidelberg (2012). https://doi.org/10.1007/978-3-642-32759-9_14

10. Doherty, S., Groves, L., Luchangco, V., Moir, M.: Formal verification of a practical lock-free queue algorithm. In: Formal Techniques for Networked and Distributed Systems - FORTE 2004, pp. 97–114. Springer, Heidelberg (2004). https://doi.org/10.1007/978-3-540-30232-2_7

11. Fraser, K.: Practical Lock-Freedom. Tech. rep., University of Cambridge, Computer Laboratory (2004). https://doi.org/10.48456/tr-579

12. Gidron, E., Keidar, I., Perelman, D., Perez, Y.: SALSA: scalable and low synchronization NUMA-aware algorithm for producer-consumer pools. In: Proceedings of the 24th ACM symposium on Parallelism in algorithms and architectures - SPAA '12, p. 151. ACM Press, Pittsburgh (2012). https://doi.org/10.1145/2312005.2312035

13. Gidron, E., Keidar, I., Perelman, D., Perez, Y.: SALSA: scalable and low synchronization NUMA-aware algorithm for producer-consumer pools. Tech. rep., Technion (2012). https://ece.technion.ac.il/wp-content/uploads/2021/01/publication_807-1.pdf

14. Hackett, F., Wrench, E., Macko, P., Davis, A.J.J., Wei, Y., Beschastnikh, I.: Trace Validation of Unmodified Concurrent Systems with OmniLink (2026). https://arxiv.org/abs/2601.11836

15. Herlihy, M.P., Wing, J.M.: Linearizability: a correctness condition for concurrent objects. ACM Trans. Program. Lang. Syst. **12**(3), 463–492 (1990). https://doi.org/10.1145/78969.78972

16. Hurault, A., Quéinnec, P.: Proving a non-blocking algorithm for process renaming with TLA. In: Tests and Proofs, pp. 147–166. Springer International Publishing (2019). https://doi.org/10.1007/978-3-030-31157-5_10

17. Jackson, D.: Alloy: a lightweight object modelling notation. ACM Trans. Softw. Eng. Methodol. **11**(2), 256–290 (2002). https://doi.org/10.1145/505145.505149

18. Jung, R., Krebbers, R., Jourdan, J.H., Bizjak, A., Birkedal, L., Dreyer, D.: Iris from the ground up: a modular foundation for higher-order concurrent separation logic. J. Funct. Programm. **28** (2018). https://doi.org/10.1017/S0956796818000151

19. Konnov, I., Kukovec, J., Tran, T.H.: TLA+ Model checking made symbolic. Proc. ACM Program. Lang. **3**(OOPSLA) (2019). https://doi.org/10.1145/3360549

20. Lamport, L.: The temporal logic of actions. ACM Trans. Program. Lang. Syst. **16**(3), 872–923 (1994). https://doi.org/10.1145/177492.177726

21. Lamport, L.: Specifying concurrent systems with TLA+. Calculational System Design, pp. 183–247 (1999). https://www.microsoft.com/en-us/research/publication/specifying-concurrent-systems-tla/

22. Lamport, L.: The PlusCal algorithm language. In: Theoretical Aspects of Computing - ICTAC 2009, pp. 36–60. Springer, Heidelberg (2009). https://doi.org/10.1007/978-3-642-03466-4_2

23. Newcombe, C., Rath, T., Zhang, F., Munteanu, B., Brooker, M., Deardeuff, M.: How amazon web services uses formal methods. Commun. ACM **58**(4), 66–73 (2015). https://doi.org/10.1145/2699417
24. Nipkow, T., Klein, G.: Concrete Semantics. Springer, Cham (2014). https://doi.org/10.1007/978-3-319-10542-0
25. Reif, W., Schellhorn, G., Stenzel, K., Balser, M.: Structured Specifications and Interactive Proofs with KIV, pp. 13–39. Springer (1998). https://doi.org/10.1007/978-94-017-0435-9_1
26. Tofan, B., Schellhorn, G., Reif, W.: Formal verification of a lock-free stack with hazard pointers. In: Cerone, A., Pihlajasaari, P. (eds.) ICTAC 2011. LNCS, vol. 6916, pp. 239–255. Springer, Heidelberg (2011). https://doi.org/10.1007/978-3-642-23283-1_16
27. Vindum, S.F., Frumin, D., Birkedal, L.: Mechanized verification of a fine-grained concurrent queue from meta's folly library. In: Proceedings of the 11th ACM SIGPLAN International Conference on Certified Programs and Proofs, New York, NY, USA, pp. 100–115 (2022). https://doi.org/10.1145/3497775.3503689
28. Xiao, L., Hou, Z., Zhu, H., He, M., Qin, S.: Specifying and verifying programs over the MCA ARMv8 architecture with TLA. J. Circ. Syst. Comput. **35**(01) (2026). DOI: https://doi.org/10.1142/S0218126625300089
29. Yu, Y., Manolios, P., Lamport, L.: Model checking TLA+ specifications. In: Correct Hardware Design and Verification Methods, pp. 54–66. Springer, Heidelberg (1999). https://doi.org/10.1007/3-540-48153-2_6

Slicing Models for Equiconsistency with Alloy

Marc Thieme[1], Shobhit Singh[1(✉)], Terru Stübinger[1],
Romain Pascual[2], and Mattias Ulbrich[1]

[1] Karlsruhe Institute of Technology, Karlsruhe, Germany
shobhit.singh@kit.edu
[2] MICS, CentraleSupélec, Université Paris-Saclay, Gif-sur-Yvette, France

Abstract. Model-driven development enables collaborative design across heterogeneous modelling domains, but it also raises the risk of inconsistent models. We study the problem of extracting minimal submodels that preserve cross-domain consistency. Concretely, given two sets of models related by a consistency specification and a model from the first set, we seek an equiconsistent slice, that is, a submodel that preserves the same consistency relationships with models of the second set. Since the definition of equiconsistency quantifies over the complete second set, a direct computation is infeasible (and undecidable in general). Thus, we formulate slicing as a declarative synthesis problem and solve it using counterexample-guided inductive synthesis (CEGIS). The procedure iteratively proposes candidate slices and refines them using counterexamples (models obtained as violation witnesses if a candidate is not a valid slice). Iterating the CEGIS loop converges to equiconsistent, minimal slices within the bounds used by the model finder. We instantiate the abstract equiconsistency slice problem using attributed typed graphs as models, express consistency relations declaratively, and further realize it using relational logic and SAT-based solving. We then obtain an automated synthesis of equiconsistent slices based only on the consistency relation. We evaluate the method on a synthetic dataset to compare three CEGIS implementations: an explicit loop in Alloy, an explicit loop in Alloy*, and a quantified encoding in Alloy*. We highlight their practical trade-offs.

Keywords: Model-Driven Engineering · Slicing · Consistency · Alloy

1 Introduction

Model-driven development [3,13] relies on a collection of models, that encodes domain-specific information about the system under development. Since these models describe overlapping aspects of the same system, they must satisfy cross-model consistency relations [27]. As systems become more complex, models grow larger, and consistency checking becomes more expensive. Still, large parts of the models may be irrelevant for a given consistency specification [26].

© The Author(s), under exclusive license to Springer Nature Switzerland AG 2026
F. Ishikawa and A. Cunha (Eds.): ABZ 2026, LNCS 16579, pp. 191–209, 2026.
https://doi.org/10.1007/978-3-032-26752-8_12

Model slicing can mitigate this complexity. Originating from static program analysis [6,7,20,30,32], slicing improves comprehensibility, performance, and debugging. For models, slicing means extracting a submodel that preserves a given *slicing criterion*. Model slicing can speed up analyses [26] and help developers focus on the aspects of a model relevant for a given purpose [4]. Still, most existing model slicing work targets behavioral or structural slicing criteria [4,8,19].

Inter-model consistency is inherently *relational*: whether a model is consistent is not intrinsic but depends on the other models used in the system description. When accounting for model evolution, i.e., when some models change due to edits through the design process, consistency then needs to be considered with respect to all possible counterpart models. For instance, removing elements of a model might introduce or eliminate consistency partners, making any slicing that considers only the current set of models unsound for consistency analysis.

We address this issue by introducing *equiconsistency slicing*, building on the notion of equiconsistency from [12,23]. Given a consistency relation between two sets of models $\mathcal{M}_1$ and $\mathcal{M}_2$, two models $m, n \in \mathcal{M}_1$ are equiconsistent if they are consistent with exactly the same models in $\mathcal{M}_2$. An equiconsistent slice preserves this property. Intuitively, an equiconsistency slice retains precisely the information required to determine inter-model consistency. For instance, a consistency condition between two circuit diagrams of different components of a system that share a common databus is that no two elements ever write onto the bus at the same time. To analyze this consistency, all components in the circuit diagrams that have no impact on the contents of the bus can be safely removed without altering the consistency status.

Equiconsistency slicing reduces model sizes while preserving consistency with the related models describing the system under development. It enables analysis of smaller representations without altering consistency and exposes which parts of a model actually influence it. Therefore, slices can help support scalable analysis and the understanding or debugging of consistency relations by isolating the elements that matter semantically.

Computing an equiconsistent slice for $m \in \mathcal{M}_1$ is challenging because it involves universal quantification over the counterpart models in $\mathcal{M}_2$. We formulate the problem as a declarative synthesis task and solve it using the counterexample-guided inductive synthesis (CEGIS) approach [1,17]. Candidate slices are iteratively refined by using the counterexample generated while trying to prove equiconsistency. Once a valid slice has been obtained, the whole procedure is iterated and converges to a minimal equiconsistent slice.

Practically, we represent models as attributed typed graphs [11], which we encode in Alloy [16]. Adding a description of the consistency relations in Alloy's specification language then provides a bounded implementation, relying on SAT-solving as a backend routine in the CEGIS loop. Within the given scope, the analyzer either finds a counterexample or establishes equiconsistency.

Contributions. This paper contributes (1) a formal notion of equiconsistent model slicing, (2) a CEGIS-based procedure ensuring minimality of the generated slice, (3) an Alloy implementation demonstrating practical feasibility, and (4) an empirical comparison of explicit Alloy, explicit Alloy*, and internal Alloy* implementations, done on synthetic model instances to assess scalability.

2   Related Work

Program Slicing and Semantic Preservation. Program slicing, introduced by Weiser [32], extracts program fragments preserving a variable's value at a given program point. Classical methods use syntactic dependencies, such as control and data dependence graphs [15]. Later work generalized slicing to semantic criteria, e.g., conditioned [10], assertion-based [5], and abstract slicing based on abstract interpretation [14]. In these approaches, the slice preserves satisfaction of a specification rather than execution traces. Our work follows this semantic view but preserves a relational property: consistency with models of another domain.

Model Slicing. Slicing has been transferred from programs to models, including state-based systems [18], UML models [2,19], and heterogeneous megamodels [25]. Most approaches are dependency-based: a set of model elements defines the criterion, and dependencies determine the slice [4]. Incremental techniques exploit edit histories or model evolution assumptions [24,28]. In contrast, our slicing criterion is not element-based but property-based. The slice is defined solely by preservation of a logical relation.

Consistency-Preserving Slicing. Constraint-oriented slicing has been studied for UML/OCL models, where slices preserve satisfaction of constraints within a model [26]. Such approaches reason about a single model and its predicates. We instead consider relations between models of different metamodels and preserve the entire set of consistent partner models (equiconsistency [12,23]).

Synthesis-Based Slicing. Some approaches separate candidate generation from verification and view slicing as a search problem guided by counterexamples [6]. We adopt this perspective and formulate slicing as a synthesis problem solved using counterexample-guided inductive synthesis (CEGIS) [1,17], where counterexamples are inconsistent partner models.

Positioning. Existing slicing techniques preserve behavior or predicate satisfaction within a single artifact. We instead introduce relational semantic slicing: the preserved property is a model relation, and slices are synthesized rather than derived from dependency analysis.

3   Equiconsistency Slicing

Model-driven development relies on multiple interrelated models describing different aspects of a system. Each model is an instance of a *metamodel* that determines the admissible structures. Examples include well-formed UML class diagrams, Simulink models, Event-B machines, or compilable Java programs. Following [23], we identify a metamodel with the set of its valid instances.

When multiple models describe the same system, they may create contradictions that hinder its realizability. In that sense, consistency denotes the absence of such contradictions and, thus, appears as a weak form of correctness, representing the notion of "joint realizability" [9]. Following [23], we consider consistency as a relation between models: either they are, or they are not consistent.

Formally, we consider two metamodels $\mathcal{M}_1$ and $\mathcal{M}_2$, together with a *consistency relation* $CR \subseteq \mathcal{M}_1 \times \mathcal{M}_2$, where $CR(m_1, m_2)$ means that m_1 and m_2 are consistent. This abstract description is enough to state the problem addressed in this paper, and will be refined in Sect. 5 for the practical implementation.

3.1   Model Slicing

In practice, large models often contain information irrelevant to cross-model consistency. Engineers, therefore, wish to remove unnecessary parts while preserving the model's consistent behavior. A solution is to slice the model and remove the irrelevant parts. Intuitively, a *slice* of a model is a smaller model that preserves a given property of the original one, called the *slicing criterion* [19]. Model slicing techniques can be broadly classified into two categories. *Syntactic slicing*, originating in program analysis, constructs slices by computing dependency relations between elements and taking their transitive closure, as introduced by Weiser [32]. In contrast, *declarative slicing* defines slices implicitly via a preservation criterion where candidate submodels are validated against a property specification. In this paper, we adopt a declarative slicing approach, where slices are characterized by equiconsistency rather than explicitly computed dependency structures. We define model slicing using a structural reduction relation and an equivalence relation as the slicing criterion.

Definition 1 (Model Slicing). Let $\mathcal{M}$ be a metamodel, $\preceq$ a partial order on $\mathcal{M}$ and S an equivalence relation on $\mathcal{M}$. A model $m' \in \mathcal{M}$ is a slice of $m \in \mathcal{M}$ with respect to S if $m' \preceq m$ and $S(m', m)$. Additionally, the model is a proper slice if $m' \prec m$, where $\prec$ is the strict partial order induced by $\preceq$.

In this paper, the order $\preceq$ corresponds to the submodel relation, which will be made explicit in Sect. 5. The remaining question is: Which property must be preserved such that a slice is similar to the original model consistency-wise?

3.2   Equiconsistency

The relevant property for consistency-based slicing is *equiconsistency* [12], which captures the idea that two models are indistinguishable with respect to consistency against all models of the second metamodel.

Definition 2 (Equiconsistency – [12, Def. 2]). Two models m_1 and m_1' in $\mathcal{M}_1$ are equiconsistent for CR, written $m_1 \sim_1^{CR} m_1'$, if

$$\forall m_2 \in \mathcal{M}_2, \ CR(m_1, m_2) \iff CR(m_1', m_2) \ . \tag{1}$$

Consequently, a given consistency relation CR induces two equiconsistency relations $\sim_1^{CR} \subseteq \mathcal{M}_1 \times \mathcal{M}_1$ and $\sim_2^{CR} \subseteq \mathcal{M}_2 \times \mathcal{M}_2$, both being equivalence relations on their associated metamodels [12]. In this paper, we will consider equiconsistency on $\mathcal{M}_1$ and make it explicit only when it might be ambiguous. Since CR is assumed fixed, we will then write $\sim$ instead of $\sim_1^{CR}$. Since equiconsistency means that no model of $\mathcal{M}_2$ can distinguish m_1 and m_1' with respect to consistency, it is the natural candidate for a slicing criterion, which leads us first to consider the following problem:

Equiconsistency Slicing Problem (ESP). Given two metamodels $\mathcal{M}_1$ and $\mathcal{M}_2$, a consistency relation $CR \subseteq \mathcal{M}_1 \times \mathcal{M}_2$, and a model $m_1 \in \mathcal{M}_1$, find an equiconsistent proper slice m_1' of m_1, i.e., find $m_1' \in \mathcal{M}_1$ such that $m_1' \prec m_1$ and $m_1' \sim m_1$.

Finding an equiconsistent slice means finding a model m_1' that is a strict submodel of m_1 and is equiconsistent with m_1. Among all slices of a model, we are particularly interested in *minimal* ones, which leads to the following problem:

Minimal Equiconsistency Slicing Problem (MESP). Given two metamodels $\mathcal{M}_1$ and $\mathcal{M}_2$, a consistency relation $CR \subseteq \mathcal{M}_1 \times \mathcal{M}_2$, and a model $m_1 \in \mathcal{M}_1$, find $m_1' \preceq m_1$ such that $m_1' \sim m_1$ and for all $m_1'' \prec m_1'$, $m_1'' \nsim m_1$.

Note that we relax the strictness condition in the definition of slice to allow for the possibility that the original model is already minimal, i.e., relaxing the proper slice condition $m_1' \prec m_1$ to $m_1' \preceq m_1$. In that sense, the existence of at least one minimal equiconsistent slice is guaranteed.

3.3   Undecidability of Equiconsistency Slicing

Equiconsistency is a strong property that requires checking consistency against all models of the second metamodel. This universal quantification makes equiconsistency undecidable in general, which hinders the feasibility of equiconsistency slicing. Consider the following decision problem:

Equiconsistency Problem (EP). Given two metamodels $\mathcal{M}_1$ and $\mathcal{M}_2$, a consistency relation $CR \subseteq \mathcal{M}_1 \times \mathcal{M}_2$, and two models $m_1, m_1' \in \mathcal{M}_1$, does $m_1 \sim m_1'$ hold?

Theorem 1 (Undecidability of Equiconsistency). *EP is undecidable.*

Proof (Sketch). Consider an alphabet Σ and $\mathcal{T}, \mathcal{T}'$ two Turing machines over Σ. We can consider the instance of the equiconsistency problem given by

- $\mathcal{M}_1 = \{\mathcal{T}, \mathcal{T}'\}$, $\mathcal{M}_2 = \Sigma^*$,
- $CR \subseteq \mathcal{M}_1 \times \mathcal{M}_2$ such that for any $t \in \mathcal{M}_1$ and $w \in \mathcal{M}_2$, $CR(t, w)$ iff $w \in L(t)$, where $L(t)$ is the language accepted by the Turing machine t,

- $m_1 = \mathcal{T}$, and $m_1' = \mathcal{T}'$.

Equiconsistency in this case becomes the equality of the languages accepted by the Turing machines, which is undecidable by Rice's theorem.

Essentially, the undecidability of equiconsistency comes from the undecidability of membership in CR. The consequence is that any practical algorithm for equiconsistency slicing must rely on restrictions or approximations.

3.4 Finite Approximation

To obtain a computable approximation of equiconsistency, we restrict the set of models of $\mathcal{M}_2$ used to check consistency. This restriction leads to a notion of constrained equiconsistency over a (finite) subset E of $\mathcal{M}_2$. In the implementation, E will correspond to the bounded exploration space of models (see Sect. 5).

Definition 3 (Constrained Equiconsistency). Let $E \subseteq \mathcal{M}_2$. Two models m_1 and m_1' in $\mathcal{M}_1$ are equiconsistent for CR with respect to E, written $m_1 \sim_E m_1'$, if for all $e \in E$, $CR(m_1, e) \iff CR(m_1', e)$.

Proposition 1. *The constrained equiconsistency relation $\sim_E$ is an equivalence relation on $\mathcal{M}_1$.*

Constrained equiconsistency is an over-approximation of full equiconsistency, which we can iteratively refine by adding more models of $\mathcal{M}_2$ to the set E. The idea is to add counterexamples that distinguish non-equiconsistent models, which we can find by checking the consistency of the candidate slice against models of $\mathcal{M}_2$. Formally, a counterexample for non-equiconsistent models $m_1, m_1' \in \mathcal{M}_1$ is a model $m_2 \in \mathcal{M}_2$ such that $CR(m_1, m_2) \not\iff CR(m_1', m_2)$. Full equiconsistency holds if and only if no counterexample exists, which naturally suggests an iterative refinement process: start with some finite set E, search for a candidate slice, and enlarge E whenever a counterexample is found. This idea serves as the basis for the CEGIS procedure introduced in the next section.

3.5 Motivating Example

We illustrate equiconsistency slicing on a simplified excerpt of an automotive body comfort system described by Lity et al. [21]. The system is described using two modeling viewpoints: an architectural model capturing hardware structure and a behavioral model describing control logic.

Metamodels and Models. The architectural metamodel *BCSComponents* (Fig. 1a) represents components that communicate via input and output ports. The behavioral metamodel *StateMachine* (Fig. 1b) describes controller logic using regions and transitions labeled by trigger and effect signals. Figures 2 and 3 show example instances of both metamodels. Intuitively, the architecture specifies which signals exist in the system, while the state machine specifies how those signals are produced and consumed.

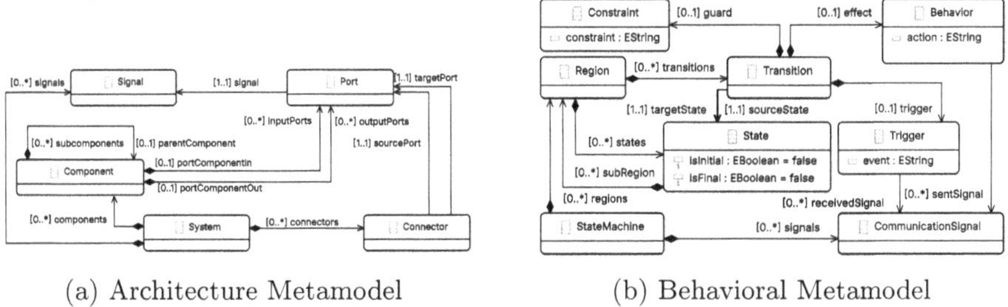

(a) Architecture Metamodel   (b) Behavioral Metamodel

Fig. 1. Metamodel: (a) Component diagram, (b) State machine.

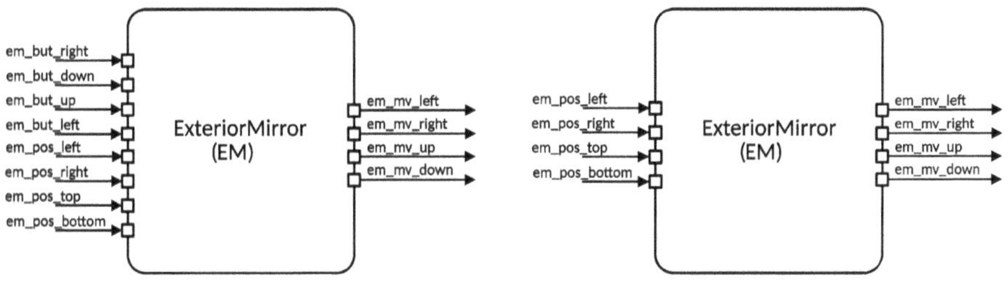

(a) Consistent with the model in Fig. 3   (b) Inconsistent with the model in Fig. 3

Fig. 2. Two instances for the metamodel from Fig. 1a (adapted from [21]).

Consistency Relation. Both models describe the same communication interface. Informally, the architecture determines which signals must appear in the behavior. More precisely, the models are consistent if:

- every input port named x is realized by a transition receiving signal x,
- every output port named x is realized by a transition emitting signal x.

Thus, consistency depends only on the presence of signal names, and not on the state machine's detailed control structure. For instance, the models of Figs. 2a and 3 are consistent, while the models of Figs. 2b and 3 are not, since some signals from the state machine do not appear as a port in the component diagram.

Slicing Problem. Consider the state machine in Fig. 3. Many transitions manipulate signals that appear elsewhere. Removing such redundant transitions does not change whether the behavioral model satisfies the architectural requirements. However, not all reductions are valid. An *equiconsistent slice* therefore preserves exactly the same consistency relationships as the original model: it keeps all information relevant to cross-model consistency, while discarding irrelevant behavioral detail. For instance, it should remain consistent with the model of Fig. 2a and inconsistent with the model of Fig. 2b. The part highlighted in blue in Fig. 3 shows an equiconsistent slice. The resulting model contains only the transitions necessary to witness the required signals; states and redundant occurrences

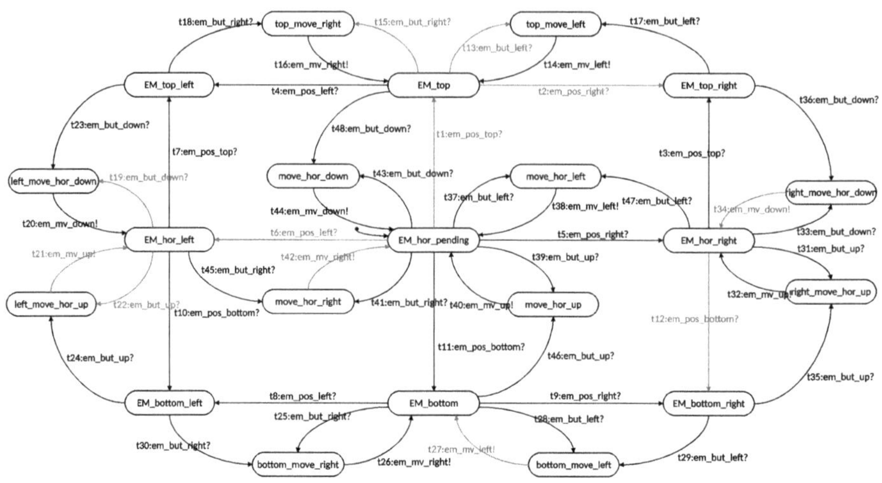

Fig. 3. State machine instance (adapted from [21]).

disappear because they do not influence consistency. In this example, we deliberately relaxed the metamodel so that the multiplicity constraints in Fig. 1b are ignored. Depending on the use case, where the metamodel itself may be fixed and not subject to change, the approach allows also encoding these multiplicities to enforce the original metamodel. The goal of this paper is to compute slices automatically from the consistency relation alone, without designing a dedicated slicer for each modeling language or constraint set.

4   Approach: Equiconsistency Slicing via CEGIS

In our declarative approach to equiconsistency slicing, the solution is split into two steps that are iterated alternately: generating a candidate slice and checking its equiconsistency with the initial model. This check requires assessing consistency for *all* possible models of the second metamodel. The universal quantification (see Eq. 1) makes the problem undecidable in general (Theorem 1) and also practically infeasible even for finite metamodels, as the number of possible instances grows exponentially with the bound on model size. We propose to use *Counterexample-Guided Inductive Synthesis (CEGIS)* to iteratively approximate this universal condition with a growing set of counterexamples. Intuitively, this means that checking the equiconsistency of the candidate slice is replaced by searching for a model (in the second metamodel) that violates equiconsistency. Each found counterexample refines the constraints imposed on future candidates. When no counterexample can be found within the bounds, the candidate is considered equiconsistent.

Algorithm 1. Equiconsistency slicing via CEGIS

1: **procedure** EQUICONSISTENTSLICE(m)
2:   $E^+ \leftarrow \emptyset,\ E^- \leftarrow \emptyset,\ s \leftarrow m$
3:   **loop**
4:     $e \leftarrow$ FINDCOUNTEREXAMPLE(m, s)
5:     **if** $e = \bot$ **then return** s
6:     **if** CONSISTENT(m, e) **then** $E^+ \leftarrow E^+ \cup e$
7:     **else** $E^- \leftarrow E^- \cup e$
8:     $s \leftarrow$ SYNTHESIZESLICE(m, E^+, E^-)

4.1   Oracles

The procedure relies on three decision problems:

1. *Counterexample search:* Given a model m and a slice s, check if there exists a model e such that $CR(m, e) \not\Leftrightarrow CR(s, e)$. If such a model exists, it is returned as a counterexample.
2. *Counterexample classification:* Given a counterexample e, find if it is consistent with the original model m. This partitions the counterexamples into $E^+ = \{e \mid CR(m, e)\}$ and $E^- = \{e \mid \neg CR(m, e)\}$.
3. *Slice synthesis:* Given E^+ and E^-, compute a slice $s \prec m$ such that

$$(\forall e \in E^+,\ CR(s, e)) \ \wedge\ (\forall e \in E^-,\ \neg CR(s, e)). \tag{2}$$

The slice s is constrained equiconsistent to m with respect to $E^+ \cup E^-$ (Definition 3).

4.2   CEGIS Procedure

The algorithm (Algorithm 1) builds the sets E^+ and E^- incrementally: they are both initially empty (meaning any submodel of m is a valid candidate), and each iteration then refines the set of admissible candidates. The algorithm terminates when the checker no longer finds a counterexample, indicating that the slice satisfies the bounded specification.

Partitioning the collected counterexamples into E^+ and E^- effectively caches the consistency status $CR(m, e)$ for each counterexample $e \in E$, and thus relieves the synthesis step from repeatedly referring to the original model m. In practice, this simplifies the synthesis constraints and reduces solver effort. The alternative formulation to (2) would be to require that $CR(m, e) \Leftrightarrow CR(s, e)$ for every $e \in E$.

The CEGIS loop computes an equiconsistent slice, but does not inherently guarantee minimality. To obtain minimal slices, we iteratively restart the procedure using the previously found slice as the new input model. The accumulated counterexamples are retained across runs, allowing the search to progressively shrink the model while avoiding the rediscovery of similar counterexamples. The process stops when no strictly smaller equiconsistent slice can be found.

4.3   Models as Attributed Typed Graphs

The CEGIS procedure is independent of a concrete modeling language. We only assume that models conform to metamodels and admit a notion of submodel and consistency. To make these notions precise, we represent metamodels and model instances as *attributed typed graphs* (ATGs).

A metamodel is given by a finite set of node types, edge types, and attribute types, together with typing functions that describe the admissible sources and targets. An instance model is a finite graph whose nodes and edges are typed by the metamodel and whose elements may carry attribute values. We can then consider the submodel relation as the partial order $\preceq$, such that s is a *submodel* of a model m if it is obtained by removing nodes, edges, and attribute values from m while preserving typing and incidence. Intuitively, a slice is a structure-preserving restriction of the original model.

The consistency relation CR may be defined by graph constraints, logical predicates, or model transformations. Equiconsistency only assumes that consistency can be decided on concrete model pairs. That is, consistency remains abstract, and the algorithm assumes only the availability of procedures for finding counterexamples, checking the consistency of model pairs, and synthesizing submodels under logical constraints. The following section explains how the required decision procedures are realized in practice for ATGs using Alloy.

5   Implementation

We implemented the proposed CEGIS procedure from Algorithm 1 in Alloy [16] and Kodkod [31] for the bounded relational model finder. The three oracles introduced in Sect. 4 (counterexample search, classification, and slice synthesis) are each encoded as satisfiability problems over finite relational structures. This section describes the finite relational representation used to decide the semantic conditions of Sect. 4. The encoding preserves the definitions within a bounded universe, allowing the slicing problem to be reduced to satisfiability.

5.1   Relational Encoding of the Slicing Problem

Encoding Metamodels and Models. Attributed typed graphs are interpreted as typed relational structures: each node and edge type becomes an Alloy signature, while source and target mappings are binary relations over them. Instead of the standard additional elements to encode attribution for nodes and edges [11], we represent the association of attribute values as a relation from model elements to values. To ensure decidability of the bounded analysis, attribute domains are interpreted over a finite abstraction domain. Concretely, we use a shared bounded integer universe for all attributes, which yields a finite relational structure while preserving the relational formulation of slicing. A concrete model instance is then encoded using singleton extensions of metamodel signatures for its model elements. Thus, each model corresponds to a fixed relational interpretation of the metamodel signature.

Encoding Slices as Substructures. The structural partial order $\preceq$ used for slicing is the submodel relation, which becomes the subgraph relation for attributed typed graphs (see Sect. 4.3). In the relational setting, it is enforced by inclusion constraints between interpretations. Every relation encoding the slice is required to be a restriction of the relation in the original model. Slice synthesis is then achieved as the search for a sub-interpretation satisfying a semantic preservation condition (the equiconsistency condition) rather than the removal of syntactically dependent elements.

Encoding the Consistency Relation. The consistency relation CR is represented as a logical predicate over relational structures. It is given intentionally, meaning that consistency holds when the relational constraint is satisfied, and the solver can reason directly over candidate models rather than over an explicit enumeration of consistent pairs. In practice, Alloy's relational operators are used to express CR. Thus, checking the consistency of two models boils down to solving a satisfiability problem over the combined relational structure rather than explicitly enumerating consistent partner models. As a result, counterexamples produced during CEGIS are concrete models that explicitly violate equiconsistency within the bounded universe.

5.2   Realizing the CEGIS Oracles

Each oracle in the CEGIS loop becomes a bounded model-finding task, and we use Alloy as the relational solver. It translates relational constraints into SAT and relies on off-the-shelf solvers, providing a concise specification language with an efficient search backend. The size of the counterexamples must be bounded to ensure that the program terminates. In practice, we bound the size proportionally to the original model, and the absence of counterexamples is guaranteed only within the chosen scope. Thus, bounding the search does not guarantee global convergence as a consequence of Theorem 1.

5.3   Execution Strategies

We implemented three variants of the slicing procedure, differing in how the CEGIS loop and the equiconsistency condition are realized. Two of them employ Alloy* [22], an extension of Alloy 4 that, unlike Alloy, can solve constraints with $\exists\forall$ quantifier alternations. It internally employs a CEGIS strategy like the one outlined in Algorithm 1, but does not partition counterexamples explicitly into E^+ and E^-. Instead, it invokes the SAT solver incrementally, allowing it to preserve knowledge about previously observed counterexamples as learned clauses in the solver state.

1. *Manual CEGIS*: The first implementation follows the procedure of Algorithm 1 closely. Separate solver calls perform equiconsistency check, counterexample classification, and slice synthesis, all encoded in Alloy. The main program orchestrates the CEGIS loop and maintains the sets E^+ and E^-, allowing reuse of the counterexamples across iterations.

2. *Iterative Star*: The second implementation uses Alloy* to encode equiconsistency using a solver-level $\exists\forall$ quantification. The slice is synthesized by solving $\exists s \prec m,\ \forall e,\ CR(m,e) \iff CR(s,e)$ within the chosen bounds. While equiconsistency is internalized, minimality is still obtained procedurally by invoking the slicer repeatedly.
3. *Full Star*: The third implementation extends the previous one by adding an explicit minimality constraint on the slice using an additional $\exists\forall$ quantification. We obtain a single Alloy* specification capturing both equiconsistency and minimality.

The second and third variants require the construction of a finite superstructure containing all admissible model elements within the chosen bounds to allow quantifying over all potential counterexamples. The superstructure ensures the Alloy* analyzer ranges over the intended search space rather than constructing witnesses that trivially satisfy the formula. Note that for the second variant, the drawback is that counterexamples cannot be reused across iterations, as they remain internal to the analyzer.

5.4   Code Generation

We have prototypically implemented an automatic translation that accepts ATGs (given as JSON files) and generates the corresponding Alloy declarations: (1) the metamodel declarations, (2) the model instance declarations, (3) the fixed model instances, (4) the slice declarations, and (5) declarations allowing the CEGIS loop to add counterexamples in the Manual approach. The consistency relation is to be stated as an Alloy predicate directly. Figure 5 contains the result of this translation for an example.

6   Case Study

To showcase the approach and principles of the Alloy encoding, demonstrate the feasibility of finding equiconsistent slices, and evaluate and compare the performance of the three approaches outlined in Sect. 5.3, we conducted a case study on small- to medium-sized models. The study uses two metamodels, for which we generated 72 synthetic concrete model instances, which were subjected to the implementations of the three slicing approaches. The test-case models were systematically synthesized for different sizes, different numbers of cycles, and different edge densities. The artifacts for reproducing the analysis are available as supplementary material [29] on Zenodo.

Figure 4 depicts the two metamodels $\mathcal{M}_1$ and $\mathcal{M}_2$ used in the case study. They are inspired by structural modeling languages but are synthetic in nature. Models in $\mathcal{M}_1$ describe the structure of system composition, including the communication protocols. Models of $\mathcal{M}_2$ express a more abstract view on the compositional nature of the modeled system with fewer details and connections.

The consistency relation CR_{study} used for equiconsistency slicing in this case study requires a correspondence between model elements and associations in

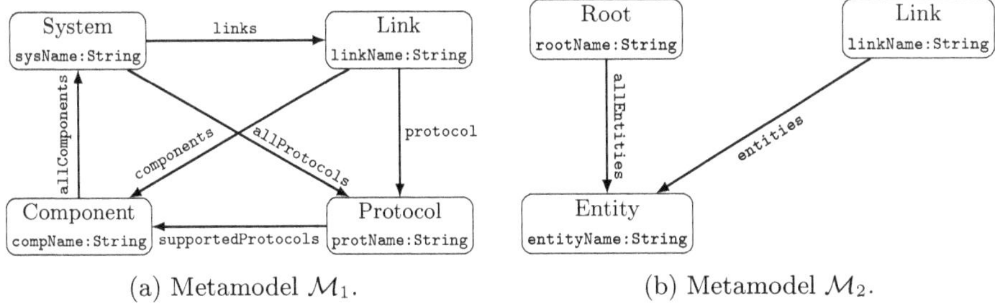

(a) Metamodel $\mathcal{M}_1$.   (b) Metamodel $\mathcal{M}_2$.

Fig. 4. Metamodels used in the empirical evaluation.

the two models. Concretely, a pair $(m_1, m_2) \in \mathcal{M}_1 \times \mathcal{M}_2$ is consistent (i.e. in CR_{study}) when

- for every **System** in m_1 there is an equally named **Root** in m_2 and vice versa;
- for every **Component** in m_1 there is an equally named **Entity** in m_2 and vice versa;
- for every **Link** in m_1 there is an equally named **Link** in m_2 and vice versa.

Moreover, if two model elements are associated in m_1 via edges in **allComponents** or **components**, then the equally named model elements in m_2 must be associated via edges in **allEntities** or **entities**, and vice versa.

The study is designed such that some elements of the metamodel are irrelevant for consistency. The presence of **Protocol** nodes in m_1 does not influence its consistency with any $m_2 \in \mathcal{M}_2$. Hence, minimal equiconsistent slices for m_1 produced by the slicing implementations omit **Protocol** nodes, all unnamed nodes, and all edges except those in **allComponents** and **components**.

6.1 Excerpts of the Study Encoded in Alloy

Figure 5 shows excerpts from the generated Full Alloy* specification. Metamodels $\mathcal{M}_1$ and $\mathcal{M}_2$ are encoded as abstract signatures. The model instance to be sliced is encoded by listing its model elements as singleton signatures. Attribute relations are defined by enumerating all attribute values. The excerpt shows a model instance representing an unnamed system with two components named 0 and 1. The figure also shows the consistency relation CR_{study} encoded as an Alloy predicate. Identifiers suffixed **_m1** and **_m2** refer to the predicate's parameter list (omitted for space reasons). The predicate first introduces abbreviations and then checks relational inclusion and equality. For example, the relations **sysName** (resp. **rootName**) capture the mapping from systems (resp. roots) to names, and **sys2root** relates equally named system/root pairs. The first checked clause ensures that every named system in **sysName** has an equally named root in **rootName**.

```
// Signatures for metamodels M_1 and M_2
abstract sig Link_1, Protocol_1, System_1, Component_1 {}
abstract sig links_1 { source: System_1, target: Link_1 }
abstract sig allProtocols_1 { source: System_1, target: Protocol_1 }
abstract sig allComponents_1 { source: Component_1, target: System_1 }
abstract sig components_1 { source: Link_1, target: Component_1 }
abstract sig protocol_1 { source: Link_1, target: Protocol_1 }
abstract sig supportedProtocols_1 { source: Protocol_1, target: Component_1 }
sig linkName_Source_1 in Link_1{linkName_1: set{v: Int | -8 < v ∧ v < 8}}
sig protName_Source_1 in Protocol_1{protName_1: set{v: Int | -8 < v ∧ v < 8}}
sig sysName_Source_1 in System_1{sysName_1: set{v: Int | -8 < v ∧ v < 8}}
sig compName_Source_1 in Component_1{compName_1: set{v: Int | -8 < v ∧ v < 8}}

abstract sig Link_2, Entity_2, Root_2 {}
abstract sig allEntities_2 { source: Root_2, target: Entity_2 }
abstract sig entities_2 { source: Link_2, target: Entity_2 }
sig linkName_Source_2 in Link_2{linkName_2: set{v: Int | -8 < x ∧ x < 8}}
sig entityName_Source_2 in Entity_2{entityName_2: set{v: Int| -8 < x ∧ x < 8}}
sig rootName_Source_2 in Root_2{rootName_2: set{v: Int | -8 < x ∧ x < 8}}
// Sample of the singleton signatures for the original model instance
one sig S1 extends System_1 {}
one sig C1, C2 extends Component_1 {}
one sig a0 extends allComponents_1 {} { source = S1 ∧ target = C1 }
one sig a0 extends allComponents_1 {} { source = S1 ∧ target = C2 }
fact { compName_1 = C1->0 + C2->1 }
...
// The signatures for the slice
sig Link_S in Link_1 {}
sig Protocol_S in Protocol_1 {}
sig System_S in System_1 {}
sig Component_S in Component_1 {}
sig links_S in links_1 {} {
    source in System_S ∧ target in Link_S }
sig allProtocols_S in allProtocols_1 {} {
    source in System_S ∧ target in Protocol_S }
sig allComponents_S in allComponents_1 {} {
    source in Component_S ∧ target in System_S }
sig components_S in components_1 {} {
    source in Link_S ∧ target in Component_S }
sig protocol_S in protocol_1 {} {
    source in Link_S ∧ target in Protocol_S }
sig supportedProtocols_S in supportedProtocols_1 {} {
    source in Protocol_S ∧ target in Component_S }
sig linkName_Source_S in linkName_Source_1 { linkName_S: set linkName_1 }
sig protName_Source_S in protName_Source_1 { protName_S: set protName_1 }
sig sysName_Source_S in sysName_Source_1 { sysName_S: set sysName_1 }
sig compName_Source_S in compName_Source_1 { compName_S: set compName_1 }

pred consistent [ /* params for model 1 (..._m1) and model 2 (..._m2) */ ] {
let allComponents = ((~source).(allComponents_m1 <: target)),
    allEntities = ((~source).(allEntities_m2 <: target)),
    entities = ~((~source).(entities_m2 <: target)),
    sys2root = sysName_m1.~rootName_m2,
    components2entity = compName_m1.~entityName_m2,
    link2link = linkName_m1.~linkName_m2
    {   sysName_m1 in sys2root.rootName_m2
        rootName_m2 in ~sys2root.sysName_m1
        compName_m1 in components2entity.entityName_m2
        entityName_m2 in ~components2entity.compName_m1
        linkName_m1 in link2link.linkName_m2
        linkName_m2 in ~link2link.linkName_m1
components2entity.entities=(components2entity.univ<: components_m1).link2link
sys2root.allEntities = (sys2root.univ <: ~allComponents).components2entity }}
// Not shown: fill the M2 signatures with nodes & edges for a complete graph
run{ all Link_m2: set Link_2, Entity_m2: set Entity_2, Root_m2: set Root_2,
    // Edges must be incident to nodes that actually belong to the graph
    allEntities_m2: set Root_m2.(~source:>allEntities_2) & target).Entity_m2,
    .., Link_m2 : Link_2 -> { x: Int | -7 ≤ x and x ≤ 7 },... |
consistent[/* signatures for slice (..._S) and signatures for m2 */]
iff consistent[/* signatures for original model (..._1) and for m2 */]
} for 0 but 4 Int
```

Fig. 5. Alloy excerpts encoding the case study using the Full Star CEGIS procedure.

6.2   Results

To evaluate and compare the scalability of the different implementations, we generated a test bench of 72 problem instances, with the configuration of the sliced model varying in size (10–15/30–45 nodes), density (low/high), and cyclicity (acyclic/cyclic). For each configuration, three random instances were added to the test bench. Experiments were conducted on an AMD EPYC 7742 CPU and 1 TiB of RAM, running Ubuntu 24.04 (kernel 6.17.0-14-generic), with multiple experiments running in parallel. The SAT solver used was SAT4J shipped with the Alloy Analyzer version 6. Alloy* is a fork of Alloy 4.2. The Java Virtual Machine was assigned a maximum heap size of 100 GB.

Figure 6 compares the three implementations. Manual CEGIS is consistently the slowest: on large, low-density acyclic graphs, it exceeds 5 h, while Iterative Star and Full Star finish in 32 s and 19 s, respectively. None of the large high-density instances terminate within the time bound for Manual CEGIS.

Density has the strongest impact on runtime (Fig. 6). On small graphs, high density multiplies runtime by 6× (Full Star), 38× (Iterative Star), and 15× (Manual CEGIS). Cycles have a comparatively moderate influence. On large graphs, cycles increase Full Star runtime by about 10×, while Iterative Star changes only marginally (1.2×). The combination of high density and cycles causes timeouts for Manual CEGIS on all large instances. Under these conditions, Iterative Star also times out in most cases, and only Full Star remains reliable.

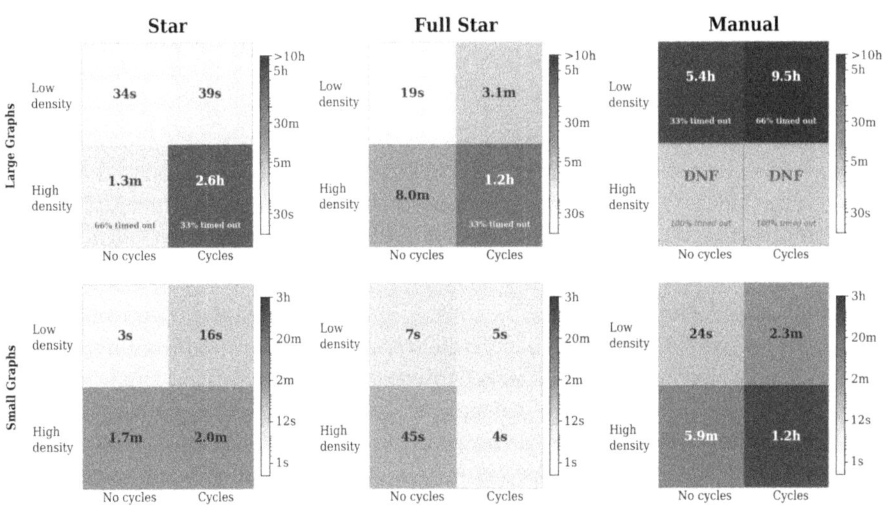

Fig. 6. Runtime Heatmaps: Effects of Density and Cycles (average of completed runs only, DNF is "did not finish within 10h").

From small to large graphs (acyclic, low density), runtime increases by about 3× for Full Star, 12× for Iterative Star, and nearly three orders of magnitude for

Manual CEGIS (24 s to over 5 h). This suggests that explicit orchestration of the synthesis loop scales poorly compared to analyzer-internal quantification. Iterative Star is the most memory-efficient implementation. On large graphs without cycles and low density, it peaks at 1.7 GB on average, compared to 5.3 GB for Full Star and 46 GB for Manual CEGIS. Manual CEGIS execution is dominated by CNF construction (about 90% of runtime), generating 100–800× more clauses than Full Star (up to 266 million), explaining runtime and memory behavior.

We also applied our approach to the motivating example from Fig. 3, an extremely sparse graph comprising 95 nodes and 226 edges. On this instance, the Manual procedure performed best and completed in 36 min (of which 35 min were spent in the SAT solver) after two iterations. Iterative Star timed out, and Full Star produced a spuriously empty result, likely because of an internal out-of-memory error in the solver. One reason for this difference may be that in this example the slice was very small (all nodes of the state chart were to be dropped), and Manual seems to favour more aggressive reductions, resulting in fewer procedure iterations (3.1 on average vs 7.1 for Star).

6.3   Discussion and Limitations

Encoding of Attributed Typed Graphs. The implementation uses a relational encoding for SAT solving rather than mirroring the theoretical ATG formulation. Attributions are represented as relations, and data values belong to bounded integer intervals. This design keeps the encoding compact and allows uniform reasoning over structure and data. The trade-off is that extending the prototype to richer ATG variants (e.g., complex data domains) would require adapting the encoding rather than directly reusing the current representation.

Performance limitation. Our implementation demonstrates feasibility, but the runtime remains too high for interactive use, partly due to the repeated analyzer calls. Nevertheless, the approach remains useful for generating meaningful test cases (representative slices or counterexamples) to support the verification and validation of the consistency relation itself, or of additional tools that act on it.

Encoding constraints. Relational encoding has a significant impact on performance. In particular, deeper signature hierarchies increase compilation time during the translation to SAT, and larger universes degrade solving time. We mitigated this by encoding attribute values over a shared value domain, reducing the number of atoms introduced into the analyzer. These observations suggest that analyzer-oriented modeling decisions have a stronger influence on performance than the abstract algorithmic structure of the slicing procedure.

Constructing the quantified set for Alloy.* Alloy* evaluates quantified formulae over a fixed universe, requiring a superstructure of all potential counterexamples. By comparison, Alloy uses bounded instance search over scoped signatures, finding counterexamples by varying these scopes. Consequently, Alloy* relies on an explicit over-approximation of candidate models, making the procedure less direct than in the standard Alloy setting.

7   Conclusion

We addressed the problem of slicing heterogeneous models linked by consistency relations. Unlike program slicing, the goal is not to preserve observable behavior but distinguishability for a consistency predicate. Thus, dependency-based slicing techniques do not apply directly; instead, we adopt a declarative approach.

We define equiconsistency slicing as a synthesis problem: given a model and a consistency predicate, we search for a minimal submodel that remains equiconsistent. This yields a language-agnostic approach independent of both the modeling and the specification formalism. The problem is solved using a CEGIS loop combining counterexample search, classification, and slide synthesis. Our empirical evaluation stresses several practical observations. First, quantified solving outperforms explicit CEGIS in most of the use cases with few outliers as exception. Second, when models are represented as graphs, structural density dominates runtime more than raw size.

Our approach still has inherent limitations. Guarantees are bounded and therefore relative to a finite domain, and the method relies on the availability of a consistency oracle, which may be expensive or undecidable in richer languages. Moreover, the workflow is currently batch-oriented and not yet incremental. These limitations suggest several research directions, including symbolic encodings for unbounded reasoning (e.g., SMT-based implementations), support for richer consistency languages such as rule-based constraints or transformations, and improved analyzer integration to make the presented approach more suitable for practical modeling environments.

Overall, this work shows that equiconsistency slicing can be understood as a synthesis problem, demonstrating how model synthesis enables language-agnostic techniques for heterogeneous models and could, for instance, be adapted to repair inconsistencies.

References

1. Abate, A., David, C., Kesseli, P., Kroening, D., Polgreen, E.: Counterexample guided inductive synthesis modulo theories. In: Chockler, H., Weissenbacher, G. (eds.) CAV 2018. LNCS, vol. 10981, pp. 270–288. Springer, Cham (2018). https://doi.org/10.1007/978-3-319-96145-3_15
2. Ahmadi, R., Posse, E., Dingel, J.: Slicing UML-based models of real-time embedded systems. In: MODELS, pp. 346–356 (2018). https://doi.org/10.1145/3239372.3239407
3. Ambler, S.W.: The Object Primer: Agile Model-Driven Development with UML 2.0, 3 edn. (2004). https://doi.org/10.1017/CBO9780511584077
4. Androutsopoulos, K., Clark, D., Harman, M., Krinke, J., Tratt, L.: State-based model slicing: a survey. ACM Comput. Surv. **45**(4), 53:1–53:36 (2013). https://doi.org/10.1145/2501654.2501667
5. Barros, J.B., da Cruz, D., Henriques, P.R., Pinto, J.S.: Assertion-based slicing and slice graphs. Form. Asp. Comput. **24**(2), 217–248 (2012). https://doi.org/10.1007/s00165-011-0196-1

6. Beckert, B., Bormer, T., Gocht, S., Herda, M., Lentzsch, D., Ulbrich, M.: Using relational verification for program slicing. In: SEFM, pp. 353–372 (2019)
7. Binkley, D., Danicic, S., Gyimóthy, T., Harman, M., Kiss, Á., Korel, B.: Theoretical foundations of dynamic program slicing. Theor. Comput. Sci. **360**(1), 23–41 (2006). https://doi.org/10.1016/j.tcs.2006.01.012
8. Blouin, A., Moha, N., Baudry, B., Sahraoui, H., Jézéquel, J.M.: Assessing the use of slicing-based visualizing techniques on the understanding of large metamodels. Inf. Softw. Technol. **62**, 124–142 (2015). https://doi.org/10.1016/j.infsof.2015.02.007
9. Bowman, H., Steen, M., Boiten, E., Derrick, J.: A formal framework for viewpoint consistency. Form. Methods Syst. Des. **21**(2), 111–166 (2002). https://doi.org/10.1023/A:1016000201864
10. Canfora, G., Cimitile, A., De Lucia, A.: Conditioned program slicing. Inf. Softw. Technol. **40**(11), 595–607 (1998). https://doi.org/10.1016/S0950-5849(98)00086-X
11. Ehrig, H., Prange, U., Taentzer, G.: Fundamental theory for typed attributed graph transformation. In: Ehrig, H., Engels, G., Parisi-Presicce, F., Rozenberg, G. (eds.) ICGT 2004. LNCS, vol. 3256, pp. 161–177. Springer, Heidelberg (2004). https://doi.org/10.1007/978-3-540-30203-2_13
12. Färber, H., Pascual, R., Stübinger, T., Ulbrich, M.: Observable semantics for characterising consistency between heterogeneous models. In: SEFM, pp. 110–128 (2026). https://doi.org/10.1007/978-3-032-10444-1_7
13. Hailpern, B., Tarr, P.: Model-driven development: the good, the bad, and the ugly. IBM Syst. J. **45**(3), 451–461 (2006). https://doi.org/10.1147/sj.453.0451
14. Halder, R., Cortesi, A.: Abstract program slicing on dependence condition graphs. Sci. Comput. Program. **78**(9), 1240–1263 (2013). https://doi.org/10.1016/j.scico.2012.05.007
15. Horwitz, S., Reps, T., Binkley, D.: Interprocedural slicing using dependence graphs. ACM Trans. Program. Lang. Syst. **12**(1), 26–60 (1990). https://doi.org/10.1145/77606.77608
16. Jackson, D.: Alloy: a lightweight object modelling notation. ACM Trans. Softw. Eng. Methodol. **11**(2), 256–290 (2002). https://doi.org/10.1145/505145.505149
17. Jha, S., Gulwani, S., Seshia, S.A., Tiwari, A.: Oracle-guided component-based program synthesis. In: ICSE, pp. 215–224 (2010). https://doi.org/10.1145/1806799.1806833
18. Korel, B., Singh, I., Tahat, L., Vaysburg, B.: Slicing of state-based models. In: ICSME, pp. 34–43 (2003). https://doi.org/10.1109/icsm.2003.1235404
19. Lano, K., Kolahdouz-Rahimi, S.: Slicing of UML models using model transformations. In: Petriu, D.C., Rouquette, N., Haugen, Ø. (eds.) MODELS 2010. LNCS, vol. 6395, pp. 228–242. Springer, Heidelberg (2010). https://doi.org/10.1007/978-3-642-16129-2_17
20. Lee, W.K., Chung, I.S., Yoon, G.S., Kwon, Y.R.: Specification-based program slicing and its applications. J. Syst. Archit. **47**(5), 427–443 (2001)
21. Lity, S., Lachmann, R., Lochau, M., Schaefer, I.: Delta-oriented software product line test models - the body comfort system case study. Technical report, TU Braunschweig (2013)
22. Milicevic, A., Near, J.P., Kang, E., Jackson, D.: Alloy*: a general-purpose higher-order relational constraint solver. Formal Methods Syst. Des. **55**(1), 1–32 (2017). https://doi.org/10.1007/s10703-016-0267-2
23. Pascual, R., Beckert, B., Ulbrich, M., Kirsten, M., Pfeifer, W.: Formal foundations of consistency in model-driven development. In: ISoLA. LNCS (2024)

24. Pietsch, C., Ohrndorf, M., Kelter, U., Kehrer, T.: Incrementally slicing editable submodels. In: ASE, pp. 913–918 (2017). https://doi.org/10.1109/ASE.2017.8115704
25. Salay, R., Kokaly, S., Chechik, M.: Heterogeneous megamodel slicing for model evolution. In: ME@MODELS, pp. 50–59 (2016)
26. Shaikh, A., Wiil, U.K., Memon, N.: Evaluation of tools and slicing techniques for efficient verification of UML/OCL class diagrams. Adv. Softw. Eng. **2011**(1), 370198 (2011). https://doi.org/10.1155/2011/370198
27. Spanoudakis, G., Zisman, A.: Inconsistency management in software engineering: survey and open research issues. In: Handbook of Software Engineering and Knowledge Engineering, pp. 329–380 (2001). https://doi.org/10.1142/9789812389718_0015
28. Taentzer, G., Kehrer, T., Pietsch, C., Kelter, U.: A formal framework for incremental model slicing. In: Russo, A., Schürr, A. (eds.) FASE 2018. LNCS, vol. 10802, pp. 3–20. Springer, Cham (2018). https://doi.org/10.1007/978-3-319-89363-1_1
29. Thieme, M.: Slicing Models for Equiconsistency with Alloy - Replication Package (2026). https://doi.org/10.5281/zenodo.18706490
30. Tip, F.: A survey of program slicing techniques. J. Program. Lang. **3**(3), 121–189 (1995)
31. Torlak, E., Jackson, D.: Kodkod: a relational model finder. In: TACAS, pp. 632–647 (2007)
32. Weiser, M.: Program slicing. IEEE Trans. Softw. Eng. **SE-10**(4), 352–357 (1984). https://doi.org/10.1109/TSE.1984.5010248

Encoding BDI Syntax with Theories in Event-B

Mengwei Xu[1]([✉]) [iD], Peter Rivière[2] [iD], Toshiaki Aoki[2] [iD], Marie Farrell[3] [iD], Yamine Aït Ameur[4] [iD], Neeraj Kumar Singh[4] [iD], and Guillaume Dupont[4] [iD]

[1] Newcastle University, Newcastle upon Tyne, UK
mengwei.xu@newcastle.ac.uk
[2] Japan Advanced Institute of Science and Technology, Nomi, Japan
{priviere,toshiaki}@jaist.ac.jp
[3] The University of Manchester, Manchester, UK
marie.farrell@manchester.ac.uk
[4] IRIT, Toulouse National Polytechnique Institute - CNRS, Université de Toulouse, Toulouse, France
{yamine,nsingh}@enseeiht.fr, guillaume.dupont@toulouse-inp.fr

Abstract. The Belief–Desire–Intention (BDI) paradigm is a popular framework in the development of autonomous systems. However, assuring the correct design of BDI agents remains difficult: existing modelling formalisms often require ad-hoc encodings of BDI agents that can be difficult to validate, maintain, and reason about. This paper focuses on modelling the syntax of BDI agents and shows how algebraic modelling in Event-B theories (e.g. inductive data types and polymorphic constructors) yields a faithful, compact, and reusable encoding of BDI syntax. Even without committing to the full BDI semantics, the encoding already supports useful reasoning, including belief entailment and belief-based invariant checking, and provides a path towards a future BDI semantic encoding via operators in theories and machine events in Event-B.

Keywords: BDI agents · Algebraic modelling · Event-B theories

1 Introduction

The Belief–Desire–Intention (BDI) paradigm [15] has been a popular framework to design and develop autonomous systems that make decisions and execute actions without human intervention, e.g. in robotics [12]. Rooted in Bratman's philosophical work [10], the (B)eliefs represent what the agent knows, the (D)esires what the agent wants to bring about, and the (I)ntentions those desires that the agent has committed to act upon. For instance, a robot may maintain

---

This work was partially supported by the Royal Academy of Engineering, EPSRC grant EP/Y001532/1, ANR-19-CE25-0010 *EBRP:EventB-Rodin-Plus* project and JST, CREST Grant Number JPMJCR23M1.

© The Author(s), under exclusive license to Springer Nature Switzerland AG 2026
F. Ishikawa and A. Cunha (Eds.): ABZ 2026, LNCS 16579, pp. 210–228, 2026.
https://doi.org/10.1007/978-3-032-26752-8_13

beliefs about its current position and nearby hazards, desires such as reaching a particular inspection location, and intentions of the current navigation plan.

However, assuring the correct design of BDI agents is challenging due to: (i) modelling expressiveness and (ii) analysis scalability. The former is limited because many existing modelling formalisms are effective for the domains that they target (e.g. communication systems) but are not tailored to BDI agents. Using these modelling languages often leads to ad-hoc encodings that are difficult to validate or reuse. The latter persists because model checking—a popular verification technique for BDI agents—suffers from state space explosion [13] as agent complexity increases for realistic scenarios, despite its high automation.

Significant work on formal modelling and analysis of BDI agents is surveyed in [26]. Many approaches adapt modelling formalisms originally intended for their target domains to BDI agents through ad-hoc encodings. For example, one of the earliest approaches [6] employs Promela [23], a modelling language for communication-based systems, to model and analyse BDI agents with the Spin model checker [22]. Similarly, the work [5,19] use re-writing logics either term-based (e.g. Maude [14]) or graph-based (e.g. Bigraphs [27]) to model BDI agents. The work [17] even avoids the modelling process by employing the program model checker Java PathFinder [20] directly on Java implementations of BDI languages e.g. Gwendolen [16]. While useful, the exhaustive state exploration in model checking leaves them vulnerable to state space explosion. To address this, recent proof-based approaches specify BDI agents in proof assistants (e.g. Isabelle/HOL [28]) using algebraic data types [24,31] on two simple BDI agents (GOAL [21] and SimpleBDI [18]) where the BDI plans only have actions (e.g. no sub-goals). In contrast, we use Event-B theories to model BDI syntax algebraically without simplification, while retaining Event-B's state-based style for future work on modelling the configuration-transition BDI semantics.

In this paper, we present an algebraic modelling approach to encode the syntax of a fully fledged BDI programming language, specified in the Conceptual Agent Notation (CAN), using Event-B formalism [1]. CAN is chosen as it includes advanced BDI agent behaviours such as declarative goals, concurrency, and failure recovery. The same modelling techniques here would apply to other BDI languages. We access algebraic modelling through Event-B theories [11] to define inductive data types and polymorphic constructors that faithfully mirror the vocabulary of the CAN syntax as written. The encoding, as implemented in Rodin [2], is both total and injective with respect to the original CAN syntax. The outcome is a suite of self-contained Event-B theories that serve as a foundation for specifying concrete BDI agent programs, keeping models reusable.

In Sect. 2, we introduce the preliminaries for the CAN language with a running example and Event-B formalism; Sect. 3 presents algebraic modelling of CAN syntax in Event-B theories; Sect. 4 shows possible reasoning mechanisms for our modelling without attaching to any specific BDI semantics; Sect. 5 discusses related work and Sect. 6 concludes and outlines future work.

2   Preliminaries

2.1   CAN Syntax

We give an overview of the syntax of the CAN language from [29,30] to which we refer for full details and a running example of CAN agents. A CAN agent consists of a belief base, $\mathcal{B}$, a plan library, Π, and an action description library, Λ. The syntax of a CAN agent is constructed by three main types of predicate symbols, namely event predicate symbols, e, belief predicate symbols, b, and action predicate symbols, act. Together with terms, they form the events, beliefs, and actions. Standard first-order terms and free/bound variables are used. For example, terms (resp. vector terms) in CAN are denoted as t (resp. $\mathbf{t}$), and we can write $e(\mathbf{t})$, $b(\mathbf{t})$, and $act(\mathbf{t})$ to denote events, beliefs, and actions, respectively.

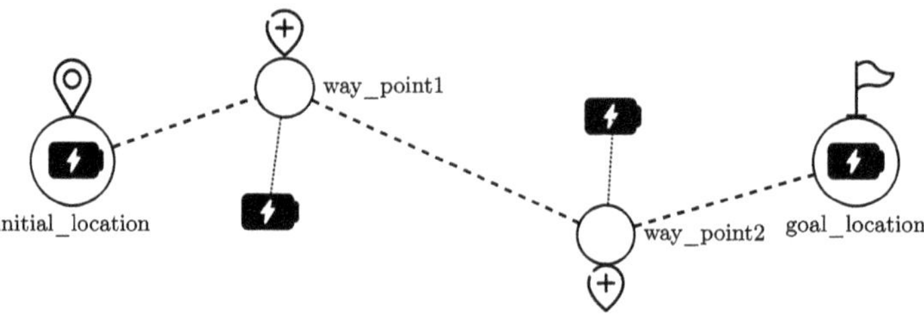

Fig. 1. Rover navigation and charging scenario with two way points.

The *belief base*, $\mathcal{B}$, represents the current beliefs of the agent. If b is a predicate symbol, and $t_1, \ldots, t_n$ are terms, then $b(t_1, \ldots, t_n)$ or $b(\mathbf{t})$ is a belief atom. Such an atom is *ground* if all terms in $\mathbf{t}$ are ground terms, i.e. it contains no variables. The belief base $\mathcal{B}$ is defined as a set of ground belief atoms.

A *plan library*, Π, contains the operational procedures and is a finite collection of plans of the form $e(\mathbf{t}) : \varphi(\mathbf{x_t}, \mathbf{y}) \leftarrow P(\mathbf{x_t}, \mathbf{y})$. Here, $e(\mathbf{t})$ is the triggering event of this plan, $\varphi(\mathbf{x_t}, \mathbf{y})$ is the context condition, and $P(\mathbf{x_t}, \mathbf{y})$ is the plan-body. The triggering event, $e(\mathbf{t})$, specifies *why* the plan is triggered, while the context condition, $\varphi(\mathbf{x_t}, \mathbf{y})$, determines *when* the plan-body P is applicable. The variable $\mathbf{x_t}$ denotes all of the free variables in the terms $\mathbf{t}$, and variables $\mathbf{y}$ are those free variables that do not appear in the triggering event but are introduced in the context condition, generally to bind objects that are to be used in the plan-body, $P(\mathbf{x_t}, \mathbf{y})$. The context condition $\varphi(\mathbf{x_t}, \mathbf{y})$ is a belief formula, built from belief atoms using the standard logical connectives, with syntax $\varphi ::= b(\mathbf{t}) \mid \neg\varphi \mid \varphi \wedge \varphi \mid \varphi \vee \varphi$. Unlike the belief base, which contains only ground belief atoms, a context condition may contain free variables. Such variables are interpreted semantically with respect to the current grounded belief base.

Events may arise either from the external environment or from within the execution of a plan-body. We write E^e for the set of external events. Events

```
 1  // Initial belief base
 2  at(init_loc), power(high), next(init_loc,WP1), next(WP1,WP2), next(WP2,goal_loc)
 3  nearest(init_loc,init_loc_charge), nearest(init_loc_charge, init_loc)
 4  nearest(WP1,WP1_charge), nearest(WP1_charge,WP1)
 5  nearest(WP2,WP2_charge), nearest(WP2_charge, WP2),
 6  nearest(goal_loc,goal_loc_charge), nearest(goal_loc_charge, goal_loc)
```

(a) Belief base.

```
 1  // Initial external events
 2  start(mission)
 3  // Plan library.
 4  start(mission):at(X)<-goal(at(goal_loc), navigate(goal_loc),power(empty)∧¬at(goal_loc))
 6  navigate(Z):at(goal_loc)<-stop(Z)
 7  navigate(Z):at(X)∧next(X,Y)∧¬power(empty)<-movement(X,Y);navigate(Z)
 8  navigate(Z):at(X)∧nearest(X,C)∧power(low) <-
 9      charge_locate(X,C); charge(C); charge_locate(C,X); navigate(Z)
10  movement(X,Y): power(high) <- move_high(X,Y)
11  movement(X,Y): power(low) <- move_low(X,Y)
```

(b) Plan library.

```
 1  // Action Description Library
 2  move_high(X,Y):at(X)∧next(X,Y)∧power(high)<- ⟨{at(Y), power(low)},{at(X), power(high)}⟩
 3  move_low(X,Y):at(X)∧next(X,Y)∧power(low)<- ⟨{at(Y), power(empty)},{at(X), power(low)}⟩
 4  charge_locate(X,C): at(X) ∧ nearest(X,C) <- ⟨{at(C)},{at(X)}⟩
 5  charge(C): at(C) ∧ power(low) <- ⟨{power(high)},{power(low)}⟩
 6  stop(Z): ⊤ <- ⟨∅,∅⟩
```

(c) Action description library

Fig. 2. BDI agent design and plan library in the rover scenario

occurring as part of a plan-body (which will be introduced next) are called *sub-events* or *internal events*. For presentation convenience, we may omit arguments of terms when they do not confuse, e.g. e in place of $e(\mathbf{t})$.

By convention e.g. in [7], the user-defined plan-body, P, may be referred to as the *program* or *agent program* and has the following syntax:

$$P::= \ act \mid ?\varphi \mid +b \mid -b \mid e \mid P_1;P_2 \mid P_1 \parallel P_2 \mid goal(\varphi_s, e, \varphi_f)$$

where act is an action, $?\varphi$ a test for φ entailment in the belief base, $+b$ and $-b$ represent belief addition and deletion respectively, and e is a sub-event (i.e. internal event). To execute a sub-event, a corresponding plan is selected and the plan-body is added in place of the event. In this way, plans can be nested. Actions, act, (from the action description library Λ) take the form $act = \psi \leftarrow \langle \phi^+, \phi^- \rangle$, where ψ is the pre-condition, and ϕ^+ and ϕ^- are the addition and deletion sets of belief atoms. There are also composite programs $P_1;P_2$ for sequence and $P_1 \parallel P_2$ for interleaved concurrency. Finally, a declarative goal, $goal(\varphi_s, e, \varphi_f)$, expresses that the state, φ_s, should be achieved through addressing the event, e, failing if φ_f is true, and re-trying if neither φ_s nor φ_f are true.

2.2   A Running Example: Rover Navigation and Charging

Figure 1 presents a rover navigation and charging scenario (adapted from [8,9, 12]). The rover must reach `goal_loc` from `init_loc` by traversing a sequence

Table 1. Structure of Event-B contexts, machines, and theories.

(a)	(b)	(c)
Context	**Machine**	**Theory**
CONTEXT Ctx	MACHINE M	THEORY Th
SETS s	SEES Ctx	IMPORT $Th1, \ldots$
CONSTANTS c	VARIABLES x	TYPE PARAMETERS $E, F, \ldots$
AXIOMS $A(s, c)$	INVARIANTS $I(x)$	DATA TYPES
THEOREMS $T_{ctx}(s, c)$	EVENTS	Type1$(E, \ldots)$
END	EVENT evt	constructors
	ANY α	cstr1$(p_1 : T_1, \ldots)$
	WHERE $G(x, a)$	AXIOMATIC DEFINITIONS
	$x :\| BAP(\alpha, x, x')$	TYPES $A_1, \ldots$
	END	OPERATORS
	...	AOp2 <nature> $(p_1 : T_1, \ldots): T_r$
	END	well$-$definedness $WD(p_1, \ldots)$
		AXIOMS $A_1, \ldots$
		END

of waypoints (WPs), and it must detour to a nearby charging station when the power is low. To capture this rover scenario in $\textsc{Can}$, we instantiate a BDI agent as follows. The initial belief base (Fig. 2a) captures the topology using belief predicates `at(X)`, `next(X,Y)`, and `nearest(X,C)`. The rover's power level is modelled using three mutually exclusive belief atoms: `power(high)`, `power(low)`, and `power(empty)`, initially set to `power(high)` on line 2.

The rover's mission is initiated by the external `start(mission)` event on line 2 of Fig. 2b. This event is addressed by the plan (line 4) through a declarative goal to achieve `at(goal_loc)` via the internal event, `navigate(goal_loc)`. The goal succeeds when the rover reaches the goal location, and fails when its power is empty and it is not at the goal location (i.e. `power(empty)`$\land\neg$`at(goal_loc)`).

Navigation proceeds in discrete steps. When the rover is not in the empty-power state, it advances along the waypoint chain using `next(X,Y)` (line 7). Rather than directly calling a movement action, the plan delegates to an internal event, `movement(X,Y)`, which branches depending on the current power status (lines 10–11). The corresponding action description (lines 2–3 of Fig. 2c) updates the location to `at(Y)` and degrades the power from high to low or low to empty.

When the rover is in the low-power mode, it can also take a charging detour (lines 8–9). Using `nearest(X,C)`, the agent relocates to the nearest charging station C via `charge_locate(X,C)`, which consumes negligible power, performs `charge(C)` to restore `power(high)`, and then returns to the original waypoint X via `charge_locate(C,X)` before resuming `navigate(Z)`. We note that, in low-power situations, the two `navigate(Z)` plans (lines 7–8) may both be applicable, and one plan is selected non-deterministically by the agent. Once `at(goal_loc)` holds, the termination plan triggers `stop(Z)` (line 6), i.e. doing nothing.

Throughout this paper, we will use this running example to illustrate how the Event-B theories in the Rodin platform can encode BDI syntax.

2.3 Event-B

We briefly recall the relevant Event-B notions we use in this paper [1]. A *context* (Table 1(a)) provides static modelling via carrier sets, s, constants, c, axioms, $A(s, c)$ and theorems, $T_{ctx}(s, c)$. A *machine* (Table 1(b)) provides a state-based model via variables, x, invariants, $I(x)$, and events (with before–after updates). Proof obligations are generated by the Rodin Platform to ensure invariant preservation, among other things. To support algebraic modelling beyond core set theory and first-order logic, we use Event-B *theories* [3,11]. A theory (Table 1(c)) can import others and define polymorphic data types and operators, either by constructors or axiomatically. We will provide further details on Event-B theories (and, later, machines and events) where required for encoding BDI agents.

```
1   THEORY TermsTheory
2   AXIOMATIC DEFINITIONS
3    TYPES:  Terms
4    OPERATORS
5      PointTerms:  ℙ(Terms)
6      TwoAryVectorTerms:  ℙ(Terms)
7        . . .
8      NAryVectorTerms:  ℙ(Terms)
9      TwoAryVectorFunction(P₁:  Terms,  P₂:  Terms)  :  Terms
10       well−definedness:
11            P₁ ∈ PointTerms
12            P₂ ∈ PointTerms
13       . . .
14      NAryVectorFunction(P₁:  Terms,  P₂:  Terms,  ⋯,  Pₙ:  Terms)  :  Terms
15       well−definedness:
16            P₁ ∈ PointTerms
17            P₂ ∈ PointTerms
18            . . .
19            Pₙ ∈ PointTerms
20   AXIOMS
21     axm1:  partition(Terms, PointTerms, TwoAryVectorTerms, ⋯, NAryVectorTerms)
22     axm2:  ∀P₁, P₂ · P₁ ∈ PointTerms ∧ P₂ ∈ PointTerms
23            ⇒ TwoAryVectorFunction(P₁, P₂) ∈ TwoAryVectorTerms
24     axm3:  ∀P · P ∈ TwoAryVectorTerms
25            ⇒ (∃P₁, P₂ · P₁ ∈ PointTerms ∧ P₂ ∈ PointTerms
26                                    ∧P = TwoAryVectorFunction(P₁, P₂))
27        . . .
```

Fig. 3. Event-B theory for terms

3 Encoding the Syntax of CAN in Event-B

In this section, we encode CAN syntax in Event-B (theories and contexts in Rodin). We treat predicate symbols (belief, event, action) and terms as primitive alphabets that are introduced axiomatically, and encode the inductive fragments (e.g. plan-bodies) using recursive data-type definitions.

```
1  CONTEXT TermsRoverNavigation
2  CONSTANTS init_loc, WP1, WP2, goal_loc, mission, empty, low, high,
3            init_loc_charge, WP1_loc_charge, WP2_loc_charge, goal_loc_charge
4  AXIOMS
5    axm1: partition(PointTerms, {init_loc}, {WP1}, {WP2}, {goal_loc}, {mission}, {empty}
6                    {low}, {high}, {init_loc_charge}, {WP1_loc_charge}, {WP2_loc_charge},
7                    {goal_loc_charge})
```

Fig. 4. Context for terms in rover scenario.

```
1  THEORY PredicateSymbolsTheory
2  AXIOMATIC DEFINITIONS
3  TYPES: Event_predicate_symbols, Belief_predicate_symbols, Action_predicate_symbols
```

Fig. 5. Event-B theory for predicate symbols.

3.1   Terms

We begin with first-order terms including point terms (i.e. non-vector terms) and vector terms. Vector terms apply an n-ary function, f, $(n \geq 2)$ to point terms, written as $f(t_1, \ldots, t_n)$ (or $\mathbf{t}$). For CAN, it suffices to restrict the arguments to point terms, without loss of generality, to illustrate our approach. We note that, although first-order logic includes variable terms, we have captured them in Event-B via the quantification and set comprehension over the domain of *ground* terms. Hence, we do not introduce variable terms as a separate syntactic category; instead, we work with the set of ground terms, defined as follows:

$$\langle \text{Terms} \rangle :: = \langle \text{Point-Terms} \rangle \mid \langle \text{Vector-Terms} \rangle$$

$$\langle \text{Vector-Terms} \rangle :: = \langle \text{N-Ary-Function} \rangle (\langle \text{Point-Terms} \rangle_1, \ldots, \langle \text{Point-Terms} \rangle_n)$$

$$\langle \text{N-Ary-Function} \rangle :: = f \text{ where } f \text{ is an } n\text{-ary function}, n \geq 2, n \in \mathbb{N}$$

The axiomatic definition in Fig. 3 models $\langle \text{Terms} \rangle$ with the user-defined type, $Terms$, as the collection of all grounded terms (line 3). A list of nullary operators e.g. $PointTerms$ and $TwoAryVectorTerms$ in OPERATORS (lines 4–19), is introduced with type $\mathbb{P}(Terms)$ to denote particular subsets of $Terms$. Here, a nullary operator is a constant that encodes an entity with an explicit type.

Meanwhile, **axm1** (line 21) specifies that the named subsets form a partition of the whole domain of terms. The $TwoAryVectorFunction$ operator (lines 9–12) constructs two-ary vector terms from two point terms. Its well-definedness ensures that both arguments lie in $PointTerms$. Both **axm2** and **axm3** formally describe the well-definedness between $PointTerms$ and $TwoAryVectorTerms$. The **axm2** specifies that applying $TwoAryVectorFunction$ to any two point terms yields an element of $TwoAryVectorTerms$. And **axm3** goes in the other direction: any element in $TwoAryVectorTerms$ arises from some pair of point terms. Similar explanations (omitted) can be given for $NAryVectorFunction$.

To provide domain-specific terms, we can import this theory and apply it to any context within any Rodin project. Recall that, in the Rover navigation scenario, the terms include all locations, `mission` to start mission, and `empty` to `high` for the battery status. To encode them in Event-B, we can have the context shown in Fig. 4. The name of this context is given in the CONTEXT clause (line 1). It first declares all constants e.g. *init_ loc* in the CONSTANTS clause. Then **axm1** (lines 5–7) assigns them as the only elements of *PointTerms*. This yields a finite, grounded set of point terms for the rover navigation scenario. We will show how to construct vector terms from point terms using the *TwoAryVectorFunction* operator when encoding the belief base.

3.2   Predicate Symbols

We have modelled terms, but predicates consist of both predicate symbols and terms. We now encode predicate symbols by introducing their types (no operators or axioms) in a separate axiomatic definition (see Fig. 5), which can be imported for domain-specific extensions. For the rover scenario, belief symbols include `at`, `next`, `nearest`, and `power`; event symbols have `start`, `navigate`, and `movement`; and action symbols contain `move_high`, `move_low`, `charge_locate`, `charge`, and `stop`. These are categorised in a context (Fig. 6).

```
1   CONTEXT  PredicateSymbolsRoverNavigation
2   CONSTANTS  at ,next ,nearest ,power ,start ,navigate , ,movement ,
3              move_high ,move_low ,charge_locate ,charge ,stop ,
4   AXIOMS
5     axm1:  partition(Belief_predicate_symbols, {at}, {next}, {nearest}, {power})
6     axm2:  partition(Event_predicate_symbols, {start}, {navigate}, {movement})
7     axm3:  partition(Action_predicate_symbols, {move_high}, {move_low}, {charge_locate},
8                    {charge}, {stop})
```

Fig. 6. Context for predicate symbols in rover scenario.

```
1   THEORY  InitialBeliefBaseExternalEventsTheory
2   IMPORT  TermDefinition ,  PredicateSymbolsDefinition
3   AXIOMATIC DEFINITIONS
4    OPERATORS
5      Initial_belief_base:  ℙ(Belief_predicate_symbols × Terms)
6      Initial_external_events:  ℙ(Event_predicate_symbols × Terms)
```

Fig. 7. Theory for initial beliefs base and external events.

```
1    CONTEXT  InitialBeliefBaseExternalEventsRoboticCleaning
2    AXIOMS
3      axm1:  Initial_belief_base = {
4             (at ↦ init_loc), (power ↦ high), (next ↦ TwoAryVectorFunction(init_loc, WP1))
5             (next ↦ TwoAryVectorFunction(WP1, WP2)),
6             (next ↦ TwoAryVectorFunction(WP2, goal_loc)),
7             (nearest ↦ TwoAryVectorFunction(init_loc, init_charge)),
8             (nearest ↦ TwoAryVectorFunction(init_charge, init_loc)),
9             (nearest ↦ TwoAryVectorFunction(WP1, WP1_charge)),
10            (nearest ↦ TwoAryVectorFunction(WP1_charge, WP1)),
11            (nearest ↦ TwoAryVectorFunction(WP2, WP2_charge)),
12            (nearest ↦ TwoAryVectorFunction(WP2_charge, WP2)),
13            (nearest ↦ TwoAryVectorFunction(goal_loc, goal_loc_charge)),
14            (nearest ↦ TwoAryVectorFunction(goal_loc_charge, goal_loc)}
15     axm2:  Initial_external_events = {(start ↦ mission)}
```

Fig. 8. Initial belief base and external events for rover scenario.

3.3 Initial Belief Base and External Events

Building on the term and predicate symbol theories, we encode the initial belief base and external events as *typed constants* (nullary operators) in an axiomatic theory. Concretely, Fig. 7 declares *Initial_belief_base* with type $\mathbb{P}(Belief\_predicate\_symbols \times Terms)$ (and similarly for the initial external events). The theory only fixes these types; a separate context instantiates them for the rover case study in Fig. 8. For example, `next(init_loc, WP1)` is encoded as $(next \mapsto TwoAryVectorFunction(init\_loc, WP1))$ on line 4, and the sole external event `start(mission)` is encoded as $(start \mapsto mission)$ on line 15.

3.4 Agent Programs

$\langle\text{UserP}\rangle ::= \langle\text{BasicP}\rangle \mid \langle\text{UserP}\rangle ; \langle\text{UserP}\rangle \mid$

$\qquad\qquad \langle\text{UserP}\rangle \| \langle\text{UserP}\rangle \mid goal(\langle\text{BeliefFormula}\rangle, \mathbf{e}, \langle\text{BeliefFormula}\rangle)$

$\langle\text{BasicP}\rangle ::= \mathbf{e} \mid \mathbf{act}$

$\langle\text{BeliefFormula}\rangle ::= \mathbf{b} \mid \neg\langle\text{BeliefFormula}\rangle \mid \langle\text{BeliefFormula}\rangle \wedge \langle\text{BeliefFormula}\rangle \mid$

$\qquad\qquad \langle\text{BeliefFormula}\rangle \vee \langle\text{BeliefFormula}\rangle \mid \top \mid \bot$

Fig. 9. Grammar for agent programs.

We now proceed to encode agent programs using inductive data types. Recall that the user-defined plan-body, P, in a plan, $\mathbf{e} : \varphi \leftarrow P$, is often called an agent program. The grammar for agent programs in CAN is formally given in Fig. 9 where the grammar category $\langle\text{UserP}\rangle$ denotes plan-body P. $\langle\text{UserP}\rangle$ can be the basic building block $\langle\text{BasicP}\rangle$ including an internal event $\mathbf{e}$ or an action $\mathbf{act}$. We have omitted the inclusion of $+b$, $-b$, and $?\varphi$ as they can be seen as special cases of actions. For example $?\varphi$ can be seen as $act : \varphi \leftarrow \langle\emptyset, \emptyset\rangle$ whereas $+b$ as $act : \top \leftarrow \langle\{b\}, \emptyset\rangle$. $\langle\text{UserP}\rangle$ can also be a declarative goal $goal(\langle\text{BeliefFormula}\rangle, e, \langle\text{BeliefFormula}\rangle)$. In a declarative goal, $\langle\text{BeliefFormula}\rangle$ represents the belief formula which is defined over a finite set of belief atoms, At, such that $\mathbf{b} \in At$ using the standard logical connectives ($\neg$, $\wedge$, and $\vee$). The first belief formula represents the success state (i.e. φ_s) to achieve through addressing an internal event, e, failing when the second belief formula representing a failure condition (i.e. φ_f) holds, and retrying as long as neither of these two belief formulas is true. Finally, $\langle\text{UserP}\rangle$ can be composed in two ways: (i) $\langle\text{UserP}\rangle ; \langle\text{UserP}\rangle$ executing those two $\langle\text{UserP}\rangle$ in sequence and (ii) $\langle\text{UserP}\rangle \| \langle\text{UserP}\rangle$ executing those two $\langle\text{UserP}\rangle$ concurrently.

The grammar for $\langle\text{UserP}\rangle$ is, by nature, recursive, and also dependent on $\langle\text{BeliefFormula}\rangle$ (which is again recursively defined). To encode $\langle\text{UserP}\rangle$, we first employ the Event-B theory to model a belief formula with an inductive

```
1   THEORY  BeliefFormulaTheory
2   DATATYPE
3     BeliefFormula(propositional_atoms)
4     CONSTRUCTORS
5       Belief_atom(atom : propositional_atoms)
6       Conjunctive_formula(
7           left_formula : BeliefFormula(propositional_atoms)
8           right_formula : BeliefFormula(propositional_atoms))
9       Disjunctive_formula(
10          left_formula : BeliefFormula(propositional_atoms)
11          right_formula : BeliefFormula(propositional_atoms))
12      Negated_formula(formula : BeliefFormula(propositional_atoms))
13      TruthFormula
14      FalseFormula
```

Fig. 10. Event-B theory for belief formula.

```
1   THEORY  AgentProgramsTheory
2   IMPORTS  BeliefFormulaTheory ,  TermsTheory ,  PredicateSymbolsTheory
3   DATATYPE
4     UserP
5     CONSTRUCTORS
6       BasicP_event_user(basic_program_event_user : Event_predicate_symbols × Terms)
7       BasicP_action_user(basic_program_action_user : Action_predicate_symbols × Terms)
8       Sequence_program_user(
9           head_program_user : UserP
10          tail_program_user : UserP)
11      Concurrency_program_user(
12          left_program_user : UserP
13          right_program_user : UserP)
14      Declarative_goal_user(
15          success_condition_user :  BeliefFormula(Belief_predicate_symbols × Terms)
16          event_user :  Event_predicate_symbols × Terms
17          failure_condition_user :  BeliefFormula(Belief_predicate_symbols × Terms))
```

Fig. 11. Event-B theory for agent programs.

data type given in Fig. 10. The DATATYPE header (line 3) makes explicit that *BeliefFormula* is parameterised by a set of propositional atoms. The six polymorphic constructors (lines 4–14) show the recursive nature of the belief formulas. *Belief_atom* (line 5) forms an atomic formula. The constructors on lines 6–12 then encode logical conjunction, disjunction, and negation over sub-formulas. As a result, formulas are built from formulas inductively. Finally, *TruthFormula* and *FalseFormula* (lines 13–14) represent truth and falsehood.

With the defined data type of *BeliefFormula*, we can encode the agent programs in Fig. 11, namely *AgentProgramsTheory* where the data type *UserP* is defined inductively. Here *UserP* builds on the earlier *BeliefFormulaTheory*, *TermsTheory*, and *PredicateSymbolsTheory* by importing them (line 2). *UserP* includes a list of constructors covering all cases from ⟨UserP⟩ in Fig. 9. For example, the constructor of *BasicP_event_user* and *BasicP_action_user* correspond to ⟨BasicP⟩ i.e. event and action. For example, to encode the action `charge(WP1)` to `charge` at the `WP1`, we can have *BasicP_action _user*($charge \mapsto WP1$) where $charge \in Action\_predicate\_symbols$ and $WP1 \in Terms$.

Similarly, compositional constructors including *Sequence_program_user* and *Concurrency_program_user* (lines 8–13) corresponds to ⟨UserP⟩; ⟨UserP⟩

```
1  THEORY  PlanLibraryActionDescriptionLibraryTheory
2  IMPORT  AgentProgramsTheory
3  AXIOMATIC DEFINITIONS
4    OPERATORS
5      plan_library : ℙ((Event_predicate_symbols × Terms)
6                      ×(BeliefFormula(Belief_predicate_symbols × Terms) × UserP))
7      action_description_library :
8        ℙ((Action_predicate_symbols × Terms)
9          ×(BeliefFormula(Belief_predicate_symbols × Terms)
10         ×(ℙ(Belief_predicate_symbols × Terms) × ℙ(Belief_predicate_symbols × Terms))))
```

Fig. 12. Event-B theory for plan/action description library

```
1   CONTEXT  PlanLibraryActionDescriptionLibraryContextRoverNavigation
2   EXTENDS  TermsRoverNavigation , PredicateSymbolsRoverNavigation
3   CONSTANTS plan1 , plan2 , plan3 , plan4 , plan5 , plan6 ,
4              act1 , act2 , act3 , act4 , act5
5   AXIOMS
6     axm1 :  plan_library = plan1 ∪ plan2 ∪ plan3 ∪ plan4 ∪ plan5 ∪ plan6
7     axm2 :  action_description_library = act1 ∪ act2 ∪ act3 ∪ act4 ∪ act5
8     axm3 :  plan1 = {triggering_event, context, plan_body, success_condition,
9                      failure_condition, procedural_program·
10                     triggering_event ∈ Event_predicate_symbols × Terms
11                     ∧triggering_event = start ↦ mission
12                     ∧context = Belief_atom(at ↦ X)
13                     ∧success_condition = Belief_atom(at ↦ goal_loc)
14                     ∧failure_condition = Conjunctive_formula(
15                             Belief_atom(power ↦ empty),
16                             Negated_formula(Belief_atom(at ↦ goal_loc)))
17                     ∧procedural_program ∈ Event_predicate_symbols × Terms
18                     ∧procedural_program = navigate ↦ goal_loc
19                     ∧plan_body = Declarative_goal_user(success_condition,
20                                       procedural_program, failure_condition)
21                     | triggering_event ↦ (context ↦ plan_body)
22                     }
```

Fig. 13. Context of plan/action description library in rover scenario

and $\langle UserP \rangle \parallel \langle UserP \rangle$ to construct sequential and interleaved agent programs over any legitimate agent program. Declarative goals are encoded via the constructor of *Declarative_goal_user*: a user-specified declarative goal is defined in terms of a success condition and a failure condition, both expressed using the *BeliefFormula* data type, along with the procedural program of an event in the middle with the type *Event_predicate_symbols × Terms*.

3.5 Plan Library and Action Description Library

We now encode the plan library, Π, and the action description library, Λ. Recall that Π contains a set of plans, $e : \varphi \leftarrow P$, where e is the triggering event, φ the belief formula, and P is an agent program. The action library, Λ, is the set of actions, $act = \psi \leftarrow \langle \phi^+, \phi^- \rangle$, where ψ is the pre-condition (i.e. a belief formula), and ϕ^+ and ϕ^- are the addition and deletion sets of belief atoms.

Figure 12 axiomatically encodes the plan library and action description library using nullary operators. For example, the nullary operator *plan_library* has type:

```
1   OPERATORS
2     belief_entail <predicate>
3           (belief_base : ℙ(propositional_atoms),
4            formula : BeliefFormula(propositional_atoms))
5     recursive definition
6       case formula :
7         Belief_atom(atom) ⇒ atom ∈ belief_base
8         Conjunctive_formula(left, right) ⇒
9               belief_entail(belief_base, left) ∧ belief_entail(belief_base, right)
10        Disjunctive_formula(left, right) ⇒
11              belief_entail(belief_base, left) ∨ belief_entail(belief_base, right)
12        Negated_formula(f) ⇒ ¬belief_entail(belief_base, f)
13        TruthFormula ⇒ ⊤
14        FalseFormula ⇒ ⊥
```

Fig. 14. Belief entail operator.

$$\mathbb{P}((Event\_predicate\_symbols \times Terms) \times$$
$$(BeliefFormula(Belief\_predicate\_symbols \times Terms) \times UserP)).$$

This means that *plan_library* is a *set of pairs*, $\big((e, t), (\varphi, P)\big)$, where (e, t) is a event predicate symbol with its term, and (φ, P) is a belief formula together with a plan body. The *action_description_library* has a similar structure.

We highlight that this axiomatic definition gives the schema for a potentially infinite set of concrete plan and action instances, especially when some components in a plan and an action, such as terms, are left free. To reason about any concrete instances, we can instantiate this schema using set comprehension, which enumerates all of the grounded plans that satisfy the constraints, such as a *typing condition*. For example, consider a BDI plan:

$$e(\mathbf{t}) : \varphi(\mathbf{x_t}, \mathbf{y}) \leftarrow P(\mathbf{x_t}, \mathbf{y}).$$

This plan defines many concrete plans, depending on the values of the variables $\mathbf{t}, \mathbf{x_t}$, and $\mathbf{y}$. To model concrete instances, we apply the constraints to this general plan rule using set comprehension in Event-B shown as follows:

$$\{\mathbf{t}, \mathbf{x_t}, \mathbf{y} \cdot C(\mathbf{t}, \mathbf{x_t}, \mathbf{y}) \mid e(\mathbf{t}) : \varphi(\mathbf{x_t}, \mathbf{y}) \leftarrow P(\mathbf{x_t}, \mathbf{y})\}.$$

This set comprehension expression captures the set of all values of $e(\mathbf{t}) : \varphi(\mathbf{x_t}, \mathbf{y}) \leftarrow P(\mathbf{x_t}, \mathbf{y})$ for all variables of $\mathbf{t}, \mathbf{x_t}, \mathbf{y}$ where the predicate $C(\mathbf{t}, \mathbf{x_t}, \mathbf{y})$ acts as a *constraint* or *typing condition* on the variables. This representation allows us to use a type schema to effectively declare the plan schema and define its instances.

We now show how to encode the plan library and action description library in Fig. 1 for the running example in the rover navigation scenario. Figure 13 gives the context for the encoded plan library and action description library. It extends the base contexts of terms and predicate symbols in Fig. 4 and Fig. 6 (line 2). The constants (line 3) encompass all 6 plans and 5 actions. As a result, the plan library is constructed by unifying all possible plans, in this case, from *plan1* to *plan6*, given by **axm1** (line 6). Each plan (with free variables) represents a set of all possible instantiated plans and is encoded through set comprehension. Here, we only describe the plan (lines 4–5) that is shown in Fig. 2b as follows:

```
start(mission): at(X) <-goal(at(goal_loc), navigate(goal_loc),
                power(low) ∧ ¬at(goal_loc))
```

We specify this in **axm3** (lines 8–22). Essentially, it encodes a set of plans with three components, namely *triggering_event*, *context*, and *plan_body* (line 8) in Fig. 13. To specify what each of these components is, a list of constraints in the form of logical conjunction is specified (lines 10–20). For example, the constraint *triggering_event* = *start* $\mapsto$ *mission* (line 11) defines what the triggering event actually is. The context is given using the constructor, *Conjunctive_formula*, to encode two negated formula (lines 14–16). To specify the *plan_body*, we provide three extra parameters, namely *success_condition*, *failure_condition*, and *procedural_program* (lines 8–9). Using these, we compose the *plan_body* as a declarative goal on lines 19–20. The set comprehension result (line 21) returns the corresponding plan mapping *triggering_event* $\mapsto$ (*context* $\mapsto$ *plan_body*) for any values satisfying the constraints, yielding the set representation of *plan*1. Due to space limits, we omit the encoding for the remaining plans and actions.

3.6   Faithful Encoding

Our encoding of the CAN syntax into Event-B is *faithful* in the following sense: (i) *coverage*—every well-formed CAN object in the syntactic categories that we model (terms, predicate symbols, belief formulas, agent programs, libraries) has a corresponding Event-B representation; and (ii) *uniqueness*—the encoding is *injective*, i.e. distinct CAN objects do not collapse to the same Event-B object.

Coverage follows because the encoding mirrors the CAN grammar: base alphabets (terms and predicate symbols) are introduced axiomatically, and the inductive fragments (e.g. belief formulas and agent programs) are defined using Event-B inductive data types by recursively translating base alphabets and then rebuilding the same syntactic representation in Event-B.

Uniqueness holds because (1) different CAN syntax elements are represented using distinct constructors, and (2) data type constructors in Event-B are injective in their arguments. The equality of encoded objects in Event-B implies the equality of the corresponding sub-components in CAN. For collections (e.g. belief bases), injectivity lifts elementwise. As a result, the encoding is a lossless syntactic encoding of CAN into Event-B.

4   Belief-Action Reasoning for CAN in Event-B

Our focus in this paper is the faithful encoding of CAN *syntax* into Event-B theories and contexts. Full reasoning about BDI behaviour typically requires an operational semantics (e.g. plan selection and event handling), which is our next step. Still, even without that semantics, we can already support useful agent reasoning via two standalone components: the *belief base* and the *action description library*. Concretely, we can (i) evaluate action applicability against the current belief base, and (ii) execute actions to check belief-based safety invariants.

```
1   MACHINE GenericActionExecution
2   SEES InitialBeliefBaseExternalEventsRoboticCleaning ,
3        PlanLibraryActionDescriptionLibraryRoboticCleaning
4   VARIABLES belief_base
5   INVARIANTS
6     inv1 :  belief_base ∈ ℙ(Belief_predicate_symbols × Terms)
7   EVENTS
8     INITIALISATION
9     THEN
10        belief_base := Initial_belief_base
11    END
12    ExecuteAction
13    ANY a , pre , adds , dels
14    WHERE
15        grd1 :  a ↦ (pre ↦ (adds ↦ dels)) ∈ action_description_library
16        grd2 :  belief_entail(belief_base, pre)
17    THEN
18        act1 :  belief_base := (belief_base \ dels) ∪ adds
19    END
```

Fig. 15. Generic action machine for $\langle \mathcal{B}, \Lambda \rangle$.

4.1   Belief Entailment

BDI languages assume a belief entailment mechanism, i.e. whether a belief formula φ follows from a belief base, $\mathcal{B}$. Here, $\mathcal{B}$ is a set of grounded belief atoms, and belief formulas are given by the inductive data type in Fig. 10. We encode belief entailment via a predicate operator **belief_entail** (Fig. 14), defined by recursion over φ: under a closed-world assumption, an atom holds iff it is in $\mathcal{B}$; conjunction/disjunction follow recursively; negation is logical negation; and $\top/\bot$ are tautology/contradiction. This suffices for evaluating action pre-conditions against the current belief base without a full BDI deliberation cycle.

```
1   MACHINE ExplicitActionExecution
2   REFINES GenericActionExecution
3   . . .
4   EVENTS
5     Charge
6     REFINES  ExecuteAction
7     ANY c
8     WHERE
9         grd1 :  c ∈ {init_loc_charge, WP1_charge, WP2_charge, goal_loc_charge}
10        grd2 :  at ↦ c ∈ belief_base
11        grd3 :  power ↦ low ∈ belief_base
12    WITH
13        act :  act = charge ↦ c
14        pre :  pre = Conjunctive_formula(Belief_atom(at ↦ c), Belief_atom(power ↦ low))
15        adds :  adds = {power ↦ high}
16        dels :  dels = {power ↦ low}
17    THEN
18        act1 :  belief_base := (belief_base \ {power ↦ low}) ∪ {power ↦ high}
19    END
```

Fig. 16. Explicit action execution machine for $\langle \mathcal{B}, \Lambda \rangle$

4.2   A Belief-Based State Machine

We now present an Event-B machine that connects the encoded CAN syntax to a generic belief-based transition machine. This machine maintains an agent configuration $\langle \mathcal{B}, \Lambda \rangle$: the belief base $\mathcal{B}$, and a set of actions Λ. The following Event-B machine in Fig. 15 captures this belief-based transition system through executing actions. **INITIALISATION** event initialises the belief base (lines 8–11). **ExecuteAction** event (lines 12–29) non-deterministically selects an action, a, from the action description library where $belief\_entail(belief\_base, pre)$ ensures that the action is applicable only when its pre-condition holds (which also eliminates all actions with free variables) in the current belief base. The effects of an action apply standard add/delete effects, yielding a transition system over belief states, and is sufficient to support invariant-based reasoning about safety properties that are expressible purely in terms of beliefs.

```
1   MACHINE  PlanActionExecution
2   REFINES  ExplicitActionExecution
3   INVARIANTS
4      inv2:  power ↦ empty ∉ belief_base
5   EVENTS
6      Charge_plan
7      REFINES  Charge
8      ANY c
9      WHERE
10        grd1:  needToCharge = TRUE
11        grd2:  at ↦ GoToCharge ∈ belief_base
12        grd3:  power ↦ low ∈ belief_base
13     WITH
14        c:   c = GoToCharge
15     THEN
16        act1:  belief_base := (belief_base \ {power ↦ low}) ∪ {power ↦ high}
17        act2:  needToGobackFromCharge := TRUE
18        act3:  needToCharge := FALSE
19     END
```

Fig. 17. Plan-driven action execution machine for $\langle \mathcal{B}, \Lambda \rangle$..

Figure 15 defines a *generic* belief-based belief transition system: each step executes an enabled action from the action description library, and updates the belief base according to the effects of actions. While this machine is convenient, **ExecuteAction** is not explicit in regard to *which* concrete action instance was executed in a given step, which can make the subsequent proving difficult. To expose the concrete action being taken, we refine Fig. 15 to Fig. 16 by refining **ExecuteAction** by action-specific events (e.g. **Charge**), each corresponding to one action in the action description library. Technically, each concrete action-specific event *refines* **ExecuteAction** by (i) fixing the chosen action symbol and its parameters (via witnesses), and (ii) keeping the same belief update. As a result, we can reason about each individual action explicitly in Event-B.

Finally, to capture the user-intent principles [25] imposed by a plan library. Following the standard Event-B methodology [4], we refine Fig. 16 to Fig. 17 by adding a small set of *control tokens* that restricts which action may execute next. For brevity, we show only one representative refined event in Fig. 17.

The **Charge_plan** event refines the **Charge** event by additionally requiring the corresponding control flag (`needToCharge=TRUE`) and by using the plan-selected parameter (`GoToCharge`) as the charging location. The belief update remains identical to the underlying action semantics, while the control layer records progress by switching `needToCharge` off and enabling `needToGoback` `FromCharge`.

We now illustrate how the invariant-based safety reasoning can be performed in our framework. For example, The safety invariant **inv2** $power \mapsto empty \notin belief\_base$ in Fig. 17 does *not* hold for the current plan library, and the counter-example can be traced to the plan `navigate(Z): at(X)` $\wedge$ `next(X,Y)` $\wedge \neg$ `power(empty)` $\leftarrow$ `movement(X,Y); navigate(Z)`. The guard $\neg power(empty)$ is too weak: it still permits `movement(X,Y)` when the battery is *low*, resulting in $power \mapsto empty$. If the guard were strengthened to $\neg power(low)$ (i.e. movement is allowed only when power is *high*), then re-encoding the intent of this revised plan library yields a model in which **inv2** holds, with the proof success-fully discharged. This final refined Rodin development, together with its proofs, is publicly available online[1]. We close this section by noting that **inv2** does not distinguish the rover location and therefore excludes even states in which the rover reaches the goal with an empty battery, more refined safety invariants, for example, involving both battery level and location, can likewise be formulated and proved in the same framework as the future work but out of the scope.

5   Related Work

Formal verification of BDI is well-summarised in [26]. We focus on the *modelling artefact* produced by related approaches, and contrast it with ours. The work in [6] translates a restricted finite-state fragment of AgentSpeak into Promela for analysis in Spin model checker. Agent syntax (e.g. predicate/action symbols) is encoded as integers, while core agent structures such as the belief base and events are represented using bounded Promela data structures. The resulting model is essentially an *interpreter-level* Promela program simulating the AgentSpeak.

Related rewriting-based approaches include [19], which translate BDI agent programs into a Maude rewrite theory where a *single algebraic term* encodes the whole agent configuration via nested subterms (e.g. beliefs and events), and reasoning-cycle steps are rewrite rules over this term. Meanwhile, the work in [5] encodes a propositional fragment of CAN as a bigraphical reactive system, where the agent configuration is a bigraph (place graph for structure, link graph for relations) and the operational semantics is given by bigraph reaction rules.

Recent proof-based approaches mechanise BDI agents in higher-order logic using general-purpose proof assistants (notably Isabelle/HOL). The work in [24] provides a deep embedding of a propositional fragment of GOAL: the syntax of formulas and agent constructs are represented as algebraic data types in HOL, and the operational semantics is defined in HOL as transition relations and trace-based satisfaction. The work in [31] models SimpleBDI using Z-Machines that are

---

[1] https://github.com/Mengwei-Xu/ABZ2026-Rodin-Artefact.

embedded in Isabelle/HOL, yielding a typed state record (beliefs/goals/plans) with pre/post style state-transforming operations for reasoning-cycle steps.

In contrast to the above approaches, our Event-B encoding ensures that the artefacts of the BDI syntax are reusable and modular as a supporting theory. This approach avoids interpreter-style encodings (Promela/Maude/Bigraph) and prover-internal semantics (HOL embeddings), while preserving state-based modelling and tool-supported proof/refinement. Additionally, it enables the support of more expressive plans, including sub-events and concurrency, extending beyond the simplified BDI agents typically used in proof-assistant encodings.

6   Conclusion and Future Work

This paper presented a faithful and reusable encoding of CAN syntax in Event-B by exploiting algebraic modelling in Event-B theories. The key benefit is practical: it replaces the ad-hoc, one-off syntactic encodings that typically underpin BDI verification with a typed and modular theory suite that can be reused across developments and extended systematically, without reducing BDI agents to restricted language fragments.

Importantly, our encoding of CAN syntax already supports proof-based analysis in Rodin without committing to the full CAN semantics: theory-level operators enable reasoning over the truth of beliefs (e.g. entailment), and actions can be linked to an Event-B transition model to support invariant checking over action executions. The next step is to encode the operational semantics of CAN e.g. over sequencing and concurrent agent programs, and declarative goals, enabling full semantic reasoning and proof-based analysis of CAN within Rodin.

References

1. Abrial, J.R.: Modeling in Event-B: system and software engineering. Cambridge University Press (2010)
2. Abrial, J.R., Butler, M., Hallerstede, S., Hoang, T.S., Mehta, F., Voisin, L.: Rodin: an open toolset for modelling and reasoning in Event-B. Int. J. Softw. Tools Technol. Transfer **12**(6), 447–466 (2010)
3. Abrial, J.R., Butler, M., Hallerstede, S., Leuschel, M., Schmalz, M., Voisin, L.: Proposals for mathematical extensions for Event-B (2009)
4. Ait-Ameur, Y., Baron, M., Kamel, N., Mota, J.M.: Encoding a process algebra using the Event B method: application to the validation of human-computer interactions. Int. J. Softw. Tools Technol. Transfer **11**(3), 239–253 (2009)
5. Archibald, B., Calder, M., Sevegnani, M., Xu, M.: Modelling and verifying BDI agents with Bigraphs. Sci. Comput. Program. **215**, 102760 (2022)
6. Bordini, R.H., Fisher, M., Pardavila, C., Wooldridge, M.: Model checking Agentspeak. In: Proceedings of the second international joint conference on Autonomous agents and multiagent systems, pp. 409–416 (2003)
7. Bordini, R., Hübner, J., Wooldridge, M.: Programming multi-agent systems in Agentspeak using Jason, vol. 8. John Wiley & Sons (2007)

8. Bourbouh, H., Farrell, M., Mavridou, A., Sljivo, I.: Integration and evaluation of the AdvoCATE, FRET, CoCoSim, and Event-B tools on the inspection rover case study. Tech. rep. (2020)
9. Bourbouh, H., et al.: Integrating formal verification and assurance: an inspection rover case study. In: NASA Formal Methods Symposium, pp. 53–71. Springer (2021)
10. Bratman, M.: Intention, plans, and practical reason (1987)
11. Butler, M., Maamria, I.: Practical theory extension in Event-B. In: Theories of Programming and Formal Methods: Essays Dedicated to Jifeng He on the Occasion of His 70th Birthday, pp. 67–81. Springer (2013)
12. Cardoso, R.C., Farrell, M., Luckcuck, M., Ferrando, A., Fisher, M.: Heterogeneous verification of an autonomous curiosity rover. In: Lee, R., Jha, S., Mavridou, A., Giannakopoulou, D. (eds.) NFM 2020. LNCS, vol. 12229, pp. 353–360. Springer, Cham (2020). https://doi.org/10.1007/978-3-030-55754-6_20
13. Clarke, E.M., Klieber, W., Nováček, M., Zuliani, P.: Model checking and the state explosion problem. In: LASER Summer School on Software Engineering, pp. 1–30. Springer (2011)
14. Clavel, M., et al.: Maude manual (version 3.1). SRI International (2020)
15. De Silva, L., Meneguzzi, F.R., Logan, B.: BDI agent architectures: a survey. In: Proceedings of the 29th International Joint Conference on Artificial Intelligence (IJCAI), 2020, Japão. (2020)
16. Dennis, L.A., Farwer, B.: Gwendolen: a BDI language for verifiable agents. In: Proceedings of the AISB 2008 Symposium on Logic and the Simulation of Interaction and Reasoning, Society for the Study of Artificial Intelligence and Simulation of Behaviour, pp. 16–23 (2008)
17. Dennis, L.A., Fisher, M., Webster, M.P., Bordini, R.H.: Model checking agent programming languages. Autom. Softw. Eng. **19**, 5–63 (2012)
18. Dennis, L.A., Oren, N.: Explaining BDI agent behaviour through dialogue. Auton. Agent. Multi-Agent Syst. **36**(2), 29 (2022)
19. Doan, T.T., Yao, Y., Alechina, N., Logan, B.: Verifying heterogeneous multi-agent programs. In: Proceedings of the 2014 International Conference on Autonomous Agents and Multi-agent Systems, pp. 149–156 (2014)
20. Havelund, K., Pressburger, T.: Model checking Java programs using Java pathfinder. Int. J. Softw. Tools Technol. Transfer **2**(4), 366–381 (2000)
21. Hindriks, K.V., De Boer, F.S., Van Der Hoek, W., Meyer, J.J.C.: Agent programming with declarative goals. In: International Workshop on Agent Theories, Architectures, and Languages, pp. 228–243. Springer (2000)
22. Holzmann, G.J.: The model checker SPIN. IEEE Trans. Software Eng. **23**(5), 279–295 (1997)
23. Holzmann, G.J., Lieberman, W.S.: Design and validation of computer protocols, vol. 512. Prentice hall Englewood Cliffs (1991)
24. Jensen, A.B.: Machine-checked verification of cognitive agents. In: ICAART (1), pp. 245–256 (2022)
25. Kambhampati, S., Mali, A., Srivastava, B.: Hybrid planning for partially hierarchical domains. In: AAAI/IAAI, pp. 882–888 (1998)
26. Luckcuck, M., Farrell, M., Dennis, L.A., Dixon, C., Fisher, M.: Formal specification and verification of autonomous robotic systems: a survey. ACM Comput. Surv. (CSUR) **52**(5), 1–41 (2019)
27. Milner, R.: The space and motion of communicating agents. Cambridge University Press (2009)

28. Nipkow, T., Wenzel, M., Paulson, L.C.: Isabelle/HOL: a proof assistant for higher-order logic. Springer (2002)
29. Sardina, S., Padgham, L.: A BDI agent programming language with failure handling, declarative goals, and planning. Auton. Agent. Multi-Agent Syst. **23**(1), 18–70 (2011)
30. Winikoff, M., Padgham, L., Harland, J., Thangarajah, J.: Declarative and procedural goals in intelligent agent systems. In: Proc. of KR'02. Morgan Kaufman (2002)
31. Wright, T., Dennis, L.A., Woodcock, J., Foster, S.: FormalVerification of BDI agents. In: The Combined Power of Research, Education, and Dissemination: Essays Dedicated to Tiziana Margaria on the Occasion of Her 60th Birthday, pp. 302–326. Springer (2024)

Relational Verification of Identity Disclosure Using Alloy

Seungil Yang[(✉)] [ID], Peter Rivière [ID], and Toshiaki Aoki [ID]

Japan Advanced Institute of Science and Technology (JAIST), Nomi, Japan
{s2360003,priviere,toshiaki}@jaist.ac.jp

Abstract. Data are increasingly released for secondary use, yet identity disclosure remains a persistent concern even after standard de-identification. Disclosure risk often arises not from isolated attributes, but from the relational structure of a release design and its interaction with external information. Statistical guarantees and empirical testing may therefore fail to expose structural risks at design time. This paper treats identity disclosure as a design-level relational property. We model data schemas, de-identification policies, and re-identification assumptions as explicit relations. Disclosure is reduced to a bounded relational reachability problem and analysed using Alloy as an executable verification engine. Satisfiable instances produce concrete disclosure witnesses, while unsatisfiability establishes bounded non-disclosure within the analysed scope. A healthcare-inspired setting illustrates that disclosure can emerge purely from relational composition, even when conventional criteria are satisfied. By recasting identity disclosure as a verifiable relational property, this work complements statistical privacy models with assumption-aware design-time verification. This reframing enables disclosure to be verified at design time, prior to data release.

Keywords: Identity Disclosure · Re-identification · De-identification · Relational Verification · Design-time Privacy Analysis · Alloy · Formal Methods

1 Introduction

The release of data for secondary use has become common practice across science, industry, and public administration. At the same time, concerns about identity disclosure remain persistent, even when standard de-identification techniques are applied. Numerous empirical studies have demonstrated that individuals can be re-identified from datasets believed to be non-identifying, often through linkage with auxiliary information or through unanticipated patterns of data combination [13–15].

A key reason for this difficulty is that identity disclosure is not determined solely by the presence or absence of explicit identifiers. Rather, disclosure risk

This work was supported by JST, CREST Grant Number JPMJCR23M1.

The Author(s), under exclusive license to Springer Nature Switzerland AG 2026
Ichikawa and A. Cunha (Eds.): ABZ 2026, LNCS 16579, pp. 229–247, 2026.
//doi.org/10.1007/978-3-032-26752-8_14

often emerges from the *relational structure* of a data release: how attributes, entities, and datasets are composed and linked, and how these structures interact with external information. As a consequence, data that appear innocuous in isolation may still admit identity disclosure once relational inference is taken into account.

Existing approaches to disclosure control address this problem from several perspectives. Classical statistical frameworks such as k-anonymity, l-diversity, and t-closeness aim to prevent re-identification by enforcing indistinguishability within equivalence classes [11,12,17]. Differential Privacy (DP) provides a stronger, probabilistic guarantee by bounding the influence of any single individual on query outputs [4–6]. Other approaches rely on instance-based analysis, query auditing, or empirical testing against known attacks.

While these techniques are valuable, they are often limited in their ability to expose *structural disclosure risks* that arise from the design of a data release itself, independently of any concrete dataset. In particular, statistical guarantees characterise disclosure risk in probabilistic terms, and empirical studies identify vulnerabilities only after data have been released and specific attacks have been demonstrated. As a result, they provide limited support for answering a fundamentally different question: whether a given release design *admits* identity disclosure as a logical consequence of its relational structure.

This observation motivates a shift in perspective. Rather than asking how likely identity disclosure is to occur for a particular dataset, we argue that identity disclosure should be understood as a *design-level property* of a data release. From this viewpoint, the central question becomes: *does the release design admit a logically valid inference path by which an individual can be identified, under explicitly stated assumptions?* When framed in this way, identity disclosure is no longer a matter of statistical estimation or post-hoc empirical testing, but a problem amenable to formal verification.

In this paper, we propose a formal, verification-oriented approach to identity disclosure analysis. We model data schemas, de-identification policies, and re-identification assumptions explicitly, and analyse their interaction using relational verification.

Building on existing applications of formal methods to privacy, the analysis is realised in Alloy, used not merely as a modelling language but as a verification engine for bounded exhaustive exploration of structurally admissible release designs [9,10]. In this setting, identity disclosure is formulated as a bounded relational reachability problem, allowing us to determine whether a given release design *admits* disclosure under explicitly stated assumptions.

The proposed approach yields precise and actionable outcomes. If disclosure is possible, the analysis produces a concrete disclosure witness that makes explicit the relational inference path involved. If no such witness exists within the given bounds, the result establishes bounded non-disclosure for the analysed design. This form of assurance is particularly well suited to design-time reasoning, where the objective is to assess and refine release policies before any real data are disclosed.

Contributions. This paper makes the following contributions:

- We formalise identity disclosure as a relational property arising from the composition of de-identification and re-identification relations.
- We present a design-time methodology that translates data schemas and disclosure assumptions into Alloy and enables bounded relational verification.
- We model representative families of de-identification techniques together with corresponding attacker assumptions within a uniform relational framework.
- We demonstrate, through a healthcare-inspired setting, that disclosure can arise purely from relational structure, and show how verification results provide actionable feedback for refining release designs.

Paper Outline. Section 2 surveys related work. Section 3 introduces Alloy as a verification tool. Section 4 presents the data-based abstraction and the running example. Section 6 presents the unified verification approach and its evidence. Section 7 discusses implications and limitations, and Sect. 8 concludes.

2   Related Work

Identity disclosure and privacy-preserving data release have been studied extensively across multiple research communities, including database systems, statistical disclosure control, and formal methods. This section reviews the most relevant strands of work and clarifies how our contribution addresses limitations that remain unresolved, particularly with respect to *design-level* and *structural* disclosure risks highlighted in the introduction.

Statistical Disclosure Control and Privacy Models. A substantial body of research addresses disclosure risk through statistical guarantees and formal privacy notions. Classical models such as k-anonymity, l-diversity, and t-closeness aim to prevent re-identification by enforcing indistinguishability within equivalence classes [11,12,17]. Differential Privacy (DP) provides a stronger, mathematically grounded guarantee by bounding the influence of any single individual on query outputs [4–6].

While highly influential, these approaches primarily reason about disclosure in probabilistic or statistical terms. As observed in practice, they do not directly capture disclosure risks that arise from the *relational structure* of released data, nor from deterministic inference enabled by data linkage. Moreover, they are typically evaluated on concrete datasets, which makes it difficult to assess disclosure risk at the level of release design, prior to data publication.

Linkage Attacks, Auxiliary Information, and Empirical Re-Identification. A complementary line of work demonstrates empirically that de-identified datasets can often be re-identified by linking them with external or auxiliary information. Narayanan and Shmatikov showed that de-identified movie rating data can be linked to public profiles through sparse overlap and relational similarity [14], while Ohm argued that de-identification promises often fail in the presence of auxiliary information and evolving linkage opportunities [15]. Related results also highlight that disclosure can arise from the *composition* of releases and background knowledge, even when each release appears safe in isolation [3,8]. Across application domains, empirical evidence from mobility data illustrates how few spatiotemporal points may suffice to single out individuals [13], and healthcare-oriented guidance emphasises the practical challenges of preventing linkage-driven re-identification in real release workflows [7].

These results provide compelling empirical evidence that identity disclosure is possible in practice. However, such studies are inherently retrospective: they identify vulnerabilities only after data have been released and specific attacks have been demonstrated. They therefore offer limited support for answering the *design-time* question posed in this paper: whether a given release design *admits* identity disclosure under explicitly stated assumptions.

Formal Methods and Verification-Based Approaches. Formal techniques have been applied to privacy in several contexts, including information-flow security, policy compliance, and verification of differential privacy [1,2,16]. Despite these advances, most existing formal approaches either target specific privacy definitions (e.g., differential privacy), or reason about program behaviour rather than the structure of data release designs. As a result, they typically do not model identity disclosure as a relational property emerging from the interaction between de-identification choices and attacker inference capabilities.

Positioning of this Work. Taken together, the above lines of work motivate the need for a verification perspective that operates *prior to data release* and reasons explicitly about the relational structure of a release design. This paper builds on that observation by treating identity disclosure not as a statistical outcome or an empirical phenomenon, but as a *design-level property* that can be subjected to formal verification.

We do not introduce a new privacy metric, nor do we propose a new de-identification algorithm. Instead, we model de-identification and re-identification as explicit relations and analyse their composition. By reducing identity disclosure to a bounded relational reachability problem, we enable exhaustive, design-time reasoning about disclosure risk, independent of concrete data instances or probabilistic assumptions.

Rather than proposing a new privacy metric or a new anonymisation algorithm, our contribution is to cast identity disclosure as a verification problem over the composition of de-identification and re-identification relations. The paper therefore complements existing verification-based privacy research with a concrete relational formulation for analysing design-time disclosure admissibility.

3   Alloy

Alloy is a lightweight formal specification language based on first-order relational logic with transitive closure, supported by an automated analysis engine known as the Alloy Analyzer [9,10]. Crucially, Alloy combines a relational modelling language with bounded exhaustive analysis: the relational model defines the design space, and the Analyzer explores it exhaustively within a finite scope.

In this paper, Alloy is used *both as a modelling formalism and as a verification engine*. These two roles are inseparable: identity disclosure is defined as a relational property of a release design, and Alloy provides executable semantics for checking its admissibility.

Relational Modelling. At its core, Alloy represents systems as relations over finite sets. Signatures define abstract sets of atoms, while fields, predicates, and facts constrain their relational structure. This foundation is particularly well suited to modelling data schemas, data transformations, and cross-dataset linkages, which are inherently relational.

Bounded Exhaustive Analysis. The Alloy Analyzer translates specifications into SAT problems and performs exhaustive search within a user-defined finite scope. Although bounded, the analysis is complete with respect to all structurally admissible instances within that scope, making it well suited to design-time vulnerability detection.

Why Alloy for Identity Disclosure Verification. In this work, identity disclosure is formulated as the existence of a relational inference path between original data and externally identifiable records. Such reachability properties can be stated directly in Alloy and checked automatically. By exhaustively exploring the space defined by the schema, the de-identification relation, and the attacker assumptions, Alloy provides systematic evidence of whether disclosure is *admitted by design*.

Satisfying instances serve as explicit disclosure witnesses, while unsatisfiability establishes bounded non-disclosure under explicitly stated assumptions. This tight integration of modelling and verification forms the technical backbone of the proposed approach.

4   Healthcare-Inspired Setting

This section introduces a minimal, healthcare-inspired setting used as a running example throughout the paper. Healthcare data are adopted solely as a representative application domain; the proposed verification approach is not specific to healthcare and applies equally to other structured data release scenarios.

The purpose of this section is to fix a concrete yet lightweight context in which the roles of original data, released data, and external data can be described consistently, prior to their formal treatment in the verification framework. No disclosure assumptions or verification conditions are introduced at this stage.

We consider an original dataset, denoted by D_{orig}, representing data prior to any de-identification. At an abstract level, D_{orig} consists of a finite set of items, each corresponding to an individual record instantiating a common schema.

Table 1 illustrates a simplified instance inspired by typical healthcare records. The table is provided solely for intuitive grounding; the verification results developed later do not depend on these concrete values.

Table 1. Example original dataset D_{orig}

Item	Name	Date of Birth	Drug
p_1	Alice	1985-03-12	DrugA
p_2	Bob	1990-07-24	DrugB

From D_{orig}, a released dataset D_{rel} is obtained by applying a de-identification process. Depending on the release design, attributes may be removed, generalised, or perturbed, while preserving the underlying relational structure imposed by the schema.

We further assume an external dataset D_{ext}, containing identifiable records and accessible to an attacker. The external dataset need not be complete nor share the same schema as D_{rel}; it suffices that some attributes overlap and can be compared under plausible matching assumptions.

Attributes such as *Name* are typically treated as direct identifiers, while others, such as *Date of Birth*, may act as quasi-identifiers depending on context. Their precise role is intentionally left open here and will be made explicit later, when de-identification and re-identification relations are formalised.

This setting is intentionally abstract: concrete attribute values, statistical distributions, and dataset sizes are not modelled. Its role is to fix consistent dataset roles for D_{orig}, D_{rel}, and D_{ext}, thereby providing a neutral design context for the verification-oriented analysis developed in subsequent sections.

5 Methodology

This section presents a verification-oriented methodology for analysing identity disclosure at the level of data release design. The goal is not to estimate how likely re-identification is, but to determine whether a release design *admits* identity disclosure as a logical consequence of its relational structure under explicitly stated assumptions.

The methodology adopts a *design-time verification* perspective. Rather than analysing a particular dataset instance or replaying known attacks, it reasons over the space of *all structurally admissible datasets* consistent with: (i) a schema abstraction, (ii) a de-identification design, and (iii) an explicit attacker model. This makes disclosure risk a design-level question, to be assessed before any data release.

5.1   Design-Time Verification Framework

The framework separates three concerns that are often conflated in practice: data structure, de-identification policy, and attacker assumptions. Each is specified independently, and identity disclosure is analysed only through their interaction. As a result, differences in verification outcomes can be attributed to design choices, not to accidental properties of concrete attribute values, dataset sizes, or statistical frequency.

Crucially, the analysis produces *design-time evidence*. A satisfiable result indicates that disclosure is *admitted by design* and yields a concrete witness showing the inference path involved. An unsatisfiable result establishes *bounded non-disclosure* within the chosen scope and assumptions, serving as a structural filter before empirical evaluation or deployment. This formulation makes disclosure a property of design, rather than of data instances, and enables verification prior to data release.

5.2   Verification Workflow and Alloy Encoding

The methodology is realised as a bounded verification task in Alloy. In compressed form, the workflow is:

1. **Schema abstraction:** encode the schema as relational structure, abstracting away concrete value domains.
2. **De-identification relation:** specify admissible releases as a relation T between original and released records.
3. **Re-identification relation:** specify attacker linkage assumptions as a relation R between released and external records.
4. **Disclosure condition:** express identity disclosure as a reachability condition arising from the composition $T \circ R$.
5. **Evidence and refinement:** run Alloy within a finite scope; if SAT, inspect the witness and refine T (or assumptions); if UNSAT, obtain bounded non-disclosure evidence.

Alloy provides bounded exhaustive search within the chosen scope: it either returns a concrete disclosure witness or establishes that no admissible instance satisfies the disclosure condition in that scope. The next section instantiates this workflow, fixing a common data abstraction and varying only T and R to isolate disclosure as a design-level relational property.

6   Identity Disclosure Verification

This section operationalises identity disclosure as a verifiable relational property and demonstrates how disclosure can be decided mechanically at design time. It demonstrates, through *Alloy models* that identity disclosure can be analysed as a *design-time verification problem*, rather than as a post-hoc or instance-dependent risk assessment.

Building on the data-based abstraction (Sect. 4) and the verification-oriented methodology (Sect. 5), we show that identity disclosure is primarily determined by the relational interaction between: (i) the de-identification design, (ii) explicit attacker assumptions, and (iii) their composition. No probabilistic modelling, empirical datasets, or attack simulations are required for the structural analysis considered here.

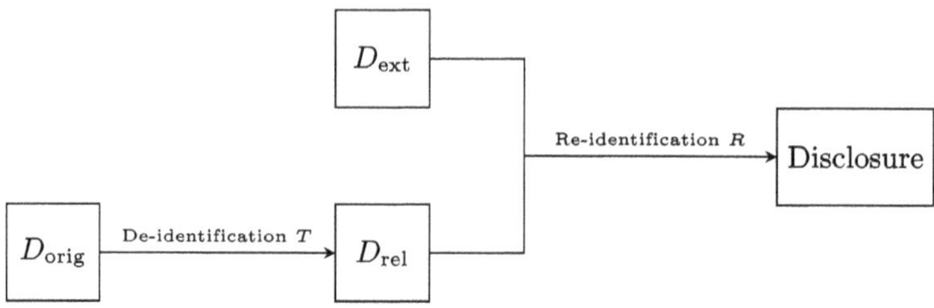

Fig. 1. Identity disclosure as relational composition. Original data D_{orig} is transformed into released data D_{rel} via a de-identification relation T. Disclosure arises when D_{rel} can be linked, through a re-identification relation R, to an external dataset D_{ext}. Thus, disclosure corresponds to the existence of a relational path from original data to identifiable external data.

Figure 1 illustrates the verification setting adopted in this section. The figure makes explicit that identity disclosure does not arise from any single dataset in isolation, but from the *composition* of two relations: a de-identification relation T and a re-identification relation R.

6.1 Verification Setting and Relational Inputs

The verification problem is parameterised by three datasets: the original dataset D_{orig}, the released dataset D_{rel}, and an external dataset D_{ext}. Verification is performed at the level of dataset items. We write $Items(D)$ for the finite set of items contained in a dataset D.

Common data-based Abstraction. To ensure that differences in verification outcomes arise solely from de-identification design choices and attacker assumptions, we fix a *single shared data-based abstraction* across all de-identification families. Each dataset item is modelled as a record over a common attribute universe A, used consistently for D_{orig}, D_{rel}, and D_{ext}.

Listing 1 presents this abstraction at the dataset level. At this stage, we introduce dataset signatures only: no de-identification, re-identification, or disclosure conditions appear here. For clarity, only the attributes relevant to the running example are shown.

Executable verification models may introduce auxiliary relational fields (e.g., connectivity links such as `deId` or `reId`). Such fields are auxiliary to verification and are not part of the abstract data schema.

```
sig D_orig { name: one Name, zip: one ZipCode, dob: one DOB,
             sex: one Sex, drugName: one DrugName,
             price: one UnitPrice, age: one Int}

sig D_rel { zip: one ZipCode, dob: one DOB,
            sex: one Sex, drugCode: one DrugCode,
            price: one UnitPrice, age: one Int}

sig D_ext { name: one Name, zip: one ZipCode, dob: one DOB, sex: one Sex,
            drugName: one DrugName, drugCode: one DrugCode,
            price: one UnitPrice, age: one Int}
```

Listing 1. Schematic data-based abstraction (pseudo-Alloy)

Relational Inputs to Verification. Given this fixed dataset abstraction, the verification task is characterised by two relations introduced in the following sections: a de-identification relation T linking D_{orig} to D_{rel}, and a re-identification relation R linking D_{rel} to D_{ext}. Identity disclosure does not arise from dataset structure alone, but from the composition of these relations.

By fixing the data model and varying only T and R, the analysis isolates identity disclosure as a *design-level relational property*, independent of concrete datasets or probabilistic assumptions.

6.2   Formalising De-Identification as Relations

De-identification is formalised at the level of release design as a relation between records in the original dataset and records in the released dataset. Rather than modelling concrete algorithms, we specify which released records are *admissible by design* as de-identified versions of original records.

Let A_{orig} and A_{rel} denote the attribute sets available in D_{orig} and D_{rel}, respectively. For records $d \in Items(D_{\mathrm{orig}})$ and $r \in Items(D_{\mathrm{rel}})$, we write $d.a$ and $r.a$ for the value of attribute a when defined. De-identification is modelled as a relation

$$T \subseteq Items(D_{\mathrm{orig}}) \times Items(D_{\mathrm{rel}}),$$

where $(d, r) \in T$ means that r is an admissible de-identified release of d.

The relation T is defined independently of attacker assumptions and captures only the design intent of the release policy: which attributes may change and which must be preserved. Its interaction with re-identification is analysed in Sect. 6.3.

In the following, T is instantiated for three representative families of de-identification techniques: generalization, deletion, and noise addition, all within the same relational framework. For readability, we reuse the predicate name `DeIdentified` across variants; each listing instantiates a different relation T (i.e., T_{gen}, T_{del}, and T_{noise}).

Generalization. Generalization-based de-identification replaces the value of a designated attribute with a coarser representation, while preserving all other released attributes. Typical examples include mapping a drug name to a drug category or an exact location to a broader region.

Let A_{orig} and A_{rel} denote the attribute sets of D_{orig} and D_{rel}, respectively. Let $x \in A_{\mathrm{orig}}$ be a generalized attribute, $y \in A_{\mathrm{rel}}$ its released counterpart, and let α_x and α_y denote their respective value domains.

A generalization function

$$g : \alpha_x \to \alpha_y$$

defines the abstraction.

The generalization relation $T_{\mathrm{gen}} \subseteq D_{\mathrm{orig}} \times D_{\mathrm{rel}}$ is defined by

$$(o, r) \in T_{\mathrm{gen}} \iff r.y = g(o.x) \land \forall z \in A_{\mathrm{orig}} \cap A_{\mathrm{rel}} \setminus \{x, y\}, \; o.z = r.z.$$

Thus, only the designated attribute is transformed via g; while all remaining shared attributes are preserved exactly. The definition extends naturally to multiple generalized attributes.

Alloy Encoding. In the Alloy model, the generalisation function g is encoded as a relation `g: DrugName -> DrugCode`. The constraint `o.drugName.g = r.drugCode` implements the equation $r.y = g(o.x)$ from the formal definition.

Listing 2 shows the corresponding encoding.

```
pred DeIdentified(o: D_orig, r: D_rel) {

    // Apply generalisation: r.drugCode = g(o.drugName)
    o.drugName.g = r.drugCode

    // Preserve all other shared attributes
    o.price = r.price
    o.zip = r.zip
    o.dob = r.dob
    o.sex = r.sex
    o.age = r.age
}
```

Listing 2. Generalization-based de-identification relation

This predicate characterises the admissible released records under generalization, independently of any re-identification assumptions.

Deletion. Deletion-based de-identification removes a designated set of attributes $I \subseteq A_{\mathrm{orig}}$ from the released dataset. At the schema level, the released attribute set is

$$A_{\mathrm{rel}} = A_{\mathrm{orig}} \setminus I.$$

Although the schema-level description suggests a reduced attribute set, in our verification setting we maintain the common data abstraction introduced in

Sect. 6.1. The deletion model is therefore realised by constraining only the attributes retained in A_{rel}, while unused attributes remain present in the shared schema but are not semantically relevant.

The deletion relation $T_{\mathrm{del}} \subseteq D_{\mathrm{orig}} \times D_{\mathrm{rel}}$ is defined by

$$(o, r) \in T_{\mathrm{del}} \iff \forall z \in A_{\mathrm{rel}}, \; r.z = o.z.$$

Thus, all attributes retained in the released schema are preserved exactly, while attributes in I are not constrained by the deletion relation and therefore carry no semantic relevance in this model.

In other words, attributes in I are treated as absent from the semantic interface of the released dataset, rather than as hidden values available for subsequent matching. Accordingly, they do not contribute to the disclosure condition.

Alloy Encoding. Attributes in I (e.g., `name`) do not appear in `D_rel`, while all attributes in A_{rel} are preserved verbatim.

Listing 3 shows the corresponding encoding.

```
pred DeIdentified(o: D_orig, r: D_rel) {

  // Preserve all attributes in A_rel
  o.zip = r.zip
  o.dob = r.dob
  o.sex = r.sex
  o.price = r.price
  o.age = r.age
  o.drugName.g = r.drugCode
}
```

Listing 3. Deletion-based de-identification relation

Noise Addition. Noise-based de-identification perturbs a numerical attribute within a bounded range, while preserving all other released attributes.

Let $x \in A_{\mathrm{orig}} \cap A_{\mathrm{rel}}$ be a numerical attribute, and let $n \geq 0$ denote the noise bound. The noise relation $T_{\mathrm{noise}} \subseteq D_{\mathrm{orig}} \times D_{\mathrm{rel}}$ is defined by

$$(o, r) \in T_{\mathrm{noise}} \iff r.x \in [o.x - n, \, o.x + n] \wedge \forall z \in (A_{\mathrm{orig}} \cap A_{\mathrm{rel}} \setminus \{x\}), \; r.z = o.z.$$

Thus, only the designated numerical attribute may vary within the specified tolerance, while all remaining shared attributes are preserved exactly.

Alloy Encoding. In the Alloy model, the attribute **age** corresponds to the numerical attribute x, and the constant **n** represents the noise bound. All other shared attributes are preserved exactly.

Listing 4 shows the corresponding encoding.

```
pred DeIdentified(o: D_orig, r: D_rel) {

  // Preserve shared attributes
  o.zip = r.zip
  o.dob = r.dob
  o.sex = r.sex
  o.price = r.price
  o.drugName.g = r.drugCode

  // Apply bounded noise to age
  let n = 2 |
    gte[r.age, sub[o.age, n]] and
    lte[r.age, add[o.age, n]]
}
```

Listing 4. Noise-based de-identification relation (pseudo-Alloy)

Summary. Across all three families, de-identification is uniformly modelled as a binary relation that specifies which attributes may change and which must be preserved. These relations characterise only the transformations that are logically admissible by design; they do not assume that re-identification occurs in practice.

Identity disclosure therefore depends solely on the relational composition of the de-identification relation T and the re-identification relation R, independent of concrete data values or statistical distributions.

6.3   Formalising Re-Identification

Re-identification models the attacker's ability to link released records to externally identifiable records using auxiliary information. Formally, it is captured as a binary relation

$$R \subseteq Items(D_{\mathrm{rel}}) \times Items(D_{\mathrm{ext}}),$$

where $(r, e) \in R$ indicates that a released record r can be plausibly matched to an external record e.

To avoid ambiguity about attribute usage, we distinguish the attribute sets of the released and external datasets. Let A_{rel} and A_{ext} denote the attribute sets of D_{rel} and D_{ext}, respectively, and let

$$A_{\cap} = A_{\mathrm{rel}} \cap A_{\mathrm{ext}}$$

be the set of attributes that can be compared across datasets. The attacker is assumed to use a subset $K \subseteq A_{\cap}$ for record linkage. As before, $r.a$ and $e.a$ denote the value of attribute a in records r and e, respectively.

Exact Matching. Exact matching assumes that the attacker can link records whenever all attributes in K coincide exactly. The exact re-identification relation R_{exact} is defined by:

$$(r, e) \in R_{\text{exact}} \iff \bigwedge_{y \in K} r.y = e.y.$$

Listing 5 shows the corresponding Alloy encoding, where $r \in D_{\text{rel}}$, $e \in D_{\text{ext}}$, and the attributes in K are realised explicitly as field equalities.

```
pred ReIdentified(r: D_rel, e: D_ext) {

  // Matching attribute set
  // K is subset of attributes common to D_rel and D_ext
  // Exact equality on all attributes in K

  r.zip = e.zip
  r.dob = e.dob
  r.sex = e.sex
  r.price = e.price
  r.drugCode = e.drugCode
  r.age = e.age
}
```

Listing 5. Exact re-identification relation

Approximate Matching. Approximate matching captures situations in which numerical attributes may differ within a tolerated bound. Let $x \in K$ be a numerical attribute, and let $\kappa \geq 0$ denote an admissible deviation. The approximate re-identification relation R_{approx} is defined by:

$$(r, e) \in R_{\text{approx}} \iff |r.x - e.x| \leq \kappa \ \wedge \bigwedge_{y \in (K \setminus \{x\})} r.y = e.y.$$

Listing 6 gives the Alloy encoding. Here, the numerical attribute x corresponds to **age**, and the constant **k** realises the bound κ.

```
pred ReIdentified(r: D_rel, e: D_ext) {

  // Exact match on categorical attributes
  r.zip = e.zip
  r.dob = e.dob
  r.sex = e.sex
  r.price = e.price
  r.drugCode = e.drugCode

  // Approximate match on numeric attribute x = age
  // abs(r.age - e.age) <= k
  let k = 2, diff = sub[r.age, e.age] |
```

```
      gte[diff, sub[0, k]] and
      lte[diff, k]
}
```

Listing 6. Approximate re-identification relation (pseudo-Alloy)

Note. The integer operators used in Listings 4 and 6 (e.g., **add**, **sub**, **gte**, **lte**) are provided by Alloy's **util/integer** module. The corresponding Alloy encodings therefore open **util/integer**.

6.4   Identity Disclosure as Relational Reachability

Identity disclosure is characterised as a *relational reachability* property arising from the composition of the de-identification relation T and the re-identification relation R.

Recall that $T \subseteq Items(D_{\mathrm{orig}}) \times Items(D_{\mathrm{rel}})$ and $R \subseteq Items(D_{\mathrm{rel}}) \times Items(D_{\mathrm{ext}})$. Disclosure arises when an original record can be connected to an externally identifiable record through an intermediate released record. Formally, this corresponds to $(d, e) \in T \circ R$, the standard relational composition of T and R.

Definition 1 (Identity Disclosure). Identity disclosure occurs if and only if

$$\exists d \in Items(D_{\mathrm{orig}}),\ e \in Items(D_{\mathrm{ext}}) \quad (d, e) \in T \circ R \,\wedge\, d.name = e.name.$$

In this abstraction, *name* is treated as a unique direct identifier. More generally, identity conditions can be defined over any designated subset of attributes representing direct identifiers.

6.5   Verification with Alloy: Evidence

Definition 1 is verified in Alloy as a satisfiability query. The datasets D_{orig}, D_{rel}, and D_{ext} are represented as signatures, and the relations T and R are encoded as predicates.

A SAT result yields a concrete disclosure witness: a triple (o, r, e) such that **DeIdentified[o,r]**, **ReIdentified[r,e]**, and $o.name = e.name$ hold simultaneously. This witness makes explicit the relational inference path from an original record to an externally identifiable one.

Listing 7 shows the Alloy encoding corresponding directly to Definition 1.

```
pred IdentityDisclosure(o: D_orig, e: D_ext) {
  some r: D_rel |
    DeIdentified[o, r] and
    ReIdentified[r, e] and
    o.name = e.name
}


run {
```

```
  some o: D_orig, e: D_ext |
    IdentityDisclosure[o, e]
}
```

Listing 7. Alloy encoding of identity disclosure as relational reachability

SAT. If the query is satisfiable, Alloy produces a witness (o, r, e) such that `DeIdentified[o,r]`, `ReIdentified[r,e]`, and $o.name = e.name$ hold. This witness explicitly realises the relational path corresponding to $(d, e) \in T \circ R$, thereby demonstrating that disclosure is admitted by the release design under the given attacker model.

UNSAT. If the query is unsatisfiable, no instance within the chosen scope satisfies the disclosure condition, establishing bounded non-disclosure.

Table 2 summarises the outcomes for the three de-identification families under the two matching assumptions.

Table 2. Verification outcomes

De-identification	Result	Interpretation
Generalization	SAT	Disclosure admitted via generalization mapping.
Deletion	SAT	Disclosure admitted under exact matching ($\kappa = 0$).
Noise + approx ($\kappa > 0$)	SAT	Disclosure admitted under approximate matching.
Noise + exact ($\kappa = 0$)	UNSAT	No disclosure admitted (bounded non-reachability).

This table highlights that disclosure is governed by the interaction between T and R, rather than by the data itself. The purpose of these experiments is not to demonstrate unexpected empirical behaviour, but to show that disclosure conditions can be made explicit and verified mechanically as a design-level property. Even in this minimal setting, the analysis distinguishes between release designs that admit disclosure and those that block relational reachability under different attacker assumptions. In particular, the contrast between exact and approximate matching in the noise-based case shows how a change in attacker assumptions can alter the verification outcome. The case study should therefore be read as a proof-of-feasibility illustration of the verification workflow, rather than as a claim of broad empirical coverage.

These results confirm that identity disclosure is determined by the relational structure of T and R, rather than by concrete data instances or statistical frequency.

7   Discussion

This section reflects on the implications of treating identity disclosure as a design-time verification problem and clarifies its relation to existing privacy models.

7.1 Design-Level Structural Evidence

The results in Sect. 6 show that identity disclosure is determined by relational design choices, not by concrete data instances. With the data abstraction fixed, changes in SAT/UNSAT outcomes are induced solely by variations in the de-identification relation T and the re-identification relation R.

A SAT result establishes that disclosure is *admitted by design* under explicitly stated assumptions, and the returned instance serves as an explicit disclosure witness. An UNSAT result establishes *bounded non-disclosure* within the analysed scope. In both cases, the evidence concerns structural admissibility, rather than empirical likelihood.

The noise-based models illustrate this point. When approximate matching is permitted ($\kappa > 0$), bounded perturbation does not prevent relational composition, and disclosure is admitted. When exact matching is enforced ($\kappa = 0$), the same design blocks reachability. The decisive factor is therefore the interaction between T and R, not any individual transformation in isolation.

7.2 Complementarity with Statistical Privacy Models

Statistical privacy models, including k-anonymity and differential privacy, characterise disclosure risk in probabilistic terms. They address the question: *How unlikely is re-identification under a given threat model?*

The present approach addresses a different question: *Does the release design admit a logically valid inference path to identity disclosure, under explicitly stated assumptions?* A SAT result indicates structural admissibility, not inevitability; an UNSAT result provides bounded evidence, not absolute safety.

Relational verification thus acts as a design-time structural filter. Designs that admit disclosure can be refined prior to deployment, while those that block relational reachability may proceed to statistical evaluation. The approach complements, rather than replaces, probabilistic guarantees.

7.3 Privacy as Non-reachability

Formally, identity disclosure occurs when the relational composition $T \circ R$ reaches an identity-defining attribute. Privacy at design time can therefore be viewed as a non-reachability property over relational composition.

This interpretation does not introduce a new privacy metric. Rather, it provides a structural invariant: a release design preserves privacy iff the composed relation does not intersect with the identity relation within the analysed scope. Such invariants can be verified independently of probability distributions or dataset size.

7.4 Scope and Limitations

The analysis is intentionally bounded. UNSAT results establish non-disclosure only within the chosen finite scope, and the models abstract away adaptive attackers and probabilistic background knowledge. These limitations are inherent to structural, design-time reasoning and are complementary to empirical and statistical methods.

Overall, the results support the view that identity disclosure can be analysed as a design-level relational property, making disclosure assumptions explicit and formally checkable prior to data release.

The present formulation treats disclosure as an existential reachability property: if an original record can be connected to an externally identifiable record through the composed relation, disclosure is considered admitted. This abstracts away from the number of reachable external candidates and from any probabilistic interpretation of attacker success. In practice, candidate multiplicity may affect the likelihood of correct identification, but this concerns a quantitative notion of risk rather than the structural admissibility question addressed in this paper.

The models are intentionally small and abstract, as the goal is to isolate structural disclosure conditions rather than to model realistic datasets in full detail. Extending the approach to richer schemas, larger scopes, and more heterogeneous release settings remains an important direction for future work.

The attacker assumptions considered here are intentionally simple, focusing on exact and approximate matching as representative linkage mechanisms. A natural extension is to analyse richer attacker models, including relational similarity, linkage attacks, and composition across multiple releases or external datasets. This distinction clarifies that our approach targets structural admissibility, not probabilistic risk estimation.

8 Conclusion

This paper has developed a relational verification perspective on identity disclosure in data release. Instead of treating disclosure as a probabilistic outcome or an instance-dependent event, we formalised it as a structural property of release design.

By modelling de-identification as a relation T between D_{orig} and D_{rel}, and re-identification as a relation R between D_{rel} and D_{ext}, identity disclosure reduces to a reachability condition over the relational composition $T \circ R$. Disclosure occurs precisely when this composition admits a path connecting an original record to an externally identifiable record.

Using Alloy, this reachability condition is checked as a bounded satisfiability query. A SAT result yields an explicit disclosure witness, demonstrating that the design admits identity disclosure under the stated assumptions. An UNSAT result establishes bounded non-reachability, providing structural evidence of non-disclosure within the analysed scope.

The case study shows that disclosure is governed by the interaction between the release relation T and the attacker model R. With the dataset abstraction fixed, changes in verification outcomes arise solely from design choices and matching assumptions, not from concrete data values or statistical distributions.

This perspective does not replace statistical privacy models. Rather, it complements them by introducing a design-time layer of structural reasoning. Relational verification functions as a pre-release filter, making disclosure assumptions explicit, formally checkable, and refutable before deployment.

Future work includes extending the framework to richer schemas and multi-release settings, integrating probabilistic guarantees with relational invariants, and investigating how bounded non-reachability can be systematically combined with quantitative privacy analyses. This shift enables privacy risks to be analysed and eliminated before data release, rather than mitigated after exposure.

References

1. Albarghouthi, A., Hsu, J., Barthe, G.: Synthesizing programmatic privacy. In: Proceedings of the ACM on Programming Languages (POPL) (2017)
2. Barthe, G., Köpf, B., Olmedo, F., Zanella-Béguelin, S.: Probabilistic relational reasoning for differential privacy. In: ACM Symposium on Principles of Programming Languages, pp. 97–110 (2013)
3. Dalenius, T.: Towards a methodology for statistical disclosure control. Statistik Tidskrift (1977)
4. Dinur, I., Nissim, K.: Revealing information while preserving privacy. In: ACM Symposium on Principles of Database Systems, pp. 202–210 (2003)
5. Dwork, C., McSherry, F., Nissim, K., Smith, A.: Calibrating noise to sensitivity in private data analysis. In: Theory of Cryptography Conference. pp. 265–284. Springer (2006)
6. Dwork, C., Roth, A.: The Algorithmic Foundations of Differential Privacy. Now Publishers (2014)
7. Emam, K.E.: Guide to the De-Identification of Personal Health Information. CRC Press (2013)
8. Ganta, S., Kasiviswanathan, S.P., Smith, A.: Composition attacks and auxiliary information in data privacy. In: ACM Conference on Computer and Communications Security (2008)
9. Jackson, D.: Alloy: a lightweight object modelling notation. ACM Trans. Softw. Eng. Methodol. **11**(2), 256–290 (2002)
10. Jackson, D.: Software Abstractions: Logic, Language, and Analysis. MIT Press, 2 edn. (2012)
11. Li, N., Li, T., Venkatasubramanian, S.: t-closeness: privacy beyond k-anonymity and l-diversity. In: International Conference on Data Engineering, pp. 106–115. IEEE (2007). https://doi.org/10.1109/ICDE.2007.367856
12. Machanavajjhala, A., Kifer, D., Gehrke, J., Venkitasubramaniam, M.: l-diversity: privacy beyond k-anonymity. In: International Conference on Data Engineering, pp. 24–35. IEEE (2006)
13. de Montjoye, Y., Hidalgo, C.A., Verleysen, M., Blondel, V.D.: Unique in the crowd: the privacy bounds of human mobility. Sci. Reports **3** (2013). https://doi.org/10.1038/srep01376
14. Narayanan, A., Shmatikov, V.: Robust de-anonymization of large sparse datasets. In: IEEE Symposium on Security and Privacy, pp. 111–125 (2008). https://doi.org/10.1109/SP.2008.33
15. Ohm, P.: Broken promises of privacy: responding to the surprising failure of anonymization. UCLA Law Rev. **57**(6), 1701–1777 (2010)

16. Sabelfeld, A., Myers, A.C.: Language-based information-flow security. IEEE J. Sel. Areas Commun. **21**(1), 5–19 (2003)
17. Sweeney, L.: k-anonymity: a model for protecting privacy. Internat. J. Uncertain. Fuzziness Knowl. Based Syst. **10**(5), 557–570 (2002). https://doi.org/10.1142/S0218488502001648

Evaluating the Practical Impact
of Parallelism in Asmeta

Andrea Bombarda$^{(\boxtimes)}$, Silvia Bonfanti , Cesar Cornejo ,
Angelo Gargantini , and Nico Pellegrinelli

University of Bergamo, Bergamo, Italy
{andrea.bombarda,silvia.bonfanti,cesar.cornejo,angelo.gargantini,
nico.pellegrinelli}@unibg.it

Abstract. Parallelism is a key semantic feature of Abstract State
Machines (ASMs), represented in the `Asmeta` tool set by the `par` construct, which enables synchronous execution of multiple rules. While its
theoretical importance is firmly grounded in the ASM formalism, which
models synchronous updates through parallel rule execution, an evaluation of its real usefulness in real-world models has received limited
attention. This paper presents an experimental study evaluating how
and when parallelism is effectively used in `Asmeta`. We analyzed existing
specifications to measure the adoption of the `par` construct, and generated sequential variants replacing `par` with `seq` to compare behavior
through randomized test suites. Our findings show that `par` is widely
adopted and useful: it rather frequently produces results different from
those obtained by sequential execution.

Keywords: Abstract State Machines · `Asmeta` · Parallelism ·
Sequential

1 Introduction

Each notation introduces a set of concepts designed to serve as core features
for practitioners who adopt it. These concepts are translated in *constructs*
that are used when writing artifacts. For instance, object-oriented programming promotes encapsulation and modularity through the constructs of classes
and objects. For *Abstract State Machines* (ASMs) [9], a core feature is the synchronous *parallelism*: within a single computation step, all enabled rules are
evaluated concurrently over the current state. Their updates are collected into
a consistency-checked update set and applied atomically, yielding the next state
of the machine [4]. This concept is represented by the `par` construct within the
`AsmetaL` notation[1] [1,8]. It allows executing multiple rules in parallel by computing their updates based on the same state, and applying them together.

---

[1] The language used in the `Asmeta` tool set.

© The Author(s), under exclusive license to Springer Nature Switzerland AG 2026
F. Ishikawa and A. Cunha (Eds.): ABZ 2026, LNCS 16579, pp. 248–255, 2026.
https://doi.org/10.1007/978-3-032-26752-8_15

In practice, with the `par` statement, modelers can express concurrent reactions of independent components and multi-location updates that would otherwise be more complex to be decomposed into sequential steps. While parallelism is a semantic feature of ASMs, `Asmeta` allows users to also model sequential control flow through the `seq` construct: each rule is executed one after the other, so later rules are evaluated over the updates produced by earlier ones. In certain cases, whether the statements are executed sequentially or in parallel has no effect on the update set obtained after all rules have been fired. Thus, one may argue on the real usefulness of the `par` statement in `Asmeta`. More specifically, while one can provide theoretical evidence that the `par` construct is useful, some doubts may remain at a practical level.

A large body of work has established parallelism as a foundational semantic feature of ASMs, justifying compact synchronous updates and parallel rule composition that `Asmeta` implements via the `par` construct [4,9,15]. Although intuitively, ASM parallelism aims to capture the essence of synchronous parallel algorithms, [13] claimed that the original theory proposed in [4] was not convincing and proposed a new and simpler one.

In this work, we conduct an empirical study to assess the use of parallelism in `Asmeta` and to analyze how system behavior is affected when sequential execution replaces parallel constructs. A classical approach when it comes to investigating the usefulness of notations in software engineering is to provide users with questionnaires and ask their opinion [3,14]. However, questionnaires risk to be not objective, especially if the user base is limited and/or respondents contributed to the development of the notation. This is the reason behind our decision to evaluate the usefulness of `par` empirically and objectively.

We evaluated the usefulness of parallelism in `Asmeta` by analyzing and experimenting on 299 specifications. Our results confirm that `par` is used in most of the considered specifications (246 out of 299), and for the specifications we are able to generate the tests for (131 out of 246), in almost half of specifications (63 out of 131) parallelism was useful to express the desired behavior.

The remainder of the paper is structured as follows. Section 2 introduces ASMs and their parallelism, with the `Asmeta` notation. Section 3 details the empirical experimental methodology we adopted in our evaluation and presents the obtained results. In Sect. 4, we discuss potential threats to the validity of our findings and experiments. Finally, Sect. 5 concludes the paper.

2   Asmeta and Parallelism

This section examines the semantics and practical relevance of parallel execution in system modeling based on the ASM formalism[2].

The `par` statement is used in `Asmeta` to express parallel behavior by executing rules in parallel. Semantically, all rules are evaluated simultaneously over the current state, and all location updates are collected into a single *update set*

---

[2] For theoretical foundations of ASMs, see [9]; for further details on `Asmeta`, see [1,8].

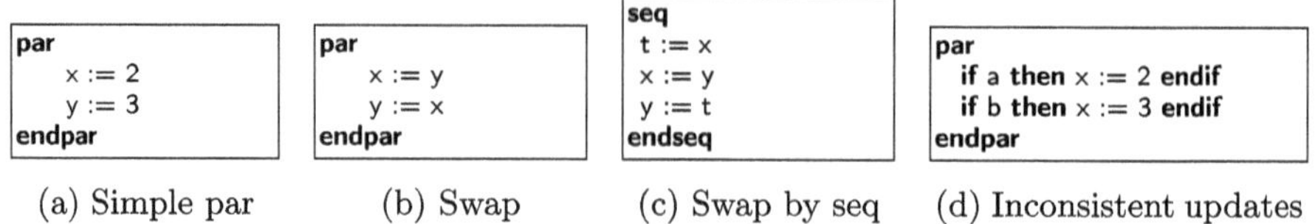

(a) Simple par   (b) Swap   (c) Swap by seq   (d) Inconsistent updates

Fig. 1. Examples of parallel and sequential blocks

that is applied atomically to produce the next state. As a consequence, the **par** construct can be interpreted as indicating that the contained statements can be executed in any order. Some examples illustrating the use of **par** in Asmeta are shown in Fig. 1. In Fig. 1a, two functions x and y are simultaneously updated, and the resulting update set is $\{x = 2, y = 3\}$. Since all terms are evaluated with respect to the current state, the **par** construct can easily express, for instance, operations such as value swapping without auxiliary variables. The code in Fig. 1b correctly swaps x and y in a single parallel step. Achieving the same effect with a sequential construct (**seq**) would require the more classical implementation shown in Fig. 1c.

As illustrated by the swap example, the use of **par** enables a more compact and declarative specification, eliminating the need for temporary variables. More generally, it facilitates the transition from one state to the next in spirit closer to the stepwise semantics of finite state machines rather than the imperative paradigm of general-purpose programming languages.

However, parallel updates may give rise to *inconsistent update* situations. As shown in Fig. 1d, when both conditions **a** and **b** are satisfied, the model attempts to assign two different values to **x** within the same step. Such inconsistencies can occur only under **par**, and their detection is beneficial, as it alerts the modeler to unintended interactions among rules. In this sense, **par** serves as a safeguard that exposes conflicting updates, thereby contributing to the correctness and clarity of the specified behavior.

3   Evaluation of the Practical Impact

In this section, we describe the empirical evaluation methodology we have adopted to assess the usefulness of parallelism and **par** construct in Asmeta. In particular, we defined two research questions (RQs) to guide our evaluation:

RQ1 Is parallelism in Asmeta used?
RQ2 Is parallelism in Asmeta useful?

RQ1: Is Parallelism in Asmeta Used? To evaluate if the **par** construct is used in Asmeta, we select all specifications from the original Asmeta GitHub repository at https://github.com/asmeta/asmeta/tree/master/asm_examples, excluding duplicates, those marked as "old," or written solely for testing purposes. Then, we count how many of the selected Asmeta specifications contain par in the main module. Specifications, scripts, and results are available online [6].

Findings: We found that par is used in 246 specifications over 299. It is therefore apparent that parallelism is a construct frequently used by modelers. However, there are cases in which parallelism is used even though it may not be strictly required. For instance, in Fig. 1a, the same behavior could have been achieved executing rules sequentially. We investigate this aspect in the following RQ.

RQ2: Is Parallelism in AsmetaUseful? To objectively evaluate the usefulness of par, we have devised the methodology depicted in Fig. 2. Given an Asmeta specification, M_{par}, containing some par blocks, we automatically generate a set of Asmeta specifications M_{seq} by replacing each par individually, one after the other[3], with a seq block (Step 1 in Fig. 2). For this, we use the *Parallel to Sequential* mutation operator defined in [5]. In this way, M_{par} and each M_{seq} differ only in the parallelism among rules, which is substituted by a more classical sequential activation. This mutation completely changes the semantics of the Asmeta specification, but it may or may not change its behavior. More precisely, if par plays a meaningful role in M_{par}, then M_{seq} exhibits different behavior. Conversely, if M_{seq} behaves identically to M_{par}, par is not useful in M_{par}.

In a specification S, we say that par is *useful* iff there is at least one par block in S that cannot be replaced by a seq block, with identical body, without changing the behavior of S.

Now, the problem of evaluating the usefulness of par is reduced to checking the behavioral equivalence between a specification (M_{par}) and a set of specifications (M_{seq}), and this can be proved or disproved in several ways. In this paper, we propose using *random test generation* and *mutation* analysis, which are effective for disproving, but not proving, behavioral equivalence.

First, a test suite TS is generated from M_{par} by using a random test generator [1] (Step 2 in Fig. 2). TS contains a set of tests in the Avalla language, which are composed by multiple step, set and check commands [11]. Being generated from M_{par}, TS will consist only of test cases that successfully execute that specification. Finally, TS is executed over all M_{seq} specifications (Step 3 in Fig. 2). If all the tests in TS pass, then we can say that the mutated specification shows an identical behavior w.r.t. the original one, and changing from par to seq did not cause any behavioral modification - at least for the behavior the tests were able to cover. Instead, if any test in TS fails, we say that the mutation is killed and we were able to find a case in which changing from par to seq would alter the behavior of the specification.

---

[3] Alternatively, we could have replaced all the pars in one shot, but this would have made impossible to assess the individual contribution of each par.

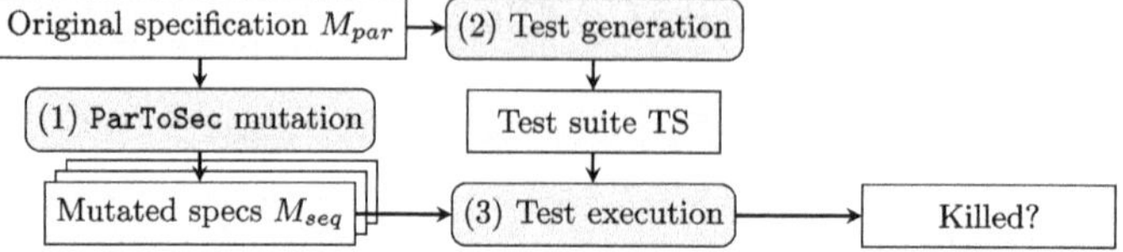

Fig. 2. Experimental process

Findings: Using the experimental methodology outlined above and considering the same set of specifications as in RQ1, we obtained the following results. Out of the 246 specifications, the full process completed successfully for 131. Mutants could be generated for all specifications, but the process could not be completed for some due to constructs not supported by either the validator or our test generator. Among the 131 successfully processed specifications, at least one mutant was killed for 63 of them (48.1%), indicating that parallelism (i.e., the use of **par**) matters in nearly half of the cases according to our definition of usefulness.

Upon analyzing the results, we were surprised by the large number of specifications (68) for which no mutant was killed. Although our findings come with certain limitations, which we discuss in the next section, we identified two peculiar scenarios in which **par** can (or cannot) be replaced by **seq**.

Fig. 3. Control State ASM

Fig. 4. **seq** order matters

Control State ASMs are ASMs in which one of the rules has a series of conditional rules checking the current state and setting a new state in case of meaningful events [10]. For these machines, the **par** is useful because omitting it would cause the ASM to skip some states during execution. For instance, in the ASM shown in Fig. 3, a sequential execution would result in the specification remaining permanently in the ON state. Overall, we observed that **par** is useful when it contains rules updating locations that are subsequently used by other rules within the same execution step.

Order Matters. In some cases, the inability (or ability) to kill mutants is instead caused by the specific ordering of rules within the **par**. For example, in the specification shown in Fig. 4, the **par** construct appears not useful solely because of the order in which the two assignments were written. If one had written the two updates in the opposite way, the **par** would have been useful.

4   Threats to Validity

In this section, we describe the main threats to validity according to the scheme proposed in [19] and elaborate on mitigation strategies.

Internal validity is a concern arising when the design of a study may compromise the accuracy of the results. To mitigate this risk, we have carefully checked the code executed in our experiments to see if other factors could have caused the outcome, such as errors in the tools or in the experimental code we wrote. However, potential threats to the internal validity still exist. First, to perform mutation analysis in RQ2, we have forced the behavior of the analyzed specifications to be deterministic even when specifications perform non-deterministic choices, to avoid flaky tests [7]. Second, in case of *inconsistent updates*, random test generation raises an exception, and it does not produce any scenario; therefore, the evaluation does not take into account the capability of the `par` construct to detect *inconsistent updates*. Initially, in the evaluation process, we had to set the number of tests and steps in each test to generate test cases. To avoid explicitly specifying the number of tests and steps, we introduced a 10 minutes timeout and iteratively increased the number of test cases with more steps, up to 20 iterations or until the first 5 iterations failed to generate any valid scenario. While this approach reduces the risk of selecting incorrect configuration parameters, it is important to acknowledge that using more tests (or steps) than those we encountered during our experiments within the timeout period could have yielded different results. By increasing timeout and max number of iterations, we may kill more mutants and increase the number of specifications for which `par` is actually useful. Likewise, when using random test cases, we cannot guarantee full coverage of the `Asmeta` specification [5]. As a result, some mutants may survive not because they behave identically to the original specification, but because the generated tests never exercise the mutated part.

Construct validity concerns arise when the link between theory and observation is weakened. A potential threat in our study lies in assuming that our chosen measures appropriately capture the usefulness of parallelism in `Asmeta`. We selected them based on established practice: usage frequency is widely used as a proxy for practical relevance [12,18], and mutation has been used in several contexts, such as assessing test suite effectiveness [16], source code optimization [17], and anomaly detection [2]. We acknowledge that the results for RQ2 are highly dependent on the definition of *usefulness* adopted in this study.

External validity is concerned with whether we can generalize the results outside the scope of the presented study. Killing mutants is a sufficient condition for proving usefulness of `par` but it is not a necessary one: it is not suitable for proving that `par` is not useful. We may explore formal proofs for that in future works, for instance using a model checker or an SMT solver. In our analysis, we considered all specifications available in the `Asmeta` GitHub repository. Although this constitutes an extensive dataset, most specifications were developed for research purposes. Nevertheless, the considered set also includes some real-world case studies, partially mitigating the external validity threat. In this paper, we applied our empirical evaluation to parallelism in `Asmeta`. However, we believe that the same methodology can be applied to other constructs or formal notations where a mutation excluding the analyzed construct exists.

5 Conclusion

In this paper, we empirically assessed the usefulness of parallelism and of the `par` construct in `Asmeta`. We found that most `Asmeta` specifications (82%) employ `par` (RQ1) and for many of them (52%) it is useful (RQ2). Thus, we can consider the `par` advantageous, at least in the presence of certain modeling styles that represent common pattern in ASMs. However, we discovered that in many other cases it could be replaced by `seq` without changing the behavior. Although parallelism is a fundamental feature of ASMs, to the best of our knowledge, this is the first work to empirically investigate whether `Asmeta` users employ `par` out of an actual need for parallelism or simply because it is the most commonly suggested composition strategy for ASMs. Also, some users may be more familiar with `seq`, while others may benefit from `par`. Further investigation of the pros and cons of parallel constructs may be needed, including required effort and ease of expressing complex behavior, e.g., via user questionnaires.

Acknowledgments. The work of Andrea Bombarda is supported by the project ANTHEM (AdvaNced Technologies for Human-centrEd Medicine) - PNC0000003 – CUP: B53C22006700001.

References

1. Arcaini, P., Bombarda, A., Bonfanti, S., Gargantini, A., Riccobene, E., Scandurra, P.: The ASMETA approach to safety assurance of software systems, pp. 215–238. Springer International Publishing, Cham (2021). https://doi.org/10.1007/978-3-030-76020-5_13

2. Arcaini, P., Gargantini, A., Riccobene, E., Vavassori, P.: A novel use of equivalent mutants for static anomaly detection in software artifacts. Inf. Softw. Technol. **81**, 52–64 (2017). https://doi.org/10.1016/j.infsof.2016.01.019

3. ter Beek, M.H., Ferrari, A.: Empirical formal methods: guidelines for performing empirical studies on formal methods. Software **1**(4), 381–416 (2022). https://doi.org/10.3390/software1040017

4. Blass, A., Gurevich, Y.: Abstract state machines capture parallel algorithms: correction and extension. ACM Trans. Comput. Logic **9**(3) (2008). https://doi.org/10.1145/1352582.1352587

5. Bombarda, A., Bonfanti, S., Cornejo, C., Gargantini, A., Pellegrinelli, N.: Evaluating coverage and fault detection capability of scenarios for the validation of asmeta specifications. In: Deshmukh, J., Havelund, K., Pinto, A. (eds.) NASA Formal Methods. Springer Nature Switzerland, Cham (2026a)

6. Bombarda, A., Bonfanti, S., Cornejo, C., Gargantini, A., Pellegrinelli, N.: Replication Package for "Evaluating the Practical Impact of Parallelism in Asmeta" (2026). https://doi.org/10.5281/zenodo.18550923

7. Bombarda, A., Bonfanti, S., Gargantini, A., Pellegrinelli, N.: Eliminating flakiness: deterministic control for validating nondeterministic asmeta specifications. In: Dutle, A., Humphrey, L., Titolo, L. (eds.) NASA Formal Methods, pp. 100–115. Springer Nature Switzerland, Cham (2025). https://doi.org/10.1007/978-3-031-93706-4_7

8. Bombarda, A., Bonfanti, S., Gargantini, A., Riccobene, E., Scandurra, P.: ASMETA tool set for rigorous system design. In: Formal Methods, pp. 492—517. Springer Nature Switzerland, Cham (2024). https://doi.org/10.1007/978-3-031-71177-0_28

9. Börger, E., Stärk, R.: Abstract state machines: a method for high-level system design and analysis. Springer Verlag (2003). https://doi.org/10.1007/978-3-642-18216-7

10. Borger, E., Stark, R.F.: Abstract State Machines. Springer, Berlin, Germany (Apr (2013)

11. Carioni, A., Gargantini, A., Riccobene, E., Scandurra, P.: A scenario-based validation language for ASMs. In: Börger, E., Butler, M., Bowen, J.P., Boca, P. (eds.) Abstract State Machines, B and Z, pp. 71–84. Springer, Berlin, Heidelberg (2008). https://doi.org/10.1007/978-3-540-87603-8_7

12. Costa, D., Andrzejak, A., Seboek, J., Lo, D.: Empirical study of usage and performance of java collections. In: Proceedings of the 8th ACM/SPEC on International Conference on Performance Engineering, pp. 389–400. Association for Computing Machinery, New York, NY, USA (2017). https://doi.org/10.1145/3030207.3030221

13. Ferrarotti, F., Schewe, K.D., Tec, L., Wang, Q.: A new thesis concerning synchronised parallel computing – simplified parallel ASM thesis. Theoret. Comput. Sci. **649**, 25–53 (2016). https://doi.org/10.1016/j.tcs.2016.08.013

14. Gross, A., Jurkiewicz, J., Doerr, J., Nawrocki, J.: Investigating the usefulness of notations in the context of requirements engineering. In: 2012 Second IEEE International Workshop on Empirical Requirements Engineering (EmpiRE), pp. 9–16 (2012). https://doi.org/10.1109/EmpiRE.2012.6347684

15. Gurevich, Y.: Abstract state machines: an overview of the project. In: Seipel, D., Turull-Torres, J.M. (eds.) FoIKS 2004. LNCS, vol. 2942, pp. 6–13. Springer, Heidelberg (2004). https://doi.org/10.1007/978-3-540-24627-5_2

16. Jia, Y., Harman, M.: An analysis and survey of the development of mutation testing. IEEE Trans. Softw. Eng. **37**(5), 649–678 (2011). https://doi.org/10.1109/TSE.2010.62

17. López, J., Kushik, N., Yevtushenko, N.: Source code optimization using equivalent mutants. Inf. Softw. Technol. **103**, 138–141 (2018). https://doi.org/10.1016/j.infsof.2018.06.013

18. Salmani Nodoushan, M.A.: Measurement theory in language testing: past traditions and current trends. i-manager's J. Educ. Psychol. **3**(2), 1–12 (2009). https://doi.org/10.26634/jpsy.3.2.1023

19. Wohlin, C., Runeson, P., Höst, M., Ohlsson, M.C., Regnell, B., Wesslén, A.: Experimentation in software engineering. Springer Berlin Heidelberg (2024). https://doi.org/10.1007/978-3-662-69306-3

Human-Centred Formal Verification: A Vision for Bridging Technical Rigour with Stakeholder Needs in Autonomous Systems

Asieh Salehi Fathabadi[(✉)] [iD] and Sebastian Stein [iD]

University of Southampton, Southampton, UK
A.Salehi@soton.ac.uk, ss2@ecs.soton.ac.uk

Abstract. Current formal verification practices for autonomous systems often develop in isolation from diverse stakeholders who interact with, operate, or are affected by these systems. Although formal methods excel at providing mathematical guarantees, they often fail to address the broader ecosystem of requirements and perspectives that determine real-world acceptance. This *vision paper* argues for human-centred formal verification that embeds stakeholder engagement throughout the verification lifecycle. We propose a framework that maintains rigour while ensuring that verification processes are accessible, inclusive, and responsive to stakeholder needs. Our approach addresses the gap between technical correctness and stakeholder confidence through participatory specification development, multi-perspective verification processes, and stakeholder-appropriate result communication. *This is a vision paper presenting a research agenda with technical details left to future work, aiming to advance discussion on integrating formal rigour with socio-technical stakeholder needs.*

1 Introduction and Related Work

Autonomous systems increasingly operate in complex socio-technical environments where success depends not only on technical correctness but also on acceptance by diverse stakeholders [26,29,33]. From autonomous vehicles to medical AI, these systems must satisfy the requirements of end-users, operators, regulators, and affected communities, each with distinct expectations and concerns. However, current formal verification practices focus predominantly on technical specifications developed by domain experts, with limited engagement from the broader stakeholder ecosystem.

The formal methods community has made significant advances in verifying properties of autonomous systems [6,23], yet a consistent gap remains between mathematical guarantees and stakeholder confidence. Specifications may omit critical stakeholder requirements, and verification results are often inaccessible to non-technical decision-makers, leading to deployment challenges despite technically sound verification [12,28]. For example, an autonomous vehicle may be

© The Author(s), under exclusive license to Springer Nature Switzerland AG 2026
F. Ishikawa and A. Cunha (Eds.): ABZ 2026, LNCS 16579, pp. 256–264, 2026.
https://doi.org/10.1007/978-3-032-26752-8_16

formally proven to avoid collisions under specific conditions while still failing to address stakeholder concerns such as pedestrian prioritisation or emergency vehicle interaction.

We argue that closing this gap requires human-centred formal verification: an approach that embeds stakeholder perspectives throughout the verification lifecycle while preserving mathematical rigour. This ensures that verification processes capture the full spectrum of stakeholder needs, increasing both technical assurance and real-world acceptance.

This paper is based on participatory design [30,31], which improves system acceptance by involving users in shaping system behaviour, and requirements engineering [14], which captures diverse stakeholder perspectives. We extend these approaches to formal verification contexts by offering (1) a framework for stakeholder-centric formal verification, (2) concrete techniques for multimodal specification development, (3) a worked example demonstrating feasibility, and (4) metrics for evaluating stakeholder engagement. Related work in visual specification languages [15], scenario-based modelling [17], explainable AI [3], and human–AI collaboration [5], along with broader human-centred design research [16], has sought to make technical systems more interpretable and usable. However, these strands of work typically support understanding or communication after development, rather than enabling stakeholders to participate directly in the creation and verification of formal specifications.

We refer to the resulting disconnect as the *stakeholder specification gap*: the mismatch between expert-authored formal specifications and the broader set of real-world needs known only to stakeholders [32]. For example, an autonomous warehouse robot may be proven safe with respect to collision avoidance yet still exhibit unpredictable or uncomfortable behaviour from a worker's perspective. Stakeholder groups often hold conflicting priorities—end-users value predictability, operators require intervention mechanisms, regulators demand auditability, and communities expect fairness and transparency [13,27]. Without systematic engagement, many of these requirements remain unrepresented in the formal model.

Prior work on participatory verification [18] and human-in-the-loop formal methods [10] explores ways for stakeholders to influence verification, but typically in isolated stages or through guidance to verification tools. Similarly, model-based systems engineering [11] and safety assurance cases [7] provide structured frameworks for requirements and assurance but do not routinely translate stakeholder concerns into formally verifiable properties. In contrast, our framework integrates socio-technical perspectives throughout the verification lifecycle and focuses on aligning stakeholder input with formal semantics through multi-modal specification techniques.

2   A Framework for Human-Centred Formal Verification

We propose a framework for human-centred formal verification that addresses the stakeholder specification gap while maintaining mathematical rigour. This framework embeds stakeholder engagement throughout the verification lifecycle[1].

Stakeholder-Centric Verification Lifecycle: An overview of the full lifecycle is shown in Fig. 1. Although shown linearly for clarity, the lifecycle is iterative, with verification outcomes and stakeholder feedback driving regular refinement.

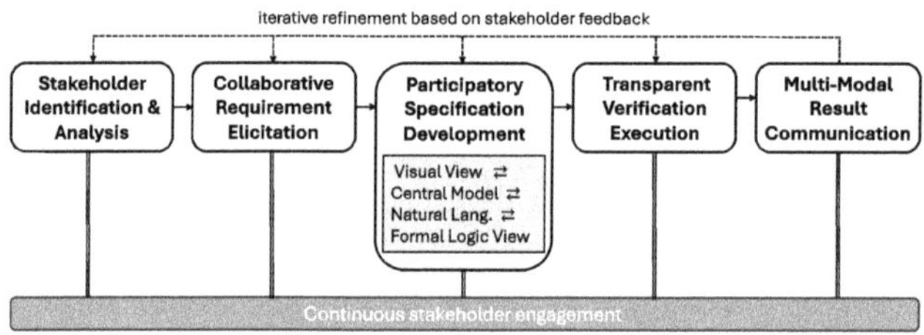

Fig. 1. Proposed human-centred formal verification lifecycle.

Our approach restructures the traditional verification process to prioritize stakeholder engagement. *Stakeholder Identification and Analysis* systematically identifies stakeholders by influence, interest, and impact, including indirect groups such as affected communities [24,25]. *Collaborative Requirement Elicitation* engages stakeholders through structured techniques [14] to capture needs and concerns and translate them into verifiable, traceable requirements. *Participatory Specification Development* involves stakeholders in iterative review of accessible representations, ensuring that formal specifications reflect their requirements [22]. *Transparent Verification Execution* supports stakeholder oversight through review of intermediate results, verification plans, and progress summaries. *Multi-Modal Result Communication* uses tailored formats such as executive summaries, visualisations, and technical reports [16].

Multi-perspective Specification Techniques: To support stakeholder participation, we use multi-modal techniques that improve accessibility while preserving formal rigour. *Visual Specifications* use graphical models such as state machines or sequence diagrams to express system behaviour and link them to formal logic through bidirectional translation. *Scenario-Based Specifications* express requirements through concrete situations that map to corresponding formal properties using structured templates. *Natural Language Interfaces* use controlled or domain-specific languages that allow stakeholders to express requirements in familiar terms and generate corresponding formal specifications [8].

---

[1] As a vision paper, we outline the rationale and leave full formalisation and tooling for future work.

Layered Specification Architecture organises requirements and properties across multiple abstraction levels, allowing stakeholders to engage at appropriate levels of detail, from high-level policies to concrete behavioural specifications.

Emergency Vehicle Priority: To demonstrate technical feasibility, consider specifying emergency vehicle priority for autonomous vehicles. Traditional formal verification might specify:

$\forall e \in EmergencyVehicles, \forall av \in AutonomousVehicles$: Approaching$(e, av) \Rightarrow$ YieldPath(av, e). Our multi-modal approach would present this as: *Natural Language:* "When an emergency vehicle approaches, autonomous vehicles must yield the right of way." *Visual Specification:* A state diagram showing autonomous vehicle states (normal driving, detecting emergency vehicle, yielding) with transitions triggered by emergency vehicle proximity. *Scenario-Based:* Concrete scenarios like "Ambulance with sirens approaches from behind on highway" with expected behaviours: "Autonomous vehicle detects siren audio signature, verifies emergency vehicle via vehicle-to-vehicle communication, safely moves to shoulder while maintaining minimum following distance." *Formal Property:* The original temporal logic formula, automatically generated from the natural language template, with additional constraints for safety (minimum distances, maximum deceleration) derived from scenarios. Stakeholder feedback might reveal missing requirements: emergency vehicles need predictable yielding behaviour, residents want noise minimization during yielding, traffic authorities require audit logs of emergency interactions. These translate to additional formal properties: deterministic yielding algorithms, acoustic impact constraints, and logging requirements. This demonstrates how stakeholder input enhances rather than compromises formal rigour by identifying missing requirements that improve system completeness and real-world effectiveness.

Feasibility and Tool Support. A key challenge is maintaining semantic consistency across visual, natural-language, and formal representations during iterative change. We propose a *model transformation pipeline* in which stakeholder-facing artefacts act as views over a central formal specification, with updates synchronised through bidirectional mappings. This builds on model-driven engineering techniques [8] and can be implemented using standard transformation frameworks with integrated consistency checking. In practice, a prototype could integrate: (1) a controlled natural language editor for structured requirement capture; (2) a diagram editor for visual state- or scenario-based models; and (3) a formal backend (e.g., Event-B [1], TLA+ [21], model checking backends Kind 2 [9] or temporal logic) for verification. Such a pipeline could be delivered as a *plugin* to existing formal specification environments, for example extending the Rodin toolset [2] for Event-B, thereby enabling seamless adoption within established verification workflows. Automated synchronisation would enable stakeholders to engage with accessible representations while formal verification is performed on an internally coherent model.

Case Study: Autonomous Vehicle Urban Deployment: Urban Autobreaknomous Vehicle (AV) involves diverse stakeholders with differing priorities, including residents, businesses, emergency services, regulators, and accessibility advocates. Engagement activities surface requirements such as predictable pedestrian interaction, reliable access management, emergency vehicle prioritisation, auditability, and inclusive interaction features. These needs are expressed using the multi-modal approach; for example, predictable pedestrian interaction becomes temporal-logic constraints on speeds, stopping distances, and warning signals, which stakeholders review through visual and scenario-based representations.

Refinement Example. We illustrate how stakeholder input tightens a baseline safety property for *emergency vehicle priority*. Let Yield denote creating right-of-way, Hazard hazard lights, Log an audit event, and $Risk > \theta$ an internal risk predicate.

Baseline property P_0: $\mathbf{G}(\text{DetectEV} \rightarrow \mathbf{F}_{\leq 2\text{s}}\text{Yield} \wedge \mathbf{G}_{\leq 10\text{s}}(\text{dist} \geq d_{\min}))$, where $\mathbf{G}$ is "globally" (always), $\mathbf{F}_{\leq t}$ is "eventually within t" (something will occur within time bound), $\mathbf{G}_{\leq t}$ is "globally for t" (something holds continuously for time duration), dist is inter-vehicle distance, and $d_{\min}$ is the safety threshold.

Stakeholder-derived constraints:

$$
\begin{array}{lll}
C_1 : \mathbf{G}(\text{StartYield} \rightarrow \mathbf{G}_{\leq T}\ \text{Maneuver} = \text{Shoulder}) & \quad \text{must move to shoulder within } T \\
C_2 : \mathbf{G}(\text{StartYield} \rightarrow \mathbf{F}_{\leq 0.5\text{s}}\text{Hazard}) & \quad \text{activate hazard lights promptly} \\
C_3 : \mathbf{G}(\text{StartYield} \rightarrow a(t) \in [-a_{\max}, a_{\max}]) & \quad \text{limit acceleration/deceleration} \\
C_4 : \mathbf{G}(\neg\text{Horn} \vee \text{Risk} > \theta) & \quad \text{horn only above risk threshold} \\
C_5 : \mathbf{G}(\text{EndInteraction} \rightarrow \mathbf{F}_{\leq 1\text{s}}\text{Log}) & \quad \text{log event within } 1\,\text{s}
\end{array}
$$

Refined property: $P_{\text{AV}} = P_0 \wedge C_1 \wedge C_2 \wedge C_3 \wedge C_4 \wedge C_5$, where each C_i reflects a stakeholder-driven refinement: C_1 shoulder maneuver, C_2 hazard lights within $0.5\,\text{s}$, C_3 acceleration limits, C_4 horn use only at high risk, C_5 interaction logging.

C_1–C_5 are generated from controlled templates and compiled to the target backend (e.g., LTL/MTL for model checking, or invariants in Event-B). For instance, C_2 becomes an Event-B proof obligation that `StartYield` leads to `HazardOn` within $0.5\,\text{s}$, leveraging approaches for modelling and verifying trust-related requirements in Event-B [4,13], where stakeholder-derived trust constraints are formalised as proof obligations to ensure both behavioural and assurance properties. Similarly, C_5 becomes a liveness property in TLA+ capturing post-interaction logging requirements. Stakeholder constraints thus *strengthen* the baseline property without weakening mathematical rigour.

3   Agenda, Evaluation, Challenges, and Mitigation

Advancing human-centred verification requires: (1) *stakeholder engagement methods* [19] capturing concerns for formalization; (2) *multi-modal specification languages* ensuring consistent visual, natural language, and formal views; and (3) *collaborative verification environments* supporting participation without sacrificing rigour. These can be assessed using requirement completeness (fraction captured), traceability to formal properties, specification accuracy (alignment with stakeholder intent), and comprehension scores.

Evaluation and Validation: combine subjective and technical measures. Subjective metrics capture stakeholder perceptions of coverage, engagement quality, and confidence. Technical metrics include the reduction of late requirement changes, the proportion of verified properties derived from stakeholder input, changes in verification effort, and the rate of issues discovered post-deployment. Together these assess whether human-centred verification improves both stakeholder confidence and formal assurance.

Expected Challenges and Mitigation Strategies. Implementing human-centred formal verification faces several anticipated challenges requiring careful consideration and mitigation strategies.

Complexity and Scalability Concerns: Engaging all stakeholders at every stage is costly. We recommend full-group involvement only for *initial elicitation* and *final review*, where consensus is critical.

Intermediate stages (e.g., iterative specification refinement, verification planning) can use *representative panels* selected for diversity of role and perspective, reducing cost while preserving coverage. Trade-offs include faster iteration but higher risk of missing niche requirements; this can be mitigated by rotating panel membership or validating interim artefacts with the wider group at predefined checkpoints. Standardised engagement protocols and lightweight online review tools further reduce coordination effort without sacrificing inclusivity.

Technical Expertise Barriers: Meaningful stakeholder participation requires some understanding of formal concepts, but stakeholders typically lack formal methods training. Mitigation strategies should develop scaffolding approaches supporting stakeholder participation without requiring deep technical expertise, including educational materials and training programs providing sufficient understanding for effective participation, interface designs abstracting technical complexity while preserving meaningful engagement opportunities, and facilitator roles bridging stakeholders and technical experts. Progressive disclosure techniques allow stakeholders to engage at appropriate technical levels.

Conflicting Stakeholder Requirements: Different stakeholder groups often have conflicting requirements requiring careful resolution without compromising verification quality. Mitigation approaches should develop systematic conflict resolution processes including stakeholder priority weighting, requirement negotiation protocols, and trade-off analysis frameworks. Use formal methods to identify requirement conflicts early and explore solution spaces. Establish governance structures for final requirement arbitration when consensus cannot be reached.

Verification Quality Concerns: Adding stakeholder engagement raises questions about whether this compromises verification quality or mathematical rigour. Mitigation strategies should establish clear boundaries between stakeholder input and technical verification requirements, develop quality gates ensuring stakeholder requirements translate into sound formal properties, use automated consistency checking to verify that multi-modal specifications maintain semantic alignment [20], and conduct regular technical reviews ensuring verification processes meet formal methods standards while incorporating stakeholder perspectives.

4   Conclusions and Future Directions

Human-centred formal verification addresses both technical correctness and stakeholder needs in autonomous systems. Our framework shows how rigour can be maintained while making verification accessible and responsive, supported by a feasibility example and an evaluation outline. Advancing this agenda requires interdisciplinary collaboration and future work on tool prototypes, empirical studies, standards, and training. Human-centred verification offers a rigorous path to integrating autonomous systems into social contexts. *As a vision paper, we outline a conceptual agenda and leave full technical development to future work.*

References

1. Abrial, J.R.: Modeling in Event-B: system and software engineering. Cambridge University Press, Cambridge, UK (2013)
2. Abrial, J., et al.: Rodin: an open toolset for modelling and reasoning in Event-B. Int. J. Softw. Tools Technol. Transf. **12**(6), 447–466 (2010)
3. Adadi, A., Berrada, M.: Peeking inside the black-box: a survey on Explainable Artificial Intelligence (XAI). IEEE Access **6**, 52138–52160 (2018)
4. Altamimi, M., Fathabadi, A.S., Yazdanpanah, V.: Formal modeling of trust in autonomous delivery vehicles. In: Integrated Formal Methods (2025)
5. Amershi, S., et al.: Guidelines for human-AI interaction. In: Proceedings of the 2019 CHI Conference on Human Factors in Computing Systems, CHI 2019, Glasgow, Scotland, UK, May 04-09, 2019. p. 3. ACM (2019)
6. Banach, R.: Autonomous system safety properties with multi-machine hybrid Event-B. In: Proceedings Sixth International Workshop on Formal Methods for Autonomous Systems, FMAS@iFM 2024, Manchester, UK, 11th and 12th of November 2024. EPTCS, vol. 411, pp. 1–19 (2024)
7. Bloomfield, R., Bishop, P., Anderson, T.: Safety and Assurance Cases: Past. Making Systems Safer, Present and Possible Future - an Adelard Perspective. In (2010)
8. Carvalho, G., Cavalcanti, A., Sampaio, A.: Modelling timed reactive systems from natural-language requirements. Formal Aspects Comput. **28**(5), 725–765 (2016). https://doi.org/10.1007/s00165-016-0387-x
9. Champion, A., Mebsout, A., Sticksel, C., Tinelli, C.: The kind 2 model checker. In: Chaudhuri, S., Farzan, A. (eds.) CAV 2016. LNCS, vol. 9780, pp. 510–517. Springer, Cham (2016). https://doi.org/10.1007/978-3-319-41540-6_29
10. Chiodo, M., Müller, D., Siewert, P., Wetherall, J.L., Yasmine, Z., Burden, J.: Formalising Human-in-the-Loop: Computational Reductions, Failure Modes, and Legal-Moral Responsibility (2025)
11. Dori, D.: Overview of ISO 19450. In: Model-based systems engineering with OPM and SysML, pp. 375–386. Springer, New York (2016). https://doi.org/10.1007/978-1-4939-3295-5_24

12. Fathabadi, A.S., Leonard, P.: Trust equals less death - it's as simple as tha : developing a socio-technical framework for trustworthy defence and security automated systems. In: Proceedings of the Second International Symposium on Trustworthy Autonomous Systems, TAS 2024, Austin, TX, USA, September 16-18, 2024, pp. 20:1–20:10. ACM (2024)
13. Fathabadi, A.S., Yazdanpanah, V.: Trust modelling and verification using Event-B. In: Proceedings Fifth International Workshop on Formal Methods for Autonomous Systems, FMAS@iFM 2023, Leiden, The Netherlands, 15th and 16th of November 2023. EPTCS, vol. 395, pp. 10–16 (2023)
14. Ferrari, A., Spoletini, P.: Formal requirements engineering and large language models: a two-way roadmap. Inf. Softw. Technol. **181**, 107697 (2025)
15. Fitzgerald, J., Larsen, P.G., Mukherjee, P., Plat, N., Verhoef, M.: Validated designs for object-oriented systems. Springer-Verlag TELOS, Santa Clara, CA, USA (2005)
16. Giacomin, J.: What is human centred design? Des. J. **17**(4), 606–623 (2014)
17. Harel, D., Marelly, R.: Come, let's play. Springer, Scenario-Based Programming Using LSCs and the Play-Engine (2003)
18. Harte, R., et al.: A human-centered design methodology to enhance the usability, human factors, and user experience of connected health systems: a three-phase methodology. JMIR Hum Factors (2017)
19. IEEE Standards Association: ISO 9241-210:2019 — Ergonomics of human-system interaction — Part 210: Human-centred design for interactive systems (2019), https://www.iso.org/standard/77520.html
20. IEEE Standards Association: IEEE Std 7001-2021 — IEEE Standard for Transparency of Autonomous Systems (2021). https://standards.ieee.org/standard/7001-2021.html
21. Lamport, L.: Specifying systems: the TLA+ language and tools for hardware and software engineers. Addison-Wesley Professional (2002)
22. Lorch, R., et al.: Formal methods in requirements engineering: survey and future directions. In: Proceedings of the 2024 IEEE/ACM 12th International Conference on Formal Methods in Software Engineering (FormaliSE), Lisbon, Portugal, April 14-15, 2024, pp. 88–99. ACM (2024)
23. Luckcuck, M., Farrell, M., Dennis, L.A., Dixon, C., Fisher, M.: formal specification and verification of autonomous robotic systems: a survey. ACM Comput. Surv. **52**(5), 100:1–100:41 (2019)
24. Mitchell, R.K., Agle, B.R., Wood, D.J.: Toward a theory of stakeholder identification andå salience: defining the principle of who and what really counts. Acad. Manag. Rev. **22**(4), 853–886 (1997)
25. O'Haire, C., et al.: Engaging stakeholders to identify and prioritize future research needs. Methods Future Research Needs Report 4, Agency for Healthcare Research and Quality (AHRQ), Rockville, MD (2011), AHRQ Publication No. 11-EHC044-EF
26. Ramchurn, S.D., et al.: A study of human-agent collaboration for multi-UAV task allocation in dynamic environments. In: Proceedings of the Twenty-Fourth International Joint Conference on Artificial Intelligence, IJCAI 2015, Buenos Aires, Argentina, July 25-31, 2015, pp. 1184–1192. AAAI Press (2015)
27. Ramchurn, S.D., Stein, S., Jennings, N.R.: Trustworthy human-AI partnerships. iScience **24**(8), 102891 (2021)
28. Fathabadi, A.S.: The trust-safety divide: a critical gap in human-robot interaction research. SCRITA / TRUST 2025 Workshop Proceedings (2025). https://arxiv.org/abs/2509.11402

29. Schmager, S., Pappas, I.O., Vassilakopoulou, P.: Understanding Human-Centred AI: a review of its defining elements and a research agenda. Behav. Inf. Technol. **44**(15), 3771–3810 (2025)
30. Schuler, D., Namioka, A.: Participatory design: principles and practices. L. Erlbaum Associates Inc., USA (1993)
31. Simonsen, J., Robertson, T. (eds.): Routledge International Handbook of Participatory Design. Routledge, London (2012). https://doi.org/10.4324/9780203108543
32. Soorati, M.D., et al.: From intelligent agents to trustworthy Human-Centred multiagent systems. AI Commun. **35**(4), 443–457 (2022)
33. Yazdanpanah, V., et al.: Reasoning about responsibility in autonomous systems: challenges and opportunities. AI Soc. **38**(4), 1453–1464 (2023)

Formal Verification of Decentralized Autonomous Organizations

Simone Valentini[1]([✉]) [iD], Sowelu Avanzo[2]([✉]) [iD], and Elvinia Riccobene[1]([✉]) [iD]

[1] University of Milan, Milan, Italy
{simone.valentini,elvinia.ricobene}@unimi.it
[2] University of Turin, Turin, Italy
soweluelios.avanzo@unito.it

Abstract. Decentralized Autonomous Organizations (DAOs) manage governance and financial processes through blockchain-based smart contracts, posing significant challenges in specification, implementation, and verification. While visual and model-driven approaches support DAO design, they lack integrated formal verification and reliable code generation mechanisms.

In this short contribution, we outline our long-term research vision aimed at integrating visual DAO specification with formal verification based on Abstract State Machines (ASMs). The proposed approach supports the verification of governance properties before deployment, thereby reducing the risk of vulnerabilities in smart contracts and enhancing assurance guarantees for stakeholders.

Keywords: Decentralized Autonomous Organization · DAO-ML · Formal Verification · Abstract State Machines · ASMETA

1 Introduction and Motivation

Decentralized Autonomous Organizations (DAOs) are blockchain-based systems that enable people to coordinate and govern themselves mediated by a set of self-executing rules deployed on a public blockchain, and whose governance is decentralized [20]. By enabling automated and decentralized execution of organizational rules, DAOs introduce novel forms of collective coordination, and have a big potential in the area of socio-technical systems in which governance and financial processes can be encoded as smart contracts deployed on public blockchains [4]. However, their design and implementation pose significant software engineering challenges, particularly due to the complexity of specifying, implementing, and verifying decentralized governance mechanisms [12].

Smart contracts on public blockchains are usually immutable: once deployed, their logic cannot be changed without costly migration or disruptive upgrades. Errors in governance design, like incorrect role hierarchies, permission assignments, or control relations, can lead to irreversible financial losses or manipulation. Ensuring correctness at design time is crucial [26].

© The Author(s), under exclusive license to Springer Nature Switzerland AG 2026
F. Ishikawa and A. Cunha (Eds.): ABZ 2026, LNCS 16579, pp. 265–273, 2026.
https://doi.org/10.1007/978-3-032-26752-8_17

Recent approaches adopt model-driven development and visual modeling languages, such as DAO-ML [7,9,17,23], to guide users in eliciting governance requirements and facilitate the design of governance structures and role-based access control. These methods improve communication with non-technical stakeholders and support code generation toward Solidity [29], the most used code language for DAO deployment on blockchain [10]. However, they lack integrated formal verification capabilities. As a result, governance properties are not systematically validated before deployment, and design errors may propagate from the visual model into the generated smart contract code.

In this short paper, we present a first step toward a formally grounded verification framework for DAO governance models. Our approach provides a formal semantics for DAO-ML [5,6] by mapping its elements into concepts specified by using the Abstract State Machine (ASM) formal method [13–15]. The formal model, automatically obtained from a DAO-ML model, can be analyzed using the ASMETA toolset [11,18], enabling simulation, model checking, and invariant verification prior to Solidity code generation. We illustrate the approach through a simplified excerpt from a realistic governance scenario involving a DAO coordinating regional tourism. This example demonstrates how governance inconsistencies can be identified and addressed at the modeling stage.

The approach adopted here has previously been used to provide formal semantics to graphical languages in other domains [3,27,28], but its application to DAO design introduces additional complexities in modeling role-based access control within socio-economic systems. In this context, the method is novel.

Recent work has addressed DAO verification; however, most approaches focus on detecting vulnerabilities at the level of the underlying blockchain smart contracts [1,16,22,24]. These techniques usually analyse code after it's been deployed or created, unlike our approach which advocates for security-by-design at the modeling stage. By placing formal analysis between visual DAO specification and code generation, we can verify governance properties before deployment, reducing the risk of design flaws propagating into immutable smart contracts and strengthening assurance guarantees for DAO stakeholders. Other methods aim to support secure-by-design development and analysis of smart contracts [2,21,25]. However, they are not specifically tailored to DAO governance structures and often require substantial expertise in formal methods or advanced formal modeling techniques.

2   The DAO-ML Language

The DAO-ML language has been developed to facilitate the specification of the organizational structure of DAOs and role-based access control [5]. Table 1 reports the DAO-ML notation and its informal description. The language notation extends that of Organization Models, defined in [30], to incorporate concepts needed to capture the specificities of decentralized governance. Elements such as *DAO*, *committee*, *governance area*, and *permission*, which are not present in the original Organization Models, have been included in DAO-ML.

Table 1. DAO-ML model elements and properties.

Element	Notation	Description
DAO		DAO system involving roles, committees, governance areas, and permissions included in the square.
Committee		Organized group of agents deliberating on a set of governance areas.
Role		Functions performed by agents in an organization.
Governance Area		Domain of interest for a committee or role.
Permission		Authorization to perform a given action.
Association	....	Assignment of a permission to a committee or role.
Control	⟶	The target entity can delegate, assign or remove permissions to/from the source entity.
Aggregation	⟶◇	The source entity is a sub-role or sub-committee of the target.
Federation		Participation of a role or committee in a target committee.

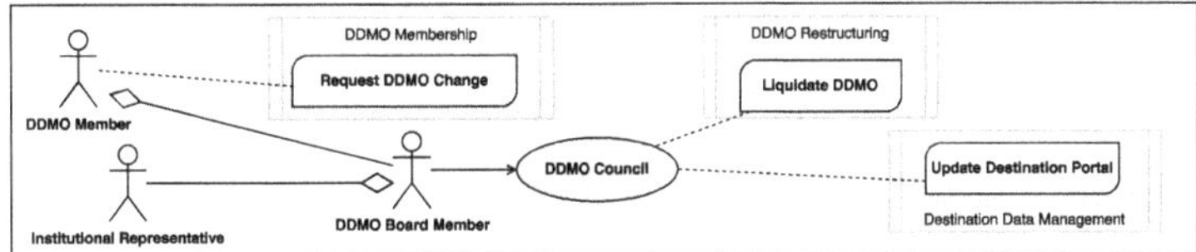

Fig. 1. Part of the Travelhive case study from [8]

As in Organization Models, *roles* represent distinct functions and responsibilities within an organization and are depicted using the UML actor icon, accompanied by a textual description. Permissions are assigned to agents through *Association* relations. An *Aggregation* relation captures inheritance between a more general and a more specialized role. Interactions among agents—namely roles and committees—also include control dynamics, whereby a controlling agent may assign or revoke permissions from a controlled agent. This capability is modeled through a *Control* relationship.

In [8], a translator is presented that generates optimized Solidity code from DAO-ML visual models. While DAO-ML supports the design phase through its user-friendly notation, it currently lacks tool support for the formal verification of DAO organizational structures. This limitation poses a significant risk: users may design and automatically generate DAO smart contracts that embed undesirable governance properties, such as incorrectly defined roles, improper permission assignments, flawed control relations, or inconsistent role hierarchies. To address this gap, we propose the first approach aimed at formally verifying the organizational structures of DAOs prior to code deployment.

Running example. Figure 1 presents a simplified excerpt from the *Travelhive* [8] case study, focusing on the organizational structure of a Decentralized Destination Management Organization (DDMO). It is a decentralized governance infrastructure that enables local stakeholders to collaboratively manage tourism

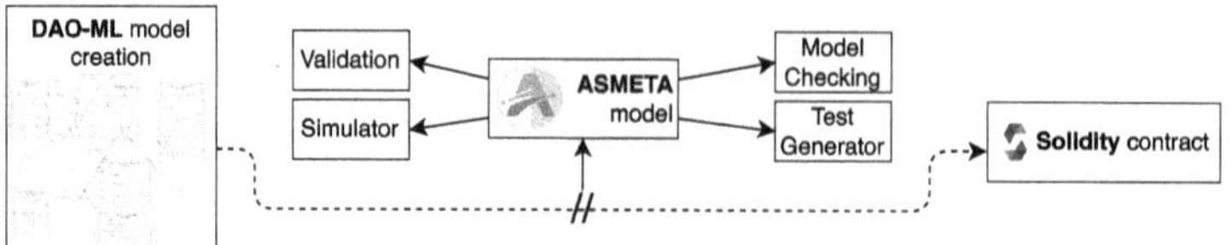

Fig. 2. Process for DAO development using DAO-ML

destinations through community-driven decision-making. Thus, local communities are empowered to define marketing strategies, promotion and token-based incentive policies, tailored to the specific characteristics of their region.

The model defines three roles: The *DDMO Member* represents any operational participant and does not possess voting or proposal rights; the *DDMO Board Member* is a restricted governance role, assigned to selected members, that grants participation rights in organizational decision-making; finally, the *Institutional Representative* is a specialized role representing institutional stakeholders. Using DAO-ML notation (Table 1), hierarchical inheritance is expressed via *aggregation* relations: the Institutional Representative is a sub-role of the DDMO Board Member, which in turn refines the DDMO Member role.

The *DDMO Council* is modeled as a *Committee*, i.e., a deliberative entity operating within defined governance areas. A *Control* relation specifies that the Council may assign or revoke permissions to the DDMO Board Member role.

Three Governance Areas are defined: *DDMO Membership*, *DDMO Restructuring*, and *Destination Data Management*. Within these areas, permissions are assigned via *Association* relations. In particular, the DDMO Member is authorized to *Request DDMO Change*, while the DDMO Council holds the permissions *Liquidate DDMO* and *Update Destination Portal*.

3 Formal Analysis of DAO-ML Models

To provide DAO-ML notation with a formal semantics and derive a formal specification from a DAO-ML model for analysis purposes, we adopt the *semantic mapping* technique of [19]. A manually defined *building function* maps DAO-ML constructs into mathematical elements expressed in `AsmetaL`, the textual language of the ASMETA toolset for Abstract State Machines. This mapping assigns semantics by translating graphical elements into abstract domains and transition rules, producing a corresponding `AsmetaL` model.

The resulting models can be analyzed using ASMETA's validation and verification facilities, including simulation (by `AsmetaS`) and model checking (by `AsmetaSMV`) of Computation Tree Logic (CTL) properties. This enables assessment of the expected dynamic behavior of a DAO-ML model *before* its translation into Solidity and deployment on the blockchain, following a process depicted in Fig. 2. Since smart contracts are typically immutable, early detection of governance inconsistencies reduces the risk of propagating design flaws into deployed code and increases confidence in the security of the resulting DAO system.

Table 2. DAO-ML model elements and properties.

DAO-ML element	ASM element
Committee	`static committeeName : Entity`
Role	`static roleName : Entity`
Permission	`static permissionName : Permission`
Governance Area	`static governanceAreaName : GovernanceArea` `controlled into : Permission -> GovernanceArea`
Association	`controlled associate : Prod(Entity, Permission) -> Boolean`
Control	`controlled controls : Prod(Entity, Entity) -> Boolean`
Aggregation	`controlled aggregation : Entity -> Entity`

3.1 Building Function Definition

Table 2 summarizes the mapping between DAO-ML elements and `AsmetaL` constructs. We introduce the abstract domains `Entity`, `Permission`, and `Governance Area` to represent the primary structural components of DAO-ML. The `Permission` and `GovernanceArea` domains directly correspond to their respective elements in DAO-ML, while the `Entity` domain encompasses both *Roles* and *Committees*. To distinguish between these, we define the enumerated domain `EntityType = {ROLE, COMMITTEE}`, which allows each `Entity` to be classified accordingly.

Each specific *Committee* or *Role* is represented as a static function (i.e., a constant) of type `Entity`, while *Permission* elements are modeled as static functions of type `Permission`. Similarly, specific *Governance Areas* are defined as static functions of type `GovernanceArea`, together with a dynamic controlled function `into` that maps a `Permission` to its corresponding `GovernanceArea`.

Relationship elements are formalized as follows. An *Association* is represented by a controlled function that checks whether a given `Entity` holds a specific `Permission`. A *Control* relation is modeled as a controlled Boolean-valued function over two `Entity` elements, returning `true` precisely when the first entity exercises control over the second. Finally, an *Aggregation* relation is captured by a controlled function mapping one `Entity` to another, thereby reflecting the hierarchical structure of the organization. The `Federation` relationship has not yet been modeled, but its absence does not affect our analysis.

In addition to the elements listed in Table 2, we define further functions and a set of transition rules to capture aspects of the intended dynamic behavior that cannot be directly expressed in the graphical notation and are typically described informally. In particular, two derived functions, `controlledBy` and `hasPermission`, are introduced to determine whether an `Entity` controls another `Entity` and whether an `Entity` possesses a specific `Permission`, respectively. Both functions account for control relationships and associations inherited through aggregation relations and inductions. Two transition rules (not reported here) model the two runtime operations of granting (`r_grantPermission`) and revoking (`r_revokePermission`) permissions. Both rules can be executed by agents that control a target entity (either a role or a committee) and possess the appropriate permission to assign or revoke privileges. The derived functions `controlledBy` and `hasPermission` are used to verify these preconditions. When they are satisfied, the controlled function `associate` is updated accordingly to grant or revoke the specified permission.

3.2   Mapping a DAO-ML Model Into an AsmetaL Model

```
1    static liquidate_ddmo : Permission
2    static update_destination_portal : Permission
3    static request_ddmo_change : Permission
4    static ddmo_member : Entity
5    static ddmo_board_member : Entity
6    static institutional_representative : Entity
7    static ddmo_council : Entity
8    ...
```

Listing 1.1: Signature of the AsmetaL model

Following the mapping rules detailed in Sect. 3, the DAO-ML model in Fig. 1 is automatically translated into an AsmetaL model whose signature is partially reported in Listing 1.1.

Once the formal model has been derived, rigorous verification activities can be performed. In particular, system requirements can be formalized as CTL formulas to verify *safety* and *liveness* properties (e.g., *a given role can eventually acquire a specific permission*), or as *invariants* to ensure that unauthorized states (e.g., *a non-council member holding the permission to liquidate the DDMO*) are never reachable. These properties are then analyzed using the ASMETA model checker to validate the correctness of the DAO organizational layer design. The following is a CTL formula defined to verify the example in Fig. 1:

```
CTLSPEC af(not hasPermission(institutional_representative, liquidate_ddmo))
```

It states that, in the future, the role `institutional_representative` will never have `liquidate_ddmo` permission. The model checker fails to validate this property because the DDMO Council committee can assign the Liquidate DDMO permission to the DDMO Board Member role, which is subsequently inherited by the Institutional Representative.

4   Conclusion and Future Work

In this paper, we presented a formally grounded approach for verifying DAO governance models by mapping DAO-ML specifications to Abstract State Machines (ASMs). This mapping enables rigorous analysis of governance structures prior to smart contract deployment. By leveraging the ASMETA toolset, simulation and model checking can identify inconsistencies in role hierarchies, permission assignments, and control relations at the modeling stage, thereby reducing the risk of propagating design errors into immutable Solidity contracts.

Future work includes automating the DAO-ML-to-ASM translation, strengthening integration with Solidity code generation, and extending the framework toward richer governance constraints and compositional verification of interacting DAOs. Our long-term objective is a unified, verification-aware workflow for secure DAO design and deployment.

Acknowledgement. This work was supported in part by project SERICS (PE00000014) under the NRRP MUR program funded by the EU - NGEU.

References

1. Altaleb, H., Fregan, B., Rajnai, Z.: Fortifying decentralized governance: introducing Decentralized Autonomous Verification (DAVe) for Decentralized Autonomous Organization (DAOs) security. In: 2024 IEEE 28th International Conference on Intelligent Engineering Systems (INES), pp. 000049–000054 (2024). https://doi. org/10.1109/INES63318.2024.10629149
2. Annenkov, D., Nielsen, J.B., Spitters, B.: ConCert: a smart contract certification framework in Coq. In: Blanchette, J., Hritcu, C. (eds.) Proceedings of the 9th ACM SIGPLAN International Conference on Certified Programs and Proofs, CPP 2020, New Orleans, LA, USA, January 20-21, 2020, pp. 215–228. ACM (2020). https:// doi.org/10.1145/3372885.3373829
3. Arcaini, P., Mirandola, R., Riccobene, E., Scandurra, P.: MSL: a pattern language for engineering self-adaptive systems. J. Syst. Softw. **164**, 110558 (2020). https:// doi.org/10.1016/J.JSS.2020.110558
4. Avanzo, S.: A model-driven method for decentralized autonomous organization development. Doctoral thesis, Università degli Studi di Torino, Turin, Italy (2025), phD in Computer Science (Ciclo 37°), Department of Computer Science. https://tesidottorato.depositolegale.it/bitstream/20.500. 14242/214884/1/ilovepdf_merged-8.pdf
5. Avanzo, S., Norta, A., Linares, J., Schifanella, C., Hattingh, M.: DAO-ML: a modelling language for the specification of decentralized autonomous organization governance. Methods **13**, 16 (2024). https://ceur-ws.org/Vol-3791/paper3.pdf
6. Avanzo, S., Norta, A., Linares, J., Schifanella, C., Hattingh, M.: Extending trusted DAPP modeling for decentralized autonomous organization development. In: Prieto, J., Vargas, R.P., Lage, O., Machado, J.M., Bálint, M. (eds.) Blockchain and Applications, 6th International Congress, pp. 140–149. Springer Nature Switzerland, Cham (2025)
7. Avanzo, S., Norta, A., Schifanella, C.: A modelling approach for a high utility decentralized autonomous organization development. In: Machado, J.M. (eds.) Blockchain and Applications, 5th International Congress, pp. 542–547. Springer Nature Switzerland, Cham (2023)
8. Avanzo, S., et al.: DAO-ML to solidity: a scalable code generation approach for decentralized autonomous organization development. In: Proceedings of the 2025 International Conference on Information Technology for Social Good, pp. 353–361. GoodIT '25, Association for Computing Machinery, New York, NY, USA (2025). https://doi.org/10.1145/3748699.3749812

9. Avanzo, S., et al.: DAOMod: a modeling method for decentralized autonomous organization development. Electronic Communications of the EASST **84** (2025). https://doi.org/10.14279/eceasst.v84.2675. https://eceasst.org/index.php/eceasst/article/view/2675

10. Bartoletti, M., et al.: Smart contract languages: a comparative analysis. Future Gener. Comput. Syst. **164**, 107563 (2025). https://doi.org/10.1016/J.FUTURE.2024.107563

11. Bombarda, A., Bonfanti, S., Gargantini, A., Riccobene, E., Scandurra, P.: ASMETA tool set for rigorous system design. In: Formal Methods - 26th International Symposium, FM 2024, Milan, Italy, September 9-13, 2024, Proceedings, Part II. Lecture Notes in Computer Science, vol. 14934, pp. 492–517. Springer (2024). https://doi.org/10.1007/978-3-031-71177-0_28

12. Bonnet, S., Teuteberg, F.: Decentralized autonomous organizations: a systematic literature review and research agenda. Int. J. Innov. Technol. Manage. (IJITM) **21**(04), 1–63 (2024)

13. Börger, E., Gervasi, V.: Structures of computing - a guide to practice-oriented theory. Springer (2024). https://doi.org/10.1007/978-3-031-54358-6

14. Börger, E., Raschke, A.: Model. Companion Softw. Pract. Springer (2018). https://doi.org/10.1007/978-3-662-56641-1

15. Börger, E., Stärk, R.F.: Abstract state machines. A Method for High-Level System Design and Analysis. Springer (2003). http://www.springer.com/computer/swe/book/978-3-540-00702-9

16. Certora: Certora Technology White Paper — Certora Prover Documentation 0.0 documentation (2024). https://docs.certora.com/en/latest/docs/whitepaper/index.html

17. Domenicale, I., Toti, C., Avanzo, S., Viano, C., Schifanella, C.: An interdisciplinary approach to the coordination layer of DAOs and the design of token economies. In: Lustenberger, M., Spychiger, F., Küng, L. (eds.) Decentralized Autonomous Organizations—Governance, Technology, and Legal Perspectives: Proceedings of the 2nd European DAO Workshop (DAWO), Zurich, Switzerland, 2025, pp. 53–68. Springer Proceedings in Business and Economics, Springer, Cham (2026). https://doi.org/10.1007/978-3-032-03273-7_4. Accessed 31 Oct 2025

18. Gargantini, A., Riccobene, E., Scandurra, P.: Model-driven language engineering: the ASMETA case study. In: Proceedings of the Third International Conference on Software Engineering Advances, ICSEA 2008, October 26-31, 2008, Sliema, Malta, pp. 373–378. IEEE Computer Society (2008). https://doi.org/10.1109/ICSEA.2008.62

19. Gargantini, A., Riccobene, E., Scandurra, P.: A semantic framework for metamodel-based languages. Autom. Softw. Eng. **16**(3–4), 415–454 (2009). https://doi.org/10.1007/S10515-009-0053-0

20. Hassan, S., De Filippi, P.: Decentralized autonomous organization. Internet Policy Rev. J. Internet Regul. **10**(2), 1–10 (2021)

21. He, Y., Dong, H., Wu, H., Duan, Q.: Formal analysis of reentrancy vulnerabilities in smart contract based on CPN. Electronics **12**(10) (2023). https://doi.org/10.3390/electronics12102152. https://www.mdpi.com/2079-9292/12/10/2152

22. Hildenbrandt, E., et al.: KEVM: a complete formal semantics of the Ethereum virtual machine. In: 31st IEEE Computer Security Foundations Symposium, CSF 2018, Oxford, United Kingdom, July 9-12, 2018, pp. 204–217. IEEE Computer Society (2018). https://doi.org/10.1109/CSF.2018.00022

23. Kaya, F., Perez, F., Dekker, J., Gordijn, J.: Decent: a domain specific language to design governance decisions. In: International Conference on Research Challenges in Information Science, pp. 603–610. Springer (2023)
24. Liao, J., Tsai, T., He, C., Tien, C.: SoliAudit: smart contract vulnerability assessment based on Machine Learning and Fuzz Testing. In: Alsmirat, M.A., Jararweh, Y. (eds.) Sixth International Conference on Internet of Things: Systems, Management and Security, IOTSMS 2019, Granada, Spain, October 22-25, 2019, pp. 458–465. IEEE (2019). https://doi.org/10.1109/IOTSMS48152.2019.8939256
25. Mavridou, A., Laszka, A., Stachtiari, E., Dubey, A.: VeriSolid: correct-by-design smart contracts for Ethereum. In: Goldberg, I., Moore, T. (eds.) FC 2019. LNCS, vol. 11598, pp. 446–465. Springer, Cham (2019). https://doi.org/10.1007/978-3-030-32101-7_27
26. Mehar, M.I., et al.: Understanding a revolutionary and flawed grand experiment in blockchain: the DAO attack. J. Cases Inf. Technol. **21**(1), 19–32 (2019). https://doi.org/10.4018/JCIT.2019010102
27. Riccobene, E., Scandurra, P.: An executable semantics of the systemc UML profile. In: Frappier, M., Glässer, U., Khurshid, S., Laleau, R., Reeves, S. (eds.) ABZ 2010. LNCS, vol. 5977, pp. 75–90. Springer, Heidelberg (2010). https://doi.org/10.1007/978-3-642-11811-1_7
28. Riccobene, E., Scandurra, P.: A formal framework for service modeling and prototyping. Formal Aspects Comput. **26**(6), 1077–1113 (2014). https://doi.org/10.1007/S00165-013-0289-0
29. Sowelu, V.: DAO-ML to solidity testing). https://github.com/SoweluAvanzo/DAO-ML_to_Solidity_testing (2025), Github repository that provides a set of solidity smart contracts automatically generated from DAO-ML models
30. Sterling, L.S., Taveter, K.: The Art of agent-oriented modeling. The MIT Press, OCLC: 1178943942

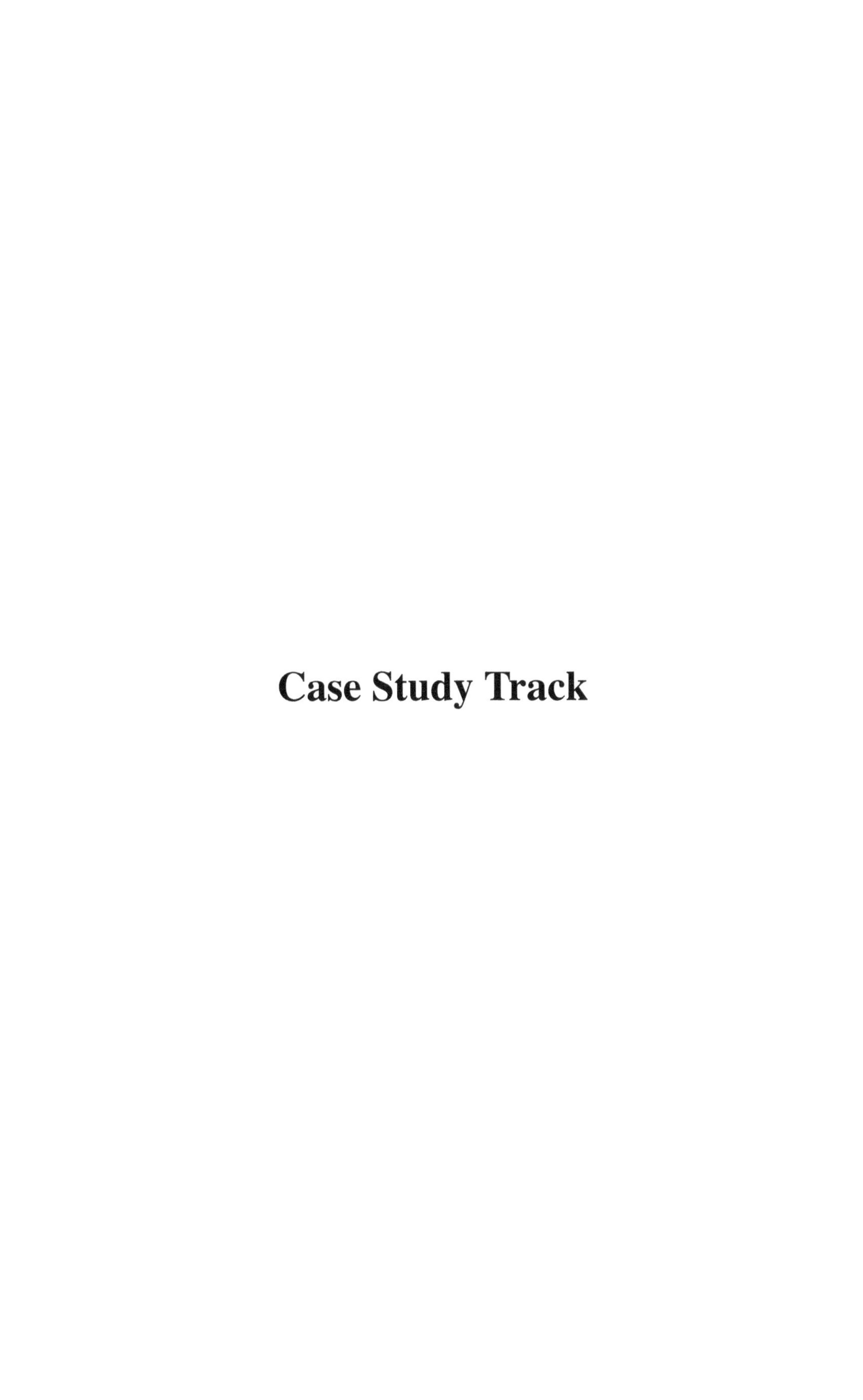

Case Study Track

ABZ 2026 Case Study: A Planetary Rover

Marie Farrell[1][(✉)] and Tsutomu Kobayashi[2]

[1] The University of Manchester, Manchester, UK
`marie.farrell@manchester.ac.uk`
[2] Japan Aerospace Exploration Agency (JAXA), Tsukuba, Japan
`kobayashi.tsutomu@jaxa.jp`

Abstract. This document summarises the ABZ 2026 case study challenge. The system under consideration is that of an autonomous planetary rover. We summarise the architecture for the rover, its requirements and the tasks that participants in the case study track should focus on. We also outline several extensions that may be considered in future work or that offer other perspectives for formal modelling and verification.

1 Introduction

We propose the case study of a semi-autonomous planetary rover undertaking an inpsection mission. This use case is adapted from [2–4] and modified in several interesting ways. The software architecture for our rover is illustrated in Fig. 2. The requirements for the components are described throughout the remainder of this document, along with several system-level requirements. The examples discussed in [2–4] were inspired by real-world missions including the Curiosity [20, 21] and Perseverance [9] planetary exploration rovers illustrated in Fig. 1. These sophisticated robotic systems have more complex architectures and functionalities than we present here including sample collection [9] and autonomous laser targetting [12] capabilities. This ABZ 2026 case study focuses on simplified, but sufficiently complex, aspects of these rover missions including waypoint inspection, failure modes and communication.

It has been well observed that formal specification and verification of autonomous robotic systems remains a challenging topic, with heterogeneous and integrated formal methods recommended to tackle the intricate complexities of these systems [1, 11, 15]. This is further complicated by the unpredictable environment in the space domain alongside our inability to provide high-fidelity testing of these systems on planet Earth [5]. More specifically, a rover must handle interactions with the planet's ground while avoiding obstacles or valleys, relying on sensors and actuators that operate within strict physical constraints. The harsh environment and physical constraints also cause problems with the battery and unreliable communication. Therefore, functionalities for detecting failures and recovery from them are vital for safety. At the same time, the large budget and human resources invested in space development raise expectations for mission achievement, which often conflict with safety.

© The Author(s), under exclusive license to Springer Nature Switzerland AG 2026
F. Ishikawa and A. Cunha (Eds.): ABZ 2026, LNCS 16579, pp. 277–290, 2026.
https://doi.org/10.1007/978-3-032-26752-8_18

Fig. 1. NASA's Curiosity (left) and Perseverance (right) rovers. Source: NASA.

2 Requirements

We begin by defining the architecture for our autonomous robotic system. This architecture is shown in Fig. 2. We include several components and sub-components. Some of these are grouped to demonstrate the system decomposition. Specifically, we have a Vision system which is used for obstacle recognition and determining the current position of the rover. Then the MapValidator is used to validate the information coming from the Vision component along with the information that was communicated by the ground station which includes the list of prioritised goal locations and charging locations. The Goal Reasoning Agent (GRA) is charged with selecting the next goal that the rover should visit. This can either be the next one in the prioritised list or a charging location depending on the remaining battery available, as calculated by the BatteryMonitor which sits inside the Battery+Hardware component shown in Fig. 2. We then have two copies of the same functionality in the ComputePlan2Charging and ComputePlan2Destination components. Each of these comprises a Planner and a Plan Reasoning Agent (PRA). The idea here is that ComputePlan2Destination produces a plan (list of waypoints) that the rover should traverse to reach the goal location. In parallel, ComputePlan2Charging provides a plan from the goal location to the nearest charging location. This ensures that the rover will have enough battery power to reach the next goal and then recharge if necessary. This is an important point and is needed to meet the system-level requirement that the rover should never run out of battery (which will be dicussed later).

As mentioned already, the Battery+Hardware component keeps track of the battery level through the BatteryMonitor. However, it also interfaces with the hardware (wheels, motors, actuators, etc.) to traverse through the waypoints in the plans that are sent to it by ComputePlan2Charging and ComputePlan2Destination. We make the SolarPanelController explicit here. When the rover reaches a charging location the solar panels should be opened and subsequently closed once charing is complete. This is a sophisticated functionality that has not been present on older rovers but it will be useful in future missions. When the solar panels are left open during an entire mission, they

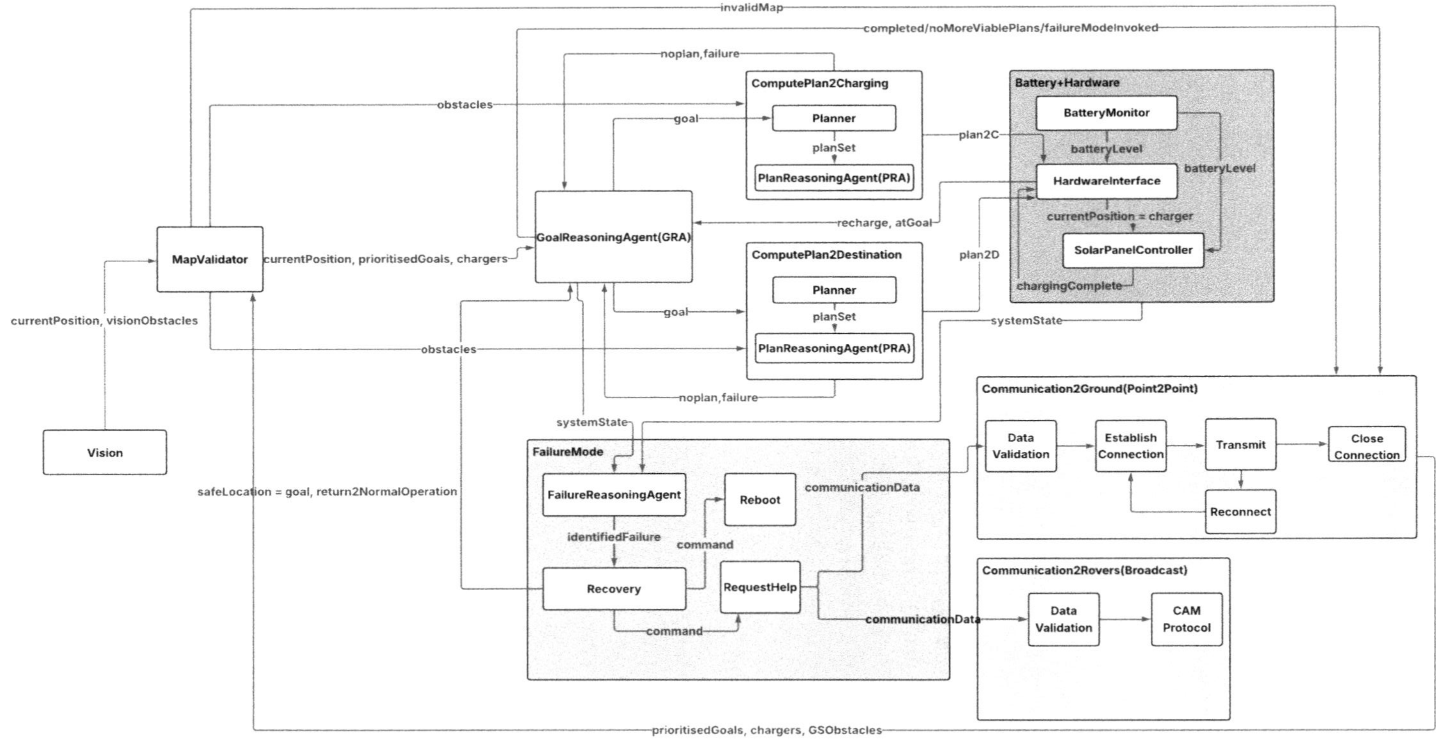

Fig. 2. System Architecture.

can become very dusty making it difficult and sometimes impossible to charge. NASA's insight lander suffered from this exact issue[1].

Distant plantary missions in hostile and unpredictable environments can experience several causes of failure. Recovery from such failures is typically not trivial. Hence, we include the FailureMode component which comprises a FailureReasoningAgent who determines the most likely cause of the failure, a Recovery component who invokes various recovery operation. These include a simple Reboot or RequestHelp. Help can be requested from the ground station via Communication2Ground or from other nearby rovers using Communication2Rovers. Each of these communication options follow a different protocol. The communication to the ground station is a point-to-point communication whereas communicating with other rovers takes place in a broadcast style. We describe the kinds of communications in a bit more detail later but we note that we do not concern ourselves with security aspects of message passing in this case study. That said, cybersecurity is especially important in space applications [17] so an extension of this case study to focus on security would be a useful contribution. When assistance is requested through the RequestHelp component, it may take some time to receive a reply from the ground (40 min round trip communication time from Earth to Mars) and from other rovers so the WaitForHelp component periodically rechecks whether a response has been received.

2.1 Variables

We provide variable names and types for the variables used in Fig. 2. Case study participants may veer from this list in their specific models to simplify and/or concretise their specifications. This list should be viewed as a guideline and actual types depend on the level of abstraction that the modelling might be done at (Table 1).

2.2 System-Level Requirements

As we defined this use case, we moved through each of the components in Fig. 2 and elicited requirements for each. We also examined the system-level requirements. These were inspired by [2–4], with the addition of a requirment related to failure modes. We summarise the system-level requirements in Table 2.

2.3 The **Vision** Component

We assume that the rover is equipped with appropriate sensors and cameras to enable perception of obstacles and localisation. We do not focus on the low-level details of localisation algorithms that are commonly used in robotic systems such as Simultaneous Localisation and Mappling (SLAM) [7]. However, we welcome

---

[1] https://www.jpl.nasa.gov/news/nasa-mars-orbiter-spots-retired-insight-lander-to-study-dust-movement/.

Table 1. Variable names and types for the variables used in Fig. 2.

Variable Name	Type
currentPosition	(x,y) where $x \in \mathbb{N}, y \in \mathbb{N}$
visionObstacles	$\{(x,y) \mid x \in \mathbb{N}, y \in \mathbb{N}\}$
safeLocation	(x,y) where $x \in \mathbb{N}, y \in \mathbb{N}^a$
return2NormalOperation	bool
obstacles	$\{(x,y) \mid x \in \mathbb{N}, y \in \mathbb{N}\}$
prioritisedGoals	$\{(x,y) \mid x \in \mathbb{N}, y \in \mathbb{N}\}$
chargers	$\{(x,y) \mid x \in \mathbb{N}, y \in \mathbb{N}\}$
invalidMap	message
completed/ noMoreViablePlans/ failureModeInvoked	message
noplan	bool
failure	bool
goal	(x,y) where $x \in \mathbb{N}, y \in \mathbb{N}$
systemState	$(\texttt{failure}, \texttt{noplan}, \mathit{messages})$
plan2C	$[(x,y) \mid x \in \mathbb{N}, y \in \mathbb{N}]$
plan2D	$[(x,y) \mid x \in \mathbb{N}, y \in \mathbb{N}]$
batteryLevel	float
chargingComplete	bool
recharge	bool
atGoal	bool
identifiedFailure	message
command	message
recheck	bool
communicationData	$(\mathit{messages}, \mathit{dataCollected}, \texttt{systemState})$
GSObstacles	$\{(x,y) \mid x \in \mathbb{N}, y \in \mathbb{N}\}$
helperID	$\mathbb{N}$
failed2Reconnect	bool

^{a}There might be multiple safe locations.

submissions that focus on these finer-grained details. We define several requirements for the Vision component in Table 3. We recognise that vision perception systems are not often completely exact in nature and this is reflected in the requirements.

2.4   The **MapValidator** Component

Recognising that both the ground station and Vision system may incorrectly label obstacles, GSObstacles, chargers, prioritisedGoals and the rover's currentPosition. We include the MapValidator component to do some sanity checking that goals, chargers and the current position of the rover do not collide with obstacles that are identified by the Vision system or the ground station. In cases where there are issues, we sent an invalidMap notification to the ground

Table 2. System-level requirements.

ID	Description
SL1	The rover shall never run out of battery.
SL2	The rover shall eventually visit all of the goal locations.
SL3	The rover shall react appropriately to failures, requesting help from the ground station and other rovers if needed.
SL4	The rover shall not collide with an obstacle.
SL5	The rover shall have a low incidence of failures.

Table 3. The Vision system requirements.

ID	Description
V1	Vision shall take input from sensors including a camera and LiDAR.
V2	Vision shall return the current position of the rover (using SLAM algorithms [7]) and a set of obstacle positions.
V3	Vision shall identify obstacles with an accuracy of over 95%.
V4	The current position of the rover identified by the Vision component shall not collide with any of the identified obstacles.
V5	The current position identified by the Vision component shall be the actual current position of the rover within $\pm 2\,\mathrm{m}$.
V6	The Vision system shall be robust to small perturbations in input data (local robustness), e.g. [13].

station where we assume that human operators can assist by either (1) updating the data that they orignally sent or (2) overriding certain perceptions of the Vision system. We include the requirements for the MapValidator in Table 4.

2.5   The Goal Reasoning Agent (GRA)

We use a symbolic Goal Reasoning Agent to choose the next waypoint that the rover should navigate to. In previous work, a similar agent was implemented using Lustre [2,3] and in Gwendolen [4]. This rules-based agent is responsible for ensuring that the rover can always reach a `charger` position from any `goal` that it selects and instructing the rover to navigate directly to a `charger` when needed. It also notifies the ground station when the current mission is completed and invokes the FailureMode as required. We summarise the requirements for the Goal Reasoning Agent in Table 5.

2.6   The ComputePlan2Charging Component

The ComputePlan2Charging component is made up of two subcomponents: a Planner and a PlanReasoningAgent(PRA) as illustrated in Fig. 2. The requirements for this component are shown in Table 6. Various path planning algorithms

Table 4. The MapValidator requirements.

ID	Description
M1	The MapValidator shall validate the `obstacles` and `currentPosition` provided by the Vision component against the `prioritisedGoals`, `GSObstacles` and `chargers` provided by the ground station.
M2	The `obstacles` sent from the MapValidator to the Goal Reasoning Agent shall not collide with the `currentPosition` of the rover.
M3	The `obstacles` sent from the MapValidator to the Goal Reasoning Agent with the `charger` positions.
M4	If the map is invalid then the MapValidator shall send a message to the ground station to seek advice, operators can update and override the original map.
M5	The `obstacles` sent from the MapValidator to the Goal Reasoning Agent shall not collide with the goal positions of the rover that are given by the ground station.

might be used by the Planner that are appropriate for robotic systems. This can range from a simple depth-first search style algorithm to more sophisticated implementations. We do not seect a specific planning algorithm so participants in the case study track may choose any suitable and/or interesting algorithm.

2.7   The **ComputePlan2Destination** Component

The ComputePlan2Destination component has the same structure as the ComputePlan2Charging component. The only difference is that is computes the plan to the destination goal, `plan2D`, rather than the charging location as default. Note that this `goal` destination might be a charging position in situations where the GRA sends the rover to recharge. In this case the `plan2C` produced would be empty because the rover will be at the charger. The requirements are listed in Table 7.

2.8   The **Battery+Hardware** Component

We group the BatteryMonitor, HardwareInterface and SolarPanelController together in Fig. 2 as these are concerned with low-level physical control and measurements. For ease of calculation, we assume that each step in any given plan for the rover consumes 1 unit of battery power. More sophisticated models could have knowledge of the terrain topography and use this to calculate battery used per plan step. For example, going up a hill may use more battery than traversing a level area. We encourage participants to consider more complicated models where possible. The HardwareInterface is responsible for sending low-level movement commands to various actuators that control motion. This rover system uses the Robot Operating System (ROS) [16] so pre-existing libraries are used

Table 5. The Goal Reasoning Agent (GRA) requirements.

ID	Description
G1	The GRA shall select the next **goal** for the rover to navigate to from the **prioritisedGoals** that were received from the ground station.
G2	Whenever the **recharge** flag is set to true then the GRA shall set the **goal** as the nearest charging position.
G3	If the **atGoal** flag is true then the GRA should remove the **goal** that was achieved from the prioritised list of goals before selecting the next one.
G4	The **goal** that is selected by the GRA shall be the one with the highest priority in the list, unless the **recharge** flag is set to true.
G5	If either planning component (ComputePlan2Charging or ComputePlan2Destination) returns **noplan** then the GRA shall inform the ground station and await instructions before proceeding.
G6	If all goals have been achieved then the GRA shall notify the ground station that the current mission has been completed.
G7	If a failure is identified by either of the planners then the GRA shall enter FailureMode and notify the ground station that it is in failure mode
G8	If failure is detected then the GRA shall send the **systemState** to the FailureMode component.
G9	The ground station can instruct the GRA to set the goal as a designated **safeLocation**, in this case, the GRA shall put this **safeLocation** as the **goal** by updating the prioritised list of goals.

Table 6. The ComputePlan2Charging requirements.

ID	Description
CPC1	The Planner shall compute a set of plans (sequences of (x,y) coordinates) from the **goal** position to the nearest **charger** position.
CPC2	The plans produced by the Planner shall not contain any obstacles.
CPC3	The shortest path to the charger, **plan2C**, shall be selected by the PRA.
CPC4	If there are no viable plans then the ComputePlan2Charging component shall return **noplan**, otherwise the **plan2C** shall be sent to the Battery+Hardware component.
CPC5	If a failure in planning occurs (e.g. timeout) the ComputePlan2Charging shall notify the GRA.

Table 7. The ComputePlan2Destination requirements.

ID	Description
CPD1	The Planner shall compute a set of plans (sequences of (x,y) coordinates) from the **currentPosition** to the **goal** that has been selected by the GRA.
CPD2	The plans produced by the Planner shall not contain any obstacles.
CPD3	The shortest path to the goal location, **plan2D**, shall be selected by the PRA.
CPD4	If there are no viable plans then the ComputePlan2Destination component shall return **noplan**, otherwise the **plan2D** shall be sent to the Battery+Hardware component.
CPD5	If a failure in planning occurs (e.g. timeout) the ComputePlan2Charging shall notify the GRA.

here such as `move_base`. We include the requirements for the Battery+Hardware component in Table 8.

Table 8. The Battery+Hardware component requirements.

ID	Description
HI1	The HardwareInterface shall set the `recharge` flag to true if the `batteryLevel` is not high enough to reach the `goal` and subsequently reach a charging location.
HI2	Once at a charging position, the rover shall remain there until the battery has been recharged.
HI3	The `atGoal` flag shall be set to true only when the `goal` position has been reached.
HI4	The HardwareInterface shall send movement and velocity commands to the actuators that control robot movement.
HI5	The commands that the HardwareInterface sends to the actuators shall eventually be received and acted upon i.e. an instruction to move left does indeed lead to the robot moving left.
HI6	When the `currentPosition` is a `charger` position then the solar panels shall be opened (and tilted towards the sun).
HI7	When charging is complete the solar panels shall be closed. This is to avoid dust accumulating while the rover is moving and protect the panels from adverse weather conditions.
BM1	The BatteryMonitor shall monitor the battery level of the rover.
BM2	The BatteryMonitor shall return the battery level as 5% less than the measured level. This is to ensure reliability under degradation.

2.9 The **Communication2Ground (Point2Point)** Component

The robot is capable of communicating with the ground station. It uses this communication link to send/receive data including updated goal lists, notify mission completed, and report erroneous behaviour. We view this as a point-to-point communication where one rover communicates with one ground station. While we do not dictate a specific protocol to use here, Fig. 2 outlines the appropriate steps that this communication should follow. We assume secure communications and are not concerned with bit flips at this stage but a more realistic communications protocol should take these things into consideration [17]. We include the requirements for this component in Table 9 and we welcome submissions exploring this aspect.

2.10 The **Communication2Rovers(Broadcast)** Component

In more futuristic space missions, we envisage teams of rovers carry out planetary tasks ranging from sample collection to habitat construction. In such scenarios, rovers work together in teams to achieve complex tasks, an aspect that we do

Table 9. The Communication2Ground requirements.

ID	Description
CG1	Communication data that is received shall be validated by the Data Validation component to ensure it is in the correct format (`invalidMap, completed, noMoreViablePlans, failureModeInvoked, communicationData`).
CG2	Communication2Ground shall establish a connection with the ground station using a standard protocol (e.g. [6,14]). This shall operate with a greater than 99% success rate.
CG3	If there is a connection failure (broken connection, timeout, etc.) then Communication2Ground shall attempt to reconnect.
CG4	Messages/data shall be transmitted within a reasonable time frame (e.g. 10 ticks).
CG5	Once all of the data is sent then Communication2Ground shall wait until a response is received (e.g. up to 1 h on Mars, up to 5 s on the Moon).
CG6	Once the response is received then Communication2Ground shall close the connection.
CG7	The response includes prioritised goals, charger and obstacle positions that shall be passed to the MapValidator component.
CG8	A failure reconnection notification shall be sent to the FailureReasoningAgent if the reconnection fails more than 3 times consecutively.

not focus on in this case study. However, we do consider the situation where rovers must assist each other. For example, when one rover gets stuck on a rock or in sand then another rover can be used to (1) provide visual data to the fground station to help operators decide the best course of action or (2) to simply push the stuck rover away from the hazard. In these situations, we assume that a broadcast style of communication is used that alerts nearby rovers of the situation. One potential protocol for doing this is the Cooperative Awareness Message (CAM) protocol that is to be used in autonomous vehicles [10]. The CAM protocol is summarised in [8,18]. Table 10 summarises the requirements for the Communication2Rovers component.

Table 10. The Communication2Rovers requirements.

ID	Description
CR1	Communication data that is received shall be validated by the Data Validation component to ensure it is in the correct format (`location, failure, etc.`).
CR2	The Communication2Rovers component shall communicate with nearby rovers using the Cooperative Awareness Message protocol [8].
CR3	Communication2Rovers shall send the `helperId` of the rover that is coming to assist so that the main rover can check it's ID when it gets there. This is a security check to ensure that the rover is not "assisted" by an adversary.

2.11   The **FailureMode** Component

Since space robotic systems operate in an unpredicatable, hazardous and hostile environment that we do not have accurate simulations or means for physically testing, we assume that these systems will fail (repeatedly) [19]. This was already evident in the communication2Ground component that we discussed earlier (Sect. 2.9). As a result, we include the FailureMode shown in Fig. 2. The purpose of this component is to react appropriately to failures that occur in other parts of the system. (The FailureMode could also fail itself, but we ignore this for now.) We include a FailureReasoningAgent to diagnose the cause of failures. This could be a rather complex component. For example, since it is impossible to predict all failures in advance for space missions, this component may incorporate some kind of learning. Alternatively, and for simplicity, submissions to the case study track may assume that it has an accurate model of all failures. We define requirements for the FailureMode in Table 11.

Table 11. The FailureMode requirements.

ID	Description
FM1	In cases of failure, the FailureMode shall be invoked by the GRA and Battery+Hardware via the sending of the `systemState` or by the Communication2Ground by sending a `failed2Reconnect` message.
FM2	The FailureReasoningAgent shall consider the `systemState` and output the most likely cause of the failure. For example, the planner times out and fails to compute a plan. This could be a planning failure or a localisation failure.
FM3	Once the failure has been identified the recovery mode shall either reboot or request help from the ground station and/or other rovers that are nearby. For example, it could be stuck in a crater and need physical help and/or manual remote control procedures to be invoked.
FM4	If the rover is instructed to wait for help then it should wait for a reasonable amount of time before rechecking if help is on the way.
FM5	In Recovery mode, while deciding what to do the rover shall be sent to a `safeLocation` (if possible). This is achieved by updating the GRA to set the next goal to be the safe position. An example would be the SolarPanelController is failing or the communication continues to fail in its current physical position (poor signal).

3   Scenarios

We list several use case/scenarios in this section.

Scenario 1: The rover autonomously navigates to the next goal location while successfully avoiding obstacles and maintaining battery power. Once it is finished it sets up a communication stream with the ground control station to transmit the data that it has collected throughout its journey. This data may include measurements, images or weather-related information.

Scenario 2: During navigation, the rover encounters a failure (e.g. one of the controllers that is responsible for the rover's physical movement reports an error). The rover must then enter failure mode where it reasons about the failure that has been encountered and chooses what course of action to take. This could be a simple reboot or it may need to request help from the ground station. In some cases the ground station may decide to send another rover to the failed rover's location to assess it and potentially intervene. The failed rover must authenticate and accept help from the rover that has been sent by the ground station.

Scenario 3: The rover uses a combination of obstacles identified by the vision component and obstacles that were identifed and uploaded from the ground control station. In some instances there may be a mismatch between these data sources. In this case the rover should contact the ground station to seek advice and provide the ground station with the lists of obstacles that conflict with one another.

4   Expectations: Case Study Track Submissions

We anticipate contributions to the ABZ 2026 case study track that tackle the rover system that is described in this document and outlined in Fig. 2. We recognise that the requirements that we have listed above have diverse characteristics, ranging from propositional logic style to incorporating probabilistic aspects that capture levels of uncertainty in movement and perception. We also include several requirements that are especially difficult to formally model and verify. We welcome submissions that focus on any combination of these aspects.

We note that the rover is built using a standard middleware such as the Robot Operating System (ROS) [16] which uses a range of in-built and contributed library functions including `move_base` for low-level movement. The majority of these library functions are not verified and reliability is usually argued based on sheer volume of use in-the-wild. While we do not instruct participants in the case study track to spend significant time worrying about modelling, specifying and verifying message passing in ROS, we would be glad to see submissions that consider this aspect. Providing formal guarantees at this level remains an open research challenge and contributions in this area would certainly be in scope for the ABZ 2026 case study track.

In an ideal world, participants should model, specify and verify the architecture shown in Fig. 2 and (at least a subset of) the requirements that we have outlined in this document. Due to the complexity of robotic systems, it is likely that a range of formal techniques as well as software testing and simulation would be needed to provide complete coverage of this system [15]. Submissions focusing on specific components, frameworks, modelling paradigms, verification tools and specification logics are thus encouraged.

Participants in the case study track are encouraged to make any simplifying assumptions about the environment, ground station functions, communication protocols, nearby rover functions, cybersecurity mitigations and precision of the onboard equipment. We expect that these assumptions are clearly outlined in the submissions.

Several components of our system embody Artificial Intelligence (AI) this includes the Vision and Goal Reasoning Agent components. The species of AI used in each is quite different with the Vision system relying on sub-symbolic AI and the Goal Reasoning Agent using symbolic AI. Verification for each of these kinds of AI is usually very different ranging from testing to formal proof and we encourage articipants to consider the AI aspects of this system using their chosen tools. They can also model/implement additional measures to provide assurance around the AI components such as the addition of safety shields and/or runtime monitoring.

References

1. Azaiez, A., Anisi, D.A., Farrell, M., Luckcuck, M.: Revisiting formal methods for autonomous robots: a structured survey. In: Annual Conference Towards Autonomous Robotic Systems, pp. 338–352. Springer (2025)
2. Bourbouh, H., Farrell, M., Mavridou, A., Sljivo, I.: Integration and evaluation of the advocate, fret, cocosim, and event-b tools on the inspection rover case study. Technical report, NASA (2020)
3. Bourbouh, H., et al.: Integrating formal verification and assurance: an inspection rover case study. In: NASA Formal Methods Symposium, pp. 53–71. Springer (2021)
4. Cardoso, R.C., Farrell, M., Luckcuck, M., Ferrando, A., Fisher, M.: Heterogeneous verification of an autonomous curiosity rover. In: NASA Formal Methods Symposium, pp. 353–360. Springer (2020)
5. Cardoso, R.C., et al.: A review of verification and validation for space autonomous systems. Curr. Robot. Rep. **2**(3), 273–283 (2021)
6. CCSDS. Overview of space communications protocols. Technical report, CCSDS (2007)
7. Davison.: Real-time simultaneous localisation and mapping with a single camera. In: Proceedings Ninth IEEE International Conference on Computer Vision, pp. 1403–1410. IEEE (2003)
8. ETSI, T.: Intelligent transport systems (its); vehicular communications; basic set of applications; part 2: specification of cooperative awareness basic service. Draft ETSI TS, vol. 20, no. 2011, pp. 448–51 (2011)
9. Farley, K.A., et al.: Mars 2020 mission overview. Space Sci. Rev. **216**(8), 142 (2020)
10. Farrell, M., et al.: Security-minded verification of cooperative awareness messages. IEEE Trans. Dependable Secure Comput. **21**(4), 4048–4065 (2023)
11. Farrell, M., Luckcuck, M., Fisher, M.: Robotics and integrated formal methods: Necessity meets opportunity. In: International Conference on Integrated Formal Methods, pp. 161–171. Springer (2018)
12. Francis, R., et al.: Aegis autonomous targeting for the curiosity rover's Chemcam instrument. In: 2015 IEEE Applied Imagery Pattern Recognition Workshop (AIPR), pp. 1–5. IEEE (2015)
13. Gopinath, D., Katz, G., Păsăreanu, C.S., Barrett, C.: Deepsafe: a data-driven approach for assessing robustness of neural networks. In: International Symposium on Automated Technology for Verification and Analysis, pp. 3–19. Springer (2018)

14. Kodheli, O., et al.: Satellite communications in the new space era: a survey and future challenges. IEEE Commun. Surv. Tutorials **23**(1), 70–109 (2020)
15. Luckcuck, M., Farrell, M., Dennis, L.A., Dixon, C., Fisher, M.: Formal specification and verification of autonomous robotic systems: a survey. ACM Comput. Surv. (CSUR) **52**(5), 1–41 (2019)
16. Macenski, S., Foote, T., Gerkey, B., Lalancette, C., Woodall, W.: Robot operating system 2: design, architecture, and uses in the wild. Sci. Robot. **7**(66), eabm6074 (2022)
17. Maple, C., et al.: Security-minded verification of space systems. In: 2020 IEEE Aerospace Conference, pp. 1–13. IEEE (2020)
18. Santa, J., Pereñíguez, F., Moragón, A., Skarmeta, A.F.: Vehicle-to-Infrastructure messaging proposal based on CAM/DENM specifications. In: 2013 IFIP Wireless Days (WD), pp. 1–7. IEEE (2013)
19. Stancliff, S., Dolan, J., Trebi-Ollennu, A.: Planning to fail: reliability as a design parameter for planetary rover missions. In: Proceedings of the 2007 Workshop on Performance Metrics for Intelligent Systems, pp. 204–208 (2007)
20. Vasavada, A.R.: Mission overview and scientific contributions from the mars science laboratory curiosity rover after eight years of surface operations. Space Sci. Rev. **218**(3), 14 (2022)
21. Welch, R., Limonadi, D., Manning, R.: Systems engineering the curiosity rover: a retrospective. In: 2013 8th International Conference on System of Systems Engineering, pp. 70–75. IEEE (2013)

Can Large Language Models Support Modeling Systems with ASMETA? A Case Study with a Planetary Rover

Andrea Bombarda(✉)🆔, Silvia Bonfanti🆔, Angelo Gargantini🆔,
and Nico Pellegrinelli🆔

University of Bergamo, Bergamo, Italy
`{andrea.bombarda,silvia.bonfanti,angelo.gargantini,`
`nico.pellegrinelli}@unibg.it`

Abstract. Formal modeling languages provide strong support for the specification, analysis, and validation of cyber-physical systems, but their adoption in practice is often hindered by the effort and expertise that are required to produce correct and complete models. In this paper, we investigate whether Large Language Models (LLMs) can support the modeling process by assisting in the generation and refinement of ASMETA specifications from natural language requirements. We propose an iterative and human-in-the-loop workflow in which an LLM is used to derive an initial ASMETA model, progressively refine it, and support scenario-based validation using existing ASMETA tools. The approach explicitly combines automated assistance with human inspection to mitigate modeling errors and potential biases introduced by the LLM. We evaluate the feasibility and effectiveness of this workflow through a case study based on the ABZ 2026 planetary rover problem, using GPT-5.2, accessed via the ChatGPT interface and leveraging the Projects functionality to support persistent and multi-iteration interactions. Our experience suggests that LLMs can significantly lower the entry barrier to formal modeling and support engineers by accelerating the creation of analyzable ASMETA artifacts, but expert oversight is necessary to ensure correctness, completeness, and alignment with stakeholder intent.

Keywords: ASMETA · Abstract State Machines · Large Language Models · Human-in-the-loop modeling

1 Introduction

Formal languages provide a disciplined way to describe software-intensive and cyber-physical systems with precision [2]. When requirements are captured in a mathematically grounded notation, a model becomes more than documentation: it becomes an analyzable artifact that can be used to run automated activities such as simulation and validation, formal verification, and even code generation. In this perspective, modeling is not only a design support, but also a practical enabler for early detection of inconsistencies, missing cases, and unintended behaviors, before implementation decisions make changes costly.

© The Author(s), under exclusive license to Springer Nature Switzerland AG 2026
F. Ishikawa and A. Cunha (Eds.): ABZ 2026, LNCS 16579, pp. 291–309, 2026.
https://doi.org/10.1007/978-3-032-26752-8_19

The ASMETA [8] framework supports system modeling through the Abstract State Machines (ASM) paradigm, offering a lightweight yet expressive language and a user-oriented environment. ASMETA specifications can be executed and analyzed with dedicated tools, allowing engineers to explore system scenarios, check properties, and derive implementation-oriented artifacts [1]. Despite these advantages, the adoption of a formal notation still poses a barrier: even when the syntax is relatively simple and the tooling is user-friendly, writing a correct and complete model requires familiarity with formal abstractions, disciplined structuring choices, and attention to details such as state representation, controlled/monitored functions[1], and rule design [11,13]. As a result, practitioners may not fully benefit from ASMETA's capabilities because the initial modeling effort is perceived as difficult or time-consuming.

This paper investigates whether Large Language Models (LLMs) can reduce this entry cost by supporting the automatic generation of ASMETA models from textual requirements. The core idea is to use natural language requirements, which are the most available and accessible form of specification in industrial settings, as input, and produce an initial formal model that can then be assessed and, possibly, refined by the engineer. We believe that this approach can both lower the skills threshold for formal modeling and support experienced engineers by reducing manual effort, shortening the time needed to obtain an analyzable artifact, and making model-based validation and verification more readily applicable in early development phases. Concretely, we envision an iterative modeling process in which an LLM assists engineers across multiple phases of the ASMETA workflow. Starting from natural language requirements, an initial ASM model is generated and progressively refined. The model is then exercised through scenarios using existing ASMETA tools, with support from the LLM. Violations and inconsistencies introduced at any of these stages are identified through human inspection, deliberately performed without LLM assistance in order to reduce potential biases, and the process is repeated. In this way, the LLM is integrated into a closed-loop workflow that combines automated analysis with human oversight, complementing existing formal modeling practices.

To investigate the efficacy of our approach, we conducted an evaluation using the planetary rover description and requirements, as provided by the ABZ 2026 case study [10]. We focus on GPT-5.2 from OpenAI, accessed via the ChatGPT interface [20], in particular leveraging its *Projects* functionality, which enables a structured workflow across multiple iterations, persistent context, and reusable artifacts. Rather than treating the LLM as a one-shot code generator, we explore an interactive process in which requirements are progressively clarified, modeling decisions are made explicit, and the produced ASMETA specification is incrementally improved. This reflects how formal modeling typically occurs in practice: through iterative refinement, feedback, and alignment with user intent.

Our evaluation shows that, even from a minimal prompt, GPT-5.2 was able to quickly produce a complete first draft of the rover model derived from the ABZ

---

[1] *Controlled* functions are modified by the machine and read by the environment. *Monitored* functions are read by the machine and modified by the environment.

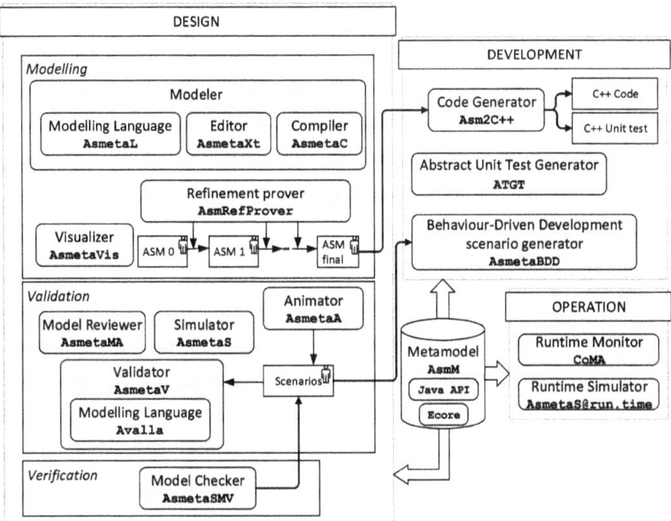

Fig. 1. The ASMETA toolset supporting the ASM development process, including modeling, validation, verification, code generation, and runtime operations.

case study, although the resulting artifacts required further iterations and some manual corrections before they became correct and complete. Scenario-based validation further showed that automatically generated scenarios were generally plausible, but often failed to exercise key behaviors (e.g., rover movement), which motivates using the LLM to craft more targeted scenarios and improve behavioral coverage. As with the ASMETA specifications, however, test scenarios generated by the LLM also required manual fixes to make them executable.

The remainder of this paper is structured as follows. Section 2 presents the ASMETA framework. Section 3 details the planetary rover case study, with focus on the part of the system subject to our analysis. Section 4 shows the envisioned LLM-based modeling and validation methodology, while Sect. 5 discusses on the challenges we faced and the lessons we learned from its adoption. Finally, Sect. 6 presents related work and Sect. 7 concludes the paper.

2   The ASMETA-Based Development Process

This work builds on Abstract State Machines (ASMs), which extend Finite State Machines (FSMs) by replacing unstructured control states with states characterized by arbitrarily complex data. In particular, we rely on the capabilities that are provided by the ASMETA toolset [1], which supports developers throughout the entire system life cycle. This life cycle is typically structured into three main phases: design, development, and operation. Each of these phases is supported by dedicated analysis tools (see Fig. 1).

For this case study, we limit ourselves to the *design* phase, in particular on the modeling and validation activities. The development process starts with the *modeling* phase. At its core is `AsmetaL`, the executable modeling language used to define ASMETA models. `AsmetaL` is designed to allow system requirements to be expressed in a form that resembles pseudo-code over abstract data structures, while maintaining a well-defined semantics. Models written in the `AsmetaL` language can be edited using the `AsmetaXt` editor, which provides editing functionalities, and compiled with the `AsmetaC` compiler.

Once the model is available, its correctness with respect to the requirements can be assessed through *validation*. The `AsmetaS` simulator supports both random and interactive execution of ASMETA models, while the `AsmetaA` animator enhances simulation with a graphical interface that offers a structured view of the system state at each step. Scenario-based validation is provided by `AsmetaV`: users specify expected behaviors in the `Avalla` language, and the tool executes them against the model to detect possible deviations from requirements.

Beyond the design phase, ASMETA supports model-driven *development* activities, such as automatic generation of test cases with `ATGT` [5, 12], which exploits a model checker or random simulation to derive `Avalla` scenarios.

3   The Planetary Rover Case Study

In this section, we report some of the details of our case study, i.e., the planetary rover proposed for the ABZ 2026 Case Study track [10]. It is a semi-autonomous planetary rover undertaking an inspection mission. In particular, in this paper, we focus on modeling and validating the components concerning the rover battery. Thus, we exclude from our analysis the components used for the communication, the validation of a map, and vision. While we believe that some of them could be considered as well, to validate our approach and evaluate its efficacy, we have chosen to limit to more simple behavior and components of the planetary rover. More specifically, we modeled the components shown in Fig. 2 and the requirements that we report in Table 1.
More specifically, we consider the following aspects:

- Selection of a charger as a current goal, when the battery is low (the `goal` message exchanged among GRA and `ComputePlan2Charging` components);
- Computation of the plan to reach a charger (the `plan2C` message exchanged among the `Planner` and `HardwareInterface` components);
- Execution of a plan step-by-step, implying the consumption of the battery;
- Handling of the battery charging status (`Battery+Hardware` component).

In the following, we detail the approach that we envisioned to model and validate such a system by the collaboration between human-in-the-loop and LLMs.

4   Modeling with LLMs

In this section, we provide a demonstration of our proposed modeling and validation approach based on the use of LLMs and a human-in-the-loop philosophy. We first introduce our methodology (Sect. 4.1). Then, we delve into the modeling (Sect. 4.2) and validation (Sect. 4.3) activities for the planetary rover.

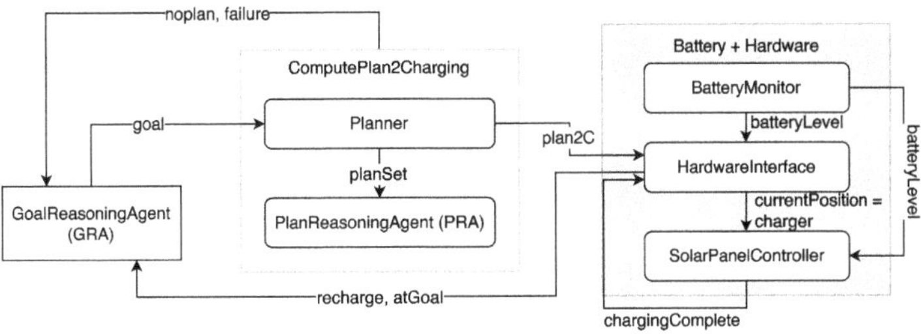

Fig. 2. System architecture.

4.1   Methodology

Figure 3 summarizes the workflow that we propose to integrate an LLM (e.g., ChatGPT) into the ASMETA-based design phase as an iterative companion to the modeler. The workflow is explicitly human-in-the-loop and alternates between LLM-assisted artifact generation/refinement and tool-supported assessment with manual inspection.

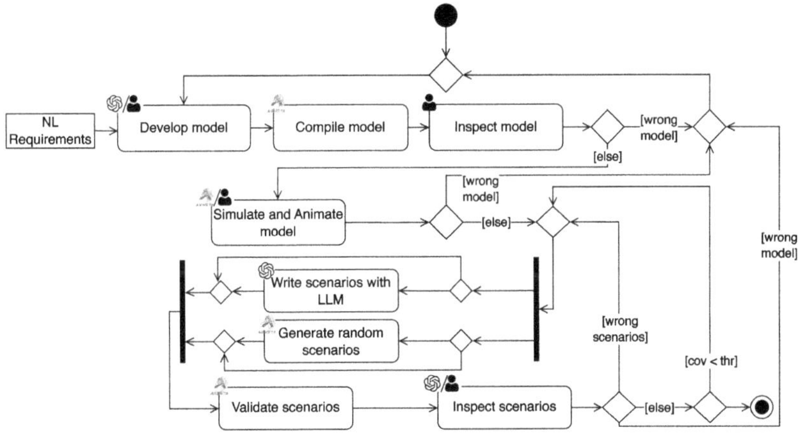

Fig. 3. The proposed modeling approach.

We assume that users interact with an LLM over multiple iterations, progressively improving results by applying one, or a combination of, the two different strategies:

- Enriching the document knowledge base that is available to the model (e.g., adding requirements excerpts, modeling guidelines, standard-library fragments, or previous versions of the model);
- Revising the instructions (e.g., domain/type conventions, preferred idioms, or project-specific modeling constraints).

Table 1. Requirements targeted by our ASMETA implementation.

Req	Description
SL1	The rover shall never run out of battery.
G2	Whenever the **recharge** flag is set to true then the GRA shall set the **goal** as the nearest charging position.
G5	If either planning component ([...]) returns **noplan** the GRA shall [...] await instructions before proceeding.
CPC3	The shortest path to the charger, **plan2C**, shall be selected by the PRA.
CPC4	If there are no viable plans then the **ComputePlan2Charging** component shall return **noplan**, otherwise the **plan2C** shall be sent to **Battery+Hardware**.
CPC5	If a failure in planning occurs (e.g., timeout) the **ComputePlan2Charging** shall notify the GRA.
HI1	The **HardwareInterface** shall set the **recharge** flag to true if the **batteryLevel** is not high enough to reach the **goal** and subsequently reach a charging location.
HI2	Once at a charging position, the rover shall remain there until the battery has been recharged.
HI6	When the **currentPosition** is a **charger** position then the solar panels shall be opened.
HI7	When charging is complete the solar panels shall be closed. [...]
BM1	The **BatteryMonitor** shall monitor the battery level of the rover.
BM2	The **BatteryMonitor** shall return the battery level as 5% less than the measured level. [...]

This enables a closed-loop process where each iteration incorporates feedback from compilation, simulation, and analysis outcomes, and where the LLM can reuse a stable context across steps (e.g., modeling conventions and architectural assumptions). In our approach, we take advantage of the Projects functionality, which enables a structured workflow across multiple iterations, persistent context, and reusable artifacts. Our approach is based on a two-step process:

Step 1 - Cooperative modeling and refinement. Starting from the natural-language requirements, the LLM proposes an ASMETA model. The user then compiles the generated specification using the **AsmetaC** compiler. The compiler feedback helps to identify syntactic and structural issues during the subsequent manual inspection of the model. If errors or inconsistencies are detected, a refinement iteration is triggered. The user may decide to be assisted by the LLM to fix the errors. This may involve adjusting the model, adding missing context to the knowledge base, or tightening instructions or prompts (e.g., concerning types/-domains and library usage). Alternatively, during a refinement step (especially in the case of minor issues such as isolated syntax errors), the user may choose to modify the model directly.

Step 2 - Model validation. Once the model compiles and the manual inspection does not reveal issues, the workflow proceeds with validation activities. The ASMETA model is simulated (with `AsmetaS`) and/or animated (with `AsmetaA`) to detect potential behavioral issues or runtime errors. If undesired behaviors or inconsistencies emerge, a new refinement iteration is started. Alternatively, scenario-based validation is performed. In particular, the user adopts two different strategies to obtain `Avalla` scenarios from the model: (a) automatically generating scenarios via the random test generator that is available in ASMETA, which exploits the random simulation offered by `AsmetaS`; (b) leveraging the LLM to generate scenarios. Scenarios are then executed with `AsmetaV`. The feedback from `AsmetaV` (PASS/FAIL verdict and coverage information [4]) supports the subsequent inspection activity. Scenarios that are generated with the aid of the LLM should be inspected manually. Conversely, randomly generated scenarios may be inspected with the support of the LLM. Therefore, the LLM plays a twofold role. First, it can support the creation and refinement of executable scenarios in the `Avalla` language. Second, during inspection, it can explain their semantics in natural language and help to assess whether they describe plausible behaviors of the modeled system. This reduces effort in constructing and interpreting scenarios. If the inspection reveals faults in the model, a new model refinement iteration is triggered, accordingly to Step 1. If the scenarios are faulty, they are corrected in a new scenario refinement iteration, either manually or with LLM guidance. When validation and inspection do not reveal errors in either the model or the scenarios, the achieved coverage is compared against a target threshold. If coverage is insufficient, a new refinement iteration is initiated with the goal of extending existing scenarios or generating new ones.

We emphasize that human oversight is an explicit de-biasing mechanism. A key design choice of the process that we envision and report in Fig. 3 is that every step involving the LLM is systematically followed by manual inspection, supported by the feedback from ASMETA tools. This ensures that corrections are grounded in human judgment and tool evidence (e.g., compiler errors and simulation traces), mitigating risks such as wrong model implementation, inconsistent type choices, accidental misuse of library functions, or missing model behavior. In practice, the user's primary role is to arbitrate intent and correctness, while the LLM accelerates drafting, restructuring, and repair across iterations.

Setup Description. To implement the previously described methodology, we use the GPT 5.2 LLM, accessed via the ChatGPT interface and its *Projects* functionalities. As a document knowledge base, we initially included a tutorial on the ASMETA language [8], the Egon Börger Festschrift paper describing all phases and activities within the ASMETA-based development process [1], the ASMETA StandardLibrary[2] the description of the ABZ 2026 case study [10], and the PDF of Fig. 2. The aim is to provide ChatGPT with the relevant context on the

---

[2] https://github.com/asmeta/asmeta/blob/master/asmeta_models/STDL/StandardLibrary.asm.

`AsmetaL` language, the case study, and the part to be modeled. Additionally, we provide the *project* with the instructions reported in Fig. 4.

The file TutorialAsmeta.pdf is a tutorial of the ASMETA formal method. It describes how systems should be modeled by using the AsmetaL notation and how validation-based scenario is performed by using the Avalla language. Further information on the AsmetaL language, together with its own metamodel are available at `https://asmeta.github.io/material/AsmetaL_quickguide.html`.

Additional information on the ASMETA framework, and on the purpose of each activity is described in the file FestschriftEgon75.pdf. The StandardLibrary.asm includes standard domains and functions. All domains not defined there should be defined in the specification.

The description of the case study under development is given within the document-v2.pdf, while the simplified architecture of the subportion of the system we consider is given in Architecture.pdf.

You should consider the information coming from these source documents to derive ASMETA models and Avalla scenarios.

Fig. 4. ChatGPT project instructions.

Replication Material. We provide all ASMETA specifications with models, scenarios, and prompts in our replication package at https://github.com/asmeta/asmeta/tree/master/asmeta_models/ABZ2026_CaseStudy.

4.2   Modeling

Once we defined the methodology outlined above in Sect. 4.1, we started modeling the planetary rover , including its requirements listed in Table 1.

Generate a set of ASMETA modules for the planetary rover case study. Please model the components involved in the reduced architecture, and focus on the requirements SL1, G2, G5, CPC3, CPC4, CPC5, HI1, HI2, HI6, HI7, BM1, and BM2.

Fig. 5. First modeling prompt.

At the beginning, we provided to the LLM a very simple prompt, as in Fig. 5. While it just specifies the target and the requirements of interest, we found it to be quite effective. Indeed, the LLM generated six ASMETA modules and one ASMETA main specification: 1. `RoverDomains` defines the basic domains of interest and utility static functions; 2. `HardwareInterface` provides the interface to the hardware, such as motors and battery; 3. `SolarPanelController` defines how and when the solar panels are opened or closed; 4. `BatteryMonitor` implements the monitoring activity of the battery (e.g., the BM2 requirement - see Table 1); 5. `ComputePlan2Charging` defines rules and functions used by the rover to define the path to reach a charger; 6. `GoalReasoningAgent` implements the reasoning capabilities of the planetary rover, such as the handling of no plans, or the definition of the next goal location; 7. `RoverReducedMain` imports all other modules, defines the main rule, and initializes all controlled functions.

We compiled and manually inspected the generated ASMETA specifications and we found, in each of them, some issue. Table 2 lists such issues, provides a description for each of them, and reports which ASMETA specifications manifested those issues. Most of these issues (I1, I2, I3, I4, I6, I7, I8, and I9) are syntax or compilation errors, while I5 concerns with an additional requirement that we would like to have in our specifications, since using `Real` instead of `Integer` may prevent the model checker to work with the ASMETA specification.

Table 2. Issues after the first ASMETA specification generation.

ID	Description	Specs.
I1	Missing `export` statement in modules	RoverDomains, HardwareInterface, SolarPanelController, BatteryMonitor, ComputePlan2Charging, GoalReasoningAgent
I2	Useless `par` when a single update rule is executed	ComputePlan2Charging
I3	Wrong usage and syntax of the `chooseone` function	ComputePlan2Charging, GoalReasoningAgent
I4	Wrong definition of domains where the product of two domains is used. The LLM uses `D1*D2` instead of `Prod(D1,D2)`	RoverDomains, HardwareInterface, ComputePlan2Charging
I5	Usage of function with `Real` domain or codomain	BatteryMonitor, RoverDomains
I6	Usage of non existing functions (such as `fst` to extract the first element of a sequence, or `snd` to extract the second)	RoverDomains
I7	Missing concrete domain initialization	RoverDomains
I8	Wrong positioning of invariants	RoverReducedMain
I9	Missing controlled functions initialization	RoverReducedMain

Considering the issues we identified, we modified the prompt and tried to fix each specification or module by adding additional details regarding the previously mentioned issues. Our second prompt is reported in Fig. 6. With this prompt, we were able to fix all previously identified issues for the `RoverDomains`, `SolarPanelController`, and `HardwareInterface` ASMETA modules. However, as shown in Table 3, some issues remained and new ones emerged.

> Generate a set of ASMETA modules for the planetary rover case study. Please model the components involved in the reduced architecture, and focus on the requirements SL1, G2, G5, CPC3, CPC4, CPC5, HI1, HI2, HI6, HI7, BM1, and BM2.
>
> For the module RoverDomains.asm you previously generated, you must fix all following issues, without changing anything else: - The module must export all (export *) functions and domains - When defining products of two domains, use Prod(D1, D2) instead of D1*D2 - Use only functions that are defined (e.g., use first instead of fst) - Initialize all concrete domains in the definitions section of the module. - Use only Integers instead of Real [...]

Fig. 6. Second modeling prompt.

Table 3. Issues after the second ASMETA specification generation.

ID	Description	Specs.
I3	Wrong usage and syntax of the **chooseone** function	ComputePlan2Charging, GoalReasoningAgent
I8	Wrong positioning of invariants	RoverReducedMain
I10	Missing **rtoi** function when real values are used in integer terms	BatteryMonitor

Given the exploratory nature of this study, and since the issues we identified were minor and further prompt refinements may introduce new inconsistencies, we corrected the models manually and verified that ASMETA could successfully parse and compile the generated specifications. An excerpt of the main ASMETA module for the planetary rover is reported in Listing 1. Note that, for example, the requirement SL1 in Table 1 is captured by an invariant.

```
asm RoverReducedMain
import ../../STDL/StandardLibrary
import RoverDomains
import BatteryMonitor
import SolarPanelController
import ComputePlan2Charging
import HardwareInterface
import GoalReasoningAgent
signature:
definitions:
    invariant inv_SL1 over batteryLevel: (batteryLevel
        > 0)

main rule r_Main = par
    r_BatteryMonitor[]
    r_ComputePlan2Charging
[]
    r_GRA[]
    r_HardwareInterface[]
    r_SolarPanelController[]
endpar
default init s0:
    function recharge = false
    function atGoal = false
    [...]
```

Listing 1. Excerpt of the ASMETA main module for the planetary rover case study.

4.3   Validation

Following the general approach introduced in Sect. 4.1, once the ASMETA specifications could be compiled and no issues were revealed by manual inspection, we proceeded with the model validation phase. In this section, we first describe model simulation and then present scenario-based validation activities.

Model Simulation. During the model simulation phase, we made extensive use of the `AsmetaS` simulator and the `AsmetaA` animator. Notably, although the ASMETA specifications compiled successfully, we identified several issues that emerged only at runtime. In the following, we describe the major issues that we identified and how we addressed them:

1. **Duplicated functions**: Although `AsmetaC` permits functions with the same name to appear in different modules, `AsmetaS` raises an error when such specifications are simulated. For example, we discovered that the `batteryLevel` function was declared as a *controlled* function in the `BatteryMonitor` module and as a *monitored* function in the `HardwareInterface` module. We inspected the LLM-generated output and found that this issue recurred multiple times, stemming from a misinterpretation of the PDF in Fig. 2. Specifically, whenever an arrow connected two components, the LLM assumed that the function labeled on the arrow was *controlled* by the source component and *monitored* by the destination component. To solve this issue, we manually revised the affected modules and added all necessary imports.

2. **Inconsistent updates**: Although the ASMETA code produced by the LLM was syntactically correct, we observed that its coding style more closely resembled that of conventional programming languages, where updates take effect immediately as they are executed, rather than the ASM style, in which updates are collected during a step and applied only at the end of the step. For this reason, we found several inconsistent[3] updates to occur. For example, Listing 2 reports an excerpt of the `HardwareIntefrace` module, where an inconsistent update occurs. It can be noticed that the `moving` function can be updated to `true` and, simultaneously, to `false` when the rover is already moving, needs to recharge, and has finished its movement plan. To address this issue, we manually revised the affected ASMETA modules and strengthened the guards on conditional rules. Although we performed such fixes manually, we may explore in the future a way to extend the LLM context (e.g., by providing additional semantic knowledge and some basic design rules for ASMs) to avoid the generation of ASMETA specifications with inconsistent updates.

3. **Concrete domain initialization**: We discover that the LLM declared some *concrete* domains, as subsets of other previously defined domains. For instance, the `RoverDomains` module in Listing 3 defines the concrete domains `Position` and `Plan` as subsets of structured domains. While this modeling

---

[3] We say that an update is *inconsistent* when the same location is updated to multiple different values during the same execution step.

```
rule r_loadPlan =
    if (not(noplan) and recharge) then par
        activePlan := plan2C
        moving := true
    endpar endif
rule r_moveOneStep = if moving then
    if not(isEmptyPlan(activePlan)) then par
        currentPosition := headPos(activePlan)
        activePlan := tailPlan(activePlan)
    endpar else moving := false endif endif
```

Listing 2. ASMETA rules generating inconsistent updates.

```
signature:
    domain Coord subsetof Integer
    // 2D discrete position (simple abstraction)
    domain Position subsetof Prod(Coord, Coord)
    // A plan is a finite sequence of positions
    domain Plan subsetof Seq(Position)
    [...]
definitions:
    // Initialize concrete domains
    domain Coord = {−10:10}
```

Listing 3. Concrete domains within the `RoverDomains` module.

choice is conceptually justified (e.g., only *Position*s within the rover's operating area are admissible), adopting it in ASMETA would require explicitly enumerating all of the values in these domains, resulting in a combinatorial explosion. Additionally, we noticed that the LLM-generated ASMETA modules did not contain such enumeration. To address this issue, we manually revised the affected ASMETA modules by redefining function domains and co-domains without relying on subset domains, for example, replacing `Position` with its supertype `Prod(Coord,Coord)`.

Given the preliminary nature of our investigation, we opted for manual corrections rather than further LLM iterations; this allowed us to obtain a set of ASMETA modules that could be simulated and animated without triggering runtime errors, and to move on to scenario-based validation.

Scenario-Based Validation To apply scenario-based validation to the ASMETA models developed and exercised through simulation, we adopted a two-pronged strategy that combines an LLM with a human-in-the-loop. First, we generate `Avalla` scenarios using `ATGT` and random test generation, and we ask the LLM to explain these scenarios and assess whether they capture plausible system behavior. Next, we investigate the use of the LLM to produce `Avalla` scenarios directly from textual descriptions. For both activities, because we had manually revised the ASMETA models, we updated GPT-5.2's documental knowledge base, by including the corrected specifications, and the instructions accordingly (see the replication package for details on the new instructions).

Random Scenario Generation. We configured `ATGT` to generate 5 `Avalla` scenarios with 5 steps each and asked GPT-5.2, by using the prompt reported in Fig. 7, to explain in natural language the system behavior that is represented by each of the scenarios and their plausibility w.r.t. system requirements, as in [10]. The more significant results of our interaction with our LLM are reported in Table 4. By reading the textual description and the plausibility evaluation, we can notice that although all scenarios are plausible, most of them are only representative for battery management and failures, while none of them address the movement of

Table 4. Excerpt of the evaluation of random scenarios through GPT-5.2.

N.	Description	Plausibility
0	It repeatedly changes `batteryLevel` and planner output; at each step the rover selects a new `plan2C` but never moves: `currentPosition` remains (0,0) and `moving` stays false. When `planningFailure` is true it sets `failure`; when it becomes false, it clears `failure` and set `awaitingInstructions`.	The battery evolution is compliant with BM2, the failure signaling is plausible.
1	It repeatedly changes `planSet`, `batteryLevel`, and `planningFailure`; the rover updates `plan2C` and `batteryLevel` but never moves or recharges. `failure` mirrors `planningFailure`, it may switch to `awaitingInstructions`.	Plausible for the BatteryMonitor mapping and planner failure signaling, but overall not very representative.
3	It repeatedly changes the sensed `battery` and planner outputs; the rover updates `batteryLevel` and `plan2C` each step but never moves or recharges. `failure` follows `planningFailure` (true at steps 2 and 5), while `awaitingInstructions` briefly becomes true when planning succeeds again under low battery.	Plausible for the BatteryMonitor relation (battery value is compliant with the model'offset) and for planner-failure signaling.

The following is an Avalla scenario for the ASMETA specification of the planetary rover. [...]

Provide a concise but clear textual explanation of its behavior (maximum 3 lines) and evaluate whether it represents plausible behavior of the modeled system, i.e., if it is compliant with system requirements.

Fig. 7. Scenario evaluation prompt.

the rover. Thanks to the manual inspection of the random scenarios we noticed that the evaluation performed by GPT-5.2 is correct: `goal` is never updated in all of the randomly generated scenarios and always remains equal to the initial position of the rover. For this reason, although the coverage achieved by the random scenarios was satisfactory (all macro rules for all modules are covered, and most of behavior, except of the movement of the rover and its arrival to a charging location, is exercised), we proceeded with further guided scenarios.

LLM-based Scenario Generation. Considering the weaknesses of the scenarios that were randomly generated by `ATGT`, we instructed GPT-5.2 to generate a new `Avalla` scenario including the movement of the planetary rover, its arrival to a charger, and the movement of solar panels. For such a scenario to be generated, we designed the prompt in Fig. 8. This scenario is a simple scenario in which, starting from a low-battery condition in the position (0,0), the rover moves trough the environment and reaches a charging location in (2,3) where it stops and opens the solar panels to start the battery charging process. An excerpt of such a scenario is reported in Listing 4.

Generate an **Avalla** scenario for the planetary rover ASMETA specification. In this scenario, the rover starts from the position (0,0) and moves to the goal (2,3), which is a charger. While moving, the rover consumes its battery and, when arrived to the goal location, it needs to recharge. Since the goal is a charger location, it opens the solar panel and starts recharging.

While writing the scenario, initialize all monitored functions at each step to reasonable values and perform, at each step, the necessary checks. Remember that in Abstract State Machines the updates are collected and performed at the end of each execution step. Thus, you cannot expect that the updated value is already available in the same step when it is assigned to a function. **Avalla** allows for setting the value of monitored function and checking that of controlled ones. It is not possible to do viceversa.

Fig. 8. Avalla scenario generated prompt.

```
scenario rover_to_charger_2_3_recharge         [...]
load ./../RoverReducedMain.asm                  check currentPosition = (2,3);
check currentPosition = (0,0); // State 0        check atGoal = true;
[...]                                            check isAtCharger = true;
step                                             set measuredBatteryLevel := 2; // State 9
set chargers := {(2,3)}; // State 1              step
set planSet := {[(1,1),(2,2),(2,3)]};            check panelState = OPEN; // State 10
set measuredBatteryLevel := 7;                   check moving = false;
```

Listing 4. Excerpt of the Avalla scenario generated by GPT-5.2.

Initially, the validation of the rover ASMETA specification with the scenario in Listing 4 failed. Thanks to the manual inspection of both the **Avalla** scenario and the ASMETA modules we found two issues:

- The LLM partially ignored our request of not setting the value of *controlled* functions. In particular, in some steps, the function `chargingComplete` was used within a `set` statement.
- Some of the guards that we manually introduced to fix the ASMETA specification to prevent inconsistent updates (see Sect. 4.3) turned out to be overly restrictive and, in some cases, incorrect, causing the scenario to fail.

After resolving the two issues and manually confirming that the generated scenario matched our intent, we executed it and successfully validated the rover specification. With this scenario, additionally, we covered all missing macro rules.

5   Discussion

In this section, we discuss lessons learned and threats to validity emerging from our study. Our results and considerations should be considered as a proof of concept aimed at validating the feasibility of the proposed approach and further experimentation on additional subjects and settings is needed. However, we consider our experience to be a solid starting point from which to derive lessons and identify possible concerns.

5.1   Lessons Learned

Here, we report the lessons that we learned during the use of an LLM to support the modeling and validation process of the planetary rover case study.

L1 - Underrepresented ASMETA *Constructs and LLM Usability.* We observed that `AsmetaL` constructs that are rarely used in available examples or are only briefly documented can be challenging for an LLM to apply correctly. When the provided documentation does not include (or does not include sufficient) references, usage patterns, or working examples for these constructs, the model tends to produce ambiguous or incorrect ASMETA specifications, or to fall back on more common constructs that only partially capture the intended semantics. This happened, for example, for the `chooseone` function or for model invariants. This suggests that improving documentation coverage (e.g., with minimal and executable examples for less common features) is essential to make LLM-assisted modeling and validation reliable.

L2 - Clearer Error Feedback is Essential When Integrating LLM-generated Code. We found it necessary to significantly improve the error messages of `AsmetaS` and `AsmetaV`, since LLM-generated code often contains multiple errors which are revealed only during simulation or validation, and fixing these issues requires first identifying where the fault originated and why it occurred. Without actionable diagnostics (e.g., precise locations or context-specific hints), debugging became slow and error-prone. This highlights that high-quality and developer-oriented feedback is a key enabler for efficiently integrating LLMs in the modeling and validation process with ASMETA.

L3 - Update Semantics in ASMETA *Specifications and LLM-generated Code.* We learned that LLM-generated ASMETA specifications can be syntactically correct yet still reflect a "sequential programming" mindset, where state updates are assumed to take effect immediately when encountered. This style clashes with ASM semantics, in which updates are collected throughout the execution of a step and applied only at the end of the step. As a consequence, generated models may compile but still exhibit unintended runtime behavior, making simulation-based validation essential to uncover and correct semantic mismatches.

L4 - LLM-generated Scenarios Help Validate Manual Fixes. After using an LLM to generate the ASMETA specification, we manually fixed several issues to obtain a compilable model. However, an LLM-generated `Avalla` scenario then failed because some of our fixes introduced overly restrictive (and sometimes wrong) guards that blocked the intended behavior. This shows that automatically generating scenarios with an LLM is valuable not only for increasing validation coverage, but also for stress-testing human-made adjustments and revealing unintended side effects. Overall, an iterative workflow that combines human-in-the-loop interventions with LLM-assisted model and scenario generation and explanation provides an effective mechanism to detect these inconsistencies.

5.2 Threats to Validity

In this section, we discuss potential threats to the validity [21] of our work. A possible threat to *internal* validity is that our observations may be influenced by the specific interaction protocol used with the LLM (prompt structure, conversation history, and any injected documentation). To mitigate this threat, we provide replication material including all prompts, reference to documentation, instructions, and generated outputs. Additionally, several issues in the generated ASMETA artifacts were corrected manually; while this reflects the intended human-in-the-loop workflow, it introduces the possibility that outcomes (e.g., the time to a working model) partly depend on the modelers' expertise and debugging choices rather than on the LLM alone. *Construct* validity is limited since our study evaluates the proposed methodology through compilation, simulation/animation, and scenario-based validation outcomes. However, these proxies do not fully capture model quality: a specification may compile and simulate without runtime errors while still deviating from intended semantics because it omits relevant and untested behaviors. To mitigate this threat, we manually reviewed all generated artifacts. *External* validity is threatened because we performed our evaluation on a single case study, LLM, and modeling notation. Different domains, modeling styles, tools, and LLMs may lead to different error patterns and different degrees of assistance. For example, we did not consider non-determinism [6] in our experiments. To mitigate this threat, we provide a set of lessons learned, which may generalize across different contexts.

6 Related Work

In this paper, we have explored the use of LLMs to support the modeling process of ASMETA specifications, including their validation activities, starting from a textual description of requirements. Our work fits within recent research efforts on supporting user adoption of formal methods through LLMs.

A growing set of approaches uses LLMs to translate natural-language requirements into formal logics or program specifications [3,14,23]. NL2CTL [24] proposes an LLM-based framework to translate natural language into CTL specifications, aiming to reduce the manual burden of formalization. Similarly, SYNTHTL [19] combines LLMs with model checking and human guidance to translate natural-language intent into temporal-logic specifications, emphasizing decomposition into simpler sub-requirements and iterative correction. Such an iterative correction is what we envision in our approach, where LLMs and humans collaborate to obtain system formal specifications. In a different but related direction, SpecGen targets automated generation of formal program specifications using LLMs, leveraging code understanding to infer precise behavioral constraints, which are expressed in JML [17]. Similarly, in [15,18], the authors proposed a way to formally model communication and security protocols using LLMs. Our work differs in the target formalism and artifacts: instead of temporal logic or program contracts, we generate ASMETA models and `Avalla` scenarios, enabling immediate simulation and validation inside the ASMETA toolchain.

Emerging research is also using LLMs with formal notations in the opposite direction, i.e., they translate formal models into understandable textual requirements. For example, in [22], the authors proposed a methodology for translating Event-B specifications into english, while in [7] the authors use an LLM to explain temporal properties.

A substantial body of work shows that LLMs trained on code can synthesize executable programs from natural language prompts and partial specifications. Codex [9] established an early baseline for NL-to-code generation and evaluated the functional correctness of the generated code, highlighting both the promise and brittleness of it when assessed via tests. Accordingly, more recent studies emphasize that small failures are common: generated programs may look plausible yet fail under rigorous behavioral checks, motivating iterative generation–validation–repair workflows [16], as we envision in our proposed approach: these findings motivate our choice to treat ASMETA and `Avalla` generation as an iterative modeling task rather than a one-shot generation.

7   Conclusion

In this paper we investigated whether Large Language Models (LLMs) can reduce the entry cost of formal modeling by assisting engineers in the generation and iterative refinement of ASMETA specifications starting from natural-language requirements, within an explicit human-in-the-loop workflow grounded on tool feedback (compilation, simulation/animation, and scenario-based validation). To evaluate the feasibility of this approach, we focused on a reduced architecture of the ABZ 2026 planetary rover case study and used GPT-5.2 through the ChatGPT interface and Projects functionality to support multi-iteration interactions and persistent context. Overall, our experience suggests that LLMs can effectively accelerate the production of an initial set of analyzable ASMETA artifacts, but expert oversight remains essential and LLMs can not be used as one-shot tools: even when generated specifications compile, important issues may only surface during simulation/animation and manual fixes may be required. This work is a proof of concept on a single case study; additional experiments on different systems, requirement styles, and modeling patterns are needed to assess generalizability and to quantify benefits more systematically. Nevertheless, we have identified a set of lessons learned which may be useful when applying the same approach to other case studies or other formalisms. As future work, we intend to apply the proposed approach to additional case studies and assess whether richer background knowledge (e.g., using RAG) or more specialized LLMs (e.g., a custom model fine-tuned on ASMETA specifications) can improve the results. We also plan to investigate integrating an LLM directly into the ASMETA toolset and extending the workflow with additional activities, such as manually crafting `Avalla` scenarios and using LLMs for their debugging.

Acknowledgments. The work of Andrea Bombarda is supported by the project ANTHEM (AdvaNced Technologies for Human-centrEd Medicine) - PNC0000003 – CUP: B53C22006700001.

References

1. Arcaini, P., Bombarda, A., Bonfanti, S., Gargantini, A., Riccobene, E., Scandurra, P.: The ASMETA approach to safety assurance of software systems, pp. 215–238. Springer International Publishing, Cham (2021). https://doi.org/10.1007/978-3-030-76020-5_13
2. Askarpour, M., Ghezzi, C., Mandrioli, D., Rossi, M., Tsigkanos, C.: Formal methods in designing critical cyber-physical systems, pp. 110–130. Springer International Publishing, Cham (2019).https://doi.org/10.1007/978-3-030-30985-5_8
3. Beg, A., O'Donoghue, D., Monahan, R.: Leveraging LLMs for Formal Software Requirements – Challenges and Prospects (2025). https://arxiv.org/abs/2507.14330
4. Bombarda, A., Bonfanti, S., Cornejo, C., Gargantini, A., Pellegrinelli, N.: Evaluating coverage and fault detection capability of scenarios for the validation of asmeta specifications. In: Deshmukh, J., Havelund, K., Pinto, A. (eds.) NASA Formal Methods. Springer Nature Switzerland, Cham (2026)
5. Bombarda, A., Bonfanti, S., Gargantini, A.: Automatic test generation with asmeta for the mechanical ventilator milano controller. In: Clark, D., Menendez, H., Cavalli, A.R. (eds.) Testing Software and Systems, pp. 65–72. Springer International Publishing, Cham (2022)
6. Bombarda, A., Bonfanti, S., Gargantini, A., Pellegrinelli, N.: Eliminating flakiness: deterministic control for validating nondeterministic asmeta specifications. In: Dutle, A., Humphrey, L., Titolo, L. (eds.) NASA Formal Methods, pp. 100–115. Springer Nature Switzerland, Cham (2025)
7. Bombarda, A., Bonfanti, S., Gargantini, A., Pellegrinelli, N.: Formalizing and validating properties in asmeta with large language models (extended abstract) (2026). https://arxiv.org/abs/2603.15375
8. Bombarda, A., Bonfanti, S., Gargantini, A., Riccobene, E., Scandurra, P.: ASMETA tool set for rigorous system design. In: Platzer, A., Rozier, K.Y., Pradella, M., Rossi, M. (eds.) Formal Methods, pp. 492–517. Springer Nature Switzerland, Cham (2025)
9. Chen, M., Tworek, J., Jun, H., Yuan, Q., et al.: Evaluating large language models trained on code (2021). https://arxiv.org/abs/2107.03374
10. Farell, M., Kobayashi, T.: ABZ 2026 case study: a planetary rover. https://github.com/trarse-nii/ABZ2026-case-study/blob/main/doc/document_v2.pdf
11. Garavel, H., ter Beek, M.H., van de Pol, J.: The 2020 expert survey on formal methods. In: ter Beek, M.H., Ničković, D. (eds.) Formal Methods for Industrial Critical Systems, pp. 3–69. Springer International Publishing, Cham (2020)
12. Gargantini, A., Riccobene, E., Rinzivillo, S.: Using spin to generate tests from ASM specifications. In: Börger, E., Gargantini, A., Riccobene, E. (eds.) Abstract State Machines 2003, pp. 263–277. Springer, Berlin, Heidelberg (2003)

13. Gleirscher, M., van de Pol, J., Woodcock, J.: A manifesto for applicable formal methods. Softw. Syst. Model. **22**(6), 1737–1749 (2023). https://doi.org/10.1007/s10270-023-01124-2
14. Klimek, R.: RE-oriented model development with LLM support and deduction-based verification. In: Proceedings of the 33rd ACM International Conference on the Foundations of Software Engineering, pp. 1297–1304. FSE Companion '25, Association for Computing Machinery, New York, NY, USA (2025). https://doi.org/10.1145/3696630.3730562
15. Li, Q., Han, J., Yuan, L., Li, X., Wang, X.: Constructing formal models of cryptographic protocols from alice & bob style specifications via LLM. Sci. Reports **15**(1) (2025). https://doi.org/10.1038/s41598-025-93373-y
16. Liventsev, V., Grishina, A., Härmä, A., Moonen, L.: Fully autonomous programming with large language models. In: Proceedings of the Genetic and Evolutionary Computation Conference, pp. 1146–1155. GECCO '23, ACM (2023). https://doi.org/10.1145/3583131.3590481
17. Ma, L., Liu, S., Li, Y., Xie, X., Bu, L.: SpecGen: automated generation of formal program specifications via large language models. In: 2025 IEEE/ACM 47th International Conference on Software Engineering (ICSE), pp. 16–28 (2025). https://doi.org/10.1109/ICSE55347.2025.00129
18. Mao, Z., Wang, J., Sun, J., Qin, S., Xiong, J.: LLM-aided automatic modeling for security protocol verification . In: 2025 IEEE/ACM 47th International Conference on Software Engineering (ICSE), pp. 642–654. IEEE Computer Society, Los Alamitos (2025). https://doi.org/10.1109/ICSE55347.2025.00197
19. Mendoza, D., Hahn, C., Trippel, C.: Translating natural language to temporal logics with large language models and model checkers. In: 2024 Formal Methods in Computer-Aided Design (FMCAD), pp. 1–11 (2024). https://doi.org/10.34727/2024/isbn.978-3-85448-065-5_17
20. OpenAI: ChatGPT (2026). https://chatgpt.com/, Accessed 18 Feb 2026
21. Runeson, P., Höst, M.: Guidelines for conducting and reporting case study research in software engineering. Empirical Softw. Engg. **14**(2), 131–164 (2009). https://doi.org/10.1007/s10664-008-9102-8
22. Vanhari, F.K.: Translating formal specs: Event-B to english. In: 2024 34th International Conference on Collaborative Advances in Software and COmputiNg (CASCON), pp. 1–6 (2024). https://doi.org/10.1109/CASCON62161.2024.10838142
23. Wang, Y., Ge, N., Liu, J., Cao, Z., Chen, Z., Hu, C.: Generating sysml behavior models via large language models: an empirical study. In: Proceedings of the 16th International Conference on Internetware, pp. 366–377. Internetware '25, Association for Computing Machinery, New York, NY, USA (2025). https://doi.org/10.1145/3755881.3755926
24. Zhao, M., Tao, R., Huang, Y., Shi, J., Qin, S., Yang, Y.: NL2CTL: automatic generation of formal requirements specifications via large language models. In: Ogata, K., Mery, D., Sun, M., Liu, S. (eds.) Formal Methods and Software Engineering, pp. 1–17. Springer Nature Singapore, Singapore (2024). https://doi.org/10.1007/978-981-96-0617-7_1

Formal Modeling and Analysis of a Planetary Rover Under Abnormal Scenarios with Quint

Riki Nakamura[(✉)], Shunichiro Nomura, Takahiro Kato, Takato Hatae, Satoshi Ikari, Ryu Funase, and Shinichi Nakasuka

The University of Tokyo, Tokyo, Japan
{nakamura,nomura,hatae.taka,ikari,funase,nakasuka}@space.t.u-tokyo.ac.jp,
kato-takahiro427@g.ecc.u-tokyo.ac.jp

Abstract. We present a partial formal analysis of the ABZ 2026 planetary rover case study, focusing on abnormal scenarios and failure-handling behavior. From a space-systems engineering perspective, we first identified representative abnormal scenarios through what-if analysis and then formalized the relevant interactions among goal reasoning, planning, map validation, communication, and recovery-related components in Quint as a shared-state transition system. We analyzed this model through simulation and bounded verification, which revealed several specification issues and ambiguities, including a gap in the interruption semantics of safe-location instructions and underspecified decision criteria in failure handling. We also explored a focused Event-B model of the FailureMode component as a complementary analysis. The study shows how lightweight formal modeling can help domain engineers clarify abnormal behavior in an autonomous space-system specification.

Keywords: Formal Methods · Planetary Rover · Specification Analysis · Abnormal Scenarios · Quint

1 Introduction

Autonomous planetary rovers operate in extreme and unpredictable environments where direct human intervention is limited or impossible. Deep-space missions must tolerate communication delays, harsh conditions, and irreversible hardware degradations. In such contexts, failure handling is not exceptional but a fundamental design requirement, and ensuring safe and coherent behavior under abnormal conditions is critical to mission success.

The ABZ 2026 planetary rover case study [3] defines a modular architecture including planning, goal reasoning, map validation, communication, and a dedicated FailureMode mechanism. While the specification describes how failures are detected and handled, it is not immediately clear how recovery behaviors interact across components under abnormal conditions. This motivates a formal examination of failure handling at the system level.

© The Author(s), under exclusive license to Springer Nature Switzerland AG 2026
F. Ishikawa and A. Cunha (Eds.): ABZ 2026, LNCS 16579, pp. 310–327, 2026.
https://doi.org/10.1007/978-3-032-26752-8_20

In this paper, we approach the case study from a space systems engineering perspective, where abnormal scenarios are treated as primary design drivers. Rather than modeling the entire system in full detail, we construct a partial state-based model in Quint, capturing interactions among selected components related to planning, reasoning, and failure handling. We use simulation to explore execution traces under nondeterministic conditions and verify safety invariants and temporal properties derived from the specification.

The objective of this study is not to claim deficiencies in the specification, but to examine how formal modeling makes abnormal behaviors explicit and supports a clearer understanding of recovery semantics across components.

The contributions of this paper are as follows:

1. A partial Quint model of the ABZ 2026 rover focused on abnormal scenarios and cross-component interactions.
2. A scenario-driven validation workflow based on what-if analysis, with representative cases analyzed as executable behaviors in Quint.
3. The identification of specification aspects related to abnormal scenarios that become ambiguous or require clarification when expressed as executable behavior.
4. An exploratory Event-B refinement study of the FailureMode component to examine causal ordering and structural constraints.

This study illustrates how formal methods can support the examination of specification robustness in autonomous space systems, particularly under abnormal operational scenarios.

2   Target System

2.1   Architecture

The Rover System defined in the ABZ 2026 case study [3] consists of the following components:

Vision Obstacle Recognition and Positioning
MapValidator Map Data Validation
Goal Reasoning Agent (GRA) Goal Selection and FailureMode Activation during Anomalies
ComputePlan2Charging/ComputePlan2Destination Path Planning
Battery+Hardware Battery monitoring and hardware control
FailureMode Fault diagnosis and recovery
Communication2Ground/Communication2Rovers Communication

Table 1. Treatment of each requirement: "Modeled" (implemented in the model), "Assumed" (treated as environmental assumption), and "Out" (not considered in this work).

Component	Modeled	Assumed	Out
System	SL3	–	SL1,2,4,5
Vision	–	V1–6	–
MapValidator	M1–5	–	–
GRA	G1–9	–	–
ComputePlan2Charging	CPC1–5	–	–
ComputePlan2Destination	CPD1–5	–	–
Battery+Hardware	HI1, 2, 3, 6, 7 BM1,2	HI5	HI4
Communication2Ground	CG7	CG1, 8	CG2, 3, 4, 5, 6
Communication2Rovers	–	CR3	CR1, 2
FailureMode	FM1–5	–	–

2.2 Requirements

The requirements considered in this paper are taken from the ABZ 2026 case-study specification [3]. Table 1 summarizes the requirement coverage and treatment used in this work.

3 Quint Modeling and Verification

3.1 Quint

Quint [4] is a specification language for describing transition-system models and checking properties over their executions. In Quint, a model is defined by state variables (`var`), an initialization action (`init`), and transition actions that update next-state values with the prime operator (`state'`).

We use both simulation and model checking in the analysis workflow. `quint run` is used for fast randomized exploration and scenario debugging, while `quint verify` is used to check invariants and temporal properties over the explored bounded state space. When a property is violated, Quint reports a counterexample trace, which we use to diagnose the exact sequence of state updates that leads to the violation. At the property level, invariants specify conditions that must hold in every reachable state, while temporal properties specify how states should evolve over time, including eventual progress and response obligations.

3.2 Modeling Approach Overview

Our Quint modeling strategy focuses on the part of the rover specification needed to analyze abnormal situations. Rather than formalizing the entire architecture at the implementation level, we model the decision and recovery flows that connect planning, reasoning, communication, and failure handling. Components whose internal algorithmic detail is not essential to that objective are represented at the level of their externally visible effects on the rest of the rover.

The resulting model is an integrated transition system over a shared state, not a collection of unrelated component descriptions. Each component contributes guarded transitions over this shared state, and their interaction is captured through state-based interfaces rather than protocol-level communication details. This makes it possible to study how abnormal conditions propagate across component boundaries while keeping the model at the level of the case-study requirements.

Non-determinism is used in a controlled way to represent environmental uncertainty and specification underspecification. In particular, the model leaves environment-controlled inputs symbolic and keeps open those internal choices that are required by the specification but not fully defined by it. This allows the analysis to explore multiple abnormal evolutions without committing to implementation-specific behavior that is outside the scope of the case study.

The integrated model supports simulation and provides the common basis for verification, but direct temporal checking of the full model is not always tractable. We therefore use requirement-focused harnesses as verification abstractions. A harness preserves the control structure relevant to a target property while abstracting away unrelated behavior through simplified environment actions and reduced domains. In this way, the harnesses retain the requirement-level phenomena of interest while making bounded verification feasible.

3.3   Model Organization and Execution Structure

The Quint model is organized into component-local modules together with a top-level integrated model and a set of requirement-focused harnesses. Each component module defines the local transition logic for one part of the rover, while the integrated model combines these modules into a single transition system used for simulation and system-level verification. The harnesses reuse the same modeling style but restrict the behavior to the fragment needed for a particular verification objective.

Interaction among components is expressed through a shared state rather than through explicit protocol models. Each module reads the part of the global state relevant to its decision and updates only the fields under its responsibility. This shared-state organization provides a uniform interface between components and makes dependencies among planning, reasoning, communication, and recovery behavior explicit at the model level.

Execution is defined in the standard Quint style using an initialization action and a top-level step relation. The initialization action constructs an initial symbolic rover state, and the step relation advances the system by nondeterministically choosing one enabled component action. In this way, component behaviors are composed by interleaving over the shared state, while guarded actions determine when each local transition is allowed to occur.

3.4 Modeling Approach Illustrated with the GRA Component

The Goal Reasoning Agent (GRA) illustrates the modeling approach used throughout the Quint model. Rather than encoding the GRA as a monolithic transition, we model it as a set of guarded actions over the shared rover state. This makes the decision flow explicit and keeps the model close to the structure of the requirements: goal selection, evaluation of planner outcomes, notification obligations, and auxiliary goal-list updates are represented as separate transitions.

The GRA is modeled as a symbolic decision component that selects the rover's next objective and coordinates hand-offs to planning and failure handling. The model captures requirements G1–G9 by combining explicit control states with guarded actions over the shared rover state record. Within this structure, the GRA consumes cross-component inputs such as `recharge`, `atGoal`, `mapValidated`, `invalidMap`, `cpcResult`, `cpdResult`, and `safeLocationInstruction`.

At the core of the model, the GRA control state is represented by `AwaitingGoal`, `AwaitingPlans`, `ReadyToRun`, `AwaitingInstructions`, and `FailureMode`. Figure 1 summarizes this control-state structure. The figure should be read as a requirement-level design view from which the guarded actions are derived: each transition in the diagram corresponds to one or more actions whose guards identify when the transition is enabled and whose updates record its effect on the shared state.

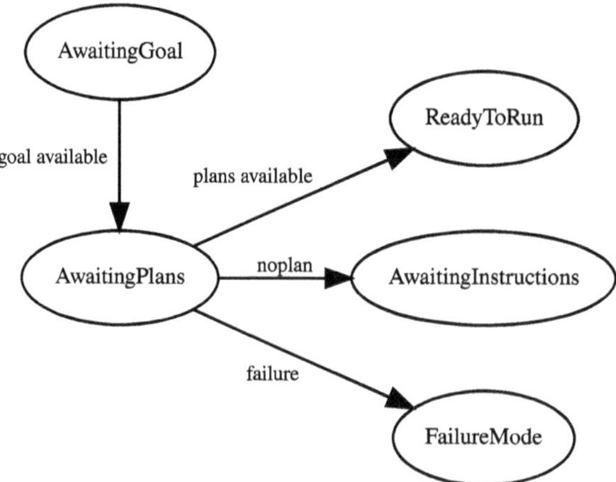

Fig. 1. State-transition diagram for the GRA control states.

Goal selection provides a representative example of this style. It is modeled as a guarded action enabled only when the map has been validated, the rover is not already at goal, and the control state is `AwaitingGoal`. The choice itself is expressed at the requirement level: if recharge is needed, the next goal is a nearest charger; otherwise, the head of the prioritized goal list is selected. Once a goal is selected, the model resets both planner results and moves to `AwaitingPlans`. Figure 2 shows the corresponding Quint fragment.

```
action selectGoal: bool = {
  val selected =
    if (state.recharge) nearestCharger(state.currentPosition, state.
        chargers)
    else highestPriorityGoal(state.prioritisedGoals)
  all {
    state.graState == AwaitingGoal,
    not(state.atGoal),
    state.mapValidated,
    not(state.invalidMap),
    match selected {
      | Some(g) => setGoalAndRequestPlanning(g)
      | None => all { state' = state }
    },
  }
}
```

Fig. 2. Representative Quint fragment for guarded goal selection in the GRA.

When planning results become available on the shared state, the GRA reacts through another compact guarded transition. Action `evaluatePlanning Results` deterministically maps the pair of planner outcomes to the next control state: `Failure` leads to `FailureMode`, `NoPlan` leads to `AwaitingInstructions`, and successful planning leads to `ReadyToRun`. This illustrates a second recurring pattern in the model: cross-component outcomes are first exposed through shared-state variables and are then consumed by a decision action that updates only the next control state. Figure 3 shows the corresponding Quint fragment.

The model then captures downstream obligations via dedicated actions: notification and instruction request on no-plan (`noMoreViablePlans`, `requested Instructions`), completion notification when all goals are consumed (`completed`), and failure escalation (`failureModeInvoked` and `systemState SentToFailureMode`). These obligations are represented as decision-level state updates and are interpreted as communication effects by the communication-related components.

In addition to the main control-flow transitions, the model includes auxiliary transitions for goal-list maintenance and safety relocation. Action `applyAtGoal` removes an achieved goal from `prioritisedGoals` when not in recharge mode, and action `applySafeLocationInstruction` prepends `safeLocation` unless it is already the list head.

```
action evaluatePlanningResults: bool = {
  val newGraState =
    if (resultsHaveFailure(state.cpcResult, state.cpdResult))
        FailureMode
    else if (resultsHaveNoPlan(state.cpcResult, state.cpdResult))
        AwaitingInstructions
    else ReadyToRun
  all {
    state.graState == AwaitingPlans,
    resultsAreFinal(state.cpcResult, state.cpdResult),
    state' = { graState: newGraState, ...state },
  }
}
```

Fig. 3. Representative Quint fragment for reaction to planner outcomes in the GRA.

Direct verification on the integrated model suffered from state-space explosion, so we verified GRA temporal requirements G1–G9 using requirement-focused harnesses. Here, a harness is a property-specific verification module that constrains initialization and environment actions to reduce unrelated behavior while preserving the GRA transitions relevant to the target property. Under this abstraction, G1, G2, G3, G4, G5, G6, G7, and G8 were verified, while G9 produced a counterexample.

For G9, the key issue is a specification gap: the requirements do not define interruption semantics for `safeLocationInstruction` when planning or execution is already in progress. In our simplified model, `safeLocationInstruction` updates `prioritisedGoals`, but does not preempt ongoing planning/execution to force immediate reselection of `goal`. As a result, there are paths where `prioritisedGoals` already contains `safeLocation` while `goal` is not updated to `safeLocation`, which yields a counterexample to `g9_instructionImpliesSafeLocationAsGoal`.

3.5   Other Components

MapValidator. The `MapValidator` component is modeled as a single guarded action `validateAndUpdateMap` that checks the consistency of map data received from `Vision` and the ground station. The action implements requirements M1–M5 by constructing the combined obstacle set $visionObstacles \cup GSObstacles$ and requiring that (i) the rover's `currentPosition` is not contained in that set, and (ii) both `visionObstacles` and `GSObstacles` are disjoint from the `chargers` and `prioritisedGoals` provided by the ground station. These checks are encoded in the pure predicate `mapIsValid`.

If the validation succeeds, `obstacles` is updated to the combined set and `mapValidated` is set to `true`; otherwise, `invalidMap` is raised and the previous `obstacles` are preserved. The invalid-map notification is not modeled as an explicit message-passing protocol but as a state update: the derived `systemState.messages` includes `InvalidMap`, and `Communication2Ground.sendPendingMessages` transfers it into `gsSent`. This captures requirement M4 that the rover requests advice when the map is invalid.

For the response path, we interpret the specification statement "operators can update and override the original map" (M4) together with CG7 as an assumption that the ground station returns corrected data. Accordingly, `Communication2Ground.updateGSStates` is constrained to produce map data that satisfies the same validity predicate against the current `Vision` output and position. The `MapValidator` then re-validates on the next step, thereby modeling a recovery from `invalidMap` when updated data arrives.

ComputePlan2Charging and ComputePlan2Destination. The `Compute Plan2Charging` and `ComputePlan2Destination` modules model requirements CPC1–CPC5 and CPD1–CPD5, respectively. The specification requires planning and shortest-path selection, but it does not prescribe a specific path-generation method. Accordingly, both modules adopt the same abstraction: two axis-aligned candidate paths are generated, obstacle avoidance is evaluated by checking whether any obstacle lies on each path segment between consecutive waypoints, and the shortest feasible candidate is returned when one exists.

The `ComputePlan2Charging` module computes a charging route from the selected goal to the nearest charger and publishes the result through `cpcResult`. The planner outcome is recorded as one of `Plan`, `NoPlan`, or `Failure`. If no feasible route exists, the module yields `NoPlan`, and if a feasible route exists, the model allows either successful planning (`Plan`) or planning failure (`Failure`) to capture runtime uncertainty. As with GRA, CPC requirements CPC1–CPC5 were verified using requirement-focused harnesses. Under this abstraction, all CPC requirements were checked as invariants, and all five properties were verified with no violation.

The `ComputePlan2Destination` module computes a route from `current Position` to the selected goal and publishes the result through `cpdResult`. As in charging planning, it reuses the same candidate construction and obstacle checks, and returns the shortest feasible plan. Unlike charging planning, this module is anchored at `currentPosition`, so missing position or missing goal immediately yields `NoPlan`. The planner outcome is recorded in `cpdResult` using the same abstract categories: `Plan`, `NoPlan`, and `Failure`. As in charging planning, route-construction failure yields `NoPlan`, and feasible routing may still yield `Failure` to represent runtime uncertainty. Together with `cpcResult`, this output provides the planner-result pair consumed by GRA decision logic. As with GRA, CPD requirements CPD1–CPD5 were verified using requirement-focused harnesses. As with CPC, all CPD requirements were checked as invariants, and all five properties were verified with no violation under the harness abstraction.

Battery+Hardware. The `BatteryHardware` module models requirements HI1–HI7 and BM1–BM2 by managing battery state, movement execution, and solar panel control.

Two boolean state variables, `recharge` and `atGoal`, are modeled as derived values rather than as variables updated by actions. This is due to the limitation of Quint where such reactive action definition that it should be always executed when some condition is met cannot be represented to the best of our knowledge.

Battery monitoring (BM1) and conservative reporting policy (BM2) are built directly into the model and thus satisfied by construction. We should note that the specification does not address the case where the battery level is less than 5%, and we adopted the flooring mechanism via this modeling process.

The module defines four guarded actions: `chargeAtCharger` (HI2) increments `batteryLevel` and sets `chargingComplete` at a charger; `executeMovement` (HI4) atomically updates `currentPosition` and decrements the battery by the path energy cost of `plan2D` upon plan execution; `openSolarPanels` (HI6) and `closeSolarPanels` (HI7) open and close the panels at a charger when closed, and upon charging completion, respectively. The eventuality of HI5 is verified as a temporal property.

We defined four temporal properties with regards to the `Battery+Hardware` component, only two of which yielded a result in a reasonable time:

- `HI2`: If at a charger and not fully charged, the rover does not leave
- `HI5`: When executed and goal exists, the rover eventually reaches the goal
- `HI6` (Verified): At a charger implies panels are eventually opened
- `HI7` (Verified): Charging complete implies panels are eventually closed

During the verification process, we found ambiguity in the requirements as to how to set the appropriate value of `recharge` flag when it cannot compute the battery level that is "high enough to reach the goal and subsequently reach a charging location." Also, because we defined `recharge` flag as a derived value, it was "too stateless" in that it does not remember the previous value when the plan becomes `Pending`, which triggers the re-computation of `recharge` flag, leading to a cycle of "Goal picked" $\rightarrow$ "Plan computed and `recharge` becomes `true` due to low battery level" $\rightarrow$ "Goal updated and plan is not yet available" $\rightarrow$ "`recharge` becomes `false`" $\rightarrow$ "Goal picked."

Communication2Ground. `Communication2Ground` is modeled only as a lightweight interface abstraction needed by other components. Concretely, `updateGSStates` nondeterministically provides updated goals/chargers/obstacles to support the `MapValidator` interface (CG7), `sendPendingMessages` transfers derived pending messages to `gsSent`, and `receiveSafeLocation Instruction` abstracts reception of a safe-location command used by GRA. Connection management and protocol-level behavior (CG2–CG6) are out of scope.

FailureMode. The `FailureMode` module models requirements FM1–FM5, which govern the rover's behaviour when failures are detected. The module introduces two constants: a help-wait timeout (FM4) and a maximum number of recheck cycles, both of which correspond to quantities left unspecified by the case study document.

The control state `fmState` is modeled as `FmIdle`, `FmDiagnosing`, `FmReco veryDeciding`, `FmRebooting`, `FmRequestingHelp`, `FmWaitingForHelp`, and `FmResolved`, with transitions returning to `FmIdle` after resolution. Invocation (FM1) is triggered when `systemStateSentToFailureMode` or `failed2Reconnect` holds.

Diagnosis and recovery selection (FM2–FM3) are modeled with non-deterministic choice over plausible causes and applicable actions, because the specification does not define ranking or selection criteria. Recovery can proceed via reboot, help request, or safe-location redirection (FM5). The help path uses a wait counter and periodic recheck (FM4), and resolution returns the machine to normal operation while resetting FailureMode-local variables.

The modeling process revealed several points where the specification is ambiguous or silent, each corresponding to a non-deterministic choice or an arbitrary constant in the model:

1. Diagnosis criteria (FM2): The specification requires "the most likely cause" but provides no basis for ranking causes. The model uses non-deterministic selection over plausible causes.
2. Recovery selection (FM3): The choice between reboot and requesting help is unspecified. The model uses non-deterministic selection over applicable actions.
3. Wait duration (FM4): "A reasonable amount of time" is undefined. The model uses an arbitrary constant (`HELP_WAIT_TIMEOUT = 5`).
4. Safe location reachability (FM5): "If possible" lacks a formal criterion. The model enables the action whenever a safe location exists, without checking reachability or battery sufficiency.
5. Recovery failure: The specification acknowledges that "the FailureMode could also fail itself, but we ignore this for now." The model does not include failure of the recovery process itself.

As with GRA, FailureMode requirements FM1–FM5 were verified using requirement-focused harnesses. Under this abstraction, FM1–FM3 were verified, while FM4 and FM5 were partially verified because full liveness depends on unbounded environmental assumptions (help arrival and safe-location availability).

4   Event-B Analysis

4.1   Refinement Model

Alongside the Quint model, we also explored a partial Event-B model focusing on the FailureMode component in order to verify structural consistency in the failure-handling logic. The model employs a five-level refinement chain (m0–m5) with corresponding context extensions (ctx0–ctx4), constructed in the Rodin platform.

Refinement Strategy. The refinement chain follows a *poco a poco* approach, introducing one conceptual layer per level:

Table 2. Event-B refinement chain and proof statistics for the FailureMode component

Level	Context	Focus	Requirements	Events	PO
m0	ctx0	Abstract	—	4	17
m1	ctx1	GRA state machine	G7, G8, CPC5, CPD5	12	139
m2	(ctx1)	Ground-station	G5, G7	14	46
m3	ctx2	FDIR selection	FM2, FM3	23	86
m4	ctx3	Help authentication	FM1, FM4, FM5, CR3	28	121
m5	ctx4	Battery consumption	SL1 (partial)	28	87

At the most abstract level (m0), the system is a two-valued automaton with three boolean variables (`systemNormal`, `failureDetected`, `noplanDetected`) and three events (`detectFailure`, `detectNoPlan`, `recover`). The key invariant at this level is mutual exclusion: failure and no-plan are never simultaneously true.

Level m1 introduces the GRA state machine with five states (`AwaitingGoal`, `AwaitingPlans`, `ReadyToRun`, `FailureMode`, `AwaitingInstructions`) and planning result types, replacing the abstract booleans via gluing invariants. The abstract `detectFailure` event is split into `computePlan2ChargingFailure` and `computePlan2DestinationFailure`, together with a `communicationFailure Detected` event for the FM1 `failed2Reconnect` path. Adding this communication-triggered path required relaxing the invariant that links `FailureMode` to planning failure results, since communication failures enter `FailureMode` without any planner returning `failure`.

Level m3 introduces the `FAILURE_TYPE` and `RECOVERY_ACTION` enumerated types and models the diagnosis and recovery selection as separate events with causal ordering enforced by invariants ($recoveryActionSelected$ = TRUE $\Rightarrow$ $failureIdentified$ = TRUE). The Quint model's non-deterministic `oneOf` selection over plausible causes corresponds to Event-B's `ANY ftype WHERE ftype` $\in$ `{communicationFailure, hardwareFailure, unknownFailure}` construct in the `identifyOtherFailure` event.

Level m4 adds the help-request protocol including `waitingForHelp`, `waitCount`, `helpReceived`, `helperAuthenticated`, and `helpSource` variables. The `authenticateHelper` event (CR3) is modeled here: the rover verifies the helper's identity before accepting assistance from a nearby rover. A key invariant ensures that authentication only succeeds when help has been received from a `nearbyRover` source.

Level m5 introduces `batteryLevel` and models energy consumption during help-wait cycles. The `recheckHelpArrival` event consumes `BATTERY_COST_PER_WAIT` units per recheck, and a `batteryEmergencyDuringWait` event forces an emergency abort when battery is critically low. An invariant $batteryLevel \in 1..FULL\_CHARGE$ encodes the safety property SL1 (never run out of battery) within the failure-handling scope.

Proof Obligations. All proof obligations across the six machines (m0–m5) were discharged in Rodin, confirming that each refinement level preserves the invariants established by its predecessors. The refinement scope together with events and PO (Proof Obligations) per level are summarized in Table 2.

4.2   Verification by Proof Obligations

The Event-B refinement model provides complementary verification through proof obligations rather than state-space exploration. The refinement chain verified the following structural properties that are difficult to express as Quint temporal formulas:

1. **Causal ordering:** The invariant chain $recoveryInProgress \Rightarrow recovery$ $ActionSelected \Rightarrow failureIdentified$ (m3, inv6–inv7) guarantees that diagnosis precedes recovery selection, which precedes recovery execution.
2. **Ground notification as precondition:** The invariant $graState =$ FailureMode $\Rightarrow (failureIdentified \lor \neg notifiedGround)$ (m3, inv8) ensures that when the ground has been notified, a failure cause has already been identified.
3. **Communication-triggered FailureMode entry:** Adding the `communica tionFailureDetected` event (FM1 via CG8) required relaxing the invariant linking FailureMode to planning failure. The relaxed invariant uses a `failed2Reconnect` flag to distinguish the two entry paths.
4. **Helper authentication (CR3):** The invariant $helperAuthenticated \Rightarrow$ $helpReceived \land helpSource =$ nearbyRover (m4, inv8) ensures that authentication only succeeds for rover-sourced help, preventing spoofed ground-station responses from bypassing security checks.
5. **Battery safety during recovery:** The invariant $batteryLevel \in$ $1 .. FULL\_CHARGE$ (m5, inv1) combined with the guard $batteryLevel >$ $BATTERY\_COST\_PER\_WAIT$ on `recheckHelpArrival` ensures that the rover never depletes its battery while waiting for help.

5   Validation

5.1   What-If Analysis and Scenario Identification

To guide the validation of abnormal behaviors, we conducted a what-if analysis inspired by risk analysis methods based on assumed fault scenarios, such as Failure Modes and Effects Analysis (FMEA), commonly used in space system design. This analysis was used to identify situations where the system might not behave as intended under abnormal conditions. The identified abnormal scenarios were classified into five categories based on functional roles in the system:

- Execution (Battery/Hardware)
- Planning (ComputePlan2Charging/ComputePlan2Destination)
- Communication (Communication2Ground/Communication2Rovers)

- Perception (Vision/MapValidator)
- Decision-making (Goal Reasoning Agent)

For each category, we examined potential deviations from nominal behavior at both component and system levels, including cross-component interactions. Through this process, we identified a total of 19 abnormal scenarios. Among these, 7 representative cases were selected and encoded in the Quint model to analyze their behavior as executable state transitions.

The following subsections present the results of these analyses.

5.2   Case 1: Handling Invalid Map Validation

This case validates the recovery path after an invalid map notification. When `invalidMap` is raised due to an inconsistency between `currentPosition` and the combined obstacle set, a ground-station update supplies corrected goals, chargers, and obstacles that satisfy the validity predicate. A subsequent `validateAndUpdateMap` clears `invalidMap` and restores `mapValidated`, demonstrating recovery once consistent map data arrives.

5.3   Case 2: No Selectable Goal

We validated the corner case where no selectable goal exists under two conditions: (i) `recharge = false` with `prioritisedGoals = []`, and (ii) `recharge = true` with `chargers = Set()`. We verified that if this no-candidate condition holds, the run eventually reaches and remains in a state where no selectable goal exists, `goal` stays unset, `graState` stays `AwaitingGoal`, and execution does not start. This result shows that when no candidate is available, the GRA does not set `goal` and does not progress to planning/execution. This suggests adding a bounded timeout-and-escalation policy for prolonged no-selectable-goal situations.

5.4   Case 3: `noplan` Followed by Persistent Waiting for Instructions

We validated the corner case where either planning component returns `noplan` and no external instruction is received afterward. We verified that after `noplan` is detected (without subsequent external instruction), the run can reach and remain in a state where the GRA stays in `AwaitingInstructions`, has requested instructions, has notified `NoMoreViablePlans`, and does not execute. This result shows that after `noplan`, the GRA can remain in `AwaitingInstructions`, waiting for ground-station guidance and unable to decide the next action. This suggests specifying a bounded timeout, fallback priority, and escalation rule for persistent `AwaitingInstructions`.

5.5   Case 4: Failure Recovery via Reboot

We validated the scenario where a planning failure triggers FailureMode, diagnosis identifies `PlanningFailure`, and recovery selects `DoReboot`. In the Quint model, starting from a state where `cpdResult = Failure` and `graState = FailureMode`, we confirmed that the trace proceeds through `fmInvoke` → `fmDiagnose` → `fmDecideRecovery` → `fmReboot` → `fmResolve`, returning `fmState` to `FmIdle` and setting `return2NormalOperation = true`. The GRA subsequently transitions back to `AwaitingGoal`.

In the Event-B model, the corresponding trace traverses `computePlan2` `DestinationFailure` (m1) → `notifyGroundStationOnFailure` (m2) → identify `PlanningFailure` (m3) → `selectRebootRecovery` (m3) → `startRecovery` (m3) → `recoverFromFailure` (m1–m5).

5.6   Case 5: Help-Wait Timeout Escalation

We validated the scenario where help is requested from the ground station but no response arrives within the timeout period. In the Quint model, starting from `FmWaitingForHelp` with `helpWaitTicks = 0`, we confirmed that after `HELP_WAIT_TIMEOUT` ticks of `fmWaitTick`, the `fmRecheck` action fires and sets the `recheck` flag.

In the Event-B model, the corresponding scenario involves `recheckHelpArrival` (m4) incrementing `waitCount` until it reaches `maxWaitCount` at which point `helpWaitTimeout` (m4, refining `timeoutWaitingInRecovery` from m3) fires and resets `recoveryActionSelected` to `FALSE`. This enables a re-diagnosis or alternative recovery path. Additionally, at level m5, `batteryEmergencyDuringWait` can preempt the timeout if $batteryLevel \leq BATTERY\_COST\_PER\_WAIT$, forcing an immediate fallback.

This escalation mechanism—timeout leading to recovery re-selection, or battery emergency forcing abort—was discovered through the Event-B refinement process.

5.7   Case 6: Communication Failure Triggering FailureMode

We validated the FM1 path where `failed2Reconnect` triggers FailureMode entry without any prior planning failure. In the Quint model, setting `failed2Reconnect = true` while `graState ≠ FailureMode` enables `fmInvoke`, and subsequent diagnosis identifies `CommunicationFailure`.

In the Event-B model, the `communicationFailureDetected` event (m1) enters FailureMode with `failed2Reconnect = TRUE`, bypassing the planning-failure path. The invariant relaxation discovered during Event-B development (as described in Sect. 4) confirms that this entry path is structurally distinct and requires separate invariant treatment.

5.8 Case 7: Statelessness of recharge Flag

Per requirement HI1, the `recharge` flag shall be set to "`true` if the `batteryLevel` is not high enough to reach the goal and subsequently reach a charging location." When `recharge` flag is set to `true`, per requirement G2, `GRA` shall set the `goal` as the nearest charging position. After the `goal` is set to the nearest charging position and before the path plan to the new goal is generated, it is technically unclear whether the `batteryLevel` is not high enough to reach the goal, which is the nearest charging position. So if we model the `recharge` flag as a derived, stateless value, it "forgets" that `batteryLevel` was low, and becomes the derived value in cases where plan is pending. It is not a flaw in the requirements per se, but suggests nonintuitive complexity in what seems like a simple flag like `recharge`.

6 Discussion

6.1 Specification Clarifications Revealed by Formalization

A central outcome of this study is the identification of specification points that required additional interpretation in order to construct an executable formal model. In the FailureMode component, the specification states that the system shall determine "the most likely cause" of a failure (FM2), yet no ranking or likelihood criteria are provided. In our Quint model, this was represented as a nondeterministic selection over a set of plausible causes (see Sect. 3.5). Similarly, the choice of recovery action (FM3) is described functionally but without a defined selection policy, which required abstraction as a selection from applicable recovery actions.

The phrase "a reasonable amount of time" in FM4 is not quantitatively defined. To enable analysis, a timeout constant was introduced in the model. Likewise, FM5 specifies that the rover should move to a safe location "if possible," but does not define feasibility conditions such as reachability under obstacle constraints or battery sufficiency.

Beyond FailureMode, the modeling of G9 exposed a semantic gap regarding safe-location overrides, as described in Sect. 3.4. In Battery+Hardware, modeling the `recharge` flag as a derived value highlighted a subtle interaction between HI1 and G2: when planning is pending, the condition "battery sufficient to reach the goal and subsequently a charger" becomes temporarily undefined, potentially leading to unintuitive oscillations. These observations do not indicate deficiencies in the case study, but rather illustrate areas where additional clarification could strengthen the intended recovery semantics.

7 Lessons Learned

7.1 Perspective from Space System Design and Development

From a space systems engineering perspective, risk analysis methods based on assumed fault scenarios, such as Failure Modes and Effects Analysis (FMEA), are commonly used to anticipate potential anomalies during design. In this study, we adopted a simplified form of such scenario-based reasoning.

In several cases, we identified behaviors that appeared potentially problematic from an operational perspective. By modeling these scenarios in Quint, we were able to explore their consequences and assess whether the system behaved as expected.

This experience suggests that formal modeling can serve as a practical complement to informal what-if analysis, allowing engineers to validate intuitions about potentially problematic behaviors and reason more concretely about their outcomes.

7.2   Scalability and Verification Strategy

Direct verification of the fully integrated model frequently encountered statespace explosion. To address this, we introduced requirement-focused harnesses that constrained environmental behavior and initialization to isolate relevant transitions. This approach enabled verification of several temporal properties within practical resource bounds.

However, this strategy also shifts part of the correctness argument to the validity of the harness assumptions. Careful documentation of modeling scope and environmental restrictions is therefore essential. For space-system developers, this reinforces an important methodological lesson: formal verification results must always be interpreted in the context of abstraction boundaries and operational assumptions.

7.3   Experience with Event-B Refinement Modeling

In parallel with the Quint work, we also explored an Event-B model of the FailureMode component on the Rodin platform [2]. This section reports practical observations from that process.

Where Refinement Was Effective. Event-B's stepwise refinement [1] proved effective for verifying causal structure within the FailureMode component. By placing invariants at successive refinement levels (e.g., *recoveryInProgress* $\Rightarrow$ *recoveryActionSelected* $\Rightarrow$ *failureIdentified*), causal ordering was enforced as proof obligations across all 28 events. When the communication-triggered FailureMode entry path (FM1's `failed2Reconnect`) was added, a conflict with an existing invariant was immediately detected as a proof obligation failure (see Sect. 4). This ability to discover implicit dependencies among invariants is a strength of Event-B not available through state-space exploration.

Practical Constraints. Event-B modeling requires the Rodin IDE [2], whose XML-based file format limits toolchain flexibility and makes version-control merging problematic. The refinement chain is inherently sequential, making parallel development difficult; in this study, Event-B was confined to a single author. Additionally, diagnosing refinement errors such as action-label collisions and proof obligation failures from NEW events required deep understanding of refinement semantics.

Effective Scope of Event-B. Based on these experiences, we consider Event-B better suited for deep verification of internal logic within a safety-critical component—where causal ordering guarantees and hierarchical invariant verification are needed—than for flat modeling of an entire system. The division of labor adopted in this study, using Quint for broad system-level exploration and Event-B for proving invariants of a critical component, represents a practical combination consistent with the recommendation by Luckcuck et al. [5] to integrate heterogeneous formal methods for autonomous robotic systems.

7.4 AI-Assisted Formal Modeling by Domain Experts

This study was conducted by researchers with backgrounds in space systems engineering rather than formal methods. Although we had practical experience in anomaly handling and autonomous system design, we were relatively new to tools such as Quint and Event-B.

In Quint, where models are defined in plain text files, AI coding agents were effective for drafting models, fixing syntax errors, and reading counterexample traces. In contrast, this style of AI-assisted coding was far less effective in Event-B. As mentioned earlier, the implementation of Event-B in Rodin is not well-suited for rapid text-level generation or modification.

However, AI assistance was useful mainly for rapid prototyping and syntactic support. Deciding whether a counterexample reflected a genuine specification gap or merely a modeling artifact still required domain knowledge and engineering judgment. Likewise, abstraction choices, requirement interpretation, and safety-relevant conclusions could not be delegated to AI tools. In our experience, AI assistance functioned best as a productivity amplifier for text-based formal modeling, while final validation remained the responsibility of domain experts.

8   Conclusion

In this paper, we presented a formal analysis of selected components of the ABZ 2026 planetary rover case study, focusing on abnormal operational scenarios. From a space systems engineering perspective, understanding recovery behavior under such conditions is essential for ensuring system robustness in deep-space environments.

Using Quint, we explored recovery transitions through simulation and bounded verification, which helped clarify how the specification behaves when expressed as executable state transitions. During this process, several aspects of failure handling—such as diagnosis selection, recovery decisions, timeout interpretation, and safe-location semantics—required additional clarification.

In parallel with the Quint work, we also explored an Event-B refinement model of the FailureMode component. This model made structural invariants and causal ordering constraints explicit.

Overall, this study shows that lightweight formal modeling combined with refinement-based reasoning can support the analysis of abnormal behavior in autonomous space systems. These approaches offer practical value for domain engineers seeking to better understand and operationalize complex system specifications.

References

1. Abrial, J.R.: Modeling in Event-B: System and Software Engineering. Cambridge University Press (2010). https://doi.org/10.1017/CBO9781139195881
2. Abrial, J.R., Butler, M., Hallerstede, S., Hoang, T.S., Mehta, F., Voisin, L.: Rodin: an open toolset for modelling and reasoning in Event-B. Int. J. Softw. Tools Technol. Transfer **12**(6), 447–466 (2010). https://doi.org/10.1007/s10009-010-0145-y
3. Farrell, M., Kobayashi, T.: ABZ 2026 case study: a planetary rover (2025). ABZ 2026 Case Study Document
4. Informal Systems: Quint (2025). https://quint-lang.org
5. Luckcuck, M., Farrell, M., Dennis, L.A., Dixon, C., Fisher, M.: Formal specification and verification of autonomous robotic systems: a survey. ACM Comput. Surv. **52**(5), 1–41 (2019). https://doi.org/10.1145/3342355

Journal-First Talk

SHARCS: Refinement-Centric Hazard Analysis of Requirements for Critical Systems

Asieh Salehi Fathabadi[(✉)] [iD], Thai Son Hoang [iD], and Michael Butler [iD]

University of Southampton, Southampton, U.K.
{a.salehi,t.s.hoang,m.j.butler}@soton.ac.uk

Abstract. The current state of art lacks a methodical, rigorous and scalable single approach to analysis of safety and security requirements. We present SHARCS (Systematic Hierarchical Analysis of Requirements for Critical Systems), addressing this gap by adopting an abstraction-based incremental approach to hazard analysis. SHARCS combines STPA-style control action analysis with Event-B formal modeling and refinement to analyze safety and security of cyber-physical systems by flowing down system-level requirements to component-level requirements. This paper summarizes our recent journal publication [6] with emphasis on two key contributions: (1) a systematic three-phase workflow (system level, component level, consolidation) that guides the incremental development process; (2) control abstraction diagrams, a novel visual notation for modeling control structures at different abstraction levels before concrete design. We demonstrate SHARCS on the Tokeneer secure enclave system, showing how these contributions enable scalable hierarchical decomposition with rigorous traceability.

1 Introduction

Safety and security are key issues in developing cyber-physical systems. Standards such as ED202A and ED203A [4,5] mandate security risk assessments at different design stages.

Systems Theoretic Process Analysis (STPA) [11] and STPA-Sec [13] systematically identify hazards through control action analysis but rely on human judgement to assess effects. Event-B [2] provides rigorous formal verification but lacks systematic guidance for modeling choices. Previous work [3,10] combined STPA with formal modeling, achieving both methodical analysis and rigorous verification, but lacks systematic support for incremental, hierarchical analysis needed for scalability.

This paper summarizes our journal publication [6] presenting SHARCS (Systematic Hierarchical Analysis of Requirements for Critical Systems), an abstraction-based incremental approach to hazard analysis. Our previous work [7] applied SHARCS to Tokeneer but did not formally specify the process. This paper advances beyond [7] with two contributions:

© The Author(s), under exclusive license to Springer Nature Switzerland AG 2026
F. Ishikawa and A. Cunha (Eds.): ABZ 2026, LNCS 16579, pp. 331–338, 2026.
https://doi.org/10.1007/978-3-032-26752-8_21

1. **SHARCS Workflow**: A systematic three-phase process with detailed steps, inputs, outputs, and decision criteria (Sect. 2).
2. **Control Abstraction Diagrams**: A visual notation for modeling control structures at different abstraction levels before concrete design (Sect. 3).

We demonstrate these using Tokeneer (Sect. 3)[1].

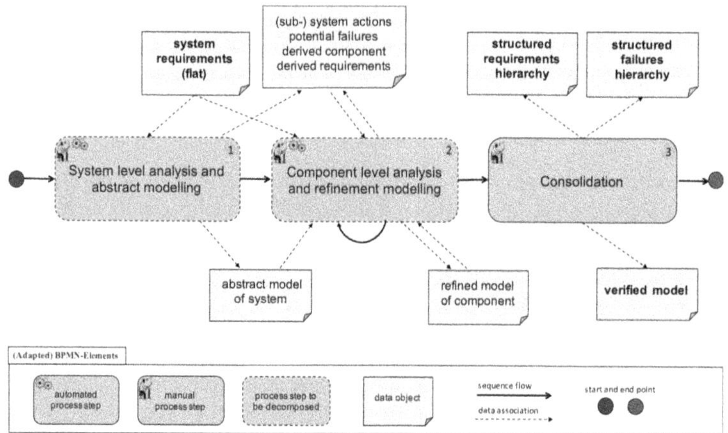

Fig. 1. SHARCS high level workflow

2 SHARCS Workflow

Figure 1 illustrates the overall SHARCS process showing the main inputs and outputs of each level of analysis. The SHARCS approach consists of three phases: (1) system level analysis and abstract modelling, (2) component level analysis and refinement modelling (repeated for each identified sub-system), and (3) consolidation phase.

System Level Analysis and Abstract Modelling: The main input to the system level analysis is a system requirements document. The requirements serve as the basis for construction of control abstraction diagrams and hence identification of system actions, potential failures, derived component requirements. These are used as input to the next component level analysis.

Each system-level consists of six steps, as shown in the expanded view of Fig. 2:

Step 1, Control Analysis: The system requirements are used to construct a control abstraction diagram showing the actors involved and the information flow

---

[1] Full understanding of the technical details may require reading the journal publication [6].

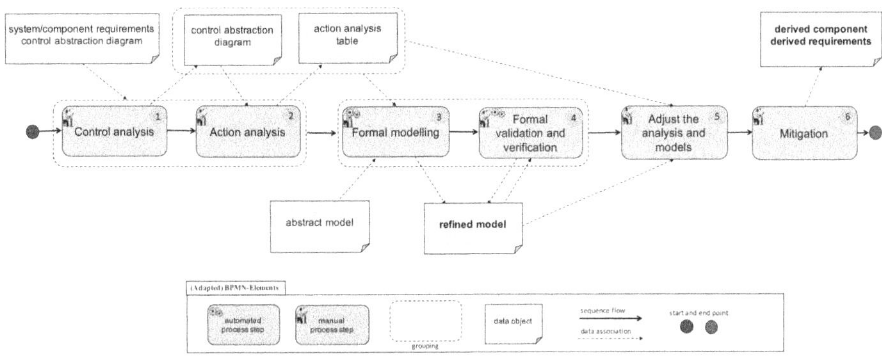

Fig. 2. Workflow for a single level of abstraction

and control between them. This diagram identifies the control actions needed in the next step.

Step 2, Action Analysis: The control abstraction diagram is used to identify behavioural actions which are analysed to identify potentially insecure or unsafe actions. An action analysis table is constructed to analyse all the possible actions that can occur at the system level and identifies the resulting failures caused by that action occurring, not occurring or occurring with the wrong timing or order.

Step 3, Formal Modelling: The actions identified in the control abstraction diagram are then formalised in an Event-B model. Control actions are modelled by events that alter the state of the system and conditions are modelled as guards of these events.

Step 4, Formal Verification and Validation: The formal model is validated using model animation and scenario playing tools. When the model behaves in an appropriate way it is verified using theorem provers to ensure that the critical invariant properties of the system are maintained.

Step 5, Adjust the Analysis and Models: Design faults are corrected and the model is revised accordingly so that verification failures are eliminated. These improvements will involve strengthening the functionality allocated to component sub-systems, or introducing additional component sub-systems.

Step 6, Mitigation and Outline Design: Each insecure or unsafe control action is considered and addressed. Mitigating actions are proposed to prevent that action from leading to a failure. The outline design identifies the sub-system components and provides their broad derived requirements which are used as inputs to the next phase.

Component Level Analysis and Refinement Modelling: Back to the high level workflow (Fig. 1), the component analysis phase is subsequently repeated if we identify further sub-components. The steps, Fig. 2, involved in the component analysis phase are similar to those of the system-level analysis. The key differences are:

334   A. Salehi Fathabadi et al.

Step 1: Elaborate the control abstraction diagrams to add the control action structure of the component(s) introduced in this phase.

Step 2: Consider the component purpose, which has been identified as part of the previous level analysis and identify component failures. For certification purposes, it is useful to record how the potential failures of this component link, via the control actions that this component addresses, to the previous level failures.

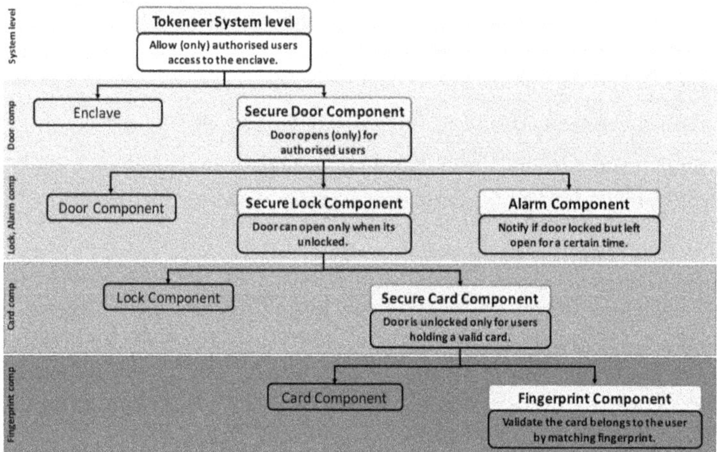

Fig. 3. Tokeneer: hierarchical component design and requirements flow-down

Step 3: Refine the abstract formal model to capture: component properties as invariants; refined/new events representing component level actions.

Step 4: Use automated theorem proving and model checking to verify constraints including the refinement proof obligations.

Consolidation Phase: In the consolidation phase (Fig. 1), we collate the results of the hierarchical analysis to produce an overview of the derived control structure and the verified derived requirements. This results in the hierarchical component structure (Fig. 3 for Tokenner case study) and hierarchical failures. The final refined version of scenarios used in the hierarchical validation form an important output from the analysis as they illustrate scenarios that could potentially lead to a failure, and provide verification evidence that the design is robust enough to mitigate them.

3   Tokeneer Case Study and Control Abstraction Diagrams

We demonstrate SHARCS through the Tokeneer system, a secure enclave consisting of components including an ID Station that interfaces to a fingerprint reader, smartcard reader, door and visual display. The primary objective is to prevent unauthorised access to the Secure Enclave while allowing authorised users to enter and exit.

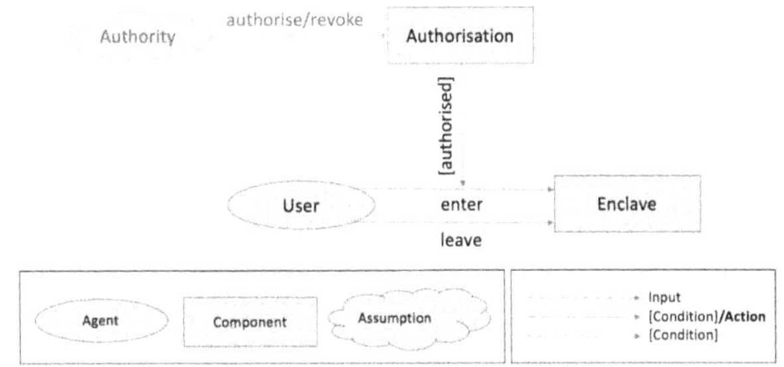

Fig. 4. Tokeneer system level control abstraction diagram

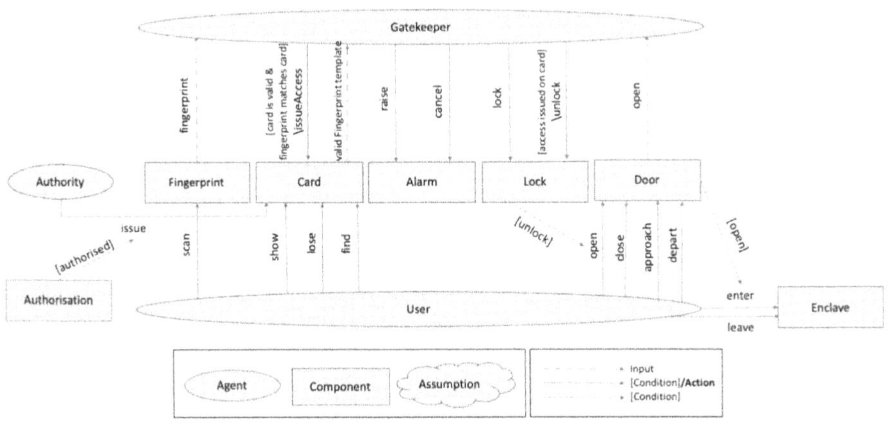

Fig. 5. Tokeneer fingerprint component level: complete control abstraction diagram

> **Control Abstraction Diagrams:** Control abstraction diagrams, see Fig. 4, visualize entities at a particular abstraction level with their information and control relationships. The diagrams show agents, components and assumptions as nodes and actions, conditions and input as links:
> **Agents** (ovals) act on components via action links (solid arrows with labels). They may constrain actions via condition links (dashed arrows with [condition] labels).
> **Components** (rectangles) are acted upon. They may be physical (enclave), conceptual (authorisation), or abstract (secure door). Abstract components are replaced by subsystems in future refinements.
> **Assumptions** (cloud shapes) annotate behavioral properties the control relies on.
> **Inputs** (dotted arrows) show information flow.

System Level, Abstract Control Structure: Figure 4 shows the Tokeneer system at the highest abstraction level. An agent, User, performs enter and leave actions on the physical component enclave. An Authorisation component imposes constraint [authorised] on the enter action. An Authority agent can grant and revoke authorisation. At this level, *how* authorization is enforced is unspecified, addressed at the next level.

Action analysis examines these actions with respect to system failures. A system failure violates the system purpose, identified by negating it[2].

Complete System: Concrete Control Structure: The hierarchical component design leads to five control components over three refinement levels: secure door, secure lock, alarm, secure card and fingerprint (See Fig. 3). Figure 5 shows the final control abstraction diagram. Components were added from right to left: door, lock, alarm, card, fingerprint. The gatekeeper agent was introduced with the lock component as the first with a physical control interface.

Considering Fig. 4 which is an "abstraction" of Fig. 5, containing 1 agents, 2 component, and 2 actions. Rather than performing hazard analysis across all the actions of the more complex Fig. 5, we commence the analysis on the smaller number of actions of Fig. 4. We then incrementally consider additional components and associated actions and analyse those additional actions for potential hazards.

Through refinements, see Fig. 3, authorization checking shifts depending on component role: abstract at system level, enforced by Secure Door, flowing down through Lock and Card to Fingerprint which validates the card holder is the authorized user.

---

[2] Full details are presented in [6].

4   Related Work and Conclusion

STPA-Sec [13] and STPA-SafeSec [8] extend STPA for security but lack formal verification and hierarchical decomposition. Existing work combines STPA with Event-B [3,10] or other formalisms [1,9] but analyzes systems at a single abstraction level.

Our key contributions are: (1) **Systematic workflow** with clear phases, steps, and decision points; (2) **Control abstraction diagrams** enabling abstraction before design with direct Event-B mapping; (3) **Refinement strategy guidance**, one of the hardest tasks in Event-B is finding useful abstractions; SHARCS provides this by incrementally introducing components; (4) **Certification evidence** supporting ED-202A/ED-203A compliance [4,5].

This paper summarizes our journal publication [6], emphasizing the SHARCS workflow and control abstraction diagrams that enable incremental decomposition from abstract system requirements to concrete component requirements. Application to Tokeneer demonstrates systematic identification of 5 component levels with formal verification across all levels[3].

Future work includes tool support for diagram-to-Event-B translation and parallel component analysis using Event-B decomposition [12].

References

1. Abdulkhaleq, A., Wagner, S., Leveson, N.: A comprehensive safety engineering approach for software-intensive systems based on STPA. Proc. Eng. **128**, 2–11 (2015). proceedings of the 3rd European STAMP Workshop 5–6 October 2015, Amsterdam
2. Abrial, J.R.: Modeling in Event-B: System and Software Engineering. Cambridge University Press (2010)
3. Colley, J., Butler, M.: A formal, systematic approach to STPA using Event-B refinement and proof (2013). https://eprints.soton.ac.uk/352155/. 21th Safety Critical System Symposium
4. Eurocae: ED-202A - airworthiness security process specification (2014). https://eshop.eurocae.net/eurocae-documents-and-reports/ed-202a/
5. Eurocae: ED-203A - airworthiness security methods and considerations (2018). https://eshop.eurocae.net/eurocae-documents-and-reports/ed-203a/
6. Fathabadi, A.S., Snook, C.F., Dghaym, D., Hoang, T.S., Alotaibi, F., Butler, M.J.: Systematic hierarchical analysis of requirements for critical systems. Innov. Syst. Softw. Eng. **21**(2), 569–593 (2025)
7. Glässer, U., Creissac Campos, J., Méry, D., Palanque, P. (eds.): ABZ 2023. LNCS, vol. 14010. Springer, Cham (2023). https://doi.org/10.1007/978-3-031-33163-3
8. Friedberg, I., McLaughlin, K., Smith, P., Laverty, D.M., Sezer, S.: STPA-SAFESEC: safety and security analysis for cyber-physical systems. J. Inf. Secur. Appl. **34**, 183–196 (2017)
9. Hata, A., Araki, K., Kusakabe, S., Omori, Y., Lin, H.: Using hazard analysis stamp/STPA in developing model-oriented formal specification toward reliable cloud service. In: 2015 International Conference on Platform Technology and Service, pp. 23–24 (2015)

---

[3] Available at https://doi.org/10.5258/SOTON/D2957.

10. Howard, G., Butler, M.J., Colley, J., Sassone, V.: A methodology for assuring the safety and security of critical infrastructure based on STPA and Event-B. Int. J. Crit. Comput. Based Syst. **9**(1/2), 56–75 (2019)
11. Leveson, N.G., Thomas, J.P.: STPA Handbook. MA USA, Cambridge (2018)
12. Silva, R., Pascal, C., Hoang, T.S., Butler, M.J.: Decomposition tool for Event-B. Softw. Pract. Exp. **41**(2), 199–208 (2011)
13. Young, W., Leveson, N.: Inside risks an integrated approach to safety and security based on systems theory: applying a more powerful new safety methodology to security risks. Commun. ACM **57**(2), 31–35 (2014)

Author Index

© The Editor(s) (if applicable) and The Author(s), under exclusive license
to Springer Nature Switzerland AG 2026
F. Ishikawa and A. Cunha (Eds.): ABZ 2026, LNCS 16579, pp. 339–340, 2026.
https://doi.org/10.1007/978-3-032-26752-8